Beyond Rules in Society and Business

NEW HORIZONS IN LEADERSHIP

Series Editor: Joanne B. Ciulla
Professor and Coston Family Chair in Leadership and Ethics,
Jepson School of Leadership Studies, University of Richmond, USA
and UNESCO Chair in Leadership Studies,
United Nations International Leadership Academy

This important series is designed to make a significant contribution to the
development of leadership studies. This field has expanded dramatically in recent
years and the series provides an invaluable forum for the publication of high quality
works of scholarship and shows the diversity of leadership issues and practices around
the world.

The main emphasis of the series is on the development and application of new and
original ideas in leadership studies. It pays particular attention to leadership in
business, economics and public policy and incorporates the wide range of disciplines
which are now part of the field. Global in its approach, it includes some of the best
theoretical and empirical work with contributions to fundamental principles, rigorous
evaluations of existing concepts and competing theories, historical surveys and future
visions.

Titles in the series include:

Moral Leadership in Action
Building and Sustaining Moral Competence in European Organizations
Edited by Heidi von Weltzien Hoivik

Beyond Rules in Society and Business
Verner C. Petersen

Beyond Rules in Society and Business

Verner C. Petersen

CREDO/Department of Organization and Management
The Aarhus School of Business

NEW HORIZONS IN LEADERSHIP

Edward Elgar
Cheltenham, UK • Northampton, MA, USA

Published by
Edward Elgar Publishing Limited
Glensanda House
Montpellier Parade
Cheltenham
Glos GL50 1UA
UK

Edward Elgar Publishing, Inc.
136 West Street
Suite 202
Northampton
Massachusetts 01060
USA

A catalogue record for this book
is available from the British Library

Library of Congress Cataloguing in Publication Data
Petersen, Verner C., 1946-
    Beyond rules in society and business / Verner C. Petersen.
        p. cm.– (New horizons in leadership series)
    Includes bibliographical references and index.
    1.Business ethics. 2.Management–Moral and ethical aspects. 3.Leadership–
Moral and ethical aspects. 4.Responsibilty. 5.Values. I.Title. II.Series.

HF5387 .P435 2002
174'.4–dc21   2001053217

ISBN 1 84064 833 3 (cased)

Printed and bound in Great Britain by MPG Books Ltd, Bodmin, Cornwall

Contents

List of tables

Foreword

We are in a challenging new era of business leadership. In the past, leaders perched on the tip of the organisational pyramid and used their positional power to command and control their organisations. Today, educated employees in democratic societies do not always respond well to orders or automatically respect authority. Complex businesses in a global economy are getting more difficult for a few people at the top to run, and the organisational pyramid is getting flatter. The sustainability of a business depends on its capacity to quickly change and adapt. This means that the power to make decisions must sink down into all levels of the organisation, so that employees can solve problems and make improvements on the spot. These kinds of business organisations cannot be run by old time bureaucracies or rule books. They operate on social and human capital, which is generated by intelligence and goodwill. In these organisations, the effectiveness and legitimacy of leaders depends on their ability to give and receive trust from their followers. The current interest in leadership comes with the realisation that today's business requires leadership from top to bottom.

I am very pleased to have Verner C. Petersen's book in the *New Horizons in Leadership* series because it tackles some of the basic questions about ethics in organisations today. Who is responsible for what? Who is responsible for whom? How do people learn and know how to answer such questions? These are not just questions about ethics, they are questions about leadership. While leadership consists of power, vision and initiative, it is also fundamentally about responsibility. Many leadership scholars now see an increasingly blurred line between leaders and followers. Businesses need employees who are willing to lead and take responsibility for the direction of the organisation and the way in which their work is accomplished. In other words, a good follower has many of the qualities of a good leader, and good leaders also know when and how to be good followers.

We all know that morality is about more than rules and regulations. Understanding what that this "more" is and what it means for leadership and management in organisations is the focus of this book. Verner C. Petersen breaks with the management theories of the 20th century that rested on the belief that social interactions could be "scientifically" engineered and the moral behaviour of employees could be controlled with regulations, sticks and motivational tricks. Many of these management theories no longer make sense today and perhaps never did. In the workplace, groups of people do not become teams because managers say they are a team. They become a team because of something that happens among themselves. Similarly, people in an organisation do not necessarily behave ethically because they follow the rules. Ethics are, as Verner C. Petersen says, part of the "social fabric" of the organisation and a moral sense that resides within its members. By trying to articulate the parts of ethics that are known but cannot be said, organisations may actually undercut a person's predilection to take moral responsibility and leadership.

This book is certain to provoke discussion and debate about a number of questions. Verner C. Petersen asks us to take a leap of faith about how we learn ethics. He argues that moral learning is tacit, not explicit. The tacit foundation of ethics is something that we cannot articulate, but we know it when we see its results. While the notion of a moral sense or feeling is easy to understand, it is not easy to control. How do we guard against people who are morally numb or who fail to pick up this unarticulated moral knowledge? Verner C. Petersen challenges us to consider the minimum of rules and organisational structures necessary for maximum performance, creativity, initiative and responsibility in the workplace. Rather than building organisational structures, he dismantles them, leaving us to wonder: How much formal structure and regulation does an organisation need to eliminate for its employees to self-organise and take responsibility for making decisions?

Verner C. Petersen's leap of faith is a leap from the old approach to management to a notion of leadership based on shared values, trust and goodwill. He joins a growing number of leadership writers in recasting the role of leader from the boss to the conveyer of values, and the role of follower from a subordinate to a partner in shared values. This entails a simple but profound conceptual shift from people working *for* someone to people working *with* each other, from ethics based on rules to ethics based on inclinations that are developed through shared values. Business leaders who are willing to take this leap will need confidence, courage, humility and a tremendous amount of faith in their employees. These virtues are not cultivated in business schools or typically found in the business community today. Some readers may find Verner C. Petersen's discourse on morality in organisations idealistic, while others may find it eminently sensible. Either way, this lively, original and engaging book will poke and prod you into reexamining your assumptions about moral learning and moral behaviour in organisations.

Joanne B. Ciulla, Ph.D.
Richmond, Virginia, USA
15 May 2001

Acknowledgements

A book like this is not brought along only by soothing words of encourage-ment. The ideas were moved along by the combined pull effects of encouragement from those who believed that there was something in my ideas and the push effects of discouragement from the disbelievers, who did not want to give up the established tools of their trade, and who would argue from the unassailable comfort of belonging to the mainstream, "where we all rest secure in the common knowledge …"

I want to thank all of you, for believing, and for disbelieving, though the disbelievers shall remain nameless.

Some of the most important encouragement for this book came from people I do not know, participants at leadership programmes, conferences and seminars. A chief nurse from Frederiksberg Hospital in Copenhagen may stand for them all. After a long afternoon presentation of the ideas on leadership in this book, she said that she had read one of my small pro-vocative articles some years ago, and that she had found that the thoughts on leadership in there corresponded more to her views of what leadership ought to be, than the management schemes she was asked to participate in. The ideas of the article had encouraged her to realise some of these views on leadership in the department she was responsible for.

I want to thank her and the many others who encouraged me in the project by showing enough confidence in the ideas to actually use them in practice, often quietly going against the mainstream.

Other direct or indirect encouragement came from people well known within their fields. From a blissful stay at the Colgate Darden Graduate School of Business Administration, at a time when the ideas were still em-bryonic, I remember the wonderfully animated discussions with Ed Free-man, and the clear words of advice from Patricia Werhane. I am also extremely grateful for the discussions with Lynn Sharpe Paine and others at the Harvard Business School and Harvard University. It was during a short stay there, arranged by Lynn, that I found the tranquillity to begin writing this book. During the process of writing, the discussions with and the e-mail repartees of Joanne Ciulla of the Jepson School of Leadership Studies, at the University of Richmond, helped keep up the spirit. I am deeply indebted to Joanne for encouraging me to have the book published by Edward Elgar, and thankful to her for providing the foreword.

Encouragement came from invitations to participate in leadership seminars, discussions, and conferences. One of the most intriguing was the invitation from the Director General and Chief Executive Officer, Hans Skov Christensen, of the Confederation of Danish Industries, to hold a series of leadership seminars at the Confederation, and co-edit a book on value-based leadership for the series. Others were important too. Lisbeth Mogensen of the Danish School of Public Administration invited me to introduce the ideas in civil servants' leadership programmes. Frants Christensen from the Institute of Service Development even organised an informal network called CREDO 2 or is it "too," of people interested in the ideas. Thanks are also due to Niels Gunder Hansen and Paul Hegedahl, who asked me to present the ideas in newspaper columns, and a series of dilemma discussions in *Ledelse i Dag* (Management Today) and Captain Kurt Alex Thomsen of the Danish Navy, who early on persuaded me to present the ideas in *Officeren* (Danish Military Officers).

Personal encouragement came in many flavours and from unlikely places. From Lone Dybkjær, a member of the European Parliament, Barbro Westerholm, a member of the Swedish parliament, Heidi von Weltzien Hoivik, of EBEN (The European Business Ethics Network) and BI, Oslo, Norway, and former German Chancellor Helmut Schmidt, who provided me with material on the Interaction Council, and was gracious enough to read and comment upon an earlier version of the chapter on leadership.

I am also extremely grateful to the former CEO, Kaj Steenkjær, and the present CEO, Anders Dam, of Jyske Bank A/S, who both believed in the ideas and had the courage to try them out in the bank and its branches over a period of years, and who supported the whole project in numerous ways. This was where one could see the elusive ideas materialise in concrete decisions, and in changes in behaviour. An experience that made me aware of the power of ideas, an experience that made me humble. Others have made the ideas materialise, among them Erik Brønserud. Thank you for the exchanges, and thank you to the other leaders who have had the courage to try out the ideas, may it be a rewarding experience for you too.

I am in debt to the other members of the research group CREDO, especially Erik Kloppenborg Madsen, Poul Bonde Jensen and Bent Martinsen, to my assistants Dorte Djien Schou, Helle Vestergaard, Birgitte Steffensen, and certainly to my imperturbable secretary Birthe Hansen, who helped keep things on an even keel and always managed to finish the most impossible tasks on time.

Finally I want to thank my editor, Alan Sturmer, for believing in the project.

Verner C. Petersen
Marcusminde
August 2001

For Lilian

Prolegomena: strings of thought

Comprehension came slowly, but some years ago it dawned upon me that the solution may have become the problem, that much of what is regarded as self-evident when attempting to regulate and manage behaviour in society as well in business, in fact carry the seeds of strange outgrowths that may turn the attempted solutions into their own problems.

Tentatively I played with the notion that explicit knowledge and the attempt to scientify all approaches to regulation of behaviour represented the wrong track, that somehow ineffable, tacit sensations of right and wrong, good and bad would be much more important.

I came to believe that self-regulation based upon an understanding of tacit knowledge, ineffable values and the processes through which they change would be important for attempts to solve problems related to un-ethical behaviour. That some form of self-regulation in which duties accompany rights and individual responsibility is reclaimed from col-lective responsibility would represent a viable alternative to the collective effort of traditional bureaucratic regulation.

I became convinced that it would be possible to show how self-organisation and value-based leadership could replace modern mechanical views of organisation and toolbox-based views of what management is about.

These notions, beliefs and convictions emerged piecemeal and pell-mell, from personal observations, research and practice. For years I want-ed to bring order into this critique of modern approaches to the regula-tion of behaviour. This book is what became of this attempt.

Part One shows the acuteness of the problems we are dealing with. Chapter 1 demonstrates how we might be losing responsibility for our own lives as a result of the schemes that are supposed to create responsible institutions. How attempts to correct unethical behaviour in society and organisations through different forms of bureaucratic regulation and codification of the right behaviour may lead to a worsening of the kind of problems that they are supposed to solve, or, in other words, represent wrong answers to some very fundamental questions in relation to social and organisational bads.

Chapter 2 on moral decay shows the small and not so small ambiguous mechanisms that bring about spirals of moral decay in business. Focusing on big scandals makes us forget that people causing these scandals may in fact behave like us, that the vicious consequences of their behaviour are reflected in the myriads of insect-eye-like facets that we, you as well as I, represent. That the only difference is the limited scope and the limited reach of influence that we possess. Attempts to create regulation to guard against the large excesses ignore that the mechanism bringing these about is found in the vicious circles of everyday life and work.

The perverting influence on behaviour of various schemes of measurement and evaluation is shown in Chapter 3. Based upon very thin assertions of scientificness, these schemes are used to create a scientific basis for regulation and management. By re-enacting a kind of scientific management using quantifiable formulas for quality, knowledge and leadership, they bring about lower quality, erosion of important aspects of knowledge, misconceptions of leadership and less ethical behaviour. Contrary to all the stated intentions.

Before I could see the vague outline of an alternative to the approaches that bring about their own problems, I had to dig deeper into an understanding of the kind of knowledge and the values we use when evaluating and deciding upon courses of action and when acting. This is how I got the idea, presented in Part Two of the book, that knowledge and values rest upon a tacit foundation.

A discussion of the important aspects of tacit knowledge thus became the subject of Chapter 4. It shows that we can know more than we can say, and demonstrates the importance of this kind of knowledge for intelligent and responsible behaviour. The implication being that attempts to make every aspect of knowledge explicit may be futile and paradoxically result in unthinking and mechanical behaviour prescribed in explicit algorithmic instructions.

This knowledge is used in Chapter 5 to discuss and demonstrate the tacit foundation of our values that we use to judge behaviour. It turns out that our judgement and our reaction to ethical problems and dilemmas may be based upon what might be called habits of the heart; habits that may show themselves in somatic reactions, a blush, a pain in the stomach and in strong actions. This foundation is eroded away when we attempt to unpack tacit knowledge and values to create explicit codes of behaviour. Perhaps tacitness is in itself an important quality, because the knowledge and the values we are not conscious of will shine through in the decisions we make and the behaviour we show, in ways that we cannot hide under a superficial gloss.

This view brought forth new problems that had to be solved, because such a tacit view might pave the way for an individualistic and relativistic view of values. Thinking about this problem for a long time I believe that I have found a solution in a more or less universal social grammar. A social grammar anchored in the history and development of human beings and human society, and containing values that are shared, non-relativistic and relatively constant. A grammar that makes communities possible.

The most convoluted argument is found in Chapter 6 on the weaving of the moral fabric. Here I attempt to unwind the most basic view of this book, and it turns out that there are layers upon layers to unwind, leaving I expect, much to be done. What is unwound is the transmission mechanism through which values can be transmitted from generation to generation, from individual to individual, without ever being stated explicitly.

Values are not constant over time and thus this chapter contains a tentative explanation of how our values change, not as a result of rational deliberation in a well-ordered context, but as a result of trials and errors and unpremeditated convergence around solutions that prove viable and consistent with the more basic values.

In Part Three I try to demonstrate how the strings of thought unwound in Part Two may help bring about changed mindsets and new ways of acting. The emphasis is on expressive action, on showing how tacit knowledge and ineffable values may be expressed in action, in responsible entrepreneurship, self-organisation and spirited, value-based leadership.

In Chapter 7 I attempt to show that modern business is both subject to and a contributor to a kind a runaway logic, pervading strategies, decision making and activities of modern business, and leading to serious problems with some of the deep values we may otherwise believe in. Instead of explicit regulation from the outside, putting a leash on a straining logic, or grafting some shiny ethical codes onto an unchanged and very powerful logic, I try to show that the logic of capital can be contained by self-regulation of business. A regulation based upon an aware-ness of emerging concerns, and the responsible entrepreneurship of indi-vidual decision makers. This might change the core of business, the processes and the products and services, instead of just putting a gloss upon existing practices.

Self-organisation held together by shared tacit structures is the subject of Chapter 8. Instead of seeing the organisation as similar to complicated Swiss analogue watches, where the actions of every element can be plan-ned and foreseen for years, the organisation is seen as a kind of intelligent anthill, or as a complex organisation. A Swiss watch is not very creative, while ants can create impressive structures.

It is inferred that self-organisation, where the actions of individuals cannot be planned and foreseen in a very determinative way, is necessary in an economy where there is less focus on repetition and more on creati-vity and renewal. The open-endedness of self-organisation emphasises the importance of the kind of knowledge and values discussed in the previous chapters.

It also demands a new view of management and leadership. This is the subject of Chapter 9 on spirited and value-based leadership. Many aspects of modern management as we know them do not seem to be com-patible with self-organisation. Modern management is too much about doing things right, about using the tools of a management toolbox, not about doing the right things. It is about using explicit algorithms on human resources, it is about using and making rules to determine actions. This is not compatible with the ideas presented in this book.

What is needed is instead a stronger emphasis on leadership, not of resources, but of thinking individuals. Spirited leadership that can make sense, show direction and support the drive of the individuals making up an organisation. Leadership that is shown in express actions, not in state-ments, credos and regulations. A leader cannot communicate and lead solely through a piece of paper. Neither the leading part of leadership, nor the forceful, but ambiguous drivers that really move members of an orga-nisation, can be left out.

A more genuine understanding of self-organisation, self-reference and self-control is thus necessary. I argue that cohesion, coordination and drive of self-organised efforts have to rely on the layers of shared knowledge and a shared social grammar in order to work. That any other alternative would tend to resurrect the spectre of a more traditional hierarchical structure.

The ambiguity of leadership is also discussed in this chapter. Successful leaders may pervert the values of the organisation, bringing about morally corrupt organisations. To find a guard against this it is necessary to recur to the discussion in Part Two, to the social grammar and the deep values held by each and every member of the organisation. This is the only anchor that prevents a strong leader from dragging the whole organisation into a vicious whirl of moral decay.

Based on ideas and theories developed in the earlier chapters the final part of the book thus represents an attempt to propose and exemplify possible trials that may help solve some of the problems that have been emphasised in the attempt to voice latent misgivings in the first chapters.

It is thus my hope that the book will help bring about the understanding that self-regulation based on values and attitudes is the only viable alternative to modern bureaucratic attempts to regulate and control behaviour in society as well as in business. What we should be striving for is not less individualism and more collectivism, but a kind of enlightened individualism, with a responsible self playing a cooperative game, in a *Gemeinschaft* of like-minded individuals.

It is my hope that the book will equip the reader with a kind of X-ray eyesight, enabling one to see the runaway logic in one's own practices, and discern the falseness, hypocrisy and inconsistency of some of the proposed and attempted solutions to counteract this logic. If this happens the voicing, proposing and exemplifying of this book might act as a catalyst for those who have felt the same misgivings and who may have a more immediate possibility of putting some of the ideas into action.

Many of the theories and thoughts found in the book may require a leap of faith on behalf of decision makers. I realise that making such a leap is difficult, because both in business and in research we communicate meaning through common references, well known and self-evident truths, like the advantages of the market, of competition, of globalisation and so on, established economic theories and well-worn models. They have created the common tracks, or ruts, that we have all fallen into, making it very difficult to persuade someone to leave this rut, or even to accept that it may just be a rut.

There is a problem of incredulity and incomprehensibility: "I am used to think that …, everyone else believes that … but surely you cannot be right." These are often heard expressions, when I present my ideas the first time to an audience, although to be sure over the past years more and more people nod quietly or even burst out that they have held ideas and notions like that, but felt that they could not express them.

With this I embark on the task of trying to lead the reader down a new and rather unused path, with less marked ruts, with unknown difficulties, but also with a potential of opening up new exiting vistas of what is possible.

PART ONE

ACUTE PROBLEMS

1 The erosion of responsibility

Had You forgotten that peace and even death are dearer to man than free-dom of choice in the knowledge of good and evil? Indeed, nothing is more beguiling to man than freedom of conscience, but nothing is more tormenting either.

Fyodor Dostoevsky

LOOK-AWAY SOCIETY

The following story was found on the front page of the weekly German newspaper *Die Zeit* in the spring of 1997.[1] A 17-year-old girl is raped in the S-Bahn in the city of Hamburg, Germany. She cries for help. Apparently there are other passengers within earshot, but nobody reacts, nobody helps her, nobody calls the police. Some passengers leave the train at the same station as the crying girl without attempting to help or comfort her. The perpetrator stays on the train for the return journey to the city. No one contacts the police.

Somehow the incident becomes known more than a month later, and it causes a certain public indignation. How could that happen? Why didn't the other passengers within earshot do something? How could something like that happen in a public place like a commuter train?

Excuses are found, apparently the fellow passengers did not realise what was happening or they misinterpreted the incident. This seems to become the official explanation. It had to be, according to the official sources, because her fellow passengers had enough chances to raise the alarm without getting involved.

In the interpretation of the newspaper, the explanation may turn out to be more sinister. The incident may show that we are living in a "*Weg-schau Gesellschaft,*" or "Look-away society." Looks are averted, shifted out of harm's way, ears are not hearing, mouths are kept closed and the mind looks away, in an attempt to minimise involvement and personal risks. As long as it doesn't happen to us. In the view of the paper, and official police speakers, we are becoming accustomed to looking away, in all sorts of situations. We may be bystanders, but we do not stand by in order to help.

There may be several different explanations for this phenomenon.[2] In the case of rude behaviour or small transgressions of an established public order or just bad behaviour we may feel that it would be overly zealous to speak up or intervene. Or we may be genuinely or conveniently unsure of what is really going on. Is the man lying on the sidewalk really ill or is he just drunk? Is the scuffle just a friendly joust or is it something more serious. As long as innocent explanations may be found we may keep our mouth shut, our hands in our pockets, and look away, although we may feel slightly ill at ease until we put some distance between the incident and ourselves; physical and timewise.

Goodin sees such a lack of reaction as being due to lack of coordination and collective intention in the group, in this case the group of bystanders, and explains that without coordination there will be no action. "Random collections of people (for instance, that group of people occupying the third carriage of the 17:27 train from London to Clacton) are incapable of forming any 'collective intention.'"[3] Although a coordinated group might have been more active, it does not really seem to explain why no one did anything.

The number of bystanders may be important. In a situation with many bystanders one might have thought that intervention might be a likely outcome. In fact the opposite might turn out to be the case. Observing a transgression together with others might actually cause everyone to look away.[4] We may feel that somebody else ought to do something, because they seem to be closer to the incident, or bigger, or several in company. With many bystanders it cannot be my duty to do something, because someone else is almost always closer or at least has not looked away as much as I have. Other excuses may be that if we all acted then we would just get in each other's way and that would be counterproductive, and so I will keep my distance. Or the opposite, to make a difference we would all have to intervene, and I cannot be sure that the others will act, if I do, and neither can they. With so many possible excuses it is no surprise that no one intervenes.

In the case of a single bystander or when a group of the bystanders know and trust each other, intervention might be more likely. If I am the only one, I cannot use the excuse that someone else ought to do some-thing, and in the case of people knowing and trusting each other, they might know that they would not be left to fend for themselves, that there might even be some informal degree of coordination. Still it might be easier to look away and do nothing, using the excuse, when asked after-wards, that I didn't see anything, or I wasn't really aware that ... Often this becomes an all too convenient excuse.[5]

This touches upon another problem. In a modern society, especially in the big cities, other factors might help explain why we look away. We usually do not know the others, the victims, the offenders, or the other bystanders. Anonymity characterises the big cities, and anonymity means that we may not be too concerned with the others, we lack confidence in each other, and feel no immediate responsibility to help.

In more traditional societies one might expect a close social control of behaviour. In a modern society this social control may have become in-effective, and as a result defective behaviour towards the others may have become more common. This defection can be illustrated quite simply in the Nordic countries. Jumping a queue is quite common, and can be ob-served everywhere, in shops, in airports and bus stops. But one does not jump a queue if it consists of people you know well.

This argument parallels Olson's argument in *The Logic of Collective Action*, although his interest differs from ours. "In any large group every-one cannot possibly know everyone else, and the group will *ipso facto* not be a friendship group; so a person will ordinarily not be affected socially if he fails to make sacrifices on behalf of his group's goals."[6]

In a way, the only positive aspect of the story from the Hamburg S-Bahn is that it became a front page story. That may mean that we can still become embarrassed when we hear of such incidents and the reactions of the bystanders. We can still become shocked when we are told that no one apparently felt it to be their responsibility to do something, call the police, comfort the girl or whatever. But the embarrassment is after the fact, distant from the incident.

The disturbing thing is that the story may indicate that our individual responsibilities towards our common lives might be less than what we would have thought or expected, especially if we have a feeling that we, too, might have looked away just like the other passengers. We might have the vague notion that it could happen to us, that we are living in a care *less* society in which individual responsibility is eroding.

Another story shows how individual responsibility is being substituted by a curious kind of institutionalised and professionalised responsibility. It is the story of the purse-snatching outside the Parrotgarden.

THE PARROTGARDEN

One evening in late September 1992,[7] around 50 public servants, the majority being heads of various sectors of the local government in Northern Jutland, gathered in a restaurant called the Parrotgarden, in the city centre of Aalborg, Denmark.

They were dining in the restaurant, in preparation for a somewhat boring evening, where they were to listen to three presentations in a lecture hall in the same building. To facilitate conversation during dinner, they were placed at three or four large tables along windows facing the park outside.

After the initial friendly greetings, sometimes accompanied by a little friendly teasing, they were served the first course, and were engaged in a lively conversation, when suddenly a loud outcry was heard:

"By God, he hit her!"

They all looked up, somewhat confused: What had happened? There were explanations and pointing of fingers as they discovered the reason for the outcry. Looking out the windows into the park, they could see an elderly woman, standing forlornly just 20 metres from where they were sitting, and a young man sprinting away with a handbag. Many rose to get a better view and most became quite agitated: "Shocking that something like that could happen here! With so many people watching."

Their own reaction, apart from watching?

One of the diners, a man in shirtsleeves, has already left the restaurant sprinting after the young man. One more gets up and follows him. That is all.

The others soon calm down and concentrate on their roast veal and potatoes. There is a lively discussion of the incident. The waiter arrives: "More veal sir?" They are not totally passive. Someone has the presence of mind to ask the waiter: "Has someone called the police?" The waiter nods.

Soon dessert is served.

Employees from the restaurant finally bring the shaking, but apparently unhurt elderly woman in from the park and make her sit down at a table in a corner of the restaurant. She is served a cup of coffee, while waiting for the police. Nobody from the group of public servants talks to her after she had been invited into the restaurant.

Later the same evening the public servants listen quietly to three presentations. The speakers present three rather different ideas as to how ethical behaviour can be encouraged in practice in a public administration. The only person missing is the man in shirtsleeves. He may still be chasing the young man, but no one knows or seems to care.

In the aftermath the lack of reactions to the incident outside the Parrotgarden was not seen as something unusual. In reality it may have become a normal reaction to these kinds of incidents, just like the reaction in the S-Bahn in Hamburg, but for the quick reaction of a man in shirtsleeves. He joined the others during the last presentation, and afterwards explained what had happened. He had been at the local police station in order to identify two young men in connection with the purse-snatching. He also said "I am not sure I would do that again, but I wasn't really thinking."

Still one might wonder why only two reacted, and the others continued eating. Somehow, their consternation and indignation seem insufficient. Could they not at least have done something to comfort the old woman?

There is a special aspect to this incident. Most of the public servants would be professionally responsible for a section of their respective local government administration. They might be among those professionally responsible for helping the elderly woman financially the next day, if her purse had not been recovered. They might even be responsible for deciding whether she ought to have psychological assistance, or other forms of help.

Some of the participants in the evening function might even become involved with the young purse-snatchers. Perhaps they would already be engaged in designing new policies, with the aim of preventing young people from becoming delinquents, or helping them out of delinquency.

They might propose, plan and help establish activity centres for the young men who have nothing to do, so that they might lose interest in snatching brown plastic purses from elderly women, thereby shaking the fragile self-confidence of these women.

They might have designed programmes, according to which the young men, if they were caught, could participate in canoe or survival trips in the wilderness of northern Sweden. A not uncommon remedy in this situation. Or programmes in which young delinquents would be encouraged to take part in a climb-the-trees programme, which supposedly would help them to stand on their own feet and somehow teach them to have confidence in their own abilities.

The curious aspect of this incident is, therefore, that the participants in the evening arrangement about ethics in public administration, as part of their daily tasks, might be very involved in helping both the victims and the perpetrators. They would even get part of their salary for doing exactly that. Together they represent a comprehensive and thorough system created with a view to prevent and redress in almost every conceivable way incidents like these.

In most cases they will even be very professional about it, because they will usually have a long education behind them and a lot of experience in dealing with such cases. Their strong professional ethos will help them decide to do the right thing in the right way.

The only thing they are not able to do is to render a small amount of improvised help in connection with the incident in front of the Parrotgarden. They seem to think that it is a matter for the police. The police will act as professionally within *their* respective areas of responsibility. The argument seems to be: Why should I get involved as a person, when we have a series of institutions taking care of such problems.

With this kind of attitude we have entrusted important parts of our lives to institutions and welfare organisations, to professional keepers of responsibility. They only have responsibility for their special area, what they are paid for and of course only during office hours.

A more individual kind of responsibility is lacking. My responsibility is inscribed in the job description. If it is not in there, I have no responsibility, almost by definition. I cannot act on my own, I can only act according to the instructions that go with my job. A society organised like ours seems to bring forth special institutions with very professional employees, with very well-defined and very special responsibilities. If something happens outside their area of responsibility they will not really care. It is not their table.

If we are right in our assumption, responsibilities will become increasingly institutionalised, and more specialised. But it may also mean that we have less and less individual responsibility in the general sense. Both in relation to our fellow human beings and in relation to our own lives.[8]

In other words, the attempt to create a welfare state in which everyone can feel safe and secure may have gone so far that we are beginning to lose individual responsibility for our fellow beings and for ourselves. It is a society in which some kind of "airbag" will save you no matter how recklessly you may be driving or living. An airbag society.

With *in vitro*-to-urn welfare and beyond, with advanced and specialised health and social care systems, with institutions for safekeeping, for aimless and mindless activity, and for education, with institution upon institution, with safeguard upon safeguard, the professionalisation of our lives has reached such an extent that we mainly have the areas of consumption and leisure left to ourselves. Even here public institutions encroach upon us, as we are treated to cultural contributions, music and theatre schemes. In some cases local government may even help establish golf courses and racetracks.

Important areas of our lives have become institutionalised and collectively insured. We may no longer have much responsibility left, confronted with this intricate, anonymous and amorphous system, whose internal workings and consistency we cannot wholly comprehend.

RIGHTS VERSUS RESPONSIBILITIES

Article 3 of the Universal Declaration of Human Rights[9] states: "Everyone has the right to life, liberty and security of person." Here is the right, now think back for a moment, if you will, to the incidents in the Hamburg S-Bahn and outside the Parrotgarden. In these incidents one might say that there was a lack of "security of person" for the 17-year-old girl and the elderly woman.

They had a right to security of person, but who is responsible for making sure that this right is upheld? The police of course. No one else? After a while one might realise that this is only part of the answer, that the courts, the legislature and perhaps even oneself might also be part of the answer.

Somehow it would seem that the responsibilities[10] have been parcelled out in bits and pieces belonging to several different institutions. The responsibilities have been institutionalised with precisely defined areas of responsibilities as we saw in the case of the public servants. Does that leave the bystanders without responsibilities? That would seem to be the

answer in the S-Bahn incident. In the Parrotgarden, someone felt responsible for calling the police, and the man in shirtsleeves even pursued the
young men, although he stated that he acted without thinking. Still, it
would seem that in general the responsibility corresponding to the
"security of person" belongs to an institutional arrangement that is somehow separated from the individuals making up society.

This view of distributed responsibility is also found in O'Neill inasmuch as she states that "a universal right to subsistence or security might
be matched by a 'distributed' obligation that assigned to each a right to
claim subsistence or protection from specified others or from specified
institutions."[11]

Still, this does not seem to represent a satisfactory answer to the question of responsibility. What do we do when institutions cannot guarantee
the security of person? Do we demand more police, more surveillance,
like video cameras in the commuter trains and in public places, and
stronger sanctions? In some cases, this is exactly what has happened.
Video surveillance is increasingly used to watch and control extensive
public places in the cities.[12] In the future, we might use video cameras in
commuter trains, too, and then every passenger might be forgiven for
thinking that it is the responsibility of someone else to intervene in incidents like the one in the S-Bahn.

In fact what we may be seeing is a more and more stand-offish approach to responsibility, almost paralleling modern smart weapon capabilities. Video cameras in public places will make it possible for everyone to
watch everyone else from afar. This would create a kind of superficially
transparent society. This fits well with the morbid interest in watching
video series showing real-time police chases and war-like actions from the
other end of the planet. I am also thinking of the smart bombs equipped
with video guidance. As used in the Gulf War they would show the intended target right up to the moment of impact signified by a sudden
white noise on the screen. It is rumoured that at least in one case one
could see the face of a scared-to-death lorry driver about to be hit. The
result would be that an incident like the rape in the S-Bahn might
actually be seen by millions of far-off bystanders. Any sense of responsibility in the distant voyeurs would have gone, what is left might be called
the thrill factor of docutainment.

In Article 19 of the Universal Declaration of Human Rights, it is
stated that "Everyone has the right to freedom of opinion and expression;

this right includes freedom to hold opinions without interference and to seek, receive and impart information and ideas through any media and regardless of frontiers."

Once more we see a right. Now where is the duty or responsibility, and who or what holds this responsibility? This is somehow rather diffuse. We might immediately think of the state. But what do we mean by that? The judiciary, the police, and how is this responsibility expressed?

I believe that now, in all welfare societies, we have a feeling that these rights are somehow taken care of by the constitution, the apparatus of the state, the courts and in certain cases by the prodding of one or the other inquisitive voices in the media perhaps, or by Amnesty International or PEN.[13] Be that as it may, responsibilities seem to be distributed in a fairly vague sort of way. In a more profound way, we may even get the idea that the responsibilities somehow ought to be held by each and everyone of us, although I am not sure that this is how we see it, when we demand our rights.

One might wonder if this is not a fairly common situation with the specification of rights and entitlements. We see the rights, but we are not too sure about who holds the obligations and the responsibilities corresponding to those rights. Somehow it seems that we can have rights without clear obligations and responsibilities. In these cases, the rights, like dangling pointers in a computer program, seem to point into thin air.

In her work on justice and virtue, O'Neill reaches the same conclusion from another direction and concludes: "The perspective of rights provides a perilous way of formulating ethical requirements since it leaves many possible obligations dangling in the air. … It is a weakness in so far as it offers a way of avoiding careful articulation of the structure of the claimed rights and of their justification, and tempts many to settle for rhetoric not matched or readily matchable by performance."[14]

As we have seen, this may represent a fairly accurate description of many of the more lofty declarations of rights or entitlements. The idea is that rights to something carry more appeal than duties to do something. It certainly seems more attractive to have the right to freedom of opinion and expression than to have the duty to be unbiased and truthful in one's expressions. In contrast to the "yoke potential" of obligations and responsibilities, there might also be a liberating potential in stating the rights, even where the corresponding obligations cannot be specified. The declaration of certain rights may create hope and open up possibilities for criticism of authoritarian regimes.

Still O'Neill thinks that it might be a good idea to begin with the obligations. "It is hard to articulate and sobering to realise who will have to contribute what for whom and at what cost if significant rights to certain goods and services – say, those that would guarantee basic standards of welfare even within a rich state – are to be established. The advantage of beginning with obligations is that taking this perspective requires one to be more realistic, clear and honest about burdens, their justification and their allocation."[15]

In September 1997 a group called the InterAction Council published a proposal for a declaration grandly called "A Universal Declaration of Human Responsibilities,"[16] mirroring in the title the "Universal Declaration of Human Rights." The declaration was endorsed by the members of the council, consisting of former statesmen from all continents, among these Helmut Schmidt, former Chancellor of the Federal Republic of Germany.[17]

This declaration was proposed in time for the fiftieth anniversary of the Universal Declaration of Human Rights. The idea being that the new Declaration of Human Responsibilities should be adopted by the UN alongside the Declaration of Human Rights.

The reasoning of the InterAction Council is interesting in relation to our attempt to show that individual responsibility might be eroding. They seem to be concerned with some of the same problems, albeit on a far larger scale. As part of the work that led to the proposal for a new declaration, the council emphasises the need for a kind of global ethics.

Leaning towards Aristotle they see human beings as social animals, needing rules and constraints, and in "a world of unprecedented change, humankind has a desperate need of an ethical base on which to stand."

More or less explicitly the council seems to believe that rights are not enough. This is where we are convinced that the members of the council are occupied with some of the same problems discussed here.

In a report laying the foundation for the new Declaration of Human Responsibilities,[18] the council is looking at the big picture, when it states: "We are convinced that a better global order cannot be created or enforced by laws, prescriptions, and conventions alone; that action in favor of rights and freedoms presumes a consciousness of responsibility and duty, and that therefore both the minds and hearts of women and men must be addressed; that rights without obligations cannot long endure, and that there will be no better global order without a global ethic."[19]

Although rights may help create freedom, there is a danger that this freedom will be a freedom of indifference; the freedom not to get involved, the freedom not to take on responsibilities. "The concept of human obligations ... serves to balance the notions of freedom and responsibility: while rights relate more to freedom, obligations are associated with responsibility. Despite this distinction, freedom and responsibility are interdependent. Responsibility, as a moral quality, serves as a natural, voluntary check for freedom. In any society, freedom can never be exercised without limits. Thus, the more freedom we enjoy, the greater the responsibility we bear, toward others as well as toward ourselves. The more talents we possess, the bigger the responsibility we have to develop them to their fullest capacity. We must move away from the freedom of indifference towards the freedom of involvement."[20]

It might be interesting, after all the lofty words, to see whether the Declaration of Human Responsibilities has anything to say in relation to the possible duties of bystanders in relation to incidents like those we have described. Under the heading "Fundamental Principles for Humanity," article 1 states: "Every person, regardless of gender, ethnic origin, social status, political opinion, language, age, nationality, or religion, has a responsibility to treat all people in a humane way." It would seem that the responsibilities of our fellow men depend on what it means to treat people in a humane way. Clearly the perpetrator does not fulfil this obligation, but what about the bystanders?

Other articles may be more explicit, though. Article 2 states: "No person should lend support to any form of inhumane behavior, but all people have a responsibility to strive for the dignity and self-esteem of all others." Article 3 ends by declaring that "Everyone has a responsibility to promote good and to avoid evil in all things." One might say that the bystanders did nothing to strive for dignity and self-esteem of the victims, nor did they try to promote good and avoid evil.

It looks as if one might actually find support for the view that the bystanders have a responsibility to do something in the Declaration of Human Responsibilities. The real question though is whether such a declaration would change the attitude and actions of the bystanders. In conclusion it might be said that the authors of the declaration may have seen the same general problem we are talking about. A lack of responsibilities in relation to rights, but it is difficult to see how their solution might change the way of solving this problem at whatever level we are talking about.

A TYPOLOGY OF RESPONSIBILITIES

The use of general notions like rights and responsibilities may limit the conclusions we draw from the above examples. We have to look more closely at the notion of responsibility. This is important if we want to get a better understanding of the phenomena we have been watching.

Leaning on the work done by O'Neill, we take a closer look at responsibilities and the relationship between responsibilities and rights. Table 1.1 represents an attempt to classify the different connections in a kind of typology of responsibilities. What follows is an attempt to explain the different types of responsibilities represented in the table.

Universal, vague responsibilities. In the incidents described above we somehow think that everyone ought to have done something. In these cases we might say that we all had a responsibility to act in order to either prevent a crime or help a victim. That would represent a vague responsibility held by all conscious and emphatic members of society, and owed to every other human being, and in a way also towards animals and nature.

To respect the life, property and dignity and worth of every human being, independent as it were of any local conditions would seem to be part of each and everyone's universal responsibility. Durkheim, in fact, regards this as the most general sphere in ethics. And the noblest in concept, for it is owed to all fellow beings.[21]

Of course, there might be excuses for not immediately jumping on the rapist or running after the purse-snatcher. There may be the question of a difference in size, a quick mental calculation may have convinced us that it would be impossible to make much of a difference and that any intervention might be dangerous. Or my physical condition is such that I would not be able to run at all, and walking after a running purse-snatcher looks like a ridiculous proposition. Actually, after all these calculations it might be too late to do something, and so the rational act of calculating the risks involved may in itself lead to no action. The more careful the calculation the less chance of any action at all.[22]

All the same, there might be something that one could do, something that would make a difference, like reporting the incident, comforting the victim. Doing nothing is not the only alternative.

Table 1.1 A typology of responsibilities

Responsibilities	Relation between right and responsibility	Owed to (examples)
Universal (held by all)	Vague (often unwritten)	Everyone (respect life, property, dignity and worth of every person, show honesty, fairness, sense of justice, keep promises, care about others, and help preserve a sense of community and the physical and biological conditions for a good life)
	Specific (often written)	Everyone (upholding the constitution, human rights etc., respecting the law)
Special (role bound)	Vague and specific	Everyone (law-making, preserving, justice, public order)
	Specific (often written)	Identifiable individuals (carrying out institutional responsibilities, observing contracts, and terms of employment)
	Vague (often unwritten)	Family members (parents towards their children)

Universal responsibilities are responsibilities we presume are held by all in society, with the exception of the mentally ill possibly, and owed to all other human beings. In a way they may be an integral part of what makes us human.

In some cases, these responsibilities are owed in a very vague sort of way. There are no strong specific connections between right-holders and those having responsibility. That may have been the case in the S-Bahn in Hamburg. It may be impossible to show that the victims' claims to "security of person" are matched in any specific way to responsibilities of other passengers. Maybe the law is not specific. Still, it would seem that every passenger within earshot ought to have had some kind of responsibility to do something. This is where the vague notions of a universal responsibility to care about others come into play. Goodin formulates it in this way: "What is no one's responsibility is everyone's. If it is right that something be done, and no one in particular has been assigned responsibility for doing it, then we are all responsible for seeing to it that it be done."[23]

In same way, we all have the vague responsibility to show honesty, fairness, sense of justice and beneficence. We might have a general responsibility to act, to keep promises, to preserve a sense of community, and to preserve the physical and biological conditions for a good life. If each and everyone in general does not show some adherence to these vague responsibilities, it might prove difficult to uphold a community and in fact all the more specific responsibilities.

O'Neill talks about universal duties without corresponding rights, and says: "Honesty and fairness, beneficence, and courage have been thought of as required of all, and as holding across many roles and activities, although lacking counterpart rights."[24]

Some of these responsibilities are present as duties in Kant's Tugend-lehre. Kant may have held the rigid version of these duties, even going as far as to say that it would be wrong to tell a lie even to someone seeking to kill a person you are protecting.

It is notable, though, that it is impossible to specify exactly when one must show these duties, what one must do, or how one must act, especially in the case of conflicting duties. We interpret this to mean that the general duty to be honest does not mean that one should never tell a lie, even presuming that it would be possible to somehow discern unequivocally between lies and non-lies, that would represent rigid interpretation. Instead, it can only mean that generally speaking, one never ought to lie, and that we cannot specify the situations in which it might be the right thing to do.

The same applies to our duty to help others. "Nonetheless, there is an 'imperfect' duty to do *something* for the sake of helping others."[25] That "something" cannot be specified in great detail in advance, it is up to us in the situation.

We have a right to expect that other people do not lie, as we have a right to expect some kind of help from other people when in distress, for instance to expect that someone would have done something in the S-Bahn incident. "The problem is how to organize group behavior around something as intangible as a desired future habit of behavior. Each individual must share knowledge of these expectations; but more important, each must also be able to rely on the support of other group members to prevent violations of these patterns of conduct."[26]

Finally we may have some vague individual responsibilities related to general character in interaction with others, such as general dependability, integrity and kindness. There may be no precise rights corresponding to these responsibilities, but somehow they still seem important. They are held by all and owed to those one lives among.

Three things are worth noting in relation to universal, vague responsibilities. The first one is that there is a lack of one-to-one correspondence between rights and responsibilities.

The second one is that the vague responsibility we are discussing here is not bound to a certain role. It is not as a member of the police corps one is bound to act, not as a public servant, but only as a human being in a society.

The third one is that this responsibility cannot be coordinated collectively with an organised division of work and responsibility. This vague responsibility cannot be divided among the individuals. In fact, all individuals carry the same potential responsibility, although they may not all land themselves in situations in which they have to show that they can act according to this responsibility.

Universal, specific responsibilities. When discussing the right to freedom of opinion and expression, we ended up by asking who was responsible for protecting this right. Our answer was state, judiciary, police and maybe groups like Amnesty International and PEN. This might be an example of responsibilities held by some adult members of society and owed to everyone else. This is a fairly general responsibility, we might not have a clear idea of how we are supposed to act upon it, but it is there somehow, and this time we are able to point to Article 19 of the Declaration of Human Rights. State constitutions and the law further specify this right and even give a more exact formulation of the responsibilities involved.

O'Neill apparently sees these responsibilities as a kind of universal, imperfect obligation. Universal, because they are to be held by all, imperfect because although the obligation bearers may be identified, we cannot identify the corresponding right-holders. She asserts that these obligations can be enacted by all but not for all.[27]

The specific responsibility owed to everyone else includes the responsibility to uphold the constitution, declarations on human rights and in general the rule of law. This type of responsibility might also include the responsibility of economic actors to uphold the basic premises of the market or other economic systems that have somehow been agreed upon, even in the absence of specific laws.

The Maastricht Treaties of the European Union contain an agreement on social policy, in a separate protocol. This agreement may be used to show the vagueness of the written treaties stating duties. Article 1 of the agreement solemnly states: "The Community and the Member States shall have as their objectives the promotion of employment, improved living and working conditions, proper social protection, dialogue between management and labour, the development of human resources with a view to lasting high employment and the combating of exclusion."[28] The community and the member states are responsible, the wording seems clear enough, but what happens to responsibility in practice? It becomes a constitutional responsibility, containing the vague wish that some politicians, civil servants, leaders of employers' federations and heads of unions will somehow feel this to be their responsibility.

We do not find any organised collectivity dividing up this type of responsibility among us all. What we find is a judiciary and a police force, but their responsibility we place under the heading of special, specific responsibilities. There may also be small pockets of organisations in the shape of human rights groups, Amnesty International and the like.

While the universal vague responsibilities were seen as belonging to us all as human beings, the universal, specific responsibilities might for similar reasons be seen as general civic responsibilities belonging to us as citizens of well-organised societies.

Special, vague and specific responsibilities. A more precise or concrete responsibility is held by those who are not only members of a society but are also in position to propose and enact laws, for instance laws concerning the freedom of expression. This is a more specific responsibility held by a few specific individuals, and owed in a way to every other human being in a society. This responsibility is somehow glued to the institution that these individuals represent. The same might be said for courts and for the state apparatus. Members of these institutions have a special responsibility owed to everyone else in society. It might be specified in a written form in law; it might also contain vaguer notions of responsibility, like the responsibility to act in the interest of all the people, the electorate and for democracy and an open society.

We cannot really characterise this responsibility as either specific or vague. It straddles these types. It is also significant that this responsibility is somehow freely chosen by specific individuals, that it does not belong to everyone. By making this choice one accepts something resembling a responsibility towards everyone in a society. The reasons for choosing this responsibility may have to do with a lust for power, a wish to change society, or something else. The important aspect is that as soon the choice is made "the object of responsibility is the *res publica*, the common cause."[29]

Here we see the beginning of a collective arrangement to hold and parcel out responsibility. Not all of us hold this responsibility, only the members of the institutions.

Responsibilities belonging to specific professions may also be placed under the heading of special, specific responsibilities. They are related to a certain education, or a certain line of work with special responsibilities. Judges, priests, teachers, scientists, engineers, doctors, nurses, soldiers, policemen, accountants, lawyers and many other groups of people characterised by their profession seem to hold specific responsibilities apart from any other member of society. Their responsibilities may be accompanied by an oath, the oath of Hippocrates, or by explicit professional codes. Not all of their responsibilities may be explicitly specified, though, in fact we would expect professional responsibilities to a certain degree to consist of special but vague responsibilities, bonded to the profession, and connected to certain attitudes and ways of doing things. That is why we have placed them separate from both the specified and the vague types of responsibility.

An attempt to elucidate various kinds of professional ethics can be found in Gorlin, while Wolgast writes about the lost responsibility of the professions[30]. What is important, though, is that the different professions may have very different or even conflicting responsibilities. Durkheim mentions the contrast between the scientist who has the duty of "developing his critical sense, of submitting his judgment to no authority other than reason ... The priest or soldier, in some respects, have a wholly different duty. Passive obedience, within prescribed limits, may for them be obligatory."[31] One may also contrast the responsibilities of a policeman and a doctor. For this reason, Durkheim talks of moral particularism or the many morals. This is very different from the universal responsibilities.

These groups of professionals as well as the institutions they represent may create pockets of self-sustaining particularistic responsibilities, apart from the rest of society, and they may evolve in directions that are in conflict with the responsibilities of every human being, citizen, or member of a family.

Special, specific responsibilities.   Institutional responsibilities may involve public servants employed in the social sector. They may have very specific responsibilities towards a number of individuals identifiable by fulfilling certain specific criteria. Only towards those, though, and only as representatives of a concrete institution. We might therefore speak of specific institutional responsibility, with members holding the specific, individual responsibility, only in so far as they represent the institution. Like the public servants (not) involved in the incident in front of the Parrotgarden, they hold a specific responsibility, and they owe it to a more or less well-defined group of people under fairly specific circumstances.

Equivalent kinds of responsibilities may be found within the state, and other institutions, organisations and companies. They belong to and are included in formal promises, and in contracts. They are to be found in every institution, every kind of organisation, in companies and contracts of the market. An employee may have a very specific responsibility towards a certain job and certain people, colleagues or managers, owners and customers, in a specific company. A social worker may have very specific responsibilities as part of the job, towards specific clients. "The tax official's responsibility for collecting taxes is not predicated on the merits of this or any taxation system but on his undertaking the office."[32] In all cases very specific responsibilities are held by very specific individuals toward identifiable other people. It is tempting to call this a 9 to 5 responsibility.

This responsibility can be seen as divided or parcelled out among institutions and more specifically among individuals. The police have their responsibility and the social sector theirs. The individual members of the police corps and the social sector have an even more specific division of responsibilities.

This responsibility is in general not only well defined, but also non-reciprocal. "The well-being, the interest, the fate of others has, by circumstance or agreement, come under my care, which means that my control *over* it involves at the same time my obligation *for* it."[33]

The parcelling out of responsibility demands some kind of orchestrated coordination. Orchestrated in formal rules, procedures, plans and in interrelated roles, informal shared "views" and experiences[34].

In contrast to the universal vague responsibilities, these individuals do not all share the same potential responsibility. They can in fact say: "This is not my table, or old woman, or train." They can say this even if they do not know if anyone else holds this responsibility, the kind that relieves the single members of an unspecified amount of responsibility; only a specified part belongs to them as long as they are in exactly that role, and only from 9 to 5.

Following the specific rules for eight hours may represent the easy way of carrying out one's responsibilities, with no questions asked and no thoughts thought, and vaguer notions of responsibility not brought into play. But if we are just following specific rules for a large part of our lives, our "spring of morality" may become slack.

With a growing division of work we may expect these professional responsibilities to play a bigger role. This concerns us, because it may mean that the vaguer individual responsibilities may erode even faster, with more and more institutions and special professions encroaching upon the vaguer responsibilities, for instance those of the family.

We are no longer talking about responsibilities belonging to us as human beings, as citizens of a well-organised society, or as professionals. We only talk about the responsibilities we have in certain situations, specified by contracts or terms of employment in a given organisation. We may call them institutional responsibilities.

Special, vague responsibilities. Here we place the responsibilities belonging to members of a family or friends or neighbours. First among these must be the special responsibility that parents may be said to hold towards some very specific individuals, their children, at least as long as they are immature. Married couples, and couples living together, might be said to hold individual responsibilities towards very specific individuals, in the shape of their spouses. Children may have special responsibilities towards their sisters and brothers, and their parents. More distant family relations may have responsibilities. Finally, friends and neighbours may have responsibilities of a vague character, with absolutely no specification.

The parents will take it that "they owe their children care and support, which their particular children, but not all children, let alone others, have a right to receive from them."[35] O'Neill, in fact, talks about special imperfect obligations, instead of responsibilities, but her argument seems to run parallel to the arguments presented here.

Nonetheless, these responsibilities are of a different hue than the responsibilities of individuals employed by child care institutions, or the public servants in the case of the Parrotgarden. They are not specific responsibilities glued to an institution and a role you can somehow discard when you leave work. Instead they are what we call 24-hour responsibilities.

This responsibility is different from the special specific responsibilities inasmuch as it is not chosen in the same way as the responsibility of someone working in the social sector. When becoming a public servant of the social sector, one accepts the institutional responsibilities that goes with the job, it may be said to be part of a contract. A parent does not in the same way choose responsibility, and does not enter into a contractual relation with his or her children. That is why Jonas talks about this as a responsibility instituted by nature in contrast to the more artificial version accepted as part of a job. "It is the distinction between natural responsibility, where the immanent 'ought-to-be' of the object claims its agent *a priori* and quite unilaterally, and contracted or appointed responsibility, which is conditional *a posteriori* upon the fact and the terms of relationship actually entered into."[36]

With the growing importance of institutions having specific responsibilities with regard to the family, a professional responsibility may force the vague responsibility belonging to the family out into marginal and less important areas. Institutions, pedagogies, child health policies, social workers may take over more and more of the natural responsibilities of the parents. In the same manner many of the other special, vague responsibilities may be substituted by more specific institutional solutions, like in the caring for the aged. But can a 9 to 5 responsibility ever substitute for a 24-hour responsibility and the closeness of a family?

In order to differentiate the special, vague responsibilities characterised here from the former types, we call them private responsibilities.

GUANO MARKINGS

The responsibility of the individuals making up institutions or employed by them can only be characterised as special according to our classification. Being institutionalised we would presume that they would be specified in every conceivable manner and written down. In this way the individual responsible becomes identifiable like the responsibilities listed in the often detailed job descriptions of public servants. Here vague responsibilities become substituted by specific formal responsibilities, and informal norms by references to formal rules.

"Underlying all formalism,…, is the fact that it is psychically cheap; it substitutes the outer for the inner as more tangible, more capable of being held before the mind without fresh expense of thought and feeling, more easily extended, therefore, and impressed upon the multitude."[37]

The formal responsibilities might be specified by law. An example is found in the so-called "Law of legal security and administration in the social area."[38] This law specifies certain responsibilities of public servants within the field of social security and likewise certain rights of the citizen. Here the responsibilities are embodied as it were in relationships between identifiable agents and recipients. They may further be characterised by a very high degree of specification of the circumstances and relationships under which they must be expressed.

We have made explicit some of the differences between responsibilities with only a vague correspondence to rights and responsibilities with a more specific relationship. This has important negative implications.

The more we attempt to anchor responsibilities in specific written statements and special institutions, the more we lose individual commitment to all the vaguer notions of responsibility. This may help us understand why no one intervened in the S-Bahn, and most of the guests in the Parrotgarden did not take any action at all. The result is that although responsibilities may become very clearly and strictly defined by written rules, this makes for some very stringent and inflexible conceptions of individual responsibilities, and it may lead to rigid behaviour by rigid representatives of rigid bureaucracies.

This fits well with Shapiro's description of rigid personalities. A rigid personality is not guided by vaguer responsibilities, attention to the circumstances of a situation and good judgement. Instead "The rigid person's behavior is guided by fixed and already established purposes and is merely technically informed by data selected according to the relevancy ..."[39]

It is perhaps fitting that this idea can be illustrated with a metaphor using the behaviour of a certain bird on the Galapagos Islands. It is called the blue-footed booby. This bird constructs a nest by marking out a ring on the ground with guano. Apparently, this blue-footed booby applies a very stringent rule with regard to its actions towards its own blue-footed booby chicks. This rule is: Care for the chicks inside the guano ring and ignore chicks outside the ring. Now, if a chick somehow gets outside the ring it will be ignored "no matter how much it struggles and twitters."[40]

Aitchison sees this behaviour as an example of a rigid system, there being only a few predefined alternatives for action. If anything un-expected happens no one will know what do to. Of course, we also see the actions of the blue-footed booby as illustrative of what happens when vaguer notions of responsibility are missing. Not that we think that the blue-footed booby has any conscious notion of responsibilities; we just use its actions as a metaphor for very rigid rule-based responsibility.

Just think of the reaction of the public servants at the Parrotgarden. Vaguer notions of responsibilities did not seem to matter. According to their institutional rings of guano markings, the old woman was outside the ring and her plight not a responsibility of theirs.

The attempt to specify responsibilities, whether the universal or the special ones, may be seen from another angle as an attempt to create an algorithmic solution to the handling of ethical problems and dilemmas.

An algorithm "is an infallible, step-by-step recipe for obtaining a pre-scribed result."[41] It is important to remember that step by step means exactly that. There is no latitude to jump over a step or carry them out in another sequence. Every step is prescribed, having carried out one step, the next step is specified. There is no uncertainty, no options, the next step is fully determined. The prototype of an algorithmic reasoning device would be the same as found in the so-called Universal Turing Machine.[42]

One of the reasons for attempting to make explicit and algorithmic-

like rules may be that relying too much on the vaguer notions of responsibility and individual discretion might be seen as relying on arbitrary and
intuitive notions. Doing this would result in particularism, because then
each and everyone could decide for him or herself in what way to
respond, for instance, in the incidents we have described. In this way, the
attempts to create algorithmic-like rules may be seen as contributing to a
more universal sense of responsibility and to a general fairness in treatment. This may help explain attempts to create a high degree of specification, explicitness, systematisation and algorithmisation, especially
with regard to the rules included under the classification of "specific
responsibility."

The result is that rules, especially in the shape of detailed guidelines,
let responsibility rest upon following certain procedures, reminding one
of the algorithms used to solve equations, or at the very least the general
form of an algorithm. Just put the problem into the decision machine,
then pull the right levers, and the solution will be generated, without
further human intervention. There is no use for judgement and discretion, the procedure would apply in an equal way to everyone fulfilling
certain conditions, and precisely for these reasons the procedural
approach might be regarded as especially impartial and fair. This will
result in a parrot-like reasoning process, just repeating the steps of the
procedure, and it will tend to reduce individual responsibility inasmuch
as we just have to learn the method and then follow it, be it located in a
computer or not. When asked how we arrived at a given result, we would
only recount the steps again and again and maybe explain the workings
of the algorithm we were using, without really understanding the why's
and how's. Discipline and mimicry will replace individual consideration
and thought.

How that may work can be shown by using a caricature version of
Searle's famous Chinese room *Gedankenexperiment*.[43] In this case a person, not knowing anything about ethics, is locked in a room and supplied
with a set of algorithmic instructions for solving ethical dilemmas. Next,
a set of written examples of ethical dilemmas is sent into the room. The
instructions for manipulating the ethical dilemmas are simple to follow.
The person in the room solves the dilemmas using the rules and sends out
the answers. The actions of the person in the ethical room would be semi-
automatic and machine-like, "following rules mindlessly, programmed."[44]
In fact, we would have an Ethical Decision Machine, though I believe

that we would not yet be prepared to accept the possibility that such a machine could really work.

We may come really close, though, in the case of a social worker who knows how to play *caring* according to certain rules in the shape of quasi-algorithms. This is the manipulation according to the rules part. But does he or she understand the relation to real world problems, or worse will he or she try to impose the "play" on the real world, thereby ignoring relevant aspects, clues, and information, making it a paper solution?

Learning only the expressible ethical rules by heart would not get us very far when looking at what we have called the vaguer notions of responsibility, whether they be of a universal or a special nature according to the characteristics we have given. There will be no predefined ways of handling a given problem. Each individual somehow has to fill out the vague notions of responsibility at their own discretion, according to their own sense of responsibility. A complete specification will be impossible, and any attempt to provide a highly specified procedural description will prove to be woefully inadequate.

It might be more reasonable to expect an algorithmic form of rules in the case of well-specified responsibilities, though even here a closer look will show that rules shaped like algorithms cannot stand alone. O'Neill argues along the same lines when she writes: "*Everyone should be punctual* prescribes a policy for time-keeping, but leaves everything else undetermined. This is true even for quite narrow and specific principles: practical principles, unlike some rules of formal systems, are necessarily indeterminate, so are never true algorithms. Even those that might be thought of as quasi-algorithms, such as practical principles that prescribe 'shadowing' certain true algorithms, will leave much open."[45]

"Leave much open" is exactly what they do, even the most detailed rules and procedures cannot specify in all detail what action one is to take. Rules are always underdetermining action. We would have to use algorithms to decide whether a certain algorithm would apply, like in the case of testing for solutions to an equation, algorithms for how to use other algorithms, and algorithms for deciding what to do with exceptions to the general rules, and so forth.

Instead of attempting to create impossible systems of interwoven algorithms we have to rely on a more general ability to make judgements. This fits well with Kant's assertion: "General logic contains ... no rules for judgment ... if it is sought to give general instructions how we are to subsume under these rules, that is, distinguish whether something does or does not come under them, that could only be by means of another rule. This in turn, for the very reason that it is a rule, again demands guidance from judgement."[46]

In spite of the algorithm-like form of many rules, they may not be more than rules of thumb; we just have to recognise them as such, but that means that we must somehow become discerning deliberators, "sensitive to each situation's particular features,"[47] and algorithms cannot make one sensitive to each situation.

Wittgenstein is also critical of the algorithmic use of rules.[48] The attempt to follow a rule means that one is ruled by a rule in a mechanical way, which will also mean that one at least attempts to leave individual responsibility and judgement out of the decision and action. This is exactly what we believe is happening, not in the simple sense that rules determine how we act in any robot-like sense, that would be impossible as algorithm-like rules are always underdetermining action, but in the sense that detailed and algorithm-like rules offload the individual of responsibility. They represent formalisations of responsibility that will weaken the individual "spring of morality." They represent as it were lazy solutions that because of the rule-format will tend to weaken the consideration of informal and vaguer aspects of responsibility.

The nightmare version of Orwell's *1984* comes to mind. Newspeak was an algorithm-like language developed to prevent people from thinking subversive thoughts, or committing thought crimes. In our case, detailed algorithm-like instructions may lead a crime of non-thinking negligence.

Rules cannot specify the conditions in which they are to be used. Rules are interpreted not according to rules, but according to shared and tacitly agreed upon beliefs. In this way rules can never completely codify responsibility.

Finally, it should be noted that rules cannot in themselves initiate actions by individuals, something separate from rules must initiate action. There must be some kind of commitment to actually do something. One might of course be forced, you either do this or ... It is, however, difficult to see how this shows a sense of responsibility. The alternative may be a strong will, a strong feeling, or some nervous disposition, some almost Pavlovian reaction, as in the Parrotgarden where a man in shirtsleeves just got up and chased the purse-snatcher without thinking.

HOW MORE REGULATION MAY LEAD TO LESS RESPONSI-BILITY

What we are interested in here is first of all to throw light upon the attitudes behind, the reasons for, and the processes giving rise to constant
demands for new regulation encompassing rights, responsibilities and
behaviour. Secondly, we want to see how a more and more detailed
regulation may contribute to an erosion of an individual sense of
responsibility.

In 1994, the Danish Consumer Ombudsman published a set of
guidelines for the advisory activities of banks in relation to private
customers.[49] The guidelines were a direct result of the negotiations
between the Consumer Ombudsman, a public institution, the Finance
Council representing the banks, the Consumer Council representing
consumers and the Trade Council representing the trades. Indirectly, the
guidelines were a result of a series of complaints about banks giving bad
advice, and even some scandals where banks' employees apparently sold
worthless bonds to private customers.

The guidelines were supposed to point out and specify what would
constitute good advice, and furthermore point out the duties of the bank
when giving advice, especially in relation to private customers and small
businesses; the reasoning evidently being that big business ought to be
able to look after their own interests. The guidelines should accordingly
protect and safeguard the rights of the customer *vis-à-vis* the bank, and
point out to the banks what their duties would be when giving advice to
private customers.

In an introduction to the guidelines, it is stated that they supplement
the existing marketing statute.[50] Although it is not stated explicitly in the
guidelines, it would seem that they also supplement a statute which
demands that certain price information in relation to goods and services
always be given.[51]

The guidelines consist of 12 clauses stating what a bank and employees of a bank ought to do to safeguard the rights and fulfil certain expectations of the consumer. Terms like *must, must make sure, must advise, take
care that* are used throughout in the 12 clauses, although the guidelines as
such have an unsure legal status.

Among other things the bank must make sure "that all essential
agreements are made or certified in writing" (Clause 11). This pre-

sumably ought to make sure that the customer and the bank adviser have the same understanding of the agreement.

According to another clause, the bank "must take care to furnish sufficient information about its products and services, including differences in prices and conditions of alternative products that may cover the needs of the customer" (Clause 3).

Three years later, it turned out that some banks apparently did not follow the spirit of the guidelines. They did not necessarily tell their customers how they could save money by using alternative products and services, nor did they tell them that their interest payments on loans might be reduced, when a general lowering of interest levels occurred.

This led to new meetings in the summer of 1997 between the original authors of the guidelines. Later that year, a set of guidelines was published that would supposedly take care of some of the problems raised, and lessen the ambiguousness of certain formulations.[52] The new guidelines[53] were exactly the same as the old guidelines, though. What the group had done was to give a page-long interpretation of each clause in the hope that the clauses and interpretations together would close certain loopholes.

This attempt to create a finer and finer mesh (or is it mess?) of rules, beginning with the statutes, and at the time of writing ending with interpretations of ethical guidelines, helps illustrate the points made in the section on algorithm-like reasoning. Rules for using rules cannot be a substitute for judgement and vaguer forms of responsibility on behalf of the individuals involved.

Later examples and demands from the Consumer Council have shown that the loopholes were not closed, and of course not even the demand for written agreements is enough. Recently, a case involving apparently bad advice given by a bank was taken to court, and the customer was awarded compensation. This made the bank involved in the case put forward the suggestion that meetings with customers should be videotaped, in order to be able to show what went on during the meeting. We have seen how the use of video cameras was considered as a solution in other instances, and now we see a suggestion that they might be used to record the meetings between bank employees and customers.

Recent discussions in a Danish committee looking into the responsibility of advice-giving[54] also discussed the idea that unfulfilled, but justified expectations of customers ought to lead to claims for compensation payments.

It would seem that vague notions of trust, honesty, dependability and promise-keeping are not enough in these cases; that they must somehow be supplemented and/or substituted by specific responsibility in the shape of written rules, whether they be laws, guidelines or interpretations. In certain cases we even want to have some technical evidence of transactions between a bank and its customers.

What will happen to the vaguer notions of responsibility in this case? Judging from the experience with the ethical guidelines we might easily get the idea that the vaguer notions are pushed aside. We no longer look to the spirit of the rule, we look to the letter of the rule. That would at least explain the necessity of having interpretations that will help pinpoint the right behaviour and the precise institutional responsibilities of the banks. A bank employee will only have to act according to the letter of the guidelines. If this is what is happening, the attempt to create institutional responsibility will again reduce individual responsibility, and may even create a demand for more guidelines, and interpretations. One might get the strong suspicion that the more ethical guidelines are used the less ethical behaviour will we experience.

The former Minister of Trade and Industry may have had the same idea when she talked about how rules take away the initiative of the individual and continued by saying: "What is even worse is that we pacify the weakest, all those, that do not have enough strength and power to say: 'This is enough'".[55]

The many rule-based attempts to safeguard the rights of citizens and customers represent an attempt to create specific universal and special responsibilities according to the typology presented. All these attempts would seem to be based upon the belief that by specifying to a higher and higher degree the respective responsibilities of travel operators, banks and every other actor on society's stage, responsibilities are somehow apportioned and made more concrete and real. Specific responsibilities are seen as a substitute for the vaguer notions of responsibility.

On the surface, it might be a good idea to increase the specific responsibilities using detailed rules, guidelines and ethical codices. It would represent an answer to the critical voices talking cynically about rights without corresponding responsibilities. With the rules parcelling out responsibilities it would become clear who and what had the responsibility to make decisions and to act, and what circumstances. The rest can stand aside.

The incidents and examples show some of the consequences of this line of thinking. The loss of vague responsibilities also represents a loss in individual responsibility. There is nothing strange about that. The vaguer notions only exist in as far as they are carried by individuals and are being demonstrated in the everyday practice of these individuals, in their reasoning, their decisions, their behaviour, in their actions so to speak.

The detailed specification of responsibility institutionalises the responsibilities, or at least reduces responsibility to certain specific circumstances as we have seen. It is even worse though. An unintended consequence of attempts to make responsibility explicit is that it leads to erosion of the vaguer universal and special responsibilities of each and every one of us. With the erosion of the vaguer notions, the vague adherence to the specific responsibilities may weaken. Responsibilities somehow become located and anchored outside the individual. They are prescribed by the law or the code, I do not have to carry them about, I do not have to observe some vague demands, only the specific ones mentioned explicitly in the law or code.

Everyone may feel free to use loopholes in the law or code, in fact that is everyone's right. Only transgressions of the letter of the law or code can be sanctioned, anything else would be unfair or unjust.

But this is not the only effect of the erosion of the vague notions. How can we expect everyone to comply with a specific law or code if there is no test for compliance, and a sanction for non-compliance or alternatively a reward for compliance?

The answer of course is that we cannot, just think of the incidents we have described. If this is correct, there will be a further need for specific agencies for testing or rather controlling for compliance and for metering out sanctions or paying rewards depending on the specifications in the law or code.

This means that a power apparatus must exist, taking care of control and metering out sanctions. This apparatus itself would have to be checked, because *Quis custodiet ipsos custodes.*

There would be a tendency to pay lip-service to the rules specifying one's responsibilities. Securing a high degree of compliance would in many cases be costly. Making sure that loopholes were closed would occupy energy and time and make the rules even more detailed, specific and more complex without really making everyone feel more responsible, only forcing everyone to act as if, or as long as they are under observation.

What we have here is the dynamic of a vicious circle or rather a spiral. With more rules and specifications there will be a need for even more detailed rules and specifications. This would tend to increase the complexity and incomprehensibility of rules. With more complex and incomprehensible rules there will be less and less compliance, if not for other reasons then because only a few persons will know and understand the rules. The vaguer notions of responsibility are overruled.

DEFECTING ON OURSELVES

The erosion of individual responsibility is made more problematic because we seem to defect not only on others but also on ourselves. The reason for this is that the individual is dissolving into a collection of roles or masks. By putting on masks belonging to the different roles we play, we do not even recognise ourselves.

We try to act in accordance with the mask we carry at a given moment. As a parent of a child with a DAMP syndrome we demand special facilities and care, while at the same time trying to keep costs under control as members of the school board. Driving the new fast car we may fume about the speed bumps popping up like pimples everywhere, forgetting that we took the initiative in writing a petition and collecting signatures to be sent to the local authorities, demanding that something be done about speeding motorists on our quiet residential road. Finally, as patients waiting in line we may certainly see the need for good hospital care, while as taxpayers we fight tax increases to be used for what might be the local version of the NHS.

What I am asserting is that we are playing a kind of prisoner's dilemma game against ourselves. The players in this game are represented by the different masks we carry. If we follow a strategy of defection we are in fact defecting on the other masks we carry.

In this way we lose all sense of relatedness, of coherence, and of the common good, whatever that may be. One of the consequences is that bigger and bigger gaps can develop between the expectations and demands we have when carrying one mask and the results we experience when carrying other masks. We will not even be able to act in solidarity with ourselves. When that happens, we will all experience the bad results of an expansive defection strategy. It will not be easy to see that part of the problem lies with ourselves. Instead we may increase our demands. The politicians have to do more, the authorities, the police, the companies, the management of the company in which we work.

In this masquerade version of society, we may react individually by restricting responsibility to the 9 to 5 institutionalised version and perhaps to our closest family and friends. Only here the vaguer notions of individual responsibility may survive together with non-institutionalised care. Yet, as Lerner writes, "much of what we want most in the world – loving relationships, mutual recognition, friendships based on loyalty and commitment, physical and emotional safety, a sense of purpose and meaning for our lives – cannot be sustained in a world that is continually narrowing the circles of caring, because this very process of narrowing creates an ethos of selfishness that undermines loving relationships."[56]

What we have here may only be a mocking trick-mirror of what I call mask-egoism. It may not be totally correct as a mirror. It may enlarge certain problematic features. Nevertheless, I believe that traits of this mask-individualism can be found in most modern societies.

Mask-egoism may multiply the expectations, wishes, demands and needs that we have. They are directed towards somebody else, towards the local council, when we demand speed bumps to reduce the speed of cars, towards the schools when our children cannot spell, or keep quiet, towards the authorities when we do not feel safe in local commuter trains, or when walking outside the Parrotgarden restaurant.

We cheat on the system, by using smart tax evasion schemes, while at the same time demanding more of the services paid for by taxation. If we can get a concrete advantage by cheating this system or by getting something apparently for free, we cannot be bothered with the diffuse and very small disadvantage that everyone else incurs because of that. No concrete person is really hurt. It is still a game with a large and dumb opponent. One can cheat on the sucker time and time again, and it really does not mind. What a game. The trick is that one is not playing against another person, who would soon change his or her tactics to suit yours in a repeated game.

Who and what can make sure that there is some kind of relatedness, of coherence, and some idea of a common good? If I am right, the onerous responsibility falls to an increasing degree on the institutions, and then we are back with the problem of institutional responsibility. Not only that, politicians may also be part of the game, no longer representing individual voters, but increasingly strong groups of individuals carrying a certain kind of mask and characterised by having a strong voice.

The result is that we do not see that many of the things we do not like or do not accept are a direct or indirect consequence of our own behaviour. We just put on our mask and ask "What is best for me? Or what is in it for me?", which is exactly the attitude that may have created some of the problems in the first place.

The alternative to an institutional response might be a solution in which each and everyone of us regards it as our responsibility to act in accordance with deeply held common values, with universal vague responsibilities and special vague responsibilities.

Instead of an empty appeal to community there may be a need for more rather than less individualism; individualism though that would partly substitute the pseudo-solidarity that is safeguarded by systems of regulation, control and sanctions, for an individual responsibility; individualism where we do not defect on the other individuals that are mirror images of us, and on ourselves in our different roles.

It is only as responsible individuals, not dependent on the particularity of the mask, that we can grasp and engage in something that is bigger than the mask we carry at any given moment. It may sound paradoxical, but this kind of individualism may be an important condition for any real sense of responsibility and community.

NOTES

[1]   Gaschke (1997), p. 1.
[2]   See for instance Huston & Korte (1976), Latané & Darley (1970) and Latané & Darley (1968).
[3]   Goodin (1996), p. 35.
[4]   Evidence for this has been found by Latané and Darley (1968, 1970) Peter Grottian in Germany (according to Die Zeit 25 April 1997). See also Held (1970).
[5]   See also Austin (1957).
[6]   Olson (1973), p. 62.
[7]   The incident happened 22 September, 1992. It is described in Petersen (1995).
[8]   Goodin has a curious argument in the opposite direction as it were. Talking about exculpating individuals, and inculpating states, he says "the argument ... that makes the 'no individual responsibility' excuse work to exculpate individuals from respons-

ibility also works to inculpate collectivities, imposing upon them responsbilities to act so as to provide the needed coordination of individual's behavior" (Goodin 1996, p. 41).

9   On 10 December, 1948 the General Assembly of the United Nations adopted and proclaimed the Universal Declaration of Human Rights, calling upon all member states "to cause it to be dessimated, displayed, read and expounded in schools and other educational institutions." The full text can be found in various places on the Word Wide Web. Since then the number of conventions, covenants, pacts and international agreements have become too numerous to mention. There are rights of self-determination, prevention of discrimination, rights of women, rights of the child, freedom of information, freedom of association, employment, marriage, social welfare, even rights to culture.

10   We are aware that different meanings may be attached to responsibility. When we say, "she was responsible for the accident" we may just mean that "she" caused it. Here we are using the expression "responsible" in a causal sense. When we say, "she was responsible for the care of the children," we mean that "she" had to look after the children, for instance making sure that they came to no harm. Here we are using "responsible" in a moral and substantive sense, and this is the meaning of responsibility we discuss here. To be responsible one must first of all have causal power, that is, be capable of making a difference, next be able to act in a accord with one's will, and finally have some idea of consequences of one's actions. This idea of responsibility is partly based upon Jonas' theory of responsibility in Jonas (1984). Jonas' idea of substantive responsibility may be expressed like this: "One is responsible even for one's most irresponsible deeds."

11   O'Neill (1996), p. 130.

12   In Britain video surveillance of the public places of whole town areas has come into use, for example in Bradford, where a large number of video cameras have been installed. "The system will enable constant, random pan, and 'walks' monitoring – that means the ability to watch someone as they walk from one end of the town to another." (KDIS Online, CCTV – Big Brother in Bradford 9 December 1998). The London Borough of Newham has installed a system for face recognition using high resolution cameras in public places according to Privacy International. In oral evidence before the House of Lords Select Committee on Science and Technology it is estimated that 200 000 cameras are monitoring public places in Britain (Privacy International, 23 October, 1997). In Norway Aftenposten reports of plans for video surveillance of the areas surrounding the railway station and Karl Johan Gaten in the Center of Oslo in Norway (Århus Stiftstidende 2 November 1998). A Danish TV channel reports of an idea to put male kindergarten pedagogues under video-

surveillance, after a few reported incidents of child abuse (TV-2, 9 November 1998). Finally there is the enormous growth in the number of webcams, showing real-time or almost real-time video of everything than can be watched with a video camera. In this way parents can watch their children in the kindergarten, their spouses at work, their home when travelling abroad and employees can be watched from afar. The potential for this superficial transparency seems almost unlimited.

13 International organization of writers. PEN is an acronym standing for poets, playwrights, editors, essayists and novelists.

14 O'Neill (1996) p. 134.

15 Ibid., p. 135.

16 A Universal Declaration of Human Reponsibilities, proposed by the InterAction Council, 1 September 1997. The text of the declaration can be found at the Tokyo Secretariat, interact@asiawide.or.jp.

17 Others members are: Malcolm Fraser, former Prime Minister of Australia; Jimmy Carter, former President of the United States; Michael Gorbachev, former President of the Union of Socialist Republics; Kenneth Kaunda, former President of Zambia; Lew Kuan Yew, former Prime Minister of Singapore and many more.

18 In Search of Global Ethical Standards, Report prepared by InterAction Council, and presented in Vienna 22–24 March 1996. The text of the report can be found at the Tokyo Secretariat, interact@asiawide.or.jp.

19 Ibid.

20 A Universal Declaration of Human Reponsibilities, Report on the Conclusions and Recommendations, InterAction Council, Vienna 20–22 April 1997.

21 Durkheim (1957).

22 Olson has the argument that even if a member of a large group neglects his own interest, his effort may not help bring any perceptible benefit to others. In this case the effort would be futile, like trying to hold back a flood with a single pail (Olson 1973, p. 64). I am not sure that Olson is right, or rather his argument may be too limited, because in real life this seemingly futile action might be exactly what is needed to change the behaviour of others, and then suddenly there might be thousands of pails. This is also the standard problem of explaining why anyone would vote at a national election, because in doing that one might have as much influence as the man with the pail.

23 Goodin (1996), p. 32.

24 O'Neill (1996), p. 137.

25 Richardson (1994), p. 71. This refers to Kant's *Tugendlehre*.

26 Deacon (1997), p. 400.

27 O'Neill (1996), p. 148.

28 Agreement on social policy concluded between the Member States of the European Community with the exception of the United Kingdom, Great Britain and Northern Ireland. *Treaty on the European Union*, Council of The European Communities, Luxembourg.

29 Jonas (1984).

30 See Gorlin (1990), Wolgast (1992) and French (1972, 1984).

31 Durkheim (1957), p. 5.

32 Jonas (1984), p. 95.

33 Ibid., p. 93.

34 Goodin discusses what a lack of coordination means for responsibility (Goodin 1996).

35 O'Neill (1996), p. 151.

36 Jonas (1984), p. 95.

37 Cooley quoted in Angell (1958), p. 91.

38 Lov om retssikkerhed og administration på det sociale område, Lov nr. 453 af 10. juni 1997.

39 Shapiro quoted in Berofsky (1995), p. 177.

40 Aitchison (1996), p. 28.

41 Haugeland (1985), p. 64.

42 For a description of the Universal Turing Machine see Hodges (1987).

43 See Searle (1980).

44 Penrose (1989), p. 531.

45 O'Neill (1996), p. 75.

46 Excerpt from Kant (1781). *Critique of Pure Reason,* quoted here from O'Neill (1996), p. 80.

47 Richardson (1994), p. 133.

48 Wittgenstein (1958). See also Holtzman & Leach (1981).

40 *Retningslinier om etik i pengeinstitutternes rådgivning* (1994).

50 Lov nr. 428 af 1. juni 1994.

51 Lov om prismærkning.

52 *God rådgivning – Forbrugerombudsmandens retningslinier om etik i pengeinstitutternes rådgivning* (1997). In the meantime new ethical guidelines and rules had been published in related areas, although not always in full agreement. See for instance: *Børsetiske regler* (1997) and *Retningslinier om etik i realkreditinstitutioner* (1995).

53 *God Rådgivning* (1997).

54 Udvalget om rådgiveransvar. This discussion is referred in Hillestrøm (1998), p. 50.

55 Excerpt from a speech given when she visited CREDO, at the Aarhus School of Business, in 1996. The excerpt can be found in her so-called "speaking paper": (Talepapir

for Erhvervsminister Mimi Jakobsen 1996, p. 7). At that time the Minister of Trade and Industry had initiated a small project called Project Pinocchio, the idea being to find ways of removing rules that acted as the strings holding up Pinocchio.

56   Lerner (1997), p. 15.

2 Ambiguous spirals of decay

Thus Vice nurs'd Ingenuity,
Which join'd with Time and Industry,
Had carry'd Life's conveniencies,
It's real Pleasures, Comforts, Ease,
To such a Height, the very Poor
Liv'd better than the Rich before.

Bernard Mandeville

DIRTY COFFEE CUPS

Many companies experience the problem of the dirty coffee cups. In order to keep up energy and attention employees and management need inordinate amounts of coffee during a working day. All sorts of arrangements exist to cater for this necessity. Coffee machines abound in offices, sometimes employees even bring their own coffee machines. More or less official coffee breaks make it possible to get a refill and catch up on bits and pieces of company gossip. All fairly harmless but apparently regarded as necessary to keep people content. In fact the culture of a company may well be judged from a study of its coffee drinking habits.

Whenever employees or management have to start work again after a coffee break the soft throw-away plastic cups are thrown into the nearest bin or are left half empty on some horizontal surface, the window sill, the corner of an office desk, a computer, a file cabinet, or on somebody else's shelves. Environmentally conscious companies may use real cups, made of porcelain or plastic, and in this case almost all cups are left on some horizontal surface.

Visitors may get the idea that all these dirty coffee cups left everywhere are somehow a sign of sloppiness. This also dawns on someone from personnel in one of these companies, and she suggests that a couple of notices may put an end to this sloppiness. Accordingly a couple of handcrafted signs are taped to the wall above the coffee machines to remind everyone to bring the coffee cups back to the lunch room and the dishwasher.

The few people who have always done that, signs or no signs, are grateful for the signs, now everyone must surely do as they have always done. A few more people actually see the notices and remember to bring the cups back after the coffee break. The rest still leave their dirty coffee cups out there.

Why can't everyone just bring back their cups? When people are asked why they do not bring the coffee cups back, the answers are something like: "Oh I didn't see the sign;" "I don't care;" "No one else does." Some even suggest that they cannot be bothered, that it is not their responsibility: "It is surely a matter for those cleaning the offices."

It is suggested that more official signs might help, because they would convey the message in a more authoritative way, and it would then become part of the official company policy.

With the blessings of management bigger and more professional signs are ordered. They are put up in several places. Now surely everyone must see them and act accordingly. The immediate effect is that a few more coffee cups are brought back. Most people continue to ignore the request, including, it is rumoured, some of the busy managers. After a while most of those initially complying with the request seem to become more lax, and again ignore the signs. After a short while it looks as if the bigger, more official signs have had even less effect than the original handwritten signs. A few steadfast people continue to bring back their coffee cups, but they did this even before the first signs.

Somehow those who took the initiative must have expected that people would comply with the signs when they were put up. One may speculate why. Did they expect that people were not aware of the problem and that they just had to be made aware? That would presume that most, if not all, of the non-followers were somehow potentially ready to follow the request, they just had to be reminded.

Or did they expect that people would follow the signs because they were there, and somehow signified a formal company policy? The argument for bigger, more official signs must certainly have rested upon such an assumption. This would presume that people usually followed formal company policy, and that it would be either embarrassing or at least reproachable to be caught not complying. It turned out that the assumptions were wrong in this case.

Only a few felt they had to comply, but they were regarded as slightly funny by the rest. They were seen as somewhat unimaginative and sticklers for formal ways of doing things, a bit pedantic in their attitude and not really the up-and-coming people of the company.

This points to a certain ambiguity in this story. On the one hand the dirty coffee cups were seen as a problem, and management accepted that by their decision to put up the signs. On the other hand it seems evident that those who ignored the signs acted more in accordance with the real attitudes of the company.

The dirty coffee cup example may sound somewhat ludicrous, the problem being so unimportant. Incidentally the same problem was mentioned as a small, but an annoying problem in a branch office of Jyske Bank during an interview session carried out by members of CREDO.[1] While talking about examples of persistent problems in the branch office, the problem of coffee pots that were never emptied popped up. "It is very evident in the case, where they [the employees] never empty the coffee pots. It has been said 750 times, and they have never got [so far as to] empty them. When you are standing there in the evening, you see 700 pots with coffee in them. Why can't they just empty them? One has to turn it into something positive though. It is better to say, if there are just three who have emptied them, 'it is really nice of you to have done this,' without sounding sarcastic."[2]

The interviewer next asks what the person being interviewed did, whether he emptied the pots, and the answer was: "That is a little difficult when you don't drink coffee yourself." Perhaps this explains why they had a problem.

During presentations on value-based leadership I often hear managers tell stories of the same kind of annoying small problems in their companies. Therefore I expect that in reality such problems tie up an inordinate amount time and energy in many companies.

IT MAKES NO DIFFERENCE WHETHER I DO OR DON'T

In the case of the dirty coffee cups an unknown number of people may have agreed with the good intention of the request. Individually they may have recognised that it would be better for the company if certain forms of behaviour did not occur. Still they did not in general comply with the request, their argument being that they did not think it would help if they complied. As long as nearly everyone was leaving the coffee cups behind, their individual change of behaviour would not matter. They would just feel stupid if they brought their cups back, and so they did not change their behaviour, even though they agreed with the intention. They all had the same kind of excuse: "I would willingly do it, if it would help, but it makes no difference whether or not I do it."[3]

Competition in a free market economy may also lead to this excuse cropping up. To see how we take a look at the example involving balls.

Tom N is responsible for buying children's toys for a department store. At the moment he is standing in front of a series of Samurai Tiger Rats based on a recent television series. Tom lifts one of the boxes with a Samurai Tiger Rat placed in a Rat-Pack Megabody. Apparently this was some kind of vehicle for the tiger rats. Tom was lost in thought for a moment. Samurai tiger rats with battle cars, who might have thought up a weird idea like that? Perhaps someone inspired by sick cartoon characters?

Privately he was not especially proud of selling such toys. He squinted towards the baskets with soccer footballs. Would it not be a better idea to give children something like that, instead of some mutant rats with the honour code of a Japanese Samurai? He went over and took up one of the leather footballs and became lost in thought.

He was still delighted that he had succeeded in getting those footballs. He had really outsmarted the competitors with these quality leather balls. He thought of his difficult negotiations with new suppliers in Pakistan. One of them had shown a real devil-may-care attitude and invited him to see the factory where the leather footballs were made. Tom suddenly remembered the warm, dark, dusty room in the barn-like building where the balls were sewn. After the strong sunlight he had trouble seeing anything, but after a while he could see the children sewing the balls. They were quite young. He had been shown how meticulously the balls were made, and had been told how well they were compared to balls produced in the West costing a lot more. Absentmindedly he had replied: "Yes but we have to compete with plastic balls."

He had wanted to ask how old the children were, and how much they were paid, whether they went to school or not, but he had forgotten, because of the drawn-out negotiations. And what the hell, nobody could see that the footballs were made by children. Although, now he came to think of it, somebody had told him that international organisations had taken up cases involving child labour and forced labour. Tom suddenly had a strange sinking feeling in his guts. What if someone became interested in *his* footballs?

Then he thought of the alternatives. At least the balls were better toys than the tiger rats. And what would the alternative be for the children engaged in the production should he choose to boycott products based on the child labour? Other buyers with fewer scruples would offer lower prices because there would no longer be competition between the buyers, and then the conditions for the children might become worse.

Besides, why should it be his problem? People wanted these products. In the last instance it was the customers who decided what would be sold, wasn't it? Not him and not his company. If they couldn't find the footballs in his department store, people would just buy them somewhere else. And what could he do about that? If his company stopped selling these balls they would just lose their market share, apart from that nothing else would change.

Tom dropped the football back into the basket, he had decided to get something else as a present for his son.

And so, realising many of the aspects of this dilemma, Tom decided that it would not help to stop buying toys made by children because his actions would make no difference. He would wait for a concerted action or for legislation that would make the sale of products made by children illegal. Then his competitors would also have to stop selling those toys.

A longer version of this example was published as an ethical dilemma in a Danish journal.[5] The dilemma gave rise to responses from a representative of a council representing the toy trade and the manager of a toy company. Parts of their responses are interesting in relation to discussion here.

One respondent asserted that the inspiration for new toys comes from American television cartoons: "This is a development that the Danish toy trade does not have many chances of influencing, because it happens through a growing internationalisation of the media-industry."[5] Accordingly, there is nothing we can do about it. Likewise competition today makes it necessary to "import from regions that have lower production – including wage costs than most European countries."

This means that a dilemma like the one in the example has to be seen in a larger international perspective: "It will thus be very difficult as an individual Danish importer to set up higher demands than what is valid internationally, because he will be in a weak negotiating position and furthermore will be weakened competition-wise by higher prices."

It is argued that it is important to act together and that a step in this direction has been taken by the toy manufacturers of Europe in the form of a code. According to the code one cannot use children below the age of 18 and convicts in toy production. The second respondent argued that many young girls of 18 years and older are in a privileged position. Working in the toy industry they get higher wages and better working conditions than elsewhere.

Speaking of footballs, the respondent had just been negotiating with a supplier of footballs. The factory producing the footballs had been visited, and: "No form of child labour is found," but then he continues: "But some of the balls are sewn in private homes and delivered to the factory ... accordingly we cannot guarantee that children have not been involved in the process in the individual homes. We have received guarantee that this is not the case, but we cannot be sure."[6]

The two respondents' arguments are stated clearly and may sound reasonable. Still they contain versions of the "it makes no difference" excuse and we-do-not-want-to-know-too-much attitude, and although inspections are carried out and guarantees demanded, one might also detect some form of look-away argument. In fact it may be a sensible reaction to demands for more accountability in relation to working conditions, to demand a written guarantee from the supplier solemnly declaring that no child labour or forced labour has been used in the production of the product in question. In this way the companies selling those products have their backs free, although they may in fact never care to check whether these guarantees are more than a piece of paper, looking, perhaps knowingly, away from their own suspicions and knowledge.

In the case of the dirty coffee cups, and the leather footballs the excuse that "it makes no difference" means that the individual contribution is so small as to be almost undetectable.

Glover talks about a discrimination threshold: "This is where a single person's act will push a situation slightly further in a certain direction, but where his contribution, although real, may be too small to be detected when its effects are spread through the community."[7]

In a different approach using two small experiments Kerr and Kaufman-Gilliland showed a justification-via-inefficacy effect in relation to social dilemmas. We tell ourselves that we would not be able to make a difference anyway.[8]

"It makes no difference" may also be used as an excuse for not voting in a general election, but here I am not sure the excuse would be accepted, realising what it would mean for the system of voting in a democratic society. In some cases of course the potential problems are taken care of by making voting compulsory. Still this only works as long people actually make a choice in the ballot box.

An argument against the "it makes no difference" attitude would be that intelligent individuals might reason that if everyone else was thinking and acting like this in every situation, it would soon lead to major problems. Accordingly they may feel a vague responsibility to do their share even if it is negligible, in the not unreasonable hope that everyone else will reason in the same way, and do their share too. Elster sees the voter reasoning like this: "If I cooperate, there is a good chance that the other will cooperate too. Being like me, he will act like me. Let me, therefore, cooperate to bring it about that he does too."[9] This reasoning seems to be borne out by an experiment of Quattrone and Tversky.[10]

CREATING A CORROSIVE ATMOSPHERE

M is the conscientious branch manager of a bank. He is trying to uphold certain standards in his branch. The standards are found in the rules and administrative guidelines for banks, official policies of the bank, written rules, and in his belief that he has to uphold certain unwritten standards belonging to his profession or stemming from his own experience in the bank. He feels both a vague and a specific responsibility to live up to these standards, and he attempts to hold all the employees in his branch to the same high standards.

Some time later a change in the general management of the bank is accompanied by rumours of a new aggressively competitive policy, aimed at gaining market shares and making the bank more profitable. Aggressive marketing, campaigns for a whole range of new products, introduction of personal campaign goals and performance-based pay are the new instruments used by management.

Soon M's branch is merged with another branch and moved to a more central location. The new head of the branch is B, who is seen by the bank's management as having the right potential under the new policy. He has shown some very good results in his former position.

B, who has a somewhat extravagant taste and very few scruples, lets the bank pay for his and his wife's membership of a yacht club, the excuse being that he will generate more business by mixing with its potential important customers.

During the next year he generates new business, not in the least thanks to his membership of the yacht club. The bank finances a substantial part of a couple of large building projects, among these the construction of a new entertainment complex with several small cinemas, restaurants and a shopping arcade. During construction there are some cost overruns, but the whole complex gets a very favourable press coverage when it is finished. The bank becomes rather heavily involved, but as a new branch in that part of the city they want to attract business, and the branch manager is seen as one of the up-and-coming people.

Somehow his enthusiasm also fires the employees, with a few exceptions. The former branch manager M has some qualms about some of the larger projects the branch has become involved in, but his objections are swept aside with someone mumbling that these objections are to be expected, that he is just envious. M is still respected, but is regarded as being too obsessed with doing things the right way whether the talk is about the new risky engagements, the bloated expense accounts or dirty coffee cups. His is a lost cause. His colleagues take their lead from the new manager, and there is an intense competition to exceed personal goals. Existing rules and guidelines are soon ignored, with no consequences as the amount of business is growing faster than elsewhere in the bank.

M feels that his position has become untenable and leaves the bank to take over the local branch of a savings bank. Some of his former employees accompany him. They are in fact choosing what Hirschman in his famous analysis calls the exit alternative.[11]

B states that the slow-moving and back-striving part of the branch has left and feels free to generate even more business. He raises the goals for the branch and for every employee for the next year. Some young ambitious employees see this as their chance and being very good at their job they generate a lot of new business. As a result they get pay rises and special benefits. With a few exceptions the other employees try to follow in their tracks. Business is booming, and the reports to the main office of the bank are getting more and more optimistic.

In the bank there are rumours that some of the business generated is rather risky, that the reports look too rosy, and that the bank stands to lose tens of millions of Danish kroner. It is also said that some of the best people are operating outside the instructions of the bank.

Experts from the main office are flown in. They soon discover major problems in the branch office and find that there is risk of losing money on many of the large engagements. Many small irregularities are also discovered, and it becomes evident that rules and guidelines have been ignored. The branch is certainly no longer seen as quite as successful, although some of the large engagements are saved.

What had happened? According to the stories told in the bank, employees were attracted by the money they could earn, and they got their inspiration from B. His relaxed attitude towards guidelines lessened their own qualms. The argument used by all of them was invariably: "If I didn't do it then one of my colleagues surely would have." Maybe they tacitly thought, "and why shouldn't I be the one to gain from this?"

Although it is a small matter the bank finally becomes aware that they are paying the yacht club fees of B and his wife. This is used as an excuse for firing B.

Is this example a case of one bad apple, B, spoiling the whole barrel? In the case of one rotten apple leading to the rapid decay of all apples in a barrel of apples there is a convincing scientific explanation. When apples ripen, they give off ethylene gas. Ethylene is a natural ripening agent, and the gas speeds up the ripening of other apples whereby even more ethylene is given off leading first to the ripening of all apples and then rapid decay, even of those apples that do not touch the already ripe or rotten apples. Ethylene is thus necessary for the ripening process, but too much ethylene too early may spoil the fruit before it can be sold. This fact is used in attempts to preserve fresh fruit, by removing the surplus ethylene from containers storing the fruit.[12]

It is in the air. The ethylene of an organisation may be represented by rumours, stories, anecdotes and habits, but in the case of the bank also by the aggressive marketing campaigns, the introduction of personal campaign goals and pay according to performance.

Again there is a certain ambiguity in the example. As with real apples the ethylene of an organisation may be seen as something positive; we usually want apples to become ripe, just as we want a business to grow. In this case ethylene may be seen as a positive attractive force luring people with chances of personal rewards, with activity, with excitement, with all sorts of positive aspects and possibilities.

The former branch manager M may have given off too little ethylene by acting too much on the safe side with little chance of ever ripening and certainly no risk of spoiling the whole barrel.

The new branch manager B on the other hand gave off enough ethylene not only to ripen business, but also to spoil the whole branch. In this case his activities led to rapid decay, to bad and problematic attitudes that again gave off more ethylene in the shape of rumours, stories, anecdotes and habits that led to ever expanding vicious circles of bad attitudes. This is apparently what happened in the branch. Too much ethylene spoilt most of the business of this branch.

The ethylene analogy may help us to understand that the simple remedy of throwing away the bad apple would already be too late, or that dismissing a manager misusing his expense account may not be enough. Neither might it have been a good idea just to keep on doing business the way M did. The problem is not only the apple or the person, it is the ethylene of the organisation, and this kind of ethylene is much more difficult to supply and remove in the right dosage and quality than the ethylene of real apples. We cannot just siphon off the excess amounts of ethylene.

The vicious spirals of unwanted behaviour may be slowed down but only through the added costs of more rules, closer surveillance and heavier sanctions. Measures that do not really influence the attitudes of management and employees in a way that will lead to a heightened sense of individual responsibility and better behaviour.

PERVERTING APPRAISALS AND INCENTIVES

In a survey carried out by CREDO, a bank employee tells a story of how campaign goals for the sale of certain pension products influence the advice given to a customer.

It is Thursday evening in the branch and the employee is engaged in a conversation with a prospective customer on one of the different pension schemes the bank is selling. There is a choice between two schemes, and the customer expects the bank employee to advise him on which scheme would be most favourable for him. Incidentally this Thursday is also the last day of an intensive campaign to sell a given type of pension scheme. And then, in the words of the employee telling the story: "The human factor is so that the bank adviser will easily be tempted to say to the customer: 'Actually I believe that my best advice to you is …,"[13] Nothing more is said in the interview, but the implication is evident, the employee just did not want to say it out loud.

What is happening is that some campaign goals for a certain product which may be accompanied by different forms of incentives influence the advice given to the customer.[14] The product sold may not be the best for the customer, but it may fulfil campaign goals and carry rewards for the employee selling it.

Here we see the first signs of how campaign goals, rewards, incentives and perhaps appraisals influence the actions of employees in a way that is not in the interest of the customer. What we are focusing on are the forms of individual performance-based incentive schemes, preferably based on pecuniary rewards. The critical arguments presented may become weaker the more general the schemes become. Basing them on teams or on the combined results achieved by all in a company may lessen their negative impact.

In order to use a pecuniary incentive system, for instance in the form of a performance-based scheme, it will be necessary to focus on performance that can somehow be measured. The more such performance measures are used, the more one can expect that vaguer goals that cannot be made operational in the same way are ignored. It is no longer the goal to find the best solution in the case of the pension scheme. The important goals are the goals that can be scaled and measured, not conceptions of a more general character.

This also seems to be the conclusion drawn in Bok's study of how executives and professionals are paid and how it affects America. One of his examples is taken from medicine: "Incentive schemes that reward doctors for working harder may induce them to perform too many services, whereas bonuses aimed at making them more cost-conscious may cause them to perform too few."[15]Under such conditions one might expect pronounced bias or skewness of goals to develop.

Although goals may be skewed individual employees will be forced to concentrate on exactly the tasks that result in better performance measures in relation to these goals and be forced to disregard as much as possible the tasks that are not part of this measurement scheme. They may personally be convinced that other tasks are more important if more general long-term goals are to be achieved, but it does not matter. They may believe that a performance-based pay system will pervert their efforts, but it does not matter. They may know that the demands of the customers are not really served by the products and services they have to sell, but it does not matter. They may even think that some of the performance they are rewarded for has problematic or unethical consequences for themselves, the environment or the society outside the company or organisation, but it does not matter.

They have to become narrow-minded and self-serving in their outlook. Someone else will have to take care of the consequences. The result is what Bento and Ferreira have called materialistic foregrounding. The foregrounding term simply meaning that materialistic and pecuniary considerations become more prominent than other considerations. In an organisational culture characterised by this foregrounding, "the emphasis is on task, outcomes, growth, efficiency, speed, winning; job stress is perceived as part of the game, conflict is acceptable, and work demands take precedence over personal life and relationships."[16]

In the short run this materialistic foregrounding may lead to higher output and better performance, with no apparent drawbacks. In the long run though it is to be expected that disregarding the other aspects in the background will have a negative influence, perhaps not as much on the company or organisation in question, as on employees. If personal life is suffering because the focus is exclusively on performance, it may not only influence the company, but the future life of the employees.

In relation to work motives Knouse mentions that psychologists might argue "that tangible rewards, such as money or objects earned, may actually reduce intrinsic motivation – doing something for its own sake."[17]

An attempt to use pay according to measured performance might actually reduce or erase the motivation to do the job because one derives a certain satisfaction from doing it, or because it represents a mental challenge, like a crossword puzzle, or a physical challenge, like a bike race. Or because it is seen as important or meaningful. Or because it increases one's self-esteem, influence or power.[18] Or because of some intangible benefits. Or because of the praise one receives.

No wonder Lepper and Green can talk about the hidden costs of reward.[19] With pay based on performance all these reasons and motives are more or less reduced to one, to pecuniary rewards. Others may be acknowledged, but only as something that one has to remember apart from the really important one, pecuniary reward based on performance; the assumption being that employees as well as managers will work harder to achieve goals when they are paid according to performance.

Strangely enough we have to conclude that such schemes may lead to more and more dirty coffee cups, less conscientious employees with a less caring and a more irresponsible attitude – and many cases of the bad apples spoiling the whole organisation.

PEER PRESSURE

A small example may show how peer pressure works. A female university lecturer tries to hold the students to certain standards in her classes. She expects them to be on time, be well prepared and make good presentations and reports. She is used to students accepting her demands after a short period of time, and usually the students are quite satisfied with her approach when they finish her courses. Sometimes she thinks that the way she is doing her teaching and the standards she keeps are more important than the content of what she teaches.

A few weeks into one autumn term she discovers that some students seem to have become more critical of her attempt to hold them to certain standards. When asked what the problem is, they have a very concrete complaint; they point to their written reports and ask her if it is really necessary to correct their spelling mistakes and in some cases reduce their grades on account of that. She tells them that she found that the many spelling mistakes detracted from the quality of the reports. They find that unfair inasmuch as her colleagues did not comment on their spelling, and that in general their demands were not nearly as stringent as hers. No one else complained if they were a little late for classes. Finally they tell her that quite frankly some of her colleagues had suggested that they should complain formally, referring to the grading practice of other teachers and mentioning her overzealousness.

In this case a number, presumably even the majority of her colleagues, have relaxed formal demands on the students, perhaps with the unspoken agreement that this will help them get better evaluations from the students which again will mean less bother, and less time expenditure for dealing with non-compliance and complaints.

The teacher being criticised feels the pressure from her peers, if not directly, then through her students. In the beginning she decides to keep up her standards. Slowly though she discovers that students are choosing the courses of her colleagues in preference to her own. As a result she decides to relax her demands and promises herself that the next time she grades she will disregard most of the spelling mistakes and let all grades slip a little upwards.

She is unhappy because she really believes that the standards have become too low and that she will now contribute to this lowering of standards. It becomes a dilemma that nags at her conscience, she has a bad feeling about it, it disturbs her sleep and her stomach. Her hope is that these problems will go away after a while when she gets used to what she is doing.

A very short-sighted solution perhaps, but what can a single individual, in this case a teacher, do, as long as everyone else is contributing to this lowering of standards? Some might think that she ought to blow the whistle on those practices, but would that really work? It would be difficult for her just to contemplate, she knows it will be unpopular and she knows what that will mean. She also doubts that any goodwill come of it, as long she is alone in seeing this as a problem.

Peer pressure is almost always a negative push factor. Pushing people to accept and change attitudes generally in accord with the way the majority sees it, and isolating those individuals who will not play ball, pushing them into peripheral positions or even beyond the periphery, out of their jobs or even their lives. In experiments Asch has analysed how group pressure modifies and distorts judgments.[20]

How does peer pressure work in theory? According to Kandel and Lazear[21] two conditions must be fulfilled for peer pressure to function as a motivational device. The first is that the actions of one of the members of a given organisation somehow affect the rest of the organisation. Kandel and Lazear talk about the well-being of the rest being affected. If this is not the case there is no incentive for the rest to exert peer pressure.

The second condition is that members of an organisation somehow have the ability to influence the choices and behaviour of the member brought under peer pressure.

Kandel and Lazear's analyses of peer pressure seem narrowly defined by the interest in peer pressure as a motivational force in a team with payment according to the performance of a team. Their view of peer pressure is too constricted. In fact the influence that one member has upon the rest of the organisation may only indirectly affect their well-being. In some way it may be enough that the behaviour of one member is different from others without directly affecting them. Strangely enough Kandel and Lazear mention in passing that "sociologist often think of peer pressure as arising when individuals deviate from a well-established group norm."[22]

In the bank case it may be enough that some of the employees take greater care, are more conscientious and observe the guidelines, even though their actions do not directly affect the rest apart from a slight drag on the combined performance of the branch. The thing really nagging the majority is that someone acts holier than they. In itself this might be enough, but if it is combined with some vague feeling of insecurity, perhaps with those exerting the pressure asking themselves: What if the few are right, and am I not really doing what I should even though the majority is acting in the same way as I am?

The second condition would seem to presume that there are cases where peer pressure cannot be brought to bear. In an organisation it is difficult to think of situations in which peer pressure cannot be brought to bear. In our view peer pressure can always be brought to bear, at least if there are no countervailing forces in the shape of different groupings in the organisation.

Peer pressure may be exerted in many ways. In the beginning there may be a slow closing off against the individual with attitudes and behaviour that deviate from the group norm; not letting someone in on gossip, new information, and talks during coffee breaks and ignoring input from the individual brought under pressure. The individual in question may never be able to do things quite right according to the rest. Next may follow more active forms of pressure. Assigning more administrative work, or giving difficult tasks to the individual under pressure. Finally more open forms of mental and physical harassment may be used by the peers, sometimes accompanied by veiled or open threats.

It may be argued that peer pressure *per se* may be seen as rather neutral in its effects. It may work in a negative mode contributing to the creation of ever widening spirals of bad behaviour, or it may work in a positive mode helping to weed out bad and problematic behaviour. It might help bring about better standards even in the case of the dirty coffee cups, except that it would be difficult to talk about peer pressure when the majority is indifferent as in the case of the dirty coffee cups. Still one might speculate whether the negative mode of peer pressure will not outweigh the positive one. In effect peer pressure means pressure is put in a more or less overt way on people in order to make them comply with what is usually the view of the majority. This pressure might in itself be regarded as something negative. If people do not follow the views of the majority, they are put under pressure to comply with the views of the majority. It may be doubtful whether the views of the majority ever represent something that one would wish to strive for, whether they are not in fact often mediocre and limiting in their effect.

In fact I am assuming that peer pressure is very poor and in most instances a very bad substitute for an attitude based on a strong sense of individual responsibility, preferably of the vague kind, where no detailed specifications are needed. It is difficult to see how at least the crude kinds of peer pressure discussed here will ever be able to contribute to such attitudes. Instead one may expect that this kind of peer pressure will just force individuals into a common mould, in which responsibility does not have a very important role to play as long as one follows the direction of the pressure. Thus peer pressure may very well contribute to a reduced individual responsibility.

SUBMITTING TO POWER AND AUTHORITY

"I had to do it or my career would be in jeopardy." This might be the response of an employee who had fiddled with the result of test procedures for measuring the presence of materials dangerous to the environment in the discharge of waste water from a chemical plant. Management may have made it very clear to the person in charge of these measurements that the results ought to show that the relevant values were well within the limits imposed by public environmental regulation. The person in charge may have been told by a management representative that this was what he was to aim for if he wanted to keep his job. Wanting to keep his job the employee may have diluted the samples to show that the amount of toxic stuff was well below the limit imposed, even though he had fairly good reason to believe that unadulterated samples would show values above the limit.

The person in question may have had absolutely no wish to fiddle with the samples if he was not forced to. His standards may have been the standards of a good laboratory technician. Still he did it because management told him to do so. In his imagination he may have thought of all the possible consequences of disobeying this wish of management. Not only would he probably lose his job under some pretext having nothing to do with the problem in question, he also feared that management might try to influence the possibilities for future employment by misrecommending him when some prospective employer asked about his time at the company. For family reasons he thought he could not cope with that. He may have said to himself: "Had I been alone, I would not have given in to the pressure from management." Pressure from management and a feeling of responsibility towards his family make the employee bend the rules.

It must not be forgotten that the same kind of threats and subtle forms of power may be used in situations where someone in power actually wants to make someone else, employee or soldier, behave according to the rules or the ethical code. For instance when a supervisor tries to force an employee to give up a certain dangerous behaviour by threatening with disciplinary action and dismissal if he continues his present behaviour. A behaviour that may endanger either himself: "You must use the hard hat, when you are working in this area or you risk serious head injury"; or someone else: "You must be more careful when handling these containers, or you will endanger the health of everyone in a 10-metre radius."

What is common in all these cases is the threat of using some kind of power or influence to make employees, or subordinates, behave in a certain way. In all instances the use of power or rather the threat of using power is meant to make someone else change their behaviour for the bad or for the good.

In the cases discussed here power seems to represent the ability of someone, the management or the police, to influence the behaviour of someone else. This is not enough though, information may also influence someone's behaviour as may love or infatuation. Power includes the ability to induce someone else to do something that he or she would not have wanted to do as in: "I would not have done that, if I hadn't been forced to." This attempt to get a handle on power is quite close to Dahl's classic definition.[23] In front of our inner eye we may see a video of police action where perpetrators are being forced into handcuffs and led away. But this "stay on the ground or I will hit you with my night stick" expression of power is still too simple.

Power may be expressed much more subtly than that. A manager may have the power not only to dismiss employees, but also to promote employees. The promise of promotion may have the same effect on behaviour of employees as the threat of dismissal, but can we say that an employee is forced to comply when he or she changes his or her behaviour in response to promises of promotion? A more encompassing understanding of power may be had by saying that power represents ability to force through one's will in the face of opposition.[24] Power might then represent physical force, ability to influence the future choices for others, the knowledge and charisma to persuade someone or the cunning to outmanoeuvre the opposition in various ways. This is the power we find evidence of in Crenson's work or Lukes' theories, perhaps it even includes Foucault's concept of micro-power.[25]

It is certainly also the power we find in Machiavelli's *The Prince*; the power of deviousness, the ability to use every trick in the book to achieve one's will. "How commendable in a Prince it is to keepe his word, and live with integrity, not making use of cunning and subtlety, every one knows well: yet wee see by experience in these our dayes, that those Princes have affected great matters, who have made small reckoning of keeping their words, and have known by their craft to turne and wind men about, and in the end have overcome those who have grounded upon the truth."[26]

We must not forget that the will to control, and the will to power may be something inherent in a human being. With power one can control important aspects of one's own existence and destiny. In the more extreme form one may think of the active positive force represented in Nietzsche's will to power. This is the almost innocent power of a fierce predator, it may be destructive and endanger others, but it is also a prime mover.[27]

According to Hegel's *Herrschaft und Knechtschaft*,[28] power is a complementary relation between people. To be in command means that someone must be under command. To exercise power means to exercise power over someone who has less power or is powerless; someone who in a way allows this power to be exercised.

Milgram's experiments may show how easily we may give in to authority.[29] In his famous experiment two persons take part in an experiment that is supposed to investigate the effect of punishment on learning.

One person administers the punishment, the other acts as the student who is supposed to learn a list of word pairs by heart. Every time the student gives a wrong answer, the teacher is to punish him with an electric chock. The teacher can use voltages from say 15 to 450 volts. When the student gives a wrong answer, the teacher must administer a jolt by using a switch, first from the low end of the scale and then increasing the voltage when more mistakes are made. The student in question does not really get any electric chocks, but he has been instructed to act as if the jolts are real and hurting.

The real purpose of the experiment is to find out how far the teacher is willing to go in following the instructions. In the experiment the teachers in general seem willing to follow the instructions and administer the punishment almost with abandon.

This conclusion seems to be supported by what is known as Zimbardo's "Stanford prison experiment." The idea behind the experiment was to place normal persons in a simulated prison as inmates and wardens respectively and then observe the results. "The prisoners experienced a loss of personal identity ... In contrast, the guards (with rare exceptions) experienced a marked gain in social power, status and group identification which made role-playing rewarding."[30]

On the basis of experiments like these one may conclude that people under certain conditions may be willing to follow instructions to inflict pain on other people. The experience of war seems to bear this out whether we are talking about the atrocities committed during the Second World War or the terrors of the recent civil war in former Yugoslavia.

I do not believe that either Milgram's experiments or the "Stanford prison experiment" as such can tell us very much about the complex processes that lead people to commit such atrocities. The explanation may be too simple; we may have to include the effects of rabid leaders, the effects of escalating reciprocal atrocities or just stories of escalating atrocities committed by the enemy, the effects of peer pressure that we have already looked upon and threats of various kinds of punishments: "It is either you or them."

This submission to authority somehow depends on certain conditions like the existence of what we may regard as legitimate authority, in this case the leader of the experiment. In a situation where we are novices or feel insecure we may leave decisions to the person apparently in control. One may well ask what else we are supposed to do, but if we accept that, then we might also accept that the reactions of the persons who thought they administered the electric jolts were the reactions of persons following the instructions of someone in authority. The test persons acting as teachers may have said to themselves: "They would know what they are doing, would they not? They would not have designed an experiment that is dangerous or illegal, would they?"

A test person administering the electric jolt may feel that the leader of the experiment holds the responsibility for the experiment; as a test person I just follow the instructions, that is my responsibility and not much more. This may also happen in relation to the other examples mentioned. In each case we give up responsibility, because those in the know, those who are in charge, must certainly hold the responsibility; I cannot have any responsibility within their field of authority. We listen to the voice of authority, we obey it. Maybe it is worth remembering that obedience stems from the Latin *ob audire*, to listen to.

In private business we may expect to find someone who has a formal responsibility and the authority to make decisions for the rest. The more responsibility and authority is concentrated in this way, the less responsibility the individual employee holds. This is at least what might be expected to be the case in traditional industries.

An example may be the scandal that led to the closure of the formerly well-regarded Danish company Nordisk Fjerfabrik Holding A/S. In the book *Ledelse og vildledelse* Krogsgaard characterises the situation in the company before bankruptcy and scandal destroyed it. "It was well known that disagreement with the management was tantamount to dismissal ... The chairman of the board, whose personality was charismatic and strongly domineering, selected his closest managers on the basis of their susceptibility to these qualities and accordingly their ability to follow his directives without objections."[31]

It may be understandable if employees and managers over the years can be drilled into a kind of misguided loyalty and obedience, when all those who have resisted the drill have left the company either in disgust or with a vague feeling of something being fundamentally wrong. If the employees and managers become used to bowing to the command of a powerful and charismatic leader, they may become like well-drilled obedient soldiers surrounded as they are by what they believe are followers of the leader. Fearful of uttering criticism, when they see glimpses of what is going on, because everybody else acts unaffected, they relax their own standards and accept more and more transgressions of rules and ethical standards, until there is an open scandal, with everyone staring in disbelief at each other wondering how it could have come so far.

Arbitrary shifts of opinions and attitudes can take place under such a system. Today someone in the company can be a hero, tomorrow the same person can be a villain and has to be denounced by everyone. There is no independent opinion.

An organisational integrity is missing. In the parallelogram of forces one just follows the resultant force no matter what direction it is pointing in. Opposition and disobedience cannot be tolerated in organisations like this, but must be subdued or removed. This is how authoritarian government works too, in contrast to democracies where opposition and disagreement may actually help solve problems, create solutions and move the whole society along.

BOTTOM-LINE SHORTSIGHTEDNESS

After getting a question about how the bank would handle engagements with questionable ethical profiles after a major Danish pension fund had announced publicly that ethical considerations would become important for their investment strategies, the CEO of a Danish bank bursts out: "I believe that it's hypocritical nonsense with all those pension funds that want to get a little PR by investing ethically. It sounds d… good. Now, let me tell you one thing … this is one of my hobby-horses. I visit a number of customers, on just one day in Copenhagen I can manage 4–5 customers. Three of the companies that I visited were doing trade with China. They import from China, at [wages of] one Kroner per hour, … is that ethical? Does one know whether there is child labour involved? No! Does one know whether they are extremely polluting? No, one doesn't! Don't they have terrible dictatorship out there? Oh yes! Almost everything is wrong with China, nevertheless we are all doing trade with them."[32]

What the CEO is saying is: This after all is business. As long as we stick to laws applicable for what we are doing, it is all right to focus on the bottom line and the interests of the shareholders. We have no further duty.

The words of the CEO sound almost as if they may have come from the mouth of Adam Smith or Milton Friedman. In a free economy "there is one and only one social responsibility of business – to use its resources and engage in activities designed to increase its profits as long as it stays within the rules of the game, which is to say, engages in open and free competition, without deception or fraud."[33]

In cases where members of CREDO have been involved in courses on value-based management and leadership, participants have been asked to contribute dilemmas from their own experience. In these dilemmas questions of legality and ethics versus potential revenue are rather frequent.

Many cases straddle the same borderline of profit, legality and ethics, and it is evident that many branch managers will accept the business if they do not overstep the limits of legality. They may sense or even know that certain business propositions involve attempts to avoid paying taxes or to circumvent other government regulation. Still most of the managers prefer to think that this is none of their business as long *they* stay within the law. If there is a problem the state ought to take care of it through new laws. If there are no laws curbing a certain behaviour, then why should I act holier than thou. I would just hurt my own business.

The same type of engagement, involving tax evasion, is commented on by the chief legal adviser of another Danish bank, and his somewhat guarded comment is: "… one may ask, is it our fault? We have made the monetary transaction, but is it the fault of the accountant, or is it the fault of their lawyer, or is it the fault of the [customer]? There are many, and I do not believe that one is better than the other. I know it certainly affects management a lot."[34]

Perhaps unknown to representatives of the banks, they seem to be asking some of the same rhetorical questions Friedman asks. Either, "Can self-selected private individuals decide what the social interest is?" Or perhaps more relevant in these situations, "Is it tolerable that these public functions of taxation, expenditure, and control be exercised by the people who happen at the moment to be in charge of particular enterprises …?"[35]

In Friedman's examples the rules of the game seem simple and clear-cut, as are his examples ranging from price controls to labour agreements and potentially dangerous medicine. In all cases intervention in a free economy will tend to reduce the benefits for all. Friedman sees only a small regulating role for government, for instance in relation to "neighborhood effects." Only in this case Friedman seems to accept that some kind of collective intervention is necessary.

Similar views seem to be held by Baumol and Blackman in their discussion of the dangers of leaving the social responsibility to the voluntary actions of business managers. They regard it as a frightening idea to have managers use the resources they command to "influence the social and political events". "... who is to determine in what way these events ought to be influenced? Who is to select these goals? If it is management itself, the power of interference with our lives and the lives of others that management is asked to assume is surely intolerable."[36]

The opinions of Danish bank managers seem to support such a view. They cannot be the moral guardians of their customers, can they? They just have to watch their part of the business. It is evident that many of the managers express the belief that this is the way to act. Having expressed this as their opinion it soon becomes evident that they are in doubt.

Many of the managers would not like to have their names and the name of the bank associated with certain types of business and certain customers even though there may be no question of illegality. A decisive factor seems to be that they would not want to be associated with certain deals and customers, and this consideration colours their decision on whether to accept or reject a business proposition. The reason for not wanting to be associated with certain business deals and customers is of course influenced by what is quietly seen as acceptable in the bank, and this again seems to have much to do with the media. Recent scandals in certain types of businesses seem to make them weary of certain engagements.

Thus Friedman's arguments seem oddly insufficient and problematic as Arrow has showed. Other considerations are necessary for the market to function.[37] He argues that there are situations in which it will be desirable to have some idea of social responsibility, some kind of duty, whether ethical, moral or legal: "[E]thical elements enter in some measure into every contract; without them, no market could function. There is an element of trust in every transaction."[38]

Although many may subscribe to Friedman's view in their words, in their deeds they seem to be somewhat more prudent and regardful in the practices, in the sense that they keep their minds open to other consider-ations. This openness often represents no more than a glimpse in the rear-view mirror towards past scandals and problem experiences. Most of the time the eyes and the mind are glued to view the bottom line in the short term.

One may wonder whether this emphasis on the short-term bottom line will not result in unforeseen problems, even if one attempts to act prudently on the information in the rear-view mirror. It is after all only a furtive rear-view look made to make sure that one's back is free. In a given branch of business many insiders may know of other unethical or even illegal practices or of potential future problems, but as long as no one outside business has seen them, they may to a certain extent be disregarded. This may work as long as the asymmetry of information that Arrow talked about exists. But what happens if they are suddenly made public?

Estes presents us with an array of examples of what happens when a company focuses too narrowly on the bottom line.[39] They include Bhopal, the Dalkon shield case, and fraud cases involving the defence industry. They also include cases where a company leaves behind heavy pollution to be taken care of by the taxpayers and local councils. In the asbestos cases, companies knowingly ignored the dangerous effects of asbestos, not only on workers in the industry, but on all those coming into contact with it.

It would seem that a narrow focus on short-term profits may actually have some very bad effects. In the asbestos case a leading producer of asbestos apparently as far back as 1933 settled asbestos workers' compensation cases out of court, and as Estes dryly comments: "A common procedure then and now to avoid a public record of guilt."[40] It is worth noting that the asbestos industry knew of the potential lethal consequences of working with or handling asbestos at a very early point in time. Still it took many years before this was recognised openly by the industry. This is also the story of a parallel Danish asbestos case.[41]

Estes talks of a record of "distortion and suppression of data that could have saved workers' lives, of 'studies' bought and paid for by the asbestos industry, of coverup and obfuscation."[42] All the while the asbestos production was kept going with few concessions to the workers. Apparently the problems brought about by working with asbestos were partly ignored, partly covered up. In a way the real problem was dumped outside the industry, on the workers, their families, pension funds, insurance companies, communities and the state. In this way the costs were not borne by those responsible for the problem.

It is of course easy to condemn the asbestos industry today. I expect that almost any one could do that. But it might not have been as easy in the 1930s or even in the early post-war years. This means that those who prefer to think that what happened here is so evidently unethical, if not strictly illegal, think that nothing like that could happen today. That is not the point though; the point is that the industry must have known about the dangers of asbestos at an early time, without really doing something about it, apart from giving out misinformation, if we are to believe Estes.

Might the same thing not be happening today? That a company knows or ought to know that it is involved in potentially dangerous practices, giving rise to potential dangers or future problems, while the employees, customers and the public are mostly unaware of these dangers and problems, or if they have a suspicion, are hindered in their attempts to gain more information. This would represent a close parallel to the asbestos case – before the acknowledgement of the terrible consequences.

A list of issues that today may contain seeds of potential troubles might include the following, in many instances overlapping, topics:

- disregarding potential dangers of products and their use;
- disregarding dangers to the environment;
- disregarding working conditions;
- disregarding human rights and questions of democracy;
- disregarding issues of social responsibility.

On the other hand, it seems evident from our examples that business today runs a severe risk of getting into very big trouble by focusing too narrowly on the bottom line, at least the bottom line in the short run. Business will be running foul of a whole series of potential conflicts, involving accusations of having made unethical decisions and being involved in unethical behaviour.

A proponent of the bottom-line approach, perhaps even our outspoken CEO talking about hypocritical nonsense may now argue: And this is what you, the customer wants, so you have to share the blame with us.

You, as a customer want asbestos firewalls, asbestos roofs, cigarettes, hand guns; cheap, but well-made leather footballs; financial schemes that will help reduce the taxes you have to pay; clothing made of natural fibres, perhaps because they are regarded as more healthy than the synthetic alternatives; you even want our gigantic bananas, not the small shrivelled bananas that the EU is trying to force down your throats, in order to help former European colonies to get rid of their produce. And of course you, the customer, will want cheap petrol for your cars, so we have to keep production costs down, or you will just go to our competitors, not because of some ideal boycott action, but because the price of our competitors would be lower. Unless you, the customer, change your attitude, it will be difficult for us to see your arguments as being very sincere.

Customers may even be employees of the companies criticised and what employee would wish that the company he or she worked for had to give up business, at least as long as there was no immediate danger of lung disease as in the case of working with asbestos fibres. Employees may look to their own personal bottom line, perhaps looking away from potential problems just like the managers and owners of the business they are employed by. No collusion between management and employees is needed, they just have to have a shared interest; not necessarily as regards the bottom line, but at least in the survival of the company and their jobs.

The recent spate of publications on shareholder value[43] seems to indicate that companies have to keep the focus on the bottom line and ignore other considerations. Although in order to avoid anything that may cause the share prices to fall, the companies would also have to keep an eye on potential problems, like being caught doing something unethical, selling products made by children in Pakistan for instance, or something illegal, like dumping toxic waste or participating in price cartels. In this case the important thing is not whether something is unethical or not, or illegal or not. The important thing is what it means for the share values.

Perhaps we have to realise that it is easier to see ethical dilemmas if one's own self-interest is not endangered, meaning that it is easier to accuse a company of unethical dealings with an authoritarian regime as long as one is not employed by that company, and as long as one does not have shares in the company or any other interest that would in essence make the company's trouble with such an ethical dilemma one's own trouble.

If we are employed by the company or own shares in it, we may have the same excuses as every other manager or employee or shareholder of a company being accused of unethical dealings. We therefore have to realise that managers are not alone responsible for the actions we deem unethical, and that our own actions may be part of the problem.

AMBIGUITIES

Looking back through the preceding discussions it may strike us that most topics contain certain ambiguities.

Although the problem of the dirty coffee cups pointed to a certain laxness in the attitudes of management as well as employees, it was evident that by ignoring small problems, like those consisting of dirty coffee cups, the company may have worked in a more efficient way with employees concentrating on matters of substance instead of mere trivialities. The employees obeying the signs were not the employees who would make the company thrive; they were perhaps acting more like well-drilled house slaves, perhaps representing Nietzsche's moral of the weak.

On the other hand if signs and other attempts to regulate, prevent or further a certain behaviour, are consistently ignored, it is to be expected that at some point this will lead to problems that may interfere with general conduct as well as efficiency, leading perhaps to vicious spirals of decay.

The excuses related to "It makes no difference whether I do or don't" seem plausible at first sight. But as we have attempted to show, things are not that simple. Such an attitude would wreak havoc on certain institutions, like voting. Therefore it would seem that it does make a difference "whether I do," even in situations with no discrimination thresholds. Somehow my actions may galvanise others into action: "If he can so can I." Perhaps this would also help solve the problem of the inactive bystanders in cases where people need assistance.

In the bank case we saw that the problem discussed perhaps could be compared to the problem of controlling the amount of ethylene gas. Too little and nothing ripens, too much and the fruit decays rapidly. Appraisals and incentives may be important for efficiency, but as we have seen, at least in some cases, appraisals and incentives may in fact bring along new problems, leading not only to problems of long-run efficiency, but also problems of attitude and responsibility, thereby perhaps perverting existing values: "I am not being paid to watch your table!"

The same ambiguity characterises peer pressure. Peer pressure probably is an unavoidable phenomenon, but as we have seen it may make it impossible for a single person to act according to a standard that is very much different from this person's peers. Peer pressure will tend to lead to a spiral of decay as in the case of the teacher, but in certain cases peer pressure may help protect certain standards. This at least must be the reasoning behind the scientific process of peer reviewing, although of course this might also represent sticking to a certain status quo where new ideas will be met with a critique from one's peers.

Comparable ambiguities characterise power. Power relations presumably cannot be avoided. In some cases power seems to have a corrupting influence, leading to a decay in moral standards. But power or the will to power also seems to represent a force necessary to break through established bonds. It would seem that many if not all of the values we somehow hold to be self-evident today are a result of power struggles or even open conflict and war.

The bottom-line short-sightedness may, as we have seen, lead one to disregard ethical dilemmas. It seems to represent the primary explanation for many of the problems and scandals we have witnessed: "We could not have acted otherwise or we would have gone out of business." To some it may represent an almost evil force that has to be harnessed through regulation, ethical codes of conduct, ombudsmen and so on. But this bottom-line view did not only give us a Bhopal disaster or an asbestos case, it is at the same time a primary factor in economic development.

Mandeville tells an ingenious story of the beneficial public consequences of private vices,[44] the simple explanation for this being that private vices of luxury, avarice and prodigality are what leads to the production of more and more products, by more and more people, thereby raising everyone's standards of living.[45]

"The prodigality, I call a noble Sin is ... that agreeable good-natur'd Vice that makes the Chimney smoke, and all Tradesmen smile."[46] All such vices of economic intemperance contribute to public benefits. Private economic virtues like frugality would not be beneficial to society.

Mandeville reasons that even thieves create a demand for locks and locksmiths. In today's terms that might perhaps be translated into the beneficial consequences of drug trafficking and other illegal activities. But why stop here? Activities that may land people in hospitals also contribute to employment for doctors and for other hospital personnel, and all this contributes to a larger gross domestic product.

Then again we may not agree with Mandeville's formula for public benefits from private vices. Or at least we would want either to make some judgements as to the quality of the vices (or pleasures) like Mill[47] or put the activities through a kind of benefit–cost analysis first. His examples of wealthy capitalists engaged in commerce, trying to outdo each other, bring to mind Carr's more recent assertion that business can be likened to a game of poker. The behaviour may not live up to the demands of the golden rule, but once again their private vices are to the benefit of society.

As in every game there must be rules. Commerce and division of labour depends on the certain conditions like the property rights, contracts and more generally a sense of security. Thus "The *Meum* and *Tuum* must be secur'd, Crimes punish'd, and all other Laws concerning the Administration of Justice, wisely contriv'd and strictly executed."[48]

Etzioni seems to express the same idea when he talks about a hypothetical curvilinear relationship between social bonds and competition: "*[C]ompetition thrives not in impersonal, calculative systems* of independent actors unbound by social relations, as implied by the neoclassical paradigm, *nor in the socially tight world of communal societies, but in the middle range*, where social bonds are strong enough to sustain mutual trust and low transaction costs but strong enough to suppress exchange orientations."[49]

Perhaps something like a multidimensional curvilinear relationship may explain the ambiguities surrounding the attitudes and mechanism we have discussed here. Not that it is always possible to illustrate more than one end of the relationship.

Too little laxness and too much regulation and order, and individual responsibility and decision-making ability suffer from suffocation. Too much laxness and individuals become careless and irresponsible.

Too many excuses like "It makes no difference ..." and no one acts even on the gravest transgression of social norms and laws.

Too much focus on concrete material incentives will pervert attitudes and behaviour. Too few incentives may bring individual activity to a halt.

Too weak peer pressure and social norms break down, too much peer pressure and independence and individual initiative break down.

Too strong concentrations of power lead to arbitrariness and corruption, too much concentration of authority and everyone loses responsibility for what they are doing. Too little authority and concentration of power and anarchy sets in.

Too short-sighted a focus on the bottom line and the company gets out of tune with surrounding society and contributes to the creation of more and more social and environmental problems. Too little bottom-line focus and the company loses out in the competition.

The discussions of the preceding sections and the ambiguities and potential curvilinear relationships may help in understanding why attempts to avoid and solve ethical and social problems and dilemmas by some simple remedy may be impossible.

NOTES

[1] CREDO is the Centre for Research in Ethics and Decision-making in Organisations, located at the Department of Organization and Management, The Aarhus School of Business. CREDO was started by the author.

[2] The interview stems from a survey on value-based leadership carried out by members of CREDO in a branch of Jyske Bank A/S in Copenhagen.

[3] Glover (1975).

[4] Petersen & Jensen (1996).

[5] Selbach (1996), p. 45.

[6] Gjørup (1996), p. 47.

[7] Glover (1975), p. 127.

[8] Kerr & Kaufman-Gilliland (1997).

[9] Elster (1989), p. 197.

[10] Quattrone & Tversky (1986).

[11] Hirschman (1970).

[12] Ethylene Control, Inc. claims that controlling the ethylene gas after picking will extend the life cycle of a commodity – allowing them to be held for a much longer period of time. And Ethylene Control, Inc. has the products to do that. Cf. http://www.ethylenecontrol.com.

[13] Petersen (1997), p. 36.

[14] In itself there may already be a problem in talking about advice. What the bank adviser is doing is selling a product and not really giving advice. This problem has been a discussion topic for some time and has been investigated by Andersen and Møgelvang-Hansen who asserts "When sales efforts are camouflaged as 'advice-giving', there is a risk that the realities will not correspond to the expectations of the customer, and that it may even be misleading" (Andersen & Møgelvang-Hansen 1997, p. 13).

[15] Bok (1993), p. 243.

[16] Bento & Ferreira (1992), p. 166.

[17] Knouse (1995), p. 18.

[18] See for instance Deci & Ryan (1985).

[19]   Lepper & Green (1978).

[20]   Asch (1969).

[21]   Kandel & Lazear (1992).

[22]   Ibid., p. 809.

[23]   See for instance Dahl (1957) and Dahl (1961).

[24]   See also Weber's definition (Weber 1956).

[25]   See Crenson (1971), Lukes (1974) and Foucault (1977).

[26]   Machiavelli (1513/1929), p. 78.

[27]   Nietzsche (1886a/1968).

[28]   Hegel (1973 ed.).

[29]   Milgram (1974).

[30]   Haney et al. (1973), p. 69. The experiment seems to find support in real prison experiments as it were. Palden Gyatso, a Tibetan monk incarcerated in Tibet by the Chinese, tells how prisoners could be made to denounce each other and beat up each other by the prison wardens (Gyatso 1997).

        The recollections of KZ guards and the ordeals of KZ inmates ought also to be relevant here, and perhaps they may give a more realistic and many-sided picture than the experiments of Milgram and others.

[31]   Krogsgaard (1992), p. 287.

[32]   Verbal comment from the CEO of a major Danish bank, as recorded by members of CREDO, during a survey on value-based leadership. 17 March 1997.

[33]   Friedman (1962), p. 133. See also Friedman (1970).

[34]   Said by the chief legal adviser of Den Danske Bank, in a survey of value-based leadership in the bank (Petersen 1997).

[35]   Friedman (1962), passim.

[36]   Baumol & Blackman (1991), p. 51.

[37]   Arrow (1973b).

[38]   Arrow (1973a), p. 24.

[39]   Estes (1996).

[40]   Ibid., p. 140.

[41]   Handberg (1990).

[42]   Estes (1996), p. 140.

[43]   See for instance Rappaport (1997), Bennett (1991), Knight (1997), McTaggart & Kontes (1994).

[44]   Mandeville (1924/1988).

[45]   Goldsmith (1985).

[46]   Ibid., p. 146.

[47]   Mill (1977 ed.).

[48]   Goldsmith (1985), p. 145.
[49]   Etzioni (1988), p. 211. Etzioni talks of a capsule consisting of social bonds and public regulation that contains competition.

3 Deceptive measures

Not all calculators of the National Debt can tell me the capacity for good or evil, for love or hatred, for patriotism or discontent, for the decomposition of virtue into vice, or the reverse, at any single moment in the soul of one of these its quiet servants, with the composed faces and the regulated actions. There is no mystery in it; there is an unfathomable mystery in the meanest of them, for ever. Supposing we were to reserve our arithmetic for material objects, and to govern these awful unknown quantities by other means!

Charles Dickens

CAN EVERYTHING THAT COUNTS BE COUNTED?

According to Garvin managers have known for long that "if you can't measure it, you can't manage it."[1] Maybe that explains why so many attempt to measure the unmeasurable, perhaps like Dickens' Mr Gradgrind: "With a rule and a pair of scales, and the multiplication table always in his pocket, sir, ready to weigh and measure any parcel of human nature, and tell you exactly what it comes to."[2]

Today we are inundated with attempts to put life into tabular form. Everybody has had the experience of being asked to fill out a questionnaire on topics touching on all imaginable aspects of human life. Some of these attempts actually try to get a measure of life, like attempts to measure the quality of life, making the quality of life immediately comparable over time and across borders. Others satisfy themselves with attempts to measure the degree of morality of different societies, with measuring the perception of ethics in American business, or simpler things like the quality of leadership or management, or the intellectual capital of a company. Perhaps it would be too frivolous to call this measure the company IQ.

In fairly recent attempts to make it possible to measure, compare and define quality, the research performance of the staff of Danish universities and business schools is graded using a curious mixture of measurement schemes. A scheme may be used for weighing and adding up different kinds of publications. A working paper published in Danish may rate 1 point, an article published in English in a refereed journal may rate 3 points and a textbook 12 points. Apparently realising that research might be published using the World Wide Web, Internet visits to one's homepage may also be counted and rated.[3]

Now, how will such schemes influence the attitude and behaviour of those being measured, not to speak of those using the results of research, the decision makers, the students and the informed public in general? One would suppose that the research effort will be concentrated on those publications and activities that receive the highest counts for the least effort. In this case perhaps refereed articles. Now the quality of articles is not really scored, in fact they may never be read by those making the assessments. The only relevant criteria are whether they are in English or not and whether they are refereed or not. It does not matter whether the journal is obscure, little read, with a small circulation and of doubtful quality. The rating just follows the criteria mentioned.

In relation to the curious measure of visits to one's homepage an easier approach is possible; it ought to be easy to design a macro that would perform a thousand or more visits to a certain homepage, and in this way a given standard is easily fulfilled.

In the simple cases presented here it is easy to see that being under pressure to perform, the standards of research may slip, and attitudes and behaviour of those actually doing research may change in a way that certainly will not further more demanding standards of quality. I am asserting that the methods of appraisal will influence the attitude and behaviour of those measured by such schemes, and that some important intangible aspects may be lost in the process.

Just as detailed written behavioural rules will relieve one of individual responsibility, "if I follow the rules I have no further responsibility," centrally designed schemes for measuring and appraising individual efforts will relieve the individual of insight and having a personal stance; in fact relieving the individual of responsibilities. When I have achieved the necessary score I do not have to speculate on whether the goals are the right ones or what the consequences of striving for these goals will be.

STANDARDS OF QUALITY – QUALITY OF STANDARDS

"One factor above all others – quality – drives the market share. And where superior quality and large market share are both present, profitability is virtually guaranteed."[4]

The importance of the quality aspect is explained by mentioning the increased national and global competition, the growing demands of ever more discerning customers, and increased public demands on products and services. Although this would seem to represent a rather vague explanation there has been a surge of interest in quality since the 1980s[5].

This interest is manifested for instance in the so-called Malcolm Baldridge National Quality Award, and by the first really international quality assurance standards, the ISO 9000 series by the International Organization for Standardization.[6] Associations and organisations have been established to promote the acceptance of a strategy of quality intended to increase competitiveness. Awards and prizes like the European Quality Award, the European Quality Prize, and a series of national and sectoral awards, have been promoted.

We are not concerned with the proliferation of standards and awards as such, only with seeing what the concepts of quality are, how they are used in the awards and standards and how this may influence the conduct of business in general and the attitude and behaviour of managers and employees in particular.

The ISO 9000 series, and supporting tools in the shape of the ISO 10000 series represent a number of standards that establish requirements for a quality management system of a company. According to Davis the essence of the ISO 9000 series can be expressed as:[7]

- Say what you do;
- Do what you say;
- Write it down;
- Check what you do;
- Make continuous improvements.

This seems to put the emphasis on documentation, and documentation certainly seems to play an important role in the specification of the standards. In the guidelines for selection and use of the standards as they can be found in ISO 9000-1, documentation is emphasised everywhere:[8]

- processes should be defined;
- procedures should be appropriately documented;
- the organisation should be functioning as documented;
- records should be kept to verify that the procedures are being followed.

In the most comprehensive of the 9000 series of standards, ISO 9001, there are 20 quality system requirements. Among these are: Management Responsibility, Quality System, Document and Data Control, Process Control, Corrective and Preventive action.

Management Responsibility encompasses the development and formulation of a quality policy. Management must define the objectives, assign responsibility and assure clear lines of authority, especially for the implementation, maintenance and reviewing of the quality system. It must also assign "the proper level of resources to activities that impact [on] quality."[9]

The Quality System consists of a quality manual "to express how its products and services conform to the stipulated requirements,"[10] and a quality plan that defines and documents how the requirements will be met and continuously improved.

Document and Data Control requires a system for documentation and control of all the data, documentation and information necessary for maintaining and updating the quality system. Furthermore "[i]t should ensure that obsolete documents are removed from all areas."[11]

Process Control concerns the documentation of production and work processes in order to ensure that the end product or service has the quality described in the quality system. Some of the elements are: "Documenting procedures where their absence could adversely affect quality;" "Continuous monitoring and control of the process parameters by qualified personnel;" "Maintaining records for qualified processes, equipment and personnel as appropriate."[12]

The Corrective and Preventive requirement concerns procedures in relation to customer complaints, and reports of sub-standard products and services according to the quality prescribed. "The firm specifies how it determines what went wrong, who should fix it, how that person is to be accurately informed, when the problem is to be solved, how it controls that the problem is solved and how to prevent a reoccurrence."[13]

A large number of companies and organisations have sought to create quality systems based on the ISO 9000 series. According to Harrington and Mathers more than 95 000 organisations had been registered worldwide in 1995.[14] This is reason enough to take a closer look at some of the aspects of this so-called quality system that may be relevant to the issues that concern us here. This means that we are focusing especially on some of the more prominent problematic aspects.

Arbitrary standards. It is worth emphasising that the ISO 9000 series does not contain a definition of quality as such, nor is ISO 9000 certification a guarantee that a company delivers high-quality products or services.[15] In fact the ISO certification only means that the company in question lives up to its own defined standards, whatever they may be.

Davis mentions that a company "can be certified to produce tables with seventeen legs, or lightbulbs that 'pop' after three uses."[16] An ISO certification only means that a company has stated in writing that it will play according to certain rules, within the legal framework of course, and also in writing that it will live up to these rules of the game in its transactions with its customers. In other words standards may be low but they have to be documented and met consistently.

This means of course that the standards may be said to have certain arbitrariness, that they may have very little to do with what is ordinarily seen as fundamental to quality. Although it may sound ridiculous, these standards may mean that a company for instance will focus on how to deal with customer complaints, instead of how to avoid customer complaints. "You have a complaint, well, just a moment, according to our standards you will receive an answer within 14 days." This may be the kind of standard that such a system promotes.

What this means for the attitude of employees is evident. If one only sticks to the standards, one would not expect to get into trouble. Individual insight in what may further quality or what may cause a decline in quality is certainly not enhanced. In fact one might say that: "Any change the workers make to the plan is fatal to success."[17]

Arbitrary descriptions of the quality system. The remarkable thing about the quality system is that there must be an unstated belief in the possibility of specifying all relevant aspects with the necessary detail, and that these specifications will somehow encompass all the relevant aspects that will have an influence on the achievement of the stated standards of prod-

ucts and services. The implicit assumption seems to be that it is possible
to write a manual detailing all these procedures and not leaving anything
important out.

One wonders if that is really possible, even for fairly simple operations, or whether we would be caught in a kind of infinite regress. This is
a problem of describing operations at the right level of detail, the right
level of understanding and the right degree of rigidity or flexibility. Only
what is the right level of detail, and how rigid should operations be? It is
difficult to envision how this is in fact possible in a modern organisation
which in many cases will need a certain latitude for discretionary decision
making in different parts of the organisation.

With this approach to the setting of standards, the emphasis will be
on processes and things that can be observed, registered, described, not
on other aspects that may somehow be important to a customer's impression of quality, not on the invisible or ineffable aspects of processes and
things, not the tacit knowledge, or attitudes and motives of managers and
employees.

In addition to problems of description already mentioned, there is the
fundamental problem of emphasising the right things. If one has no clear
idea of what makes up quality it would seem to be difficult to emphasise
the right aspects and assign them the right relative weight in the process.
It may be easy to state that there should be a certain limit to the time it
takes to answer a complaint, but how important is that compared to other
aspects of customer relations, and on what basis does one decide to
emphasise one aspect and not another?

It might be argued a that surveys of customer priorities will make it
possible to assign weights to the various aspects, but would customers really be able to state the relative weight of different aspects of quality explicitly? Would that not be like asking the customers to specify the different
parts of their preference functions? I doubt that we would get meaningful
results, although I do not doubt that customers attach different weights to
different aspects of a product or a service. I just cannot see how it is possible to reveal these weights explicitly in any consistent manner.

The focus of an ISO 9000 quality system will inevitably shift towards
descriptions of the right way to do things, not whether the things are the
right ones to do. The only thing that one may be reasonably sure of in
such an approach is that those standards that are easily enumerated and
put in writing may carry a lot more weight than the more intangible

aspects of quality. This may mean that the attention of management as well as employees may be led astray, inasmuch as they focus on the arbitrarily emphasised aspects and forget about important aspects that cannot be put into a written standard.

Emphasis on documentation. In order to get ISO certification a company has to go through a fairly arduous documentation process, specifying in detail what standards are to apply where in the company. As stated in *The Complete ISO 9000 Manual*: "Any organisation has a Quality System in place when all members of the organisation are implementing its *Quality System Documentation*"[18] (emphasis added).

Part of this documentation is the framework documentation, which consists of: policy manuals, procedures manuals, work instructions, forms, internal documents, external documents and external forms. Now changes to the framework documentation "can only be made with the authorisation of the Management Representative." The procedure to be followed in this case is specified: "Request for any changes should be made on a Request for a Change Form, QSF 006. This is submitted to the Management Representative who, after due consultation with interested parties, and perhaps after discussion in a Management Review Meeting, may issue an amendment to the documentation,"[19] in accordance, to be sure, with detailed steps outlined elsewhere.

Details of procedures are specified; it is even specified what constitutes a customer complaint. In case of a complaint the Customer Complaint and Corrective Action Report form must be used. On the surface this may sound like a good idea, it may show that everyone in the company knows what to do, how to do it and when to do it.

In a negative perspective this high degree of specification with manuals and procedures for each operation is not necessarily a good thing, for at least two reasons. In a system where an employee only has to follow a certain procedure stated in detail in a manual, we may expect that the "head" is somehow bypassed. What I mean is that the employee does not have to think about the relevance, the meaning, the importance, or the interrelatedness of what he or she is supposed to do. He or she just has to follow the description given in the manual. One might also add that even if the employee discovers that some procedures are faulty or inflexible, or discovers that it is possible to do some things in a better way, saving resources or making a better contribution, he or she may still choose to operate according to the standards of a given procedure. If the phone has to be answered by the fifth ringing, he or she may choose to let it ring until this limit is reached, although he or she might on many occasions be able to react immediately.

This critique does not even take into account the amount of energy and time that must be spent on establishing all the documentation, procedures and detailed descriptions in the first place. In the view of those involved in constructing a quality system: "… the greatest challenge was probably to unify the construction of the system with the requirement that the daily work had to be done."[20] What may happen already in the preparatory work to get the certification is that resources and energies are directed away from other important tasks in order to decide upon and write down all the details.

Rigidity and inherent bureaucracy. It is difficult to see how one can avoid falling into the trap of acting in a more and more bureaucratic way, following procedures instead of solving problems or finding better ways of doing things, or even inventing better products or services.

There seems to be an inherent danger of creating a rigid system in which rigid procedures based on written manuals become more and more important. Davis states that ISO 9000 standards "clearly lead to greater formalism in work processes," mentioning it as an advantage "that it is no longer so important to 'remember' what one has to do."[21] The disadvantage being more paperwork.

I am not sure that *not* remembering what one has to do is an advantage. In fact it may represent one of the really nasty problems in relation to ISO certification. To illustrate this one may use what the German philosopher of war von Clausewitz used in order to poke fun at all those who tried to write complete and systematic theories of war. The illustration is an excerpt from a Prussian Fire regulation:

"Wenn ein Haus brennt, so muß man vor allen Dingen die rechte Wand des zur Linken stehenden Hauses und hingegen die linke Wand des zur Rechten stehenden Hauses zu decken suchen; denn wenn man zum Exempel die linke Wand des zur Linken stehenden Hauses decken wollte, so liegt ja die rechte Wand des Hauses der linken Wand zur rechten, und folglich, da das Feuer auch dieser Wand und der rechten Wand zur Rechten liegt (denn wir haben ja angenommen, daß das Haus dem Feuer zur Linken liege), so liegt die rechte Wand dem Feuer näher als die linke, und die rechte Wand des Hauses könnte abbrennen, wenn sie nicht gedeckt würde, ehe das Feuer an die linke, die gedeckt wird, käme; folglich könnte etwas abbrennen, das man nicht deckt, und zwar eher, als etwas anderes abbrennen würde, auch wenn man es nicht deckte; folglich muß man dieses lassen und jenes decken."[22]

I am sure that the fire regulation is coherent and consistent, as far as I can tell, but attempting to understand and follow this rule in case of fire would presumably mean that both houses burn would down before the gist of the rule was understood. Even so, this could easily be part of a modern day ISO standard and the result would be the same.

There is a clear tendency towards algorithmisation in the quality systems; a tendency to specify in detail exactly what one is to do in given situations. Still, no matter how much energy and effort is spent on the attempts to give a full description of all the processes somehow regarded as important, the attempt to create quasi-algorithms for every aspect of business will turn out to be futile. In fact one may expect that every attempt at giving a precise description of what to do, by whom and when, will turn out to be indeterminate, that is it will never be enough to determine that precisely this will happen.

The other problem with the tendency to create quasi-algorithms is that they promote a head-under-the-arm-attitude and erosion of every kind of individual responsibility. Here we find a clear parallel to the observations made in relation to the proliferation of detailed behavioural rules in society and in the form of personnel policies in companies. Instead of having the individual responsibility to act according to certain general norms and values, an employee now only has to observe the rules, whether they are relevant or not. Individual responsibility, insight and forethought are not really demanded as the procedures are described in detail. In this way the demand for documentation and detailed description in itself may become a hindrance to change and development in an organisation, to more flexible working procedures and decentralised, independent decision making and problem solving.

In a planned economy there is a need for very detailed planning as a substitute for the price mechanism and the market. We now know that this system stifled innovation and led to all sorts of inefficiencies. I wonder whether ISO certification with its detailed manuals will not stifle innovation and lead to all sorts of inefficiencies in the companies that take this quality system for real.

For those responsible for implementing and maintaining the ISO certification of a company, this work may become their *raison d'être*, whatever the real importance or lack of importance. For this part of the organisation it may be important that the quality system sucks up more and more resources. This is the way to become important. Relevance and original intentions will of course be left behind.

Loss of ownership. In a guide to help bust bureaucracy in connection within this kind of quality system Davis[23] quotes some of the frustration of managers, when they discover that it may be difficult for employees to get really involved in the process. They ask "How do we get people to do it willingly?" "How do we encourage people to own responsibility?" "How do we encourage people to believe that it matters?" One gets the impression that in the attempt to implement a quality system the employees somehow lose ownership of the process; it becomes something exterior to them. They just have to act according to certain standards, but the whole system is something pulled down over their heads; it is not really something they feel responsible for.

The emphasis on standards, on control and audits may in fact lead to a kind of "blame culture," in which one may become preoccupied with avoiding blame, by shifting blame to someone else. In a sense responsibility tends to disappear. Although it may in fact be part of the intention of the quality system to avoid this shifting around of blame, the approach itself may lead to this happening. Perhaps this shows how an attempted solution may become part of the problem.

Continuation of scientific management with other means. Somehow one gets the impression that what is happening when these quality systems are being implemented is in a way the continuation of what is known as scientific management,[24] this time just with other means.

The ISO quality system shows its classic industrial process roots and orientation in its demands, and this may lead to a very mechanistic understanding of how a complex organisation involving thinking human beings operates and develops. A modern organisation does not work like a machine, and human beings are not just resources that can be fitted into a rigorous scheme. What such a quality system may represent is a Tayloristic system lifted to an nth power, not really something that will distance one from this mechanistic view.

The demands of an ISO system will certainly not fit an organisation in which many activities cannot really be described in advance without severely disabling the innovative potential and individual abilities to handle complex dilemmas and problems with no clear-cut solutions. The attempt to introduce an ISO system in such cases may result in a planned economy attitude paying lip-service to all the manuals and in reality caring less and less about the products and services of the organisation.

Davis sees a danger somewhat related to this in relation to ISO certification of public sector institutions: "Rules and regulations ... encourage people to be oriented inwards – towards doing the job as they feel it should be done – rather than outwards, towards the users of public services."[25]

Lack of documented results. In the light of this critique it is astonishing that so many companies and even public institutions have become ISO certified or are striving to become certified.

Many reasons are given for ISO certification. It can function as quality assurance in a buyer–supplier relation, standardise and simplify relations between companies, or in relation to customers, increase the quality of the products and services delivered, thereby resulting in gains in competitiveness.

Apart from these reasons some companies argue that they seek certification because others do. Whatever their view of the ISO 9000 standards they deem it necessary to get certification because competitors have it. They may see the ISO certification as irrelevant to their view of quality, regard the resources spent on the certification process as squandered, and still do it because everyone else is doing it, which may lead buyers to demand it. Brown mentions that suppliers may feel "blackmailed" to begin an ISO 9000 certification process, blackmailed by their buyers that is.[26] If this view is accepted ISO quality systems may represent an enormous exercise in futility, not really something that is of utmost importance to quality. This fits well with the very doubtful documentation of the benefits of being certified.[27]

The reason for a quality certification of public institutions may be that certification gives a stamp of approval, and that it may act as a high-profile activity that can cover up deficiencies in areas not so much open to public scrutiny. This also seems to be Davis' view: "It gave public organizations the opportunity to demonstrate that they were just as efficient as private firms."[28]

Davis quotes research results that show that ISO certification is not that important to buyers, that in fact ISO certification was long down the list. A look at the number of registered companies would also indicate that although Britain has the most ISO companies it does not necessarily have the companies with the best name for quality. A flippant observation: to a customer buying a car, the sign "made in Germany," instead of "made in England," may still mean much more than the number of ISO registrations.

SCORING TOTAL QUALITY

Many companies and advocates of quality may come to the same conclusion that we have drawn here. For some the solution is called Total Quality Management, known as TQM.

In contrast to the ISO quality system, TQM does not stop with the question of whether things are done the right way. According to Zinck TQM asks whether the right things are made – "Ob *das Richtige gemacht wird*."[29] In this relation there is an absolute emphasis on the customer. Quality is not just related to products and services, but includes all the processes of a company, the working conditions and the environment.

Quality is no longer just a technical standard, but more a way of working in the whole organisation. This means that this concept of quality also includes organisational and management questions. Omachonu and Ross declare that TQM "is the integration of all functions and processes within an organisation in order to achieve continuous improvement of the quality of goods and services. The goal is customer satisfaction."[30]

A somewhat more operational definition stresses the systematic approach to customer satisfaction using tools and techniques: "TQM means that the organization's culture is defined by and supports the constant attainment of customer satisfaction through an integrated system of tools, techniques and training. This involves the continuous improvement of organizational processes."[31]

Satisfaction must be satisfaction in relation to the expectations of customers, and expectations are not given in any absolute sense. In fact it is to be assumed that the expectations of customers are affected by products and services they find on the market. Thus the quality expectations of customers are affected precisely by the actions of the companies, who try to fulfil these expectations.

This leads to a fundamental problem. A simple example may show why. If a company producing typewriters in the late 1970s would have tried to fulfil customer expectations as found in customer surveys, it might have focused on producing a good typewriter with exchangeable type wheels and smart error correction possibilities. It is evident that this would not have been such a good idea. At that time the possibility of using word processors was already demonstrated in practice, although the equipment was rather costly. Customers may be unaware of the potential of the new technique, but manufacturers of typewriters certainly ought to be, and they ought to use this knowledge to produce electronic word processing equipment and thereby raise the expectations of customers.

This fictitious example shows that those who know the potential of new techniques and new ways of doing things are the producers, and that accordingly they ought not only to satisfy manifested customers' wants and expectations, but to raise these if they really want to produce quality. This is seldom realised, but Denton mentions that 3M's Chief Executive argues for the need "to do a better job of what we call discovering unarticulated needs."[32]

At least the simpler versions of TQM do not seem to take this into account with its focus on tools and techniques to measure existing levels of satisfaction.

As an example one might take a look at the Baldridge Award. It is said that this award has "set a national standard for quality" and that "hundreds of major corporations use the criteria in the application form as a basic guide for quality improvement programs." In this way, it is asserted, the award has created "a benchmark for quality in the U.S. industry."[33]

In order to apply for the award the applicants must address seven categories which carry different weight as specified below:

1. Leadership, 95
2. Information and Analysis, 75
3. Strategic Quality Planning, 60
4. Human Resource Development and Management, 150
5. Management of Process Quality, 140
6. Quality and Operational Results, 180
7. Customer Focus and Satisfaction, 300

If we look at the category of Leadership, the maximum point values are distributed on three items: senior executive leadership (45), management for quality (25) and public responsibility and corporate citizenship (25).

The topics examined in relation to these items are for instance "senior executives' personal leadership and involvement in creating and sustaining a customer focus and clear and visible quality values" or the way "quality values are integrated into the company's management system and reflected in the manner in which the company addresses its public responsibilities and corporate citizenship."[34]

It cannot be easy to get a meaningful score of these rather diffuse aspects of leadership and management, but a helping hand is given in the shape of a set of evaluation guidelines. According to these the different aspects are scored on scales ranging from 0 per cent in those cases where no data, or only anecdotal evidence is found, to 100 per cent in cases where a degree of excellence that can stand every comparison is clearly demonstrated. Even with such guidelines this must still be regarded as a rather ambiguous basis for awarding scores in all the categories.

One may also wonder about the weight of the different categories: their meaning and their relevance; why these weights and not others? especially when comparing these categories with the categories addressed in the European Quality Award. Even though the EFQM, or the European Foundation for Quality Management model, resembles the Baldridge model somewhat, the weights attached are different, and some of the basic categories are also different, or at least divided up in a different way.

This difference presumably means that there is a basic difference in the American and European understanding of quality. What is not so clear is how the different categories and weights are explained. Why exactly are these categories important? And why exactly are those weights the right ones to attach to the different categories? They are evidently important for the final score that a company can achieve.

It would seem that there is no substantial theory behind the scoring models and the selection of the categories. There is no deep understanding of the interdependence or independence of the categories, and no real rationale for the weights attached. The only thing that is evident is that customer orientation weighs heavily in both models. In other words the whole model may just be a result of a compromise view of what is defined as important by those who initiated these models, and here big traditional companies apparently played an important role.

Hummeltenberg draws attention to the fact that the Baldridge model has a clearer result orientation than the European model. His explanation is that "der Baldridge Quality Award über mehrere Jahre hinweg aus dem Geist einer nationalen Herausforderung heraus in enger Partnerschaft zwischen Industrie und Regierung entstanden ist."[35] The European model he regards as an answer to the Japanese and American challenge. An answer "die als Konses technikorientierter europäischer Grossunternehmen gefunden wurde." In other words a measure concocted by business itself.

It seems strange that models with such a lack of theoretical underpinnings, lack of explanation, with such ambiguous categories, very composite and doubtful scoring methods and strange weights should ever be seen as an important benchmark for quality. If the scores achieved really have a meaning, it is very difficult to see what the meaning might be. Still many companies seem to participate in the competition to get a high score and receive the prestigious award.

To the degree that companies really strive for the respective awards, one may presume that they in fact regard them as an important benchmark for something, if not quality, then for something else. And this something else could very well be the publicity of the awards themselves. Now that the awards have become known, the real value lies not in having a high score as such, but in the value of the scores and especially the award as a marketing tool, as a "stamp of quality" printed on a sash and worn at public occasions.

In this way it might be likened to a more mundane competition, the annual beauty contests, where I suppose the award also leads to substantial improvement in market value, and where the criteria are somewhat more evident, although seldom, if ever, all encompassing. Forgive me for thinking that the hallowed Baldridge Award maybe ought to be called the Miss Baldridge 2001 award, or something to that effect.

This is not necessarily a problem; one might compete for many strange awards that could help the marketing effort. One might even strive to end up in the *Guinness Book of Records*. The more serious question is, does striving for a quality award distort, hinder or destroy important developments in other areas of the company in question that perhaps may carry more weight in the end? This is not just a whimsical question. "[S]ince it is the firms themselves that fashion their own systems, they may choose words and structures that reflect not what is best for them, or their customers – but what they feel the certifying body will like. The Malcolm Baldridge National Quality Award, similarly has been subject to the criticism that it 'can be bought': i.e. that it rewards companies that spend money specifically on those aspects of quality assurances that meet the Baldridge criteria, neglecting other areas."[36]

With a lack of coherent theory behind the models this is exactly what may happen. What these attempts to promote quality may have as a result is that the wrong attitudes are promoted. That a company only has to carry the stamp of quality, it does not have to be an inherent attitude shared by every employee, and shown in every one of their activities, as well as every activity of the company, including those that are neither visible nor scored in the TQM models. This may lead to a particular kind of shortsightedness, and hypocrisy.

It is strange to compare arguments of the quality systems movement and the TQM movement with some of the original ideas of Deming, who is regarded as a father of the total quality movement. Among his well-known 14 points are statements like:[37] adopt and institute leadership; drive out fear; eliminate slogans, exhortations, and targets for the work force that ask for zero defects or new levels of productivity; eliminate work standards on the factory floor, substitute leadership; eliminate management by numbers, and numerical goals, substitute leadership; abolish annual or merit rating; institute a vigorous programme of education and self-improvement.

The rigorism of the standards and the focus of the awards' models would seem to drive out the leadership and self-improvement that Deming advocates, promoting instead a more systems-oriented and tool-based management view.

There is a risk that the rigorous demands of standards and the proliferation of evaluation tools will, if not put fear into people, at least make them subservient to the manuals and measurement objectives. It would seem that in some cases the ISO certification and the striving to get awards will lead to sloganism and incomprehensible targets for the employees. In the companies that orally adhere to the TQM not all forms of quotas are banned. They are part and parcel of some of the new performance appraisal models. Management by numbers seems to be inherent in all the approaches to quality discussed here. In fact it may look as if a quality that cannot be quantified is not quality. Annual or merit rating seems to be resurrected in an attempt to design a pay scheme based on performance. Self-improvement is not exactly an evident result of the approach to quality shown here, because one does not really have to do one's own thinking. Someone will have done it for you. Finally the call for everybody to work to accomplish the transformation seems only partially heeded in the TQM movement.

DEMANDING MEASUREMENTS AND COMMON CHAIRS

To measure is the act or process of ascertaining the extent, dimensions, quantity and so on of something, especially by comparison with a standard. I suppose that fits quite well with most people's idea of measurement. In measurement theory "measurement is the assignment of numerals to things according to any determinative, non-degenerate rule."[38] Determinative, meaning that the same numerals would be assigned to the same things under the same conditions. Non-degenerate, meaning that different things, or the same things under different conditions, would be assigned different numerals. Usually we would not be satisfied with the simple assignment of numerals. Measurement in the sense normally used demands measurement of quantities at least at the level of an ordinal scale. In most cases though the preferred scale is a more demanding interval or cardinal scale.[39]

Then there is the question of validity. Validity in the sense that measurement differences represent true differences in the objects or qualities that we attempt to measure, and validity in the sense that the object or quality measured possesses some characteristic reflected in the measurement, remembering that the "presumed characteristic is not something which can be pointed to or identified with some specific kind of behavior, rather it is an abstraction, a construct."[40] In other words to make valid measurements it is necessary to have a well-formed idea, or rather a theory, of the characteristic in question.

Finally in order to use the measurements to infer what it means to possess certain quantities of one or another characteristic, we must have some idea of the causal relationships connecting the presence of the characteristic we attempt to measure and some form of overt behaviour. This is necessary if the measurements are to be used as an ingredient in attempts to make conscious changes of the organisation in question or predicting what will happen to future behaviour. "In the pragmatic approach to validity, the interest is in the usefulness of the measures as an indicator or predictor of some other behavior or characteristic …"[41]

How can attempts to measure the unmeasurable be valid measurements according to these definitions and requirements?

Take a simple example: what is the measure of a chair? Before grabbing a measure and running off to measure the next available chair one would want to know more. What kind of chair are we talking about and what properties do we want measured? Without answers to these questions many kinds of measures are possible. We can start by measuring the height, the depth, the width and sitting height of a chair, the angle of the seat and the back and the angle between the seat and the back. Having done that we may feel that something is missing. Accordingly we begin measuring the amount of weight that the chair will support before collapsing, the number of times we may rock it back and forth on its hind legs before its legs become loose, the resistance to abrasion of the material of the frame and the seat and seat back.

Next we see that colour and material might be important. To measure colour we may use scientific measures like the wavelength of light, or just compare with Pantone colour slips, and classify the colours according to the names on the colour slips. Then we become aware of the texture of the material and start classifying the texture and the materials. Then we suddenly get the idea that we want to know what the chairishness of this chair is, its quality as a chair. Inspired by the total quality models we may add up all the different measures, after adjusting each with a certain weight.

I suppose the resulting measure could not be used for very much; it would certainly give no idea of the quality of the chair, but it could of course be used in an absurd way to compare chairs.

What I am trying to show is that even a chair, which ought to be easier to get the measure of than a human being, intellectual capital or achievements of a learning organisation, is difficult to measure if we lack a very clear idea of what a chair is, and what we want to use it for.

I suppose that everyone will have noticed that the measures discussed are different in many ways; somehow we would feel quite confident measuring the height, width and weight of the chair. We can use a common ruler graded in centimetres or inches, but what about chairishness? I suppose most would find that to be somewhat artificial. We would certainly not have a scale immediately available, and we have difficulty in establishing a reference and a measure of the difference in chairishness. In reality I expect that we do this measuring every day, we are just not aware of what we are doing, but our backs and bottoms apparently are.

This leads to the question of the scale of scales. On the one hand we have scales, measurement procedures and scalable objects that somehow we all agree on. That would be represented by the measure of length, height or weight. On the other hand there would be scales, measurement procedures and unscaleable objects represented by proxy measures, or strange compound measures like chairishness.

We can be fairly confident about the first kind of measures, but I doubt if we can be equally confident of the detailed measurement, when we are in doubt of the scale, the procedure and what in fact we are measuring. Many of the measures we criticise are of this kind. It is not measurement as such that is put into question; it is only the attempts to get a meaningful measure of these unscalable fleeting objects, where we resort to proxy measures and questionable procedures and where we in fact only have the haziest idea of what we are measuring.

After all these attempts to get the measure of the chair, we may find that in the end we do not really depend on the measures, but on trials, on the looks, the feel and the knowledge of how it was made, who made it, where and when.

MEASURING FLEETING GESTALTS

Intellectual capital, learning organisations and other modern organisational and managerial constructs would seem to be more fleeting gestalts than a chair. How would one measure such a fleeting form? Would one not need to have an idea of these fleeting forms in the same way that we need to have an idea of a chair before we begin measuring?

I am not sure that we have an equally good idea of either intellectual capital or learning organisations, and if we do not, what are we measuring then?[42] Edvinsson and Malone[43] answer this question by using a metaphor to give an idea of the intellectual capital of a company. They want us to think of a tree. An investor may look at the visible parts of the tree in order to see whether it will be able to produce something of value. Only judging the visible aspects of a tree would be a problem. One has to look at the roots, too, in order to get an idea of potential possibilities and problems. The roots would represent the intellectual capital.

I am not sure I get their idea; in a certain way the root is as visible as the rest of the tree. Intellectual capital seems to be a much more elusive concept, more akin perhaps to the genetic material of a tree before we have any idea of genes and any possibility of identifying them.

Edvinsson and Malone mention in passing that intellectual capital consists of the sum of knowledge, experience and abilities of management and employees. No precise definition is given. Stewart apparently sees it as something that you cannot touch, but which makes you wealthy.[44] Again not a very operative definition.

Goodwill may be seen as representing the intellectual capital of a company according to Labarre who mentions that these immaterial assets may represent more than 80 per cent of the total value of a company.[45]

We may have exaggerated the problems of measuring intellectual capital, because it may also be seen as consisting of aspects that can be counted. According to Edvinsson and Malone intellectual capital includes among other things inventions, techniques, processes, data, programmes and publications. It may also include employee training or even response times in relation to customer calls.

A simple kind of measurement may be had by listing all these things and it may even be possible to find a way to count each of the different aspects by using one of the more basic methods of measurement. Even so there is a problem of adding it all together into something called intellectual capital.

Breaking up intellectual capital into its large molecules, Edvinsson and Malone find that one of the important molecules is human capital which according to them includes knowledge, skills, creativeness and qualifications of the employees, as well as values, culture and philosophy of the company.

How is one to measure knowledge, skills, understanding and creative abilities located in the people making up a given organisation?[46] A proxy measure may of course consist in adding up their intellectual products in the form of inventions, computer programs and publications. But how many programs of average ability are equivalent to one creative thought that will spawn whole new families of programs, if it is programs we are into? How will one measure the ability to get these ideas and how does one rate the originality and potential of a new thought?

It gets more complicated though, knowledge, skills, understanding and creative abilities seem to have a sort of hidden nature. Some of the most important parts seem to be ineffable or tacit. Stewart recognises the problem in his discussion of intellectual capital,[47] and gives a series of small examples of tacit knowledge. For instance that it is the kind of knowledge found around the water cooler. Interestingly he asserts that it is necessary to make tacit knowledge explicit. One just has to identify the tacit knowledge and then make the important part explicit.[48]

The question is, should one attempt to make tacit knowledge explicit and scalable, and if the answer is affirmative, will it be possible? In a later chapter we show that tacit knowledge is not only important in decision making, but also that an attempt to make tacit knowledge explicit is futile. It may prove impossible, in the double sense that we cannot devise a technique to pull out this knowledge, without losing something, and we cannot use tacit knowledge made explicit as a substitute for tacit knowledge. Any extricated tacit knowledge would tend to become rigid and algorithmic, making it necessary to rely on tacit knowledge in order to use it.

Finally, there is the question of whether knowledge is just a stock that can be contained and regarded in isolation, or whether it is something that interrelates in various ways with the environment. Is someone innovative on his or her own, whatever the circumstances, or is the innovativeness heavily dependent on being surrounded by people with supplementary or like abilities or working under certain conditions.

As a simple example think of a man who has worked for 15 years in a certain company. He may have acquired knowledge that he himself is not even aware of, knowledge that is bound to the company in question, knowledge showing itself in the ability to find solutions to everyday problems that might take someone with less experience in the company a lot of time to solve. Now imagine if you will that this man was removed from the company. What then would he know? I assume that most would agree that somehow he has at least lost the ability to solve problems in the same way that he may have done in the old company. How is this kind of knowledge measured, or is that an example of something that is left along the wayside when the (ac)counting people take over, focusing on adding up the amount of formal education and other easy measures.

In a report from KPMG on social accounting the focus is on easy measures;[49] one of the measures being the number of days spent on further education per employee each year. Presumably this is according to the simple rule that more days spent on education are equal to more knowledge in the knowledge-based company. It should be evident that this can in no way be inferred, in the absence of more information, but it can of course be used to show that a given company is spending money on further education. Nothing more, nothing less.

We are in uncharted white areas of the map of knowledge and competence, and still some believe that it is possible to create a meaningful measure of intellectual or human capital. We assert that measuring such vague aspects and adding them up into a single measure for intellectual capital is impossible. Not in the sense that it is impossible to get some kind of measure of something, just that it would be like measuring the diameter and the weight of chair and dividing them into a single measure of chairishness. It may give us a cardinal measure, say a diameter–weight measure of 15 cm/kg. This number may even be used to compare the chair in question with other chairs, but we would have no idea of whether this would be a good measure of the aspects we actually wanted to know something about, and we do not have the faintest idea what we could use the diameter–weight measure for.

Like the measure of quality discussed previously such strange measures may be used because decision makers may value them, like stamp collectors may value certain qualities in used stamps just because they tacitly agree to value them.

SCALES OF LEADERSHIP

One of the attempts to put life into tabular form caught the eye some time ago. A Danish engineering company had devised a method of measuring the quality of its leaders. Every other year the employees rank their leaders on seven dimensions, using a scale from –2 to +2. The seven dimensions are: communication and cooperation; discussion of decisions and actions; employee development; delegation; consensus on goals and strategies; motivation; and prosperity of the department.

There are several problems with this attempt to scale leadership quality. First among these is the objection we have used before. To get a measure of a chair we need a good idea of what a chair is and what measures might be relevant in the concrete case.

Leadership quality seems to be a more vague concept than a chair, and there seems to be a lack of common and concrete notions of what leadership qualities may consist of. Accordingly we have only the haziest idea of what leadership quality really is. With no precise idea of the chair, or in this case leadership qualities, it would seem rather reckless to try to measure them along the seven dimensions shown here.

I cannot even begin to imagine what measures we would get if we had the same hazy idea of a chair. A combination of height, softness, weight and circumference maybe. Everyone can see how ridiculous such a measure would be in the case of a chair. The measures based upon the seven dimensions may be even more bizarre, but the lack of any clear idea of leadership works both ways; we cannot be sure that we are measuring something significant in relation to leadership quality, but neither can we show, as we could with a chair, that the measures are ridiculous. Maybe this is one of the reasons why such measures can exist; they may show something significant, we just do not know what it is.

According to a case reproduced in a Danish guide showing what to do in order to participate in the competition for the "Public Sector Quality Prize,"[50] the evaluation of management by the employees every second year using measures like the ones just discussed is supposed to create visible demands on management and as a result "develop and improve the competence of management."[51]

The idea is that the ratings that result from the measurements are discussed in the organisation, in sessions where management meets the employees. The feedback from measurements and discussions will presumably help managers focus on the areas where they have to develop management (or is it leadership?) skills.

"The experience is that evaluation of management has contributed to a process of development in the institution, in which good management is debated. The employee evaluation of management shows that the institution has got better leaders. Conversely, the effect is also that the demands on management have grown, because the employees' expectations in relation to management grow."[52] In the case in question they even conclude that as a result of the combined efforts of this and other efforts the institution has improved productivity 50 per cent during the past five years. No further data to substantiate this claim are produced though.

It is not shown how the rise in productivity is a result of the different initiatives started, nor is there anything to show how the evaluation of management by the employees has resulted in better management. In fact we are left with the assertion that the method works because the ratings have become better. To conclude that this means that management has become better may be somewhat far-fetched. Of course we cannot just conclude that the opposite is true, the reason being that we can see no causal relations, and also that we have no counter-factual evidence of what would have happened during the period had these measures not been implemented.

The quality defined by what was measured may have improved over time, but no one is able to show what happened to the unmeasurable qualities of management over the same time period though of course many may have felt what happened. The unmeasurable qualities may have declined in importance as a result of the focus on the measurable qualities.

A leader might score low on a dimension called "Consensus on goals and strategies." One might well ask what is actually being measured here. Would a better value always be a good thing? One might think of a department in which a value indicating lack of consensus actually means that the department in question is actively involved in trying out new approaches and new methods, with resulting discussions and differences of opinion, while a department where the manager scores high on the consensus scale is actually grinding to a halt in the development of new ideas, but everyone is satisfied with that situation, as long as they get their pay. Because no one wants to rock the boat, consensus is high.

The curious result is that in the first case the manager in question might show a low score on the measurement scales, but in fact be the more effective and better manager/leader. The activities changing the organisation just have the side-effect of lowering consensus, as if consensus in itself is always a good thing. The manager/leader in question may have enough insight to see how these things relate to each other. He or she may know that his or her scores will be low on something called consensus, but sincerely believe that this is in fact a not especially negative side-effect of something that is more important, although it cannot be measured.

If we are right in presuming that a consensus measure might actually be inversely related to important changes in values, attitudes, decisions and actions in an organisation, and that strict adherence to what one might naïvely infer that the measurement of the consensus means, then the application of these measures might actually lead to a decline in factors that may be important to the future of the company and those employed by it. In order to see that, insight and knowledge are very much needed. Insight and knowledge that build upon a more coherent but maybe inexpressible and unmeasurable understanding of how the different factors influence each other, and of what quality of management and leadership is all about.

In a system depending heavily on measurements, this kind of understanding may be less and less in demand, precisely because it cannot be expressed, cannot be organised into a quasi-algorithm and cannot be measured. In a way it cannot argue for its own importance, since it cannot show its results in steadily improving measurements on scales, which no one really knows how to interpret. Still there is more to come. Measurements like the ones shown here might actually influence not only the behaviour of the manager/leader but also the mindset of those doing the rating, thereby creating a vicious spiral.

Think for a moment about the female teacher brought under peer pressure because she tries to uphold a standard higher than her colleagues. Students are giving her bad ratings for her performance. The reason for their bad ratings of her may have their origin not only in her activities, but in their expectations, and their expectations are influenced by the demands that other teachers make upon them. With the lowering of her colleagues' standards her ratings get worse, and after a while she decides to lower her own expectations. This may lead to a new round of lower expectations all round, and better ratings overall.

As we can see in this imagined situation, the ratings may actually become better and better, not because the teachers become better, but because the demands on the students are lowered. Underneath the better looking ratings not only of the teachers, but also, of course, of student grades, a vicious spiral of declining quality is at work, but as it is not measured it can only be inferred and felt by some of the teachers. If not checked the result of this process may, as argued above, be mediocrity, not quality.

CHIMERICAL MEASURES

In former times workers doing a manual job were relieved of the responsibility to think about and plan their physical movements. Countless methods following in the wake of Taylor's ideas and methods for scientific management[53] made this possible.

Now, I wonder whether the belief in rational decision making, and the application of modern management theory, techniques and tool boxes may in some way represent a modern continuation of scientific management and thus contribute to solutions that cannot cure the basic problems, but only alleviate the symptoms of more basic dilemmas. This time in taking over the responsibility not only for organising the movement of the physical body, but for the organisation of the pertinent knowledge, right values and behaviour.

Perhaps I am unduly pessimistic, but some of the modern ideas, theories and methods contained in the so-called quality movement, intellectual capital movement, the learning organisations movement, pay for performance schemes, and the more general Human Resource Movement seem to contain ideas with a close affinity to classical behaviourism of Watson and Skinner or even Pavlov's salivating dog.[54]

Our discussion shows some of the problems following in the wake of an attempt to put life into a tabular form. How the attempt to measure the unmeasurable properties of organisations and individuals results in distortions of what is seen as important, for instance in relation to knowledge and quality. How attempts to measure aspects that we have no clear idea of lead to measurements that have a nonsensical relationship to the aspects we attempt to measure.

If we know nothing or only very little about the causal relations between the aspects we can measure and the qualities we want to promote, we may in fact find that measurement may be both counterproductive and distorting, inasmuch as they may have a negative influence on those subjected to this kind of evaluation. In the end we suspect that our ideas of what something means and what qualities are important will change as a result of the inherent demands of measurements.

We are tempted to call the results of all such measures chimerical. They show us a chimera, an animal with a lion's head, a goat's body and a snake's tail, an animal that cannot exist, at least not until genetic manipulation has come a stage further. Still we act as if the chimera is the real animal that we want to get the measure of.

If the real animal is represented by an elephant, the measurement attempts scorned here may remind one of the story of the seven blind men's attempt to picture an elephant. One gets a measure of the trunk, another of a hind leg and a third of ear flap, and so forth. Now adding those measures up will presumably not give a picture of an elephant, but instead some sort of a chimera that we do not even recognise. Now if we take the resulting chimera for the real elephant, we are in fact making the same kind of mistake that we make when relying on measures that are supposed to give a picture of the unmeasurable properties, whether they be the quality of management or leadership.

Like the blind men in the story, those who carry out the measurements are blind, blind on purpose that is. They close their mind's eye and ignore their insight in order to go about the measuring business in as objective a way as possible. In fact the less those carrying out the measurements know about the subject being measured, the more objective they may be. In this way we can have managers and management consultants and academics loudly insisting that the measurements actually show the whole elephant, well not the whole elephant maybe, but at least the essential parts. Just look at this significant measure, they say and point to the length of the trunk, which in their understanding is joined to the hind leg and the ear flap measure.

Somehow one is reminded of some of the more bizarre *Monty Python* dialogues, for instance the sketches involving the Hungarian dictionary or the dead parrot.

NOTES

1   Garvin (1998), p. 70.
2   Dickens (1854/1995), p. 4.
3   These examples are taken from the different schemes suggested at the Aarhus Business School in 1998, but they are fairly representative of the schemes used, because they are usually copied from each other.
4   Robert & Gale quoted in Omachonu & Ross (1994), p. 13.
5   An early pioneering work in a more classical sense is Juran (1951). The modern approach is based on Deming (1982) and Deming (1986). An overview can be found in Schildknecht (1992).
6   See for instance Green (1996).
7   Davis (1997), p. 17.
8   Taken from Harrington & Mathers (1997), p. 13.
9   Ibid., p. 60.
10   Davis (1997).p. 41.
11   Harrington & Mathers (1997), p. 62.

12 Ibid., p. 63.

13 Davis (1997), pp. 42-43.

14 Harrington & Mathers (1997), p. 24.

15 A discussion of different definitions of quality can be found in Garvin (1988). For a somewhat different view of quality, see Pirsig (1974).

16 Davis (1997), p. 25.

17 Supposedly the quote is from Frederick Winslow Taylor; it can be found in Townsend & Gephardt (1992), p. 11.

18 Green (1996), p. 73.

19 Ibid., p. 111.

20 Ellemose quoted in Davis (1997) p. 85.

21 Ibid., p. 86.

22 The excerpt is from Clausewitz (1812/1966), p. 83.

23 Davis (1993)

24 Referring of course back to the ideas of Frederick Winslow Taylor (Taylor 1911).

25 Davis (1997) p. 79.

26 Brown (1993).

27 Davis (1997).

28 Ibid., p. 71.

29 Zinck (1995).

30 Omachonu & Ross (1994), p. 3.

31 Sashkin & Kiser quoted in Knouse (1995), p. 2.

32 Quoted in Denton (1998), p. 35.

33 Omachonu & Ross (1994), p. 289.

34 Ibid., p. 290.

35 Hummeltenberg (1995), p. 181.

36 Davis (1997), p. 93.

37 Quotes are from Byrnes et al. (1994), pp. 11–12. The original 14 points can be found in Deming (1982).

38 Ellis (1968), p. 41.

39 Ellis states that a quantity relation only exists if:

   Two things A and B are comparable in respect of a given quantity q if and only if one of the following relationships connect them:

   (i) A is greater in q than B (that is $A >_q B$)

   (ii) A is equal in q to B (that is $A =_q B$)

   (iii) A is less in q than B (that is $A <_q B$).

   For a discussion of measurement theory see also Christiansen et al. (1980).

40 Sellitz et al. (1969), p. 159.

41 Ibid., p. 157.
42 Roos (1996), Roos (1998), Stewart (1991), Stewart (1994) and Stewart (1997).
43 Edvinsson & Malone (1997).
44 Stewart (1997).
45 The reference is found in Edvinsson & Malone (1997).
46 Quinn et al. (1998).
47 Stewart (1997).
48 Here one may refer to the theories of Nonaka, as found for instance in Nonaka (1991).
49 KPMG (1998). The actual use of such simple measures can be seen in a report from the Systematics company *(Intellectual Capital Report 2000* 2000).
50 *Kvalitetsprisen for den offentlige sektor – vejledning* (no year).
51 Ibid., p. 15.
52 Ibid., p. 15.
53 Taylor (1911). In a way Taylor's ideas are a continuation of the division of work principles already found with Adam Smith (Smith 1776/1974).
54 See for instance Skinner (1953).

PART TWO

TACIT FOUNDATIONS

4 Tacit knowledge and understanding

Was überzeugt mich denn, daß der Andere ein gewöhnliches Bild dreidimensional sieht? – Daß er's sagt? Unsinn–wie weiß ich denn, was er mit dieser Versicherung meint?

Nun, daß er sich darin auskennt; die Ausdrücke auf das Bild verwendet, die er auf den Raum anwendet; sich vor einem Landshaftsbild benimmt, wie vor einer Landschaft, etc. etc.

Ludwig Wittgenstein

HOG FUTURES HAVE DECLINED IN SYMPATHY ...

The subtitle is taken from a radio announcement in DeLillo's book *White Noise*.[1] It made me wonder how much knowledge is taken for granted.[2] Most educated people at least in the developed countries would probably have some gist of understanding what this announcement could mean and be able to attach some sense to it.

A child listening to an announcement like this might only understand the expression "hog," and part of the rest of the expression, which ends with: "adding bearishness to market." An educated person might understand most, but have some trouble with futures, perhaps having only the vague notion that it is somehow related to the stock exchange, to certain television programmes and special pages in the newspaper. "Bearishness" might also give trouble, but with all the interest in prices of shares and derivatives, he or she might even have an understanding of that.

To those selling and buying futures the announcement is immediately understandable, although perhaps they wonder with what the futures have declined in sympathy. The announcement might lead them to take action in reaction to the news, selling their futures, whatever.

To a farmer in the hog business the announcement might mean something else, and might even galvanise him into action, perhaps leading him to make decisions resulting in long-term changes in the production of hogs.

There are many levels of understanding, and it would seem that in order to understand the announcement the recipient would have to draw on a vast storage of preconceived notions. The announcement may be compared to a coded message that can be picked up by a recipient with the right decoding apparatus; not only an apparatus that would make it possible to make sense of the phonemes. The apparatus would have to consist of stored knowledge that would make it possible to understand the meaning of expressions like hog, hog futures, decline, sympathy, bearishness and market, and the possible relations between these expressions.

The argot of the stock exchange demands an implicit understanding with the recipient, because such an announcement is usually not accompanied by a very detailed explanation of what hogs, futures and sympathy means, or indeed what the whole expression might mean.

Some sort of taken-for-granted knowledge is necessary in all human communication. There is never enough information in the expressions we use to make them self-explanatory.[3] Context and prior knowledge are necessary. This goes to show that our everyday language rests upon a lot of built-in tacit assumptions or we would not even know what it means when someone says: "It is raining."

In order to understand common expressions we have to possess some kind of taken-for-granted knowledge. Usually we do not have to think about this knowledge, it just seems to be readily available.

In DeLillo's book the strange young boy Heinrich is asking what we know, by making the assumption that we are thrown back in prehistoric time: "What is a radio? What is the principle of a radio? Go ahead, explain. You're sitting in the middle of this circle of people. They use pebble tools. They eat grubs. Explain a radio."[4]

In an attempt to give an answer Heinrich's father says: "There's no mystery. Powerful transmitters send signals. They travel through the air, to be picked up by receivers."

Heinrich retorts: "They travel through the air. What, like birds? Why not tell them magic? ... What good is knowledge if it just floats in the air? It goes from computer to computer. It changes and grows every second of every day. But nobody actually knows anything."[5]

There may be something to Heinrich's assertion. There are not very many, if any, who could actually build radios on their own from scratch, and not everyone knows about the mechanism of a stock exchange or how to raise hogs. Most of us in fact do not have more than a vague inkling of what we are talking about.

The knowledge of building radios may be distributed over many individual minds, and in books and articles and other repositories of knowledge. When we are building a radio, we are not just assembling bits and pieces of transistors, resistors, diode and so on, but also lumps of knowledge that we cannot explain, like the knowledge of constructing a transistor or a diode.

Tentatively we assume that more and more of our knowledge is becoming outsourced. We are only left with vague notions of relationships and locations where we may find this knowledge, but we have less and less first-hand experience. In a way we come to depend more and more on the knowledge of others, knowledge that is somewhere out there.[6]

We may get the idea that knowledge not only has a large tacit, taken-for-granted part, but that it is also in some way social, shared by communities of people, lumpy as the parts of a radio and based on something like tacit conventions that we do not question or usually even think about.

Knowledge that may be dependent on upbringing and former experience is the kind of knowledge that "includes the abilities required to understand and use facts, rules and heuristics." Without this knowledge that represents our tacit, taken-for-granted knowledge, we would not be able to communicate and learn. In this way it is absolutely essential for our expressible knowledge and the evolution of this knowledge.

KNOWING MORE THAN ONE CAN SAY ...

Take a look at a skilled mountain biker, picking his way down a difficult slope. Does he know what he is doing? In a particular sense certainly, or he would not be able to stay on his bike. In another sense perhaps not. He may not be able to explain what he is doing very well. He is speeding down a complicated cross-country track without really thinking about what he is doing, letting some part of his mind and body adjust to the varying conditions without consciously thinking about what should be done. If he had to think of how a sudden obstacle could be tackled, he would either react too late or attempt an evasive manoeuvre bound to result in a fall. This I believe to be a plausible result taking into account the time it takes for the obstacle to register in the brain, the time to think consciously about the problem and then react by transmitting messages to various parts of the body, causing muscles to contract, making the knees bend, and the body sway this way or that, ultimately shifting balance and so on.

He seems to have the *problem well in hand*. In fact it is as if he is thinking with his hands or perhaps the whole body, without being involved in too much conscious thought.

Libet's experiment in the 1980s confirms at least part of this supposition. Libet made experiments in which he asked volunteers move their hands whenever they wanted to, while he was measuring the activity of the test subject's brain. It turned out that brain impulses associated with the movement of the hand began a few hundred milliseconds before the test subject reported any intent to make a movement. This would mean that the "voluntary action did not originate consciously."[7]

In the case of the skilled mountain biker it would seem that part of the brain handles processes and initiates actions independently of conscious thought. This seems to happen all the time when we move around, pick up things, write, play an instrument. A special report on this phenomenon in the *New Scientist* carried the heading: "Don't look now there's someone else running your body."[8]

In a fairly naïve way this is evidently right, at least for some of our motoric activity; we do not have to think consciously about walking in order to walk, except possibly when inebriated or handicapped in a certain way. We are interested in other aspects though, such as the tacit foundation of our knowledge and judgements.

"We say: 'Take this chair' and it doesn't occur to us that we might be mistaken, that perhaps it isn't really a chair, that later experience may show us something different."[9] But ask someone to describe a chair, and he might get into trouble. What do you mean by "chair," something to sit upon, a university chair, or the chair position in a meeting, or an organisation or something else? In Danish the problem is different. The word for chair is "stol" which of course looks like the German Stuhl or the English stool. Stol might also refer to something in a musical instrument, or parts of other objects, while the Stuhl and stool in certain cases may have a somewhat odorous meaning.

Back to the description of a chair in the meaning associated with something to sit on. When asking this question, or rather asking in

Danish for a general description of a stol, the answers take on a range from "Something to sit on" to "A horizontal plane supported by four legs, and perhaps with a back." Often the respondents describe a chair as consisting of a seat back, a seat and maybe four legs.

Checking *Webster's Dictionary* for the word chair one finds almost the same definition: "1. a seat, esp. for one person, usually having four legs for support and a rest for the back and often having rests for the arms." The dictionary of course also attempts to define the other meanings of the expression chair.[10]

The definition of a chair given in the dictionary must be of a chair in a certain configuration. The legs must be apart, of somewhat equal length, they must support the seat, whatever that means and a seat back must be attached at angle approaching 90 degrees to the seat. This does not characterise all chairs. Some modern chairs have one or three massive legs for instance, in fact the definition found would exclude a lot of chairs.

Sometimes chairs might be so strange that we only recognise them as chairs in relation to their surroundings, in their context so to speak. What is important is that we may not be able to give a general description of a chair that would cover all chairs. Instead it would seem that we have some tacit knowledge of chairishness that is used in recognising and using chairs when we encounter them. Most of us will have no trouble recognising chairs that we have never seen before, as chairs, and use them accordingly, and furthermore we seem to be able to see a certain chairishness in other objects too, when for instance using non-chair objects as chairs.[11]

In order to recognise something as a chair we need a lot of context and some tacit, gestalt-like perception of what we have come to regard as chairishness. Even the chair legs themselves would be impossible to define if they are not seen in relation to the rest. We really would not know what was meant. Legs are only relevant in relation to the rest, to the context. That means we only understand them as attached to chairs, tables, persons or as the legs of a journey. In fact we rely on something reminding us of a gestalt or a patterned definition, perhaps like the way a chess player may describe patterns in a game of chess.[12] This means that our concept of what constitutes a chair refers to a whole gestalt-like complex of meanings and interpretations relating to it.

Recognising something as a chair fit for sitting on demands more than just recognising the chairishness of the form. Somehow we also seem able to see that a certain configuration has a certain solidity. I am not sure that a chair constructed of single sheets of normal copying paper glued together in the shape of a chair would be seen as chair. Instead it might be seen as a model of a chair, a paper chair, or perhaps as a piece of art. The notion of solidity is presumably based on former experience with the solidity of materials like the ones apparently used for constructing the object, the chairishness of which we are judging. Somehow our skill to judge the ability of a chair to support our weight must be based on all sorts of hands-on experience and tacit calculations that we are unaware of.

"The expert performer knows how to proceed without any detached deliberation about his situation or actions, and without any conscious contemplation of alternatives."[13] This fits well with Polanyi, who asserts that it is a well-known fact "that the aim of skilful performance is achieved by the observance of a set of rules which are not known as such to the person following them."[14]

This is exactly the level of performance most of us have attained in order to cope with everyday problems. We recognise patterns, pictures, signs, faces and facial expressions without thinking and analysing at length.[15]

"When we turn our eyes to the face of another human being, we often seek and usually find a meaning in all that it does or fails to do. Grins, sneers, grimaces, and frowns, fleeting smiles and lingering stares, animated faces and poker faces are not merely utilitarian contractions and relaxations of the muscles, but glimpses into the heart of the other – or so it seems."[16]

We may understand "fleeting" and "lingering" in relation to facial expressions, but can we explain what the expressions mean precisely? Presumably not and still we seem to be able to read a lot into a facial expression, and make some quick inferences. That facial expressions are understood may be inferred from the reactions we show, looking for dangers if we see fear in another face, reacting with fear if we see angry expression or echoing the knowing smile of someone who sees the same joke that we did.[17]

We understand words and noises without usually having to think consciously about their meaning. We use a large part of native language as expert performers. We drive bikes, and cars, like expert performers, negotiating every day obstacle courses without much conscious thought. Spending much of our time thinking that some of our fellow rush-hour travellers are morons driving with their heads under their arms.

What these examples indicate is that from a certain level of performance we all depend upon some kind of tacit knowledge we are not really aware of.

"In some cases, we were once aware of the understandings which were subsequently internalized in our feeling for the stuff of action. In other cases, we may never have been aware of them. In both cases, however, we are usually unable to describe the knowing which our action reveals."[18]

Ryle must have had a similar idea in his mind when he wrote *The Concept of Mind*. In his meticulous way he argues that although the intellectualist legend has it that an intelligent person reflects before he acts, that execution of a task thus requires two processes, one of theorising and one of doing, that legend is false. There are many instances of intelligent behaviour evidently carried out without conscious reflection. A witty person may be able to tell good jokes, but he or she may not be able to explain how he or she does that or give any recipe for others to follow. Ryle succinctly states that efficient practice precedes the theory of it.

"Rules of correct reasoning were first extracted by Aristotle, yet men knew how to avoid and detect fallacies before they learned his lessons, just as men since Aristotle, and including Aristotle, ordinarily conduct their arguments without making any internal reference to his formulae. They do not plan their arguments before constructing them. Indeed if they had to plan what to think before thinking it they would never think at all; for this planning would itself be unplanned."[19]

In a study of the professional knowledge of nurses Josefson describes a case involving a middle-aged nurse, with many years of experience. In this case a man is admitted to her ward after surgery. After having a short conversation with the patient the nurse concludes that there is something wrong with him, although she cannot put her finger on what exactly it is that has convinced her of that. She calls a doctor, apparently someone with only little experience. He checks the patient's vital signs and finds nothing wrong. "Later in the day, the patient died, and the post mortem uncovered a complication that could not have been diagnosed by an examination of his vital signs. The nurse's comment was that she noticed something was out of the ordinary, but could not explain how she had arrived at this conclusion."[20] Previous experience was a decisive factor.

Care is central in a nurse's profession and Josefson mentions that nurses receive theoretical training that inculcates important medical knowledge and information. But this is not enough in a non-routine situation, or as Josefson sees it, when there are unexpected complications. "To deal with this degree of complexity nurses must have the ability to make a reasonable interpretation of events not covered by the descriptions in the rule book. This requires multi-faceted practical experience, through which the information acquired through formal training can be developed into knowledge. That knowledge is built up from a long series of examples which give different perspectives on an illness."[21]

One may ask whether we can learn this kind of knowledge. Wittgenstein's answer is: "Yes; some can. Not, however, by taking a course in it, but through '*experience*'. – Can someone else be a man's teacher in this? Certainly. From time to time he gives him the right *tip* – This is what 'learning' and ' teaching' are like here. – What one acquires here is not a technique; one learns correct judgement. There are also rules, but they do not form a system, and only experienced people can apply them right. Unlike calculating rules."[22]

Recent research on what has been called naturalistic decision making seems to confirm that Wittgenstein had the right idea. In empirical research it has been shown that situated and contextual learning are important for developing expertise, and insight. "[C]ontext provides examples of the conditions that call for actions, the range of permissible actions, and the consequences of actions. It provides opportunities to develop tacit knowledge about subtle features of the situation …"[23]

"But I have it in my hands" the branch manager of a Danish bank exclaimed after showing the miserable result of an attempt to write a description for making a Windsor knot in a tie. He was frustrated because he knew how to tie his tie into a Windsor knot, but he was not able to make a description of how it was done, even though his hands seemed to know what to do.

After making this experiment on more than a hundred (male) managers, it is evident that they know more than they can say and describe, at least when it concerns the art of making knots.[24] Although in fairness some descriptions were better than others. Asked how they had learned to tie a tie, a few answered that they in fact had learned it by following a set of multi-stage drawings or a set of detailed instructions. Most however had learned it from someone who knew how to do it, often their father.

Here is an example of one of the better instructions:

1. Place the tie around the neck, facing front, the thin end left – ends approximately of equal length.
2. Take the thick one, place it above the thin one, two to four buttons down.
3. Pull the thick one left around and from behind into the noose, and down behind the front part of the noose.
4. Hold the noose with the left hand and pull the thick one down until the tie tightens.
5. Try again.

A few of the managers were women, and in most cases they did not know how to tie a tie. Taking the most detailed instruction made by the male managers, a set of algorithm-like instructions, they were next asked to try to follow the instructions to the letter. In only one case out of a little more than twenty did they succeed in tying a knot; the rest failed abysmally. They usually registered the first problems with instruction 2, if they did not wear anything with buttons in front.

Even these simple instructions must rely on the user having some experience and tacit knowledge in order to understand what is to be done – and perhaps a tie.

Sometimes not much knowledge is taken for granted as in some of the examples quoted in the *New Scientist*. In one such example a small battery-powered radio comes with the following instruction: "To replace a battery, take out the old one and insert a new one."[25] I would assume that most people would smile or get annoyed when reading something as self-evident as that. Apparently we do not really want an explanation that tries to make something too explicit. What we somehow regard as self-evident need not be in there.

The tie problem may seem naïve compared with the problems that branch managers and employees of banks have to solve every day, but when they are deciding whether to lend money to a given customer or not, they apparently often find it necessary to go beyond the written instructions, and use knowledge based on experience, vague perceptions and impressions. "It is very difficult just to walk through the swing door and rate a company the first time. One has to have some experience, some knowledge, one has to have some understanding, some impression of what kind of company it is ..."[26] A branch manager agrees: "As I am often saying, this it not something that one can pronounce, it consists in looking at people, look deep into the eyes, what kind of person is this?"[27]

Experience, knowledge, understanding, impression, a look deep into the eyes. The terms used are fairly vague. It is not something that can be easily incorporated into a set of guidelines or rules for credit-rating. In fact some of the employees interviewed said that in their opinion they had to go beyond the written instructions, when credit-rating a company. "... much of it is subjective reflections."[28] It is based on a judgement involving written instructions, impressions and inexplicable notions.

An area manager talks of the need to be able to get a scent, almost like a tracker dog, when talking to the customer, apparently also listening for the things that are not said. "I am in the habit of saying that one shouldn't rely on what one is seeing. No, one must use all one's senses, it has to include Fingerspitzengefühl. The hairs at the back of one's neck have to bristle, when sitting with someone who is dangerous."[29] Dangerous in the sense that the bank may lose money on that person, if they are persuaded by his business plan.

In another bank an employee says that making decisions "has much to do with trust, and this here 'Fingerspitzengefühl', also in everyday transactions."[30]

Scents, impressions at the tip of one's fingers, bristling hairs at the back of one's neck, trust, what kind of knowledge is that? Even CEOs seem to rely on such strange sensations. The CEO of one Danish bank trusts his nose and his guts to give him an idea of how well a branch is run. He talks of relying on structured and unstructured information, from many sources when judging the branches and their managers. All these structured and unstructured impulses decide "whether I have or I haven't a good feeling in the gut."[31]

A former CEO of Danske Bank expressed a similar feeling publicly: "There are numerous examples in our daily board meetings where we declare with a clear voice, that we wouldn't touch this. This happens not only because of credit ratings, but also because they taste badly."[32]

It would seem that when judging a customer and credit rating a company, bank managers and employees rely on aspects of knowledge they cannot really explain, but which manifest themselves in feelings, impressions and physical signs like bristling hair, conditions of the stomach and taste; in a way thinking with their hands and judging with their guts, as if they possessed some kind of body knowledge.

In *The Will to Believe* James asserts that it is evident that "our non-intellectual nature does influence our convictions. There are passional tendencies and volitions which run before and others which come after belief, and it is only the latter that are too late for the fair; and they are not too late when previous passional work has already been in their own direction."[33]

It is important to note though that the impressions and feelings influencing credit rating were apparently used alongside more explicit information and knowledge when making a decision. When stating the reasons for the decisions in writing the emphasis would be on the formal knowledge, on the reference to rules, guidelines and numbers so to speak. In fact one sometimes got the impression that the decision of whether to lend money to certain customers would be based mostly on impressions, experience with the customer and be clothed in more rational terms afterwards, with explicit references to credit instructions and so forth. Bristling hair, *Gefühl*, gut feelings and taste are translated into terms of formal knowledge and almost algorithm-like reasoning. In this way the decisions are seen as resulting from such algorithm-like reasoning processes, but it is important to remember that these reasons are constructed after the decisions have been made.

It would seem that tacit knowledge is important for making professional decisions, but one feels weary using this knowledge in arguments for a certain decision. Instead making it look as if explicit or formal knowledge is the only form of knowledge used in making the decisions. Pointing to something that one cannot put one's finger on, or using expressions that may sound as if one's body and not the brain is the place where the ability to make judgements resides, somehow seems irrational and must be covered up in the written reasons given for a decision.

TENTATIVE KNOWLEDGE OF KNOWLEDGE

We know more than we can say, we use a kind of body knowledge and we seem to be able to jump to solutions, at least some people seem to have the knack of doing this in certain fields.

While writing about all these examples and reading and thinking about them at the same time, hitherto strange, unconnected lumps of knowledge about knowledge seemed to coalesce in ways beyond the control of my consciousness. They popped up and disappeared, combined and separated and made new conscious blobs of often fleeting thoughts, like the kind of tentative drafts that emerge, are pushed about, connected and correlated with what one already knows. Often the whole process involves the physical action of finding a theoretical fragment in an article or book, and/or actually the drawing of sketches of what might be termed a semantic network, or in a modern parlance mindmap, looking for relationship, inconsistencies, while the mental sketches change, under the influence of what is now stated on a piece of paper or a computer screen.

Table 4.1 Tentative typology of knowledge

What we can say:	Declarative, propositional knowledge and explicit procedural knowledge
The silent patron:	Tacit knowledge structures From–to relation, gestalt-like
Lumpy knowledge:	Stratified knowledge
Emergence:	New knowledge Unspecifiable and subliminal clues
Community and heritage:	Social knowledge and cultural knowledge
The cell walls of our minds:	Natural constraints and the "packing principle"

During one of the sketch drawing sessions, the thought that this could somehow be related to Dennett's multiple drafts model of consciousness also popped up. "According to the Multiple Drafts model, all varieties of perception – indeed, all varieties of thought or mental activity – are accomplished in the brain by parallel, multitrack processes of interpretation and elaboration of sensory inputs. Information entering the nervous system is under continuous 'editorial revision'."[34] Dennett's examples concern perception, for instance visual perception.

Most of these multiple drafts or sketches as we call them "play short-lived roles in the modulation of current activity."[35] These sketches, hastily caught on pieces of paper and in elaborate verbal sketches on the computer screen, somehow lead to new sketches, alas often only vaguely related to each other. Even so the sketches seem to contain bigger and bigger lumps, and what emerges is a tentative structure for discussing the different aspects of knowledge in a more systematic way.

The tentative typology containing some of the aspects we find important is shown in Table 4.1.

WHAT WE CAN SAY

In some of the former examples we have tried to show that one can know more than one can say. Let us now take a look at a kind of knowledge, where one can say what one knows. This knowledge is formal and can be stated explicitly.

Declarative knowledge may be represented by statements about facts, relationships, causes and states. An example of a propositional statement might be the expression "the melting point of x-material is y-degrees." Facts and formal rules used in building radios may represent propositional knowledge.

Explicit procedural knowledge describes actions, for instance encoding how to achieve a particular result. An example might be the "Sieve of Eratosthenes," a simple but tedious method for finding prime numbers.[36]

Although rather simple for people conversant with mathematics, many may have a problem understanding the meaning of a propositional statement and the Sieve of Eratosthenes may mean nothing to them, which just goes to show that although declarative or propositional knowledge can be expressed very explicitly, it stills demands a kind of implicit or taken-for-granted knowledge.

We may of course learn the words by heart and express them, but that does not mean that we know what we can say. Others would soon discover that we used the expression in connections that would show that we are in a way saying more than we knew. It would represent a kind of "inert knowledge."

We might even learn to find prime numbers by the "Sieve" or learn to solve equations by following a precise and very detailed algorithm learned by heart or perhaps just by substituting symbols on the screen in a computer program like "Mathematica." Our actions might lead to the right solutions, but in a way we would not know what we were doing. If we continue this line of reasoning long enough backwards we might of course get the idea that in a way no one does. We would rely on procedures, algorithms and knowledge we did not really understand, but could use in a way that would seem to demonstrate knowledge. A perfect recital of a sonnet by Shakespeare would not demonstrate any more knowledge than a perfect rendition by a tape recorder would.[37]

In the study of the knowledge that nurses possess, propositional knowledge is seen as that part of their knowledge that can be described in generally applicable rules. This is knowledge we would find in textbooks used in formal education. When we are not talking about mathematics or physics, but social sciences or even management science, the declarative or procedural statements are no longer quite as explicit and precise as the mathematical expressions, although they may use the same form.

Many of the declarative or procedural statements will be related to cause and effect chains, as in the expression "If the government initiates this action then it will cause employment to rise," or fall as the case might be.

The general form might be like the following, taken from Ginet's work on action: "In S's opening a door, for example, the caused event is the door's opening. S's relation to that event, in virtue of which S causes it, is S's voluntary exerting her body in connection with the door in such a way as thereby to cause the door to open."[38]

This example would make sense to most people able to understand the expression, but might also at the same time seem a little bit ridiculous; it does not seem necessary to state the obvious to quite that extent.

What about the following excerpt from a textbook on "organisational learning"? "Stress is another reason why organizations may look for solutions to problems; its presence may indicate a need for change or adaption. Stress causes the system or subsystem to learn, under pressure from the environment or from the need to succeed."[39]

Often such explanations are accompanied by diagrams with arrows showing direction of causation and influence, the importance of the contributions represented by the thickness of the arrows. In more empirical studies coefficients of correlations may take the role of the arrows.

It seems evident that this kind of declarative and explicit procedural knowledge is different from the first examples. Here we are really combining lumps or chunks of knowledge that depend on a tacit understanding, and the lumps are held together by a kind of tacit acceptance of possibility and reasonableness of such a relation. There is no mathematical logic or well-understood physical cause–effect knowledge involved, although it may superficially seem like there was.

What characterises formal knowledge is that it is overt and almost tangible, it can exist independently of an individual mind, as an expression in a book, or at an obscure Internet address. "The important thing about it is that, being formulated in texts, equations, and the like, it can be discussed, criticized, amended, compared, and rather directly taught. All this is in sharp contrast to the other kinds of knowledge ..."[40]

There is no doubt about the importance of formal knowledge in modern society where most of the knowledge is "outsourced" and located outside us, in all sorts of storages. The question is instead whether the emphasis on formal knowledge erodes the more tacit parts of knowledge that we all depend on, but cannot see or touch or transmit or store in the same way that we can with formal knowledge. I believe that this actually is happening at the moment, as a result of the current emphasis on the explicit and algorithm-like aspects of knowledge.

THE SILENT PATRON

In Fodor's *Modularity of the Mind* we may find an illustration of the kind of knowledge that does not seem to be formal, although it is stated in a textbook. "Whether John's utterance of 'Mary might do it, but Joan is above that sort of thing' is ironical, say, is a question that can't be answered short of using a lot of what you know about John, Mary and Joan. Worse yet, there doesn't seem to be any way to say, in the general case, how much, or precisely what, of what you know about them might need to be accessed in making such determinations."[41]

The kind of knowledge that one would need in order to judge whether John's utterance was meant ironically is difficult to state as formal declarative knowledge. It may represent an informal knowledge that a good friend of John, Mary, and Joan would possess, without really being able to state it explicitly. Most of the knowledge would also be tied to the specific relationships with the involved persons. Someone able to judge whether John's utterance was meant ironically might not be able to do it if some unknown person had said it; meaning that the knowledge would be situated, except of course for a general ability to discern an ironical tone or lack of same, in an utterance, if we hear it spoken out aloud.

In a series of lectures Polanyi in the 1960s tried to work out a whole structure of tacit knowing.[42] His starting point is somewhat like ours, that we can know more than we can say.

Polanyi shows that there is a certain structure to tacit knowing. He does this by recounting an experiment in which a test person being presented with words is subjected to an electric shock whenever he utters certain associations to particular "shock words." After a while the test person apparently learns to avoid the utterances that bring forth the shocks. On questioning it appeared that he could not tell what he was doing, although the experiment clearly showed that he was avoiding the shock-inducing utterances consistently.

This experiment led Polanyi to suggest a basic structure for tacit knowing consisting of two terms. "We know the electric shock, forming the second term, by attending to it, and hence the subject is *specifiably* known. But we know the shock-producing particulars only by relying on our own awareness of them for attending to something else, namely the electric shock, and hence our knowledge of them remains *tacit*.[43] Thus we rely on our awareness (in Polanyi's sense of the term) for attending to the shocks. Polanyi seems to stress a sense of awareness that emphasises sense perceptions.[44]

In the shock experiment it would seem that a silent patron of our mind takes care of the particulars, involved in recognising and avoiding the shocks, while we are attending to the shocks. We may be doing the same thing with expressions. Our patron attends to the perception of sounds and transmission into words, while we attend to the meaning of the expression. Polanyi would say that we attend *from* the silent perception of the sounds *to* the meaning of the expression. Or in face recognition, *from* the silent recognition of particular features of the face *to* the face. We somehow use the elementary features of sounds or faces to get at their joint meaning. This is what Polanyi calls the *functional* structure of knowledge.

Telling how one may explore a dark hollow with a stick Polanyi attempts to explain how the contact of the stick with objects in the hollow, the walls or whatever, is felt by the fingers and hand. The sensations are transposed into meaningful impressions of the hollow, size, shape, wall texture, hard soft, even uneven and so on. Meaningless feelings are transposed into meaningful ones. Polanyi calls this the *semantic* aspect of tacit knowing. After probing with the stick we might conclude: "This is a hollow about two feet deep and with soft mud walls," or whatever. After looking at a face, and probing with the imaginary stick of our eyes, we may say to ourselves: "I know this face ... but what's her name?"

What Polanyi seems to be saying is that we go *from* particulars *to* what may be seen as a *gestalt*. We perceive the particulars of a chair, the legs, seat, back, size, material and so on, without conscious thought and from them we move to the overall gestalt, to the phenomenon, and to the meaning of these perceptions, to the chair. We recognise the chair as a chair without recounting all these particulars, which might be dissolved in even more particular particulars, if we start thinking about what makes up a chair.

Now perhaps it is understandable that we have difficulties in giving an all encompassing definition of a chair. Even if we would somehow be able to recount all the tacit *from* relations, the particulars that give rise to the impression of a chair, we would have difficulty in defining a chair.

We tacitly seem to integrate the particulars to a whole, a chair or whatever. "Since we were not attending to the particulars in themselves, we could not identify them."[45] Polanyi draws the conclusion that too much lucidity can in fact be counter-productive. "Scrutinize closely the particulars of a comprehensive entity and their meaning is effaced, our conception of the entity is destroyed. ... Speaking more generally, the belief that, since particulars are more tangible, their knowledge offers a true conception of things is fundamentally mistaken."[46]

In our chair example this would presumably mean that an attempt to define a chair by recounting all the features, the particulars as it were, would lead to a loss of comprehension of what a chair might be. Perhaps we may also hazard the hypothesis that an attempt to isolate and enumerate the qualities of leadership might lead to a loss of comprehension of leadership and even quality.

In Borges' short story *Funes the Memorious*, we hear the story of a man who is able to remember everything. Funes would never be able to see different chairs as being all just chairs, because he would only see the particulars, and all chairs would be different from each other. In a way Funes was an idiot savant: "With no effort, he had learned English, French, Portuguese and Latin. I suspect, however, that he was not very capable of thought. To think is to forget differences, generalize, make abstractions."[47]

Somehow those who see different chairs just as chairs must be able to ignore many aspects of the chairs. It is almost as if they reduce or discard information that is irrelevant to the problem at hand without being able to explain how they do it. I wonder whether this ability hints at an important aspect of expertise.[48]

In fact the breakdown of the world into particulars, legs, seat backs and seats may get us close to a kind self-willed autism. Autistics who have become able to describe their experience reported that they could not make sense of the world. They were focused, nay obsessed with the particulars of the world and these particulars represented meaningless fragments. An article in the *New Scientist* tells how a sufferer "could not see faces, just collections of noses, eyes and mouths. Words were just strange noises."[49]

In other cases it looks as if missing parts are filled in in order to see something. This apparently happens when making sense of sentences that have lost parts in transmission. It may look as if the mind recognises something in a jumble of words or suddenly sees a meaning in an incomplete sentence, usually without much in the way of explicit analysis.

With these qualifications in mind it is important to emphasise that attempts to list all the particulars would be futile. On every level and in every profession explicit knowledge rests on tacit knowing. This assertion is important because it flies in the face of many attempts of modern science, including social science and management science.

"The declared aim of modern science is to establish a strictly detached, objective knowledge. Any falling short of this ideal is accepted only as a temporary imperfection, which we must aim at eliminating. But suppose that tacit thought forms an indispensable part of all knowledge, then the ideal of eliminating all personal elements of knowledge would, in effect, aim at the destruction of all knowledge."[50]

LUMPY KNOWLEDGE

When talking about the knowledge needed to construct a radio earlier, we reached the conclusion that knowledge had to be lumpy. The engineer constructing a radio must somehow operate with lumps of knowledge that has to be taken as given, as for instance the knowledge enclosed in a integrated circuit.

The people designing the cabinet operate with other lumps of knowledge, while those responsible for the production and sale of the radio operate with their specific lumps of knowledge.

Going in the other direction, we can see that integrated circuits are constructed and produced using lumps of knowledge that may be found in the construction and production of transistors. This knowledge may again include the lumps of knowledge of physicists working with basic research in different fields.

Using the concept of stratified knowledge and hierarchy we can argue that when we are for instance talking or writing, we use knowledge of principles belonging say to phonetics or grammar, without thinking about it. It seems to be a kind of taken-for-granted knowledge that allows us to concentrate on expressing a thought while a more tacit part of our mind takes care of grammar, spelling of words, phonemes and so on, and our hand presses keys that make some filtered version of our thoughts appear on screen, without much conscious intervention from us.

Polanyi sees this stratified knowledge as a hierarchy of entities, in which the laws, rules or principles of one level operate under the control of the level above. The voice is shaped into words belonging to a vocabulary, while the vocabulary is shaped into sentences according to the rules of a grammar, and so forth. It is important to note the use of the word "shaped." This means that the lower level is somehow controlled by the next higher. If the sentences lose control of the words the succession of words may become meaningless.

The vocabulary cannot be accounted for by the laws governing phonetics, but in order to talk, the laws of phonetics must somehow be observed.

"Accordingly, the operations of a higher level cannot be accounted for by the laws governing its particulars forming the lower level. You cannot derive a vocabulary from phonetics; you cannot derive the grammar of a language from its vocabulary ... it is impossible to represent the organizing principles of a higher level by the laws governing its isolated particulars."[51]

Knowledge of the radio "shapes" the use of integrated circuits and transistors. A jumble of integrated circuits or transistors would not work as a radio, unless we were very lucky.

A chair cannot be derived from particulars of legs, seats, knowledge of materials and so on, because "it is impossible to represent the organizing principle of a higher level by the laws governing its isolated particulars."

Poincare once said that science is built up with facts, as a house with stones. But a collection of facts is no more a science than a heap of stones is a house.[52]

Ryle, in his attack against Cartesianism,[53] talks of a category mistake. He shows what he means by an example involving a foreigner visiting Oxford or Cambridge for the first time. The foreigner is shown a number of colleges, libraries and playing fields, scientific departments and so on. Having seen all this he then asks where the university is. He has in fact been shown a heap of stones, but sees no university.

A university cannot be understood as a heap of stones and our radio cannot be derived or understood by knowing the particulars of integrated circuits and transistors. Whatever you know on this level would not be enough to get to the concept of radio.

Polanyi draws the following conclusion: "... no level can gain control over its own boundary conditions and hence cannot bring into existence a higher level, the operations of which would consist in controlling these boundary conditions. Thus the logical structure of the hierarchy implies that a higher level can come into existence only through a process not manifested in the lower level, a process which thus qualifies as an emergence."[54]

EMERGENCE

Emergence describes the phenomenon that patterns, structures and properties can arise in a way that cannot be adequately explained by referring only to the pre-existing components and their interaction. All the same a radio, as well as a chair, emerges from the local interactions between the already known components. Even so a radio cannot be adequately explained by components like transistors, resistors or other of the components it may include.

Emergent patterns are unpredictable and not deducible from the pre-existing components. Many social phenomena seem to be a result of emergence, for instance markets, states, communities, cultural and social trends.

Somewhat analogous to the example with speech we may presume that the higher levels have to obey the laws of the components, but at the same time the higher level influences the lower level components. The market is a collection of individual agents and behaviours but it also influences the behaviour of these agents.[55]

Perhaps emergence may in some vague way help us to understand the emergence of new knowledge, beginning with a hunch. Often when attempting to get to grips with something we have a hunch, but what kind of knowledge is a hunch? Apparently it just pops up like a flickering will-o'-the-wisp. When we attempt to follow the weak light, it may turn out to be nothing, or it may be the first step we are aware of when solving a problem or understanding something for the first time.

It is as if a hidden and silent patron in one's mind wants to help, by leaving a clue here and there for me to see, the me that is aware, to pick up and work with. Or by collecting a ready-made solution from some forgotten shelf of one's memory and leaving it at the doorstep of my consciousness, for me to use, without offering any further explanation. Or by suddenly presenting a new thought in one's consciousness. While being immersed in an attempt to understand something, for instance tacit knowledge, a new idea suddenly presents itself, a thought one has never had before makes itself heard in the cacophony of thoughts.[56]

In relation to a question concerning values Polanyi argued that "when originality breeds new values, it breeds them tacitly, by implication; we cannot choose explicitly a set of new values, but must submit to them by the very act of creating or adopting them."[57]

Just now I have a hunch that the whole concept as presented here, simple and complex at the same time, is perhaps not entirely convincing.

While writing this I was having fragments of several thoughts alternating in the mind at the same time, but one thing is certain I was not thinking about the computer I am sitting in front of, the keyboard, the keys, the work of my hands and fingers, nor the construction of words and sentences according to I know not what rules. This all seems to works automatically without intruding upon the conscious thoughts that I have. This cannot be said to represent a *from–to* relation in Polanyi's sense.

In fact this seems closer to the thoughts on thinking and knowing in Wittgenstein's *Remarks on the Philosophy of Psychology*. For instance when he writes: "Beobachte dich beim Schreiben, und wie die Hand die Buchstaben formt, ohne daß du es eigentlich veranlaßt. Du fühlst wohl etwas in deiner Hand, allerlei Spannungen und Drücke, aber daß *die* dazu nötig sind, diese Buchstaben zu erzeugen, davon weißt du nichts."[58]

In a way I am moving in the opposite direction of the *from–to* relation, from the *to* part, the gestalts in the shape of my thoughts, to the *from* part, the particulars, the hand and finger movements, the words on the screen, the checks of spelling and grammar. My thoughts somehow dissolve in the intricate workings of tacit skills, using the keyboard, tactile and visual feedback, to adjust position and place letters on the screen, where they assemble in expressions that seem to result from my thoughts, although in an odd way they seem to be a little different from what I was thinking. Grammar, syntax and other things may influence what I am writing, filtering out thoughts that are difficult to express or form into sentences. Perhaps this explains why the thoughts appear to come out different than the thoughts I seem to be aware of.

Tacit insight perhaps relies "on interiorizing particulars to which we are not attending and which, therefore, we may not be able to specify, and relies further on our attending from these unspecifiable particulars to a comprehensive entity connecting them in a way we cannot define."[59]

It would seem that Polanyi is simply arguing that hunches and scientific discoveries rest upon a kind a of tacit familiarity with and insight in certain topics. "[M]any of the clues used will remain unspecifiable and may indeed be subliminal."[60]

COMMUNITY AND HERITAGE

At least part of the knowledge that we find in our use of a common language seems to be based upon a kind of shared common or social knowledge. We usually come to think of the same things when we hear certain words in a certain context. "It is raining;" "This is a luxury car;" "I noticed the bike was yellowish;" "It bubbled like boiling water." In this case we are able to "make inductions in the same way as others do in the world of concerted *action.*" [61]

In some way it would seem that almost all of our knowledge is social. "Luxury"and "yellowish" would seem to be expressions that rely on some kind of common conception of what is meant. Wittgenstein gives support to this idea. "Wenn die Menschen nicht im allgemeinen über die Farben der Dinge übereinstimmten, wenn Unstimmigkeiten nicht Ausnahmen wären, könnte es unseren Farbbegriff nicht geben. Nein: – gäbe es unsern Farbbegriff nicht."[62]

But is that not the case for most of what we call knowledge?

The story of Kaspar Hauser, the strange boy who was found wandering the streets of Nuremberg in 1828 may indicate how little we know if we do not grow up among other people, and learn their knowledge conventions. Physically he was on the level of a 16 year old, mentally on the level of a small child. Later when had learned to talk he could tell that he had been held isolated in dark cave-like room (Behältnis) all his life and had only seen one other human being during his stay in the room.[63]

This community aspect of knowledge also seems to be implied in common sense. Several times we have asked participants in our courses on value-based leadership and management to answer the question: What is common sense? The direct translation of the Danish question would be something like: What is "sound reason?" They were also asked whether it was common to all.

Many answered that sound reason was individually determined and different from person to person. Others realised that there was an element of community in it, with quiet adjustments to the views of the majority, as can be seen from the answer: "Sound reason can be said to be the decision, that will win general approval with the great majority of a representative sample of a population."[64]

Still the majority felt that their sound reason was individual and different from the sound reason of others, perhaps in a curious way this is an impression they also have from the community they are living in and the organisation they are working in. It has become part of their shared and tacit cultural knowledge. One is reminded of a chorus of people shouting: "We are all individuals," in a *Monty Python* movie.

"Cultural skills include the ability to make inductions in the same way as others in the world of concerted *action*. It is our cultural skills that enable us to *make* the world of concerted *behaviour*. We do this by agreeing that a certain object is, say, a Rembrandt, or a certain symbol is an *s*. That is how we digitize the world. It is our common culture that makes it possible to come to these agreements that comprises our culture."[65]

"Our faith is faith in some one else's faith, and in the greatest matters this is mostly the case. Our belief in truth itself, for instance, that there is a truth, and that our minds and it are made for each other – what is it but a passionate affirmation of desire, in which our social system backs us up?"[66]

The same goes for science. A scientist could not really be a scientist in isolation, to work as a scientist he or she has to be part of a community working in the area he or she is working in. What scientists do would seem to be learned by taking part in a social practice involving a community of scientists, although the practice may change slightly from iteration to iteration, discarding certain parts and adding new.

Even facts seem to be part of social knowledge for "there are no mere facts in science." Facts are part of social convention for instance in a community of scientists. "A scientific fact is one that has been accepted as such by scientific opinion, both on grounds of evidence in favour of it, and because it appears sufficiently plausible in view of the current scientific conception of the nature of things. ... science is not a mere collection of facts, but a system of facts based on their scientific interpretation. It is a system endorsed by a scientific authority. ... this authority endorses a particular distribution of scientific interest intrinsic to the system, a distribution of interest established by the delicate value-judgements exercised by scientific opinion in sifting and rewarding current contributions to science. Science *is what it is*."[67]

It is supposed that most of the shared or social knowledge described here would consist of tacit taken for granted knowledge. But knowledge is not only social; in our view it is also inherited from earlier generations, like the language we use, the traditions we observe, the rites we follow, the values we hold, the culture we express. Wittgenstein expresses the idea like this: "Mein Weltbild habe ich nicht, weil ich mich von seiner Richtigkeit überzeugt habe; auch nicht weil ich von seiner Richtigkeit überzeugt bin. Sondern es ist der überkommene Hintergrund, auf welchem ich zwischen wahr und falsch unterscheide."[68]

A simple example of how shared, taken-for-granted knowledge may develop in cultural context is given by Collins. It shows that what was once explicit knowledge may slowly change into taken-for-granted knowledge, or tacit knowledge.

The example concerns a pinball machine. In the 1830s it had a very detailed set of operating instructions, while the same type of machine at the end of the century only had a short instruction like: "Insert nickel, push down handle." Later all written instructions disappeared. Everyone was supposed to know what to do without being told. Explicit knowledge thus became tacit, taken-for-granted knowledge.[69] Modern examples could include the use of personal computers and mobile phones.

In the example described it would of course still be possible to make a more explicit instruction. In other fields of tacit knowledge that would be impossible; knowledge would only exist as an ineffable inclination.

Thus knowledge, even knowledge of knowledge, may ultimately be social. I am reminded of Austin who argued that when one says: "I know," "One is not describing anything, let alone one's psychology or mental state. Instead, one is engaging in a social act, *ie.* is indicating that one is in the position (has the credentials and the reasons) to assert *p* in circumstances where it is necessary to resolve a doubt. When these conditions are satisfied, one can correctly be said to know."[70]

In a strange way this social act looks almost like the so-called Turing test for intelligent computation machines, in which Turing envisaged that if one could not distinguish between a computer and human being in a conversation based on a written question and answer session, then one would be obliged to say that the computer was thinking. In fact saying "that there [is] no way of telling that other people [are] 'thinking', or 'conscious' except by a process of comparison with oneself."[71]

Might this be translated to mean that we have knowledge about something if we are able to converse and act in way that is understandable and meaningful to others in almost the same way that speaking a language is? Act would include the ability to make predictions and what would be seen as purposeful action. It also would include that there is some consistency to conversations and acts. Paraphrasing Wittgenstein we would expect that "daß man sich darin auskennt."

THE CELL WALLS OF OUR MINDS

I wonder whether there is another sense in which knowledge might be said to be tacit than the ones we have discussed up until now. Think for instance of standing in the kitchen mixing some ingredients. Often it is important that the mixture has the right degree of viscosity, or fluidness, but when is that achieved and how does one achieve the right viscosity by adding more ingredients? The answer might be that one learns to sense when this is the case almost in the same way that one learns to tie a knot in a tie. But might there not be a something else helping us, perhaps even the mixture itself?

To Brown et al. the answer to this question is affirmative. They see problem solving as being carried out in conjunction with the environment, not solely inside the heads of the problem solver. "Instead of taking problems out of the context of their creation and providing them with an extraneous framework, JPFs [Just Plain Folks] and practitioners seem particularly adept at solving them within the framework of the context that produced them. This allows them to share the burden – of both defining and solving the problem – with the task environment as they respond directly to emerging issues. The adequacy of the solution they reach becomes apparent in relation to the role it must play in allowing activity to continue."[72]

Bates mentions the examples somewhat like these and called them cooking problems. The examples are from the work of Lévi-Strauss and concern the seemingly deep principles that underlie cooking and eating of foods across cultures. Bates concludes by noting "that the universal facts reside in the structure of the cooking problem, and not in the environment per se. Such task structures ... lie neither in the organism nor in the environment, but at some emergent level between the two."[73]

The classic example would be the creation of the hexagonal structure of the honeycombs found in beehives. This almost perfect hexagonal structure need not depend on a kind of architectural intelligence, or innate geometrical instinct of the bees. Instead it is the inevitable outcome of the packing principle, the physical laws governing the behaviour of spheres being packed under pressure from all sides. "The bees 'innate knowledge of hexagons' need to consist of nothing more than a tendency to pack wax with their hemispherical heads from a wide variety of directions."[74]

Could this perhaps be compared to for instance the operation of the market. No one needs to have much tacit nor explicit knowledge of the market. Market forces determine the result behind the back of the individual actors in a market.

On the basis of these arguments might one dare suggest that an attempt to substitute the packing principle or the market would demand, in the case of the bees, that every bee be endowed with a sense of geometry, and ability to calculate even better than it already can (for instance when communicating the distance and direction to flowers to other bees of the hive), and in the case of the market that human beings be endowed with an extremely comprehensive knowledge of economic relations and fantastic calculating abilities in order to create a command economy that would outperform the market.

NOTES

[1]   DeLillo (1984/1986) p. 149.

[2]   Before attempting to show the importance of tacit knowledge it is important to emphasise that when we are talking about knowledge we are painting with a broad brush, partly taking for granted what is meant by knowledge. In order not to leave too much to interpretation a few hints may be necessary though. In common usage one might discern between "know about" or knowledge and "knowhow" or skill, in other words between Wissen and Können. Here we see Wissen and Können as different aspects of knowledge and include both meanings. Ryle discusses "knowing how" and "knowing why" and shows the differences and parallelism in small examples. We may forget *how* to tie a reef knot, and forget *that* the German word for knife is Messer (Ryle 1949).

According to the German Duden dictionary "können" may be regarded as "erworbenes Vermögen, auf einem bestimmten Gebiet mit Sachverstand, Kunstfertigkeit o. Ä. Etwas [Besonderes] zu leisten: sportliches, handwerkliches ... While "Wissen" includes "Gesamtheit der Kenntnisse" that someone has, but also "Kenntniss, das Wissen von etw.: ein wortloses, untrügliches Wissen" (*Duden* 1996).

Bereiter and Scardamalia mention that to a cognitive psychologist, knowledge would be formal or declarative knowledge, while skills would represent procedural knowledge (Bereiter & Scardamalia 1993).

In *Philosophische Untersuchungen* Wittgenstein writes: "Die Grammatik des Wortes 'wissen' ist offenbar eng verwandt der Grammatik der Worte 'können', 'imstande sein'. Aber auch eng verwandt der des Wortes 'verstehen' (Eine Technik ' beherrschen')." (Wittgenstein 1953) part I, p. 150.

3   The letters in "It is raining" do not contain enough information to understand the expression without prior knowledge. It seems to be just a kind of shorthand convention. To see this one only has to read the absurd conversation about whether it is raining or not in DeLillo's *White Noise*, (DeLillo 1984/1986), pp. 22–25.

4   DeLillo (1984/1986), p. 148.

5   Ibid. pp 148/49.

6   In a discussion of knowledge Russell talks about two kinds of knowledge: knowledge by acquaintance and knowledge by description. Knowledge by acquaintance represents anything of which we are directly aware. That includes sense data, or the outer sense, and memory and introspection, or what Russell calls the inner sense. Russell also asserts that in addition to acquaintance with particular things we also have acquaintance with universals, "such as *whiteness, diversity, brotherhood* and, so on." When reading this one may doubt that one is acquainted with "acquainted" because it is difficult to see how one is directly acquainted with universals. In knowledge by description, "description" means "any phrase of the form 'the so-and-so' in the singular." Russell concludes that the "importance of knowledge by description is that it enables us to pass beyond the limits of our private experience." (Russell 1912). Thus it would appear that knowledge by description depends on the knowledge of others, just like in our concept.

7   Reported in Holmes (1998), p. 35.

8   *New Scientist* (5 September 1998).

9   Wittgenstein (1976), p. 397.

10 *Webster's Encyclopedic Unabridged Dictionary of the English Language* (1989).

11 Ibid., "2. Something that serves as a chair or supports like a chair."

12 Black (1990).

13 Dreyfus (1987), p. 51. See also the discussion in Dreyfus (1997) and in Bereiter & Scardamalia (1993).

14 Polanyi (1958/1962), p. 49.

15 I suddenly see that what I have written here is similar to a thought found in Wittgenstein's later work: "Wer ein Blick für Familienähnlichkeiten hat, kann

erkennen, daß zwei Leute mit einander verwandt sind, ohne sagen zu können, worin die Ähnlichkeit besteht..." Wittgenstein (1980), p. 97.

16 Russell & Fernández-Dols (1997a), p. 3.

17 Frijda & Tcherkassof (1997), pp. 85ff. Compare with Wittgenstein's remarks in Wittgenstein (1980), passim.

18 Schön (1983), p. 54.

19 Ryle (1949), p. 30.

20 Josefson (1987), p. 27.

21 Ibid., p. 26.

22 Wittgenstein (1958), parts II/XI.

23 Beach et al. (1997), p. 33.

24 The experiment was made with participants of courses on value-based management and leadership in the years 1998/1999. Participants were from banks and public authorities.

25 The examples are from *New Scientist*, 25 April 1998, p. 108.

26 Quoted in Petersen (1997).

27 Ibid.

28 Ibid.

29 Ibid.

30 Quoted from interview made by members of CREDO in Jyske Bank A/S 1996.

31 Quoted from interview with the CEO of Jyske Bank A/S 1996.

32 The CEO of Den Danske Bank quoted in Berlingske Tidende, 12 October 1996.

33 James (1896/1987), p. 206.

34 Dennett (1991), p. 111.

35 Quoted in Dennett (1991), p. 258.

36 Hoffman (1998).

37 Ryle presents this example: "The well-regulated clock keeps good time and the well-drilled circus seal performs its tricks flawlessly, yet we do not call them intelligent" (Ryle 1949, p. 28). We are not sure that Ryle is right about the seal though. Searle has an ingenious argument in shape of the Chinese room thought experiment, where he argues that perfect manipulation according to given algorithms does not represent knowledge (Searle 1980).

38 Ginet (1990), p. 6.

39 Probst & Büchel (1997), p. 45.

40 Bereiter & Scardamalia (1993), p. 62.

41 Fodor (1983), p. 88.

42 Polanyi (1967).

43 Ibid., pp. 9–10.

44   Often we interchange being aware and conscious, although as *Webster's Dictionary* stresses: "AWARE lays the emphasis on sense perceptions insofar as they are the object of conscious recognition, … COGNIZANT lays the emphasis on an outer recognition more on the level of reason and knowledge than on the sensory level alone" (*Webster's Dictionary Encyclopedic Unabridged Dictionary of the English Language* 1989).

45   Polanyi (1967), p. 18.

46   Ibid., p. 18–19.

47   Borges (1970b), p. 94.

48   Expertise is discussed in a series of articles in Chi et al. (1988).

49   McCrone (1998).

50   Polanyi (1967), p. 20

51   Ibid., p. 36.

52   This is mentioned in Aitchison (1996), p. 12.

53   Ryle (1949).

54   Polanyi (1967), p. 45.

55   As an example of how individuals and community interact one may use the following: "When ants are looking for food, they walk to a certain distance from their nest, and then they go about randomly. When one of them finds food, it goes back to the nest, dispersing pheromones on its way. These pheromones attract other ants, which disperse more pheromones, and so on. In this manner, an organized ant-trail is formed, although no-one planned it in advance. It emerges from the collective behaviour of the individual ants. A significant point is that pheromones evaporate quickly, so that once the food is finished, the trail disappears. Perhaps we should learn from this how to let go of accepted institutions and modes of thinking once they have stopped serving their original purpose" (From an interview with C. Langton from the Santa Fe Institute found at http://www.santafe.edu/~cgl/).

56   A similar idea based on somewhat different arguments is presented by many cognitive scientists. Jackendorff argues that what happens in the brain is mostly unconscious. We only become aware of the result of the activities, or as Jackendorff would have it, computations. See for instance Jackendorff (1987) and Jackendorff (1994).

57   Polanyi (1967), p. xi.

58   Wittgenstein (1980), part II/49.

59   Polanyi (1967), p. 24.

60   Ibid., p. 31.

61   Collins (1990), p. 109.

62   Wittgenstein (1970), p. 351.

63   Feuerbach (1996).

64 Results from a questionnaire used in Course 2 on Value-based leadership and management, Jyske bank A/S, 24. Silkeborg, November 1997. In a way they were saying in chorus, like the mob in *Monty Python's Life of Brian*, "We are all individuals".

65 Collins (1990), p. 109

66 James (1896/1987), p. 206.

67 Polanyi (1962), p. 68.

68 Wittgenstein (1969), p. 15. See also Haller (1981), p. 65.

69 More relevant examples today might include computers and mobile phones.

70 From *Encyclopædia Britannica Online*
    http://www.eb.co.uk:180/bol/topic?eu=108558&scnt=7

71 Hodges (1987), p. 415. The Turing test described in Hodges' book on *Alan Turing*. Turing was building on an idea of Shaw's "if a machine appeared to be doing as well as a human being, then it *was* doing as well as a human being." To this one may object that even if this is so, it still is not a human being (Hodges 1987, p. 266). See also a kind of replay from Searle, in the shape of Searle's Chinese room thought experiment Searle (1980).

72 Brown et al. (1988), p. 14.

73 Bates (1984), p. 189. The is a topic that touches upon developmental psychology, as represented in the classical ideas of Waddington, Piaget and Vygotsky, and modern attempts as found in connectionist perspectives on development. See for instance Waddington (1957), Piaget (1952), Vygotsky (1978) and Elman et al. (1996).

74 Bates (1984), p. 189.

5 Arguments for a social grammar

Kohlhaas, der du dich gesandt zu sein vorgibst, das Schwert der Gerechtig-keit zu handhaben, was unterfängst du dich, Vermessener, im Wahnsinn stockblinder Leidenschaft, du, den Ungerechtigkeit selbst vom Wirbel bis zur Sohle erfüllt? Weil der Landesherr dir, dem du untertan bist, dein Recht verweigert hat, dein Recht in dem Streit um ein nichtiges Gut, erhebst du dich, Heilloser, mit Feuer und Schwert und brichst wie der Wolf der Wüste in die friedliche Gemeinheit, die er beschirmt.

Dr Martin Luther's handbill in *Michael Kohlhaas*

REACTING TO INJUSTICE

The strange and unhappy story of Michael Kohlhaas[1] takes its beginning one day when he is travelling to Saxony with a couple of well-fed young horses.

Crossing the border he is asked to show his travel permit. Michael Kohlhaas has never heard that such a permit is necessary, and does not have money available to pay for one. Instead he leaves behind as security two black horses together with a boy who is told to care well for them. They are all placed in the care of the castle bailiff, Junker Wenzel von Tronka.

When Michael Kohlhaas later arrives in Dresden he finds out that a travel permit was not necessary. He succeeds in selling the rest of his hors-es and returns to collect his two black horses and the boy. He finds the horses in a miserable condition in a stable, while the boy has been chased away for disobedience. He is told by the bailiff that the horses have been used in the fields because there was a need for draught-horses.

Kohlhaas is incensed and refuses to accept the horses as they are. Instead he carries his case to the court, but his complaint is turned down, apparently because the bailiff, Junker Tronka, is related to the officials of the court. Later his wife goes to Berlin to deliver a petition in person. Guards hinder her in delivering the petition and by accident one of them wounds her fatally. She dies a couple of days later.

Kohlhaas swears revenge. He rides to the castle of Junker Wenzel von Tronka, and burns down everything. The Junker has already fled to Wittenberg. Kohlhaas follows him, torches part of the town, and threatens to continue until the Junker is delivered to him. The Junker flees to Leipzig with Kohlhaas at his heels. A growing number of people are following Kohlhaas. What began as a personal vendetta has grown into a small but dangerous insurrection.

At this point Dr Martin Luther enters the story. He publishes a handbill calling upon Kohlhaas to stop his mad attempts at revenge. As a result of Luther's intervention the case is reopened, while Kohlhaas receives some kind of amnesty.

Another incident involving Kohlhaas leads to his renewed arrest and a new trial against him. In this trial he is condemned to death. On the day he is being led to his execution his lawyer presents him with the sentence in the new process relating to his two black horses. The original sentence has been overturned, and Kohlhaas receives the justice that he had sought with the original complaint. His demand for compensation has been paid, all lost property has been given back and Junker Wenzel has been sentenced to two years in jail. Overwhelmed Kohlhaas kneels and declares that "his highest wish on earth has been fulfilled." Now he is ready to accept the sentence for breaking the peace of the land (Landfriedensbruch), and with this he turns to the scaffold, "wo sein Haupt unter dem Beil des Scharfrichters fiel."[2]

The story of Michael Kohlhaas may be seen as a tragic fight for justice by a single individual, against the arrogant capriciousness of the high and mighty.[3]

The story may have many parallels with individuals fighting what looks like hopeless fights against injustice and despotic regimes; from the fictional but vivid pictures of lone rangers and individual avengers of American movies, to the real terrorist or freedom fighters fighting for a new social order. On a smaller scale we may know our own Michael Kohlhaas replicas, as individuals fighting against what they regard as lies and injustices in organisations, often alone and often in a losing battle, making the fight seem pointless and difficult to understand for the more passive bystanders.

JUDGEMENT

How do we judge Michael Kohlhaas? Most people would probably agree
that he was unjustly treated, but after that agreement might disolve. Some
might see the injustice done to him as nothing more than a slight, something like this happens, he might have taken his horses and tried to forget that he was slighted. The death of his wife was a result of an accident.
Others may follow him part of the way, but not perhaps in the torching
of his enemy's castle and the destruction of the town. We may understand
his fight for justice, but not the means he employs.

One of the aspects that probably troubles us today is his almost total
disregard for the consequences of his actions, nothing seems important to
him, neither his horses, the boy taking care of them, his home, his wife,
his own life nor all the others touched by his revenge.

Which of his efforts do we condone and which do we condemn, and
what influences our judgements?

Emotions and feelings.   Hume and Hutcheson both held that reason is
insufficient for felling moral judgements.[4] To Hume reason is the slave of
passion. And passion we certainly seem to find in Michael Kohlhaas. To
Hume morality is essentially practical. It is supposed to influence actions,
going beyond the reasoned understanding.

"Since morals ... have an influence on the actions and affections, it
follows, that they cannot be deriv'd from reason; and that because reason
alone, as we have already prov'd, can never have any such influence.
Morals excite passions, and produce or prevent actions. Reason of itself is
utterly impotent in this particular. The rules of morality, therefore, are
not conclusions of our reason."[5]

Moral judgements are based on feelings. They do not and cannot represent any objective principles. What these feelings are and how they have
evolved is not really answered and this leads to serious problems with the
approach of Hume. The feelings may be strictly personal and not shared
by others, and one may question the morality of separate and different
individual moralities, although of course according to Hume one may not
have any baseline from which to do that, except perhaps – reason.

Hume in a way illustrates the consequence by asserting that when
passion is neither founded upon false suppositions nor chooses means
insufficient for the desired end, it would not be contrary to reason "to

prefer the destruction of the whole world to the scratching of my finger."
Nor would it be contrary to reason "for me to chuse my total ruin, to prevent the least uneasiness of an Indian or person wholly unknown to me."[6]

Seen from such a standpoint Michael Kohlhaas' actions cannot be
condemned. The injustice he felt he had suffered was certainly equal to
the scratching of his finger, and he did not attempt to destroy the whole
world, and neither did he choose means insufficient to achieve the desired
end, because after all, according to his own words he succeeded.

Principles.   In *Grundlegung zur Metaphysik der Sitten* Kant argued against
basing morality on emotions and feelings. He could not warn strongly
enough against smuggling empirical motives and feelings into moral
judgements.[7] Instead he maintained that all moral commands must take
the form of categorical moral imperatives, meaning that moral commands
must be independent of individual wishes and goals, of the consequences,
and individual feelings and wants. In *Grundlegung zur Metaphysik der
Sitten* his view is stated in the second proposition: "An action done from
duty has its moral worth, *not in the purpose* to be attained by it, but in the
maxim according with which it is decided upon; it depends therefore, not
on the realisation of the object of the action, but solely on the *principle* of
volition in accordance with which, irrespective of all objects of the faculty of desire, the action has been performed."[8]

We may not know what compelled Michael Kohlhaas to act in the
way he did; his actions may have been a result of something pathological,
but might also be seen as based upon a sense of duty, duty towards principles of justice, principles regarded as higher and more important than
either him or his family, with all the disastrous consequences we see in the
story.

One may insist that the principle one must follow must be a principle that would be valid for all human beings irrespective of their individual desires and inclinations. It must be a principle of reason, not of passion. Reason enters into the formulation of Kant's famous categorical
imperative: "Act only on that maxim through which you can at the same
time will that it should become a universal law." In another formulation
Kant emphasised the practical imperative: "Act in such a way that you
always treat humanity, whether in your own person or in the person of
any other, never simply as a means, but always at the same time as an
end."[9]

One of the problems with the Kantian reasoning is that it is difficult to see in what way reason may compel us to act. We do not seem to possess any moral sense that somehow drives us. Apparently Kant tried to base our motivation for acting on some kind of respect or awe for the moral law. But would this not mean that feeling would come creeping in through the back door? A feeling of reverence does not seem to be based on reason. This view is supported by Baron's work on Kantian ethics, but to Kant our feelings are feelings we decide to have. "We cannot beg of responsibility for our actions by citing a feeling that overcame us."[10] According to this view we are not a slave of our passions, but we may be misled by them if we grant them permission to do so.

How would we judge Kohlhaas from a Kantian position? We remember that "an action from duty has its moral worth, not in the purpose to be attained by it, but in the maxim according with which it is decided upon." Kohlhaas certainly stuck to a principle, but what about the Kantian maxim? Would it not be possible to interpret Kohlhaas' action as being in accordance with cartoon-like Kantian principles, and with almost total disregard for the consequences of his actions?

Consequences. "The scratching of my finger" problem in Hume would seem to be solved if one should choose to base values upon what was, I believe originally Hutcheson's dictum, "that action is best which procures the greatest happiness for the greatest number." This is the fundamental principle found in the writings of the first utilitarians and especially those expounded by Bentham.

According to Bentham and Mill, what increased happiness or pleasure was right and what decreased it wrong. "The creed which accepts as the foundation of morals, Utility or the Greatest Happiness Principle, holds that actions are right in proportion as they tend to promote happiness, wrong as they tend to produce the reverse of happiness. By happiness is intended pleasure, and the absence of pain; by unhappiness, pain, and the privation of pleasure."[11]

What counted as pleasure was up to each individual to decide, so the pleasure that Hume might achieve by destroying the world instead in order to avoid scratching his finger would count in the calculation of pleasure. I suppose that the application of such a principle to judge the case of Kohlhaas would be extremely difficult. What would count as pleasure and what as pain, and how would they be added up?

Later editions of utilitarianism, like Mill's version, qualified pleasures by dividing them into higher and lower pleasures. To Mill it was better to be Socrates dissatisfied than a satisfied fool. The argument for dividing pleasures into higher and lower is dubious, but at least it made utilitarianism more palatable, or should we say that it made utilitarian principles come closer to what was felt as being right and wrong. It is as if it was realised that some of the individual pleasures and the means to achieve them were problematic, seen from a more elevated position.

The consequentialism of Moore and perhaps Hare stressed certain things independent of pleasure. Certain things were regarded as having intrinsic value, like beauty or friendship and personal relationships in Moore's view, while Hare apparently sought to base judgement on what would be preferred by most people, if they were somehow well informed and able to think clearly.[12]

From this very summary exposition of utilitarian and consequentialist positions it is evident that the modifications of strict utilitarianism are introduced for reasons or on grounds that are difficult to reconcile with a utilitarian viewpoint. They seem to have more in common with the maxims of Kant or the passions or feelings of Hume. Even so utilitarian or consequentialist thinking underlies much of modern welfare concepts, especially those of economics of course.

Using either a strict utilitarian or consequentialist position to judge in the case of Michael Kohlhaas would seem difficult, but one might presume that many would find it abhorrent that people died in order for Kohlhaas to achieve his justice and therefore conclude that the consequences were too nasty. Kohlhaas would therefore be in the wrong.

Righteousness. In *A Theory of Justice* Rawls has a conception of social justice as fairness. Conceptually this includes the distribution of fundamental rights and duties and the division of advantages from cooperation. Justice as fairness "are the principles that free and rational persons concerned to further their own interests would accept in an initial position of equality as defining the fundamental terms of their association."[13] They are to choose these principles behind a veil of ignorance, meaning that they would not know their own position in the society for which they were to choose. "These principles are to regulate all further agreements; they specify the kinds of social cooperation that can be entered into and the forms of government that can be established. This way of regarding the principles of justice I shall call justice as fairness."[14]

There are several problems with Rawls' conception of justice. The initial situation is just a fictional device used to deduce Rawls' conception of justice. In this initial situation the participants seem already to have certain attitudes towards justice and conception of justice. Rawls presumes that they would choose a maximum amount of liberty compatible with equal liberty for others and use a maximin principle, whereby the worse off individuals would be as well off as possible. The persons deciding behind the veil of ignorance thus seem to possess precisely those qualities that will lead to the conception of justice as fairness. Or in other words, the result seems to be contained in the premises. Richardson talks of an epistemological circularity in Rawlsian deliberation.[15]

It would seem difficult to use the resulting justice as fairness principles to judge in the case of Michael Kohlhaas, although he would not appear to be following a principle of maximum liberty for himself compatible with the same for others, or any kind of maximin principle, and so the righteousness of his case is in doubt.

Other principles. There are other theories and philosophies of morals and ethics we might have used to judge the Michael Kohlhaas case. A Nietzschean appeal to the Übermensch, who would transgress the limits of the ordinary slave morality of Christianism might perhaps have been appealing. With the moral of an epic Viking without compassion "Ein hartes Harz legte Wotan mir in die Brust."[16]

Or we might appeal to some kind of intuitionism, emotivism, existentialism, modern naturalism, Jonas' ethics for a technological age, Aristotelean virtues, or even a kind of sociobiology.[17]

PRINCIPLES OF CHOICE

When judging Michael Kohlhaas there is a variety of overlapping ethical principles to choose from. What then makes us choose a certain version? Internal consistency? A feeling that one's version is the right one?

Perhaps our question is wrong, perhaps we do not have to choose, because every principle may be incomplete and represent a biased single-sided view. Perhaps our judgements of ethical dilemmas contain aspects from all these theories.

Is it of any significance that utilitarianism accompanied the rise of industrialism and modern capitalism in the United Kingdom, while the categorical imperative belongs to the continental tradition? Does the Rawlsian version of justice in fact represent a certain modern cultural and political view? In other words does the attempt to create or state a kind of universal principle reflect what they are attempting to reason about? I am not saying that they are specific in the meaning that they only reflect a particular time and culture, or they would be of only slight interest here. What I am suggesting is that they all, not just the Rawlsian version, seem to carry part of the resulting principles in their premises, premises reflecting culture, politics and ideologies.

In Hume's case, to prefer the destruction of the whole world to the scratching of my finger may in the light of our present day beliefs seem to be an outrageous example of the use of feelings, but it represents a common attitude at a time when a colonial England was subduing people in other parts of the world. If we do not find this attitude acceptable today, it is not because we hold that feelings do not matter, but because our feelings seem to be rather different today. The reason for this has nothing to do with the adoption of either of the above-stated principles, but with changes in some basic values that are apparently used to judge the feelings we may have.

Some might interject that the reason we condemn the colonialism of that time might be that we are using a Kantian universalisation criterion and that such a criterion would be sufficient.

Alas, following the Kantian maxim may also lead us to conclusions that we might not be prepared to accept, even if we cannot for the moment state the reasons for this non-acceptance. To act only on a maxim through which you can at the same time will that it should become a universal law may sound forbidding, in the sense that one might think that it would certainly guard against behaviour that we would regard as wrong, unjust or unethical. But this may be a premature conclusion.

Brandt mentions how Kant castigates certain sexual practices, "on the ground that they are contrary to nature and especially because they 'degrade' a person to the level of animals and make him 'unworthy of his humanity. He no longer deserves to be a person.'"[18] Here trouble brews, because today certain of these practices would seem to be accepted, at least not seen as unethical, and even fulfilling the Kantian maxim in that I could will that they should become a universal law. Now where did Kant get his condemnation from, if not from something apart from his own principles, from culture, religious conviction or whatever?

Brandt seems to think that neither Kant nor others holding such views came to hold these views by personal experimentation. "Doubtless they acquired these aversions in the process of culture transmission, from the preaching of puritanical parents."[19]

Another problem inherent in any attempt to use Kantian principles in practice is immediately evident. The principles may lead to insolvable conflicts, and what principle ought to guide us then?

Turning to consequentialism one might think that here at least we would have a universal principle that would be as applicable today as when the first utilitarians formulated it. The short summary given above may already have made us weary. We saw that Mill qualified the pleasures that would count. The trouble starts with question of what should count. What about the pleasures of animals versus for instance the pleasure of watching a bullfight? One might presume that what would today be added up as pleasure and what would be subtracted as pain would be rather different from what would be added and subtracted by Bentham or Mill, or even later consequentialists.

This of course would not invalidate the principle, because we would still be able to add up pleasures and subtract pains, independent of what would be regarded as pleasures and pains.

Let us leave that aside for a moment though and take a look at the pleasures. Mill's solution was to leave judgement of what pleasures are to count as pleasures to competent judges, meaning people with experience of both higher and lower pleasures. "What is there to decide whether a particular pleasure is worth purchasing at the cost of a particular pain, except the feelings and judgment of the experienced?"[20]

Would we accept that kind of judgement today, or are the pleasures that Mill's judges would advocate the pleasures of the establishment, of those in power, the aristocratic pleasures of 18th-century England? Is he not in fact saying that *these* pleasures are the pleasures that ought to count, because they are the pleasures enjoyed by those who know better? In a strange way this echoes Nietzsche's critique of the utilitarians. "Zuletzt wollen sie alle, daß die *englische* Moralität recht bekomme ... sie möchten mit allen Kräften sich beweisen, daß das Streben nach *englischem* Glück, ich meine nach comfort und fashion (und, an höchster Stelle, einem Sitz im Parlament) zugleich auch der rechte Pfad der Tugend sei."[21]

Neither the utilitarians nor the consequentialists seem to be able to explain why some things are to count as pleasures and other things as pains. In fact this seems to depend on phenomena that are outside the realm of the consequentialist thought.

Mill realised of course that independent from what ought to count as pleasure and pain, not everyone would be able to make the calculations. Instead one should be guided by general principles that in general would contribute to an increase in happiness, meaning that some individuals with the necessary abilities and experience, including Mill for instance, would be able to calculate what the effect of these principles would be, and be able to state them as general principles to be used by the less well-endowed individuals. If that could not be done, the idea of utilitarianism would collapse.[22] In fact this points to the problem of what we would call élitist reasoning. The rest of us would just have to accept the principles and rules that would be a result of someone else's reasoning and elaborate pleasure/pain calculations.

As for Rawls' conception of justice as originally formulated the instruments and the approach used to get an uncontaminated sample of pure justice in the laboratory of an imagined original situation, with decisions made behind a veil of ignorance, seem to have been contaminated by his own conceptions of how people would choose, and where did he get his conceptions?[23]

What we get from the short summary and critique of some of the major ethical theories is very ambiguous. Somewhat tentatively we propose to draw three conclusions.

First it would seem that the theories overlap and somehow turn into each other at the fringes. When judging concrete ethical cases we may think that we judge from either of these theories. What happens if we try to use some Kantian principle and this leads either to contradictions or consequences that may be horrendous? Do we shift to a utilitarian view or some kind of intuitionism and reject strict Kantian principles for such situations?

Attempts to use utilitarianism as a basis for concrete judgements would soon lead to the same kind of problems that most utilitarians after Bentham have grabbled with, that we feel that certain things and certain principles carry a value intrinsically, and that no amount of calculation can change that. Examples might be the value of family relations, friendship and compassion.

Secondly it would seem that these theories contain some elements that may seem universal and almost ahistorical. Kant's maxim is found in the golden rule, a rule whose origin seems lost in time. In a way it may be regarded as a fundamental ethical proposition, a proposition based on reciprocity, but the concrete application of this reciprocity concept is culturally and historically determined, and never found in any pure form. In relation to the Kantian maxim, "act only on that maxim through which you can at the same time will that it should become a universal law." Brandt mentions in passing that the universal law of nature, may mean "universally characteristic of human volitions." It does not have to include animals for instance, or nasty people with animal-like behaviour, does it?

The principle of rational deliberation or more precisely, the calculation of pleasures and pains also seems to belong to a universal disposition. But as we have seen this only goes for the principle of weighing pleasures against pains. Nothing is said about what pleasures and pains, over what time period they are to be weighed and calculated, and by whom.

Thirdly it would seem that all the theories that we have discussed contain important elements that are somehow irreducible and outside the theory. Where do Hume's, or for that matter Adam Smith's emotions and sentiments originate? What are pleasures and pains, why are some pleasures qualitatively better than others and why do certain pleasures carry intrinsic value?

In the Kantian theory we saw the problem with judgements like "unworthy of his humanity. He no longer deserves to be a person." In a bizarre way we would need to be very calculative in our arguments, if we wanted to find a way to use Kantian principles against Kant himself. It seems more reasonable to presume that Kant's judgements like everyone else's in this exposition are coloured by a preconceived conception of what is right, just and ethical, that cannot be explained by the theories they are expounding, but must originate somewhere else – nature, intuition, culture, ineffable inclinations, conditioned reflexes or something else.

It is as if these colorations belong not to reason, but to habits we do not question or think about, perhaps we may call them habits of the heart. We are looking for the source of colorations and irreducible values that seems to underlie all of the above theories. One of the places to look may be the theories of the previous chapter.

HABITS OF THE HEART

Suppose for a moment that making a moral judgement is in some way analogous to recognising a face of a person we knew a long time ago. It may seem strange, but please humour me for a moment. It is rather difficult to know the particulars of what makes us recognise a face that we have never seen in exactly this shape before, perhaps because it is 20 years ago that we saw this face last. We are of course presuming that the person in question does not have some very recognisable feature, like a large mole on the tip of his nose. That would give the game away.

Experts on facial recognition may be able to discern the particulars of the face, but to us it may be impossible; we may only be aware of something that we feel is familiar, and then we may exclaim: "By God, it *is* you Peter?"

We are also able to recognise a whole range of facial expressions, although we may not be able to state the particulars of this process. We just do it.[24]

If routine moral judgements are made in the same way, we may not be able to give a lot of reasons for our judgements; we may just be able to state that we feel that this would be the right or the wrong thing to do. When asked why this would be right or wrong, we are unable to appeal either to universality, utility or any other criterion. To us it might be evident almost in the same way that it would be evident that this is the face of Peter.

A simpler example might involve discerning between a genuine smile and a faked smile. I suppose that almost everyone would know immediately what I mean by a genuine and a faked smile. Not that most people know anything about the muscles of face; we just say that a faked smile would be revealed by the eyes. Damasio has the story of the particulars.[25] A smile of real joy requires the combined involuntary contraction of two muscles, the zygotic major and the orbicularis oculi. We can wilfully control the first while the orbicularis oculi is beyond wilful control. Normally we would not be able to explain that, but we recognise the effect. We see the smile of joy.

In other words something like the *from–to* relation discussed in Chapter 4 on tacit knowledge silently enables us to recognise faces, genuine smiles, faked smiles, chairs, sexual harassment, almost pathological justice seeking avengers, and judgements on strange sentences violating our moral sense.

Before we can draw such a conclusion we have to find some convincing arguments. In doing this we have to show the plausibility and importance of a tacit and ineffable foundation of our value judgements. We begin with the tentative list of sources for the habits of the heart outlined in Table 5.1.

Table 5.1 Sources for habits of the heart

The internal cautioner	Locating judgements in ourselves Individual responsibility Somatic markers Compelling reasons
The social and ethical grammar	The social foundations of our judgements The collective unconscious
Großvaters Zopf	The importance of evolution and heritage for our social grammar

THE INTERNAL CAUTIONER

A bright sun is shining through my window for the first time this spring, and suddenly I become aware of an almost irresistible urge to leave the computer and my mind wringing attempts to find a foundation for ethical judgements in some kind of ineffable ethical and social grammar. I want to go for a walk, I want to feel the first spring air after a long winter. Why am I sitting here, what keeps me inside, what kind of discipline? Perhaps the same kind of bounds that I am attempting to write about, combined with a wish to achieve something. Some inside cautioner warns me to stay in my place in spite of the urge I feel, like the cautioner in Baudelaire's poem:[26]

> *Each man who's worth the name must know*
> *A yellow Serpent is at home*
> *Within his heart, as on a throne,*
> *Which, if he says: 'I want!' says: No!'*

Written rules and explicit threats of external sanctions prohibiting or limiting a certain kind of behaviour would never be able to equal the internal tacit cautioner saying "no" to me. Is this perhaps the only place where we can locate our much sought after individual sense of responsibility? We shall see.

Perhaps we may glean some insight on this internal cautioner by employing Damasio's concept of somatic markers. Damasio sets out by raising almost the same sort of objections that we have raised against the reasoned approaches to explanation of judgements. To him this is the "high reason view," which "assumes that when we are doing our decision-making best we are the pride and joy of Plato, Descartes and Kant. Formal logic will, by itself, get us the best available solution for any problem" and in order to achieve this "emotions must be kept *out*."[27]

Instead of committing the mistake of believing that we act as advanced electronic calculators when faced with an ethical dilemma, Damasio almost follows Dennett in believing that our minds rapidly create sketches of multiple scenarios of possible responses and actions.

In the case of an ethical dilemma, a silent patron of our hearts may help us produce and evaluate the multiple fleeting sketches of possible decisions and actions, before we reason consciously about what we do. This production and evaluation seem to happen before any conscious reasoning. It comes preselected to our conscious mind. Preselected perhaps with the aid of somatic markers. A somatic marker may force "attention on the negative outcome to which a given action may lead, and functions as an automated alarm signal which says: Beware of danger ahead if you choose the option which leads to this outcome. The signal may lead you to reject, *immediately*, the negative course of action and thus make you choose among other alternatives."[28]

The important lesson we can draw is that a somatic marker may kick in, before any conscious reasoning about the problem. This marker represents a more sophisticated version of what we may call gut feeling. The unpleasant feeling that shows that we may not be comfortable with a certain decision or action. This also seems to be the reason for the name 'somatic marker'. 'Soma' for body, or bodily reactions and 'marker' because it marks the sketches of the mind. A somatic marker may act more subtly than that, no queasy feeling in the stomach is necessary, the uneasiness may show itself in a bias that we are unaware of. It may reveal itself in no more than the expression: "I feel it would be right."

Fodor concludes that it is to all intents and purposes impossible for a subject to report subphonetic linguistic distinctions, or in relation to seeing, parameters of retinal projection, "even though we have excellent theoretical grounds for supposing that such information must be registered somewhere in the course of linguistic (/visual) processing. And not *just* theoretical grounds: *we can often show that aspects of the subject's behavior are sensitive to the information that he can't report.*"[29]

A similar argument can be found in Richardson's attempt to analyse practical reasoning about final ends. "… some judgements cannot adequately be expressed except when accompanied by the appropriate emotion, this emotional layer is essential to full self-awareness. We can be left groping for words adequate to express our judgements, and forced consequently to rely upon tone of voice to add the difference. 'It was horrible!' for example is said in many ways."[30]

This fits well with the way somatic markers are supposed to be created. "When the choice of option X, which leads to bad outcome Y, is followed by punishment and thus painful body states, the somatic marker system acquires the hidden, dispositional representation of this experience-driven, noninherited, arbitrary connection."[31] We prefer to generalise this process. It does not have to be punishment; many diverse experiences such as displeasure, acceptance and praise may of course lead to the creation of somatic markers, which are activated automatically before and during our reasoning process.

Somatic markers represent special feelings generated by emotions, a conditioned feeling that we have somehow learned, and which guide and restrict our judgements.[32] We may think of them as biasing devices; they do not put us on a kind of autopilot, but subtly guide and restrict us in our judgements as well as in our actions. Somatic markers may be felt when we talk about a certain action giving us a bad taste, or a queasy feeling in the stomach. In ways we cannot individually understand and explain they signify a bias of our feelings, and there is not much we can consciously do about that.

Deacon does not talk about somatic markers, but his arguments in relation to the role of emotion in reasoning made us aware of how somatic markers may play a role in reasoning. "Powerful mental images can elicit a vicarious emotional charge that makes them capable of outcompeting current sensory stimuli and intrinsic drives for control of attention and emotion, resulting in a kind of virtual emotional experience."[33] During our reasoning we may thus be emotionally influenced by the images that are evoked.

We are not quite back with Hume; it is not just any emotion that is allowed to pass through and influence actions. We are talking about conditioned feelings, feelings like embarrassment, shame and remorse. Feelings "acquired by experience, under the control of an internal preference system and under the influence of an external set of circumstances which include not only entities and events with which the organism must interact, but also social conventions and ethical rules."[34]

Perhaps these feelings and markers are also what compel us to act, making us feel that we have to, almost without thinking. The internal cautioner may in some cases urge us to act, in other cases put up a warning sign saying: "No way!" As we have argued before, any reference to Kantian principles or any calculation of pros and cons will not be enough to compel us to act.

This may bring us an accusation of subjectivism. We might all have different forms of bias and our somatic markers may make our pulse throb, or our face blush red in widely different situations. It would seem that we might expose ourselves to the same kind of criticism we have levelled at a Ross, a Hare and a Mill.

We shall attempt to do something that is quite different from their approach though. First of all, we will try not to land in their theoretical mess, brought about by attempts to present a kind of final listing of what values are to be seen as intrinsic valuable or ethical. We shall not end up with a list of virtues or something to that effect. Instead we shall suggest another solution to the problem of making judgements based on values that cannot be presented as a finite list.

Secondly we will try to show that there might be a kind of non-subjective common foundation for the biases and somatic markers that we possess, without being able to state explicitly what these biases are.

THE SOCIAL GRAMMAR

In contrast to Hare we presume that moral judgements are made according to what might be seen as a social and ethical grammar. Here we use both terms, social and ethical, because we want to underline the social part of this grammar, realising of course that certain parts of the grammar may be social, but not necessarily have anything to do with ethics. Table manners, dress codes and so on come to mind as something that may belong to a social grammar, but have little relevance for ethics and morals.

Perhaps our concept of grammar may have more in common with Wittgenstein's "Sprachspiele." In *Philosophischen Untersuchungen* he writes "Grammatik sagt nicht, wie die Sprache gebaut sein muß, um ihre Zwecke zu erfüllen, um so und so auf die Menschen zu wirken. Sie beschreibt nur, aber erklärt in keiner Weise, den Gebrauch der Zeichen."[35]

A small example from Cosmides and Toby[36] may demonstrate how such a grammar might work. We have to consider two sentence samples:

1   If he's the victim of an unlucky tragedy, then we should pitch in to help him out.
2   If he spends his time loafing and living off others, then he doesn't deserve our help.

Contrast this with:

3   If he's the victim of an unlucky tragedy, then he doesn't deserve our help.
4   If he spends his time loafing and living off of others, then we should pitch in to help him out.

I suspect that most readers would find nothing wrong with sentences 1 and 2, while sentences 3 and 4 may seem rather odd or disturbing. Why should anyone want to say something like that? The linguistic grammar is not the problem, and there is no logical inconsistency in the sentences. In that sense sentences 3 and 4 are as good as the first two sentences. What is wrong is that sentences 3 and 4 state something that seems unjust to our moral senses, perhaps leading to us to blurt out: "This wouldn't be fair would it?"

Presumably most people intuitively see these sentences as stating something that would be unjust. It would be seen as evident, not as something that had to or could be explained. What is happening may be analogous to what is happening when we recognise a face. We cannot tell what particulars were involved, we just recognise it. It may be in this sense that the two sentences violate an ineffable grammar of ethical and social reasoning.[37] Our biases and somatic markers may be based on a shared social and ethical grammar, which may reveal itself in the feeling that there is something odd about sentences 3 and 4.

In spite of Hare's objections we therefore argue that it has meaning to talk about an analogy between a linguistic and a social grammar. Social in the sense that Cawell is talking about. "We learn and teach words in certain contexts, and then we are expected, and expect others, to be able to project them into further contexts."[38]

This is the kind of grammar that may lead us to nod approvingly at sentences 1 and 2, and to feel that there is something strange about sentences 3 and 4. It is a grammar that consists partly of overt rules and examples and partly of covert norms and predispositions,[39] making us able to judge and act in relation to specific cases, almost in the same sense that we are able to construct sentences, without looking up explicit rules or making prolonged calculations. "In the study of reasoning, a grammar is a finite set of rules that can generate all appropriate inferences while not simultaneously generating inappropriate ones. If it is a grammar of social reasoning, then these inferences are about the domain of social motivation and behaviour; an 'inappropriate' inference is defined as one that members of a social community would judge as incomprehensible or nonsensical."[40] Or, may we add, unethical.

We assume that a social grammar would be characterised by being:

- layered, and contingent, not derivable from simple principles;
- shared as a collective conscience, internalised by individuals;
- generative and non-determinative.

Layered. We have discussed the layers of ethical reasoning elsewhere.[41] On the basis of this discussion we presume that parts of the social grammar may be found in the explicit rules regulating and limiting the behaviour of people in a community, all the way from the Declaration of Human Rights, parts of national constitutions, via specific laws against corruption or sexual harassment, to family and personnel policies. These rules would seem to represent a surface layer of explicit ethical norms that either have or can be given a written expression.

Making ethical judgements apparently involves much more than following written ethical codes and laws regulating behaviour. It involves as we have seen an internalised ethical grammar, or a set of tacit norms, and a certain level of knowledge. At this intermediate level judgements seem to relate to some vaguely defined norms that we can only talk about in a roundabout way. They are not usually written down, but are expressible in a general way, like fairness or justice. They may also be likened to the tacit rules of a moderately skilful chess player, who according to Black is "guided by memories of his own previous successes and failures and, still more importantly, by the sifted experience of whole generations of masters. The accessible tradition supplies defeasible general maxims, standardised routines for accomplishing particular subtasks, detailed models for initial deployment of pieces ... and much else."[42]

We can think consciously about the norms and values, and they seem to be part of our common sense. Maybe this is the level where we can locate the philosophical discussions of ethics and instances of ethical appeal. Maybe this is the level where we can find expressions like: "It is in the interest of all ... that this kind of behaviour is not condoned." At this level we are still able to give some kind of reason for the judgements we make, although the arguments may be rather philosophical.

The explicit rules of the surface layer would then represent the upper tip of a whole root-like structure of ethical norms, experiences and knowledge. When we discuss the foundations of these norms, we are in a way attempting to follow the reasoning down along the roots, trying to understand the foundation of these rules. On the intermediate level we might find vaguely defined expressions like fairness.

An even deeper level would represent the really unconscious layers of the mind, containing ineffable ethical norms and feelings, inclinations and emotions that belong to the collective unconscious. This is the layer where the somatic markers originate.

Our layer concept may even help us avoid a problem troubling Sidg-wick[43] in a discussion of practical reasoning in the case where two practical principles overlap and in doing so give conflicting advice. This may also happen in our model. Here is part of his reasoning as represented by Richardson. "... the principles of common sense will sometimes give conflicting advice. ... Therefore ... the principles of common sense cannot be accepted as being the first principles of practical reason." He continues in a series of steps to show that even higher order principles that may seem capable of adjudicating conflicts will sometimes overlap thereby leading to new conflict. The chain of rational argumentation leads to the conclusion that there must be "exactly one first principle of practical reason of unlimited domain."[44]

Others have proposed different solutions to the same problem. McIntyre for instance prefers to invoke a kind of narrative unity.[45]

In our conception we see no need for complete hierarchical consistency, only an overall coherence, anchored in decentralised way in the collective unconscious. There is no single overriding principle either Kantian or utilitarian, only a tacit consistency between a multitude of possible practical judgements on the surface and the deeper layers; like a linguistic grammar a social grammar is in no need of a single overriding principle.[46] What we have instead are mutually supporting decentral elements.

According to our model Kant and Mill may respectively have distilled as it were some of the general elements that seem to belong to reasoning on the basis of these layers, but their ethical principles cannot be used the other way round to determine practical ethical judgement. This would be an attempt to make them into first principles, first principles that would tear up a much more subtle decentralised structure, in effect making them sterile and impotent as principles for judging concrete cases.

Shared and silent.   Angell argues that every group of people have to share something in the nature of moral order. "People cannot work together without overt or tacit standards of conduct corresponding to their common values."[47] He argues that even a family would not be held together solely by mutual affection; there has to be some moral integration, consisting of shared views of what it means to be a family and what is proper conduct for family members. Perhaps this may represent what Durkheim has called the collective conscience of a society.[48]

Here we want to emphasise something else, something we might for want of better expression call the collective unconscious. We may even use part of Jung's vocabulary and definition: "the collective unconscious ... represents a psyche that ...cannot be directly perceived or 'represented,' in contrast to the perceptible psychic phenomena, and on account of its 'irrepresentable' nature I have called it 'psychoid.'"[49]

The unconscious part of this consists in "everything of which I know, but of which I am not at the moment thinking; everything of which I was once conscious but have now forgotten; everything perceived by my senses, but not noted by my conscious mind; everything which, involuntarily and without paying attention to it, I feel, think, remember, want, and do; all the future things that are taking shape in me and will sometime come to consciousness: all this is the content of the unconscious."[50]

The unconscious may partly be personal, partly shared and thus collective. We want to emphasise the collective part of the unconscious, the part that is shared across individuals, and owes its existence not to the single individual but like a linguistic grammar is shared collectively. Jung asserts that the contents of the collective unconscious have never been individually acquired, but owe their existence exclusively to heredity.

A community would expect that the grammar they are using would be shared by everyone else in the community, so that when they act according to the grammar, they can count upon the other members of the community. We must have this implicit faith in judgement and actions of our fellow human beings or we would have no community.

"A social organism of any sort whatever, large or small, is what it is because each member proceeds to his own duty with a trust that the other members will simultaneously do theirs."[51] In fact it is the tacit belief that others will do their part that will help create the fact that will be desired by all. Or as James would have said: "There are, then, cases where a fact cannot come at all unless a preliminary faith exists in its coming. *And where faith in a fact can help create the fact ...*"[52]

To use a grammar is to observe and follow a certain social habit, usage or "rule." "Ist, was wir 'einer Regel folgen' nennen, etwas, was nur *ein* Mensch, nur *einmal* im Leben, tun könnte? ... Es kann nicht ein einziges Mal nur ein Mensch einer Regel gefolgt sein. Es kann nicht ein einziges

Mal nur eine Mitteilung gemacht, ein Befehl gegeben, oder verstanden worden sein, etc. – Einer Regel folgen, eine Mitteilung machen, einen Befehl geben, eine Schachpartie spielen sind *Gepflogenheiten* (Gebrauche, Institutionen)."[53]

There are social limits to the values that individuals and groups can hold if the community in question has to survive as a community. This is a problem of coherence. I believe that both McIntyre and Etzioni in spite of all their other differences see the breakdown of what might be seen as the social grammar as a really serious dilemma in modern societies.[54]

Different groups and communities may have different grammars,[55] but only to a certain degree, and like Cosmides and Tooby and Aitchison we assume that there are elements of a universal grammar in all the local grammars. We may guess that there has to be a certain universality in every community of people. This is part of the discussion found in the next chapter.

Examples of widely held grammars or collective consciences might be the protestant ethic described by Weber as characterising a certain period in Western capitalism,[56] while Confucianism might point to some of the basic elements of an Eastern grammar.

Generativity. We do not have to learn a preconceived set of sentences by heart, we form our own sentences. As long they are formed according to more or less tacit demands of the grammar, they may be regarded as instances of well-formed sentences. We can form sentences never heard before, and still they would be recognised as applications of the grammar. In a way it may be like playing according to well-understood general rules of a game. They define the game, but they do not define the individual actions. This shows the general generativity of a linguistic grammar. A generative grammar is thus a set of explicit and tacit rules that can be used to create new sentences, which would be regarded as well-formed and grammatical in a given language. A generative grammar will not allow the generation of sentences that are ungrammatical, meaning that they would be regarded as ill formed in a given language.[57]

Might not the social grammar allow a similar generativity, in the sense that the ineffable norms and feelings of the deeper layers of this grammar will allow many different concrete moral judgements to be generated? As long it is recognised that our judgements and actions conform to the tacitly shared social grammar, there is space for more individual expressions of morality and ethics.

An attempt to describe, say in a set of detailed written rules, all permissible ethical judgements, would limit this possibility and at the same time move responsibility away from the individual. This may indicate that the space and possibility for individual responsibility depend on the generativity of the shared, but ineffable, social grammar.

The ineffability of the grammar means that it cannot be changed at will, subjectively. It is way beyond our reach; we can only listen to it. This may also be important for individual responsibility. We cannot easily avoid the telltale signs of the somatic markers. If we could, then our judgements might become arbitrary. As Jung once said: "The conscious mind allows itself to be trained like a parrot, but the unconscious does not – which is why St. Augustine thanked God for not making him responsible for his dreams. The unconscious is an autonomous psychic entity; any efforts to drill it are only apparently successful, and moreover harmful to consciousness. It is and remains beyond the reach of subjective arbitrary control, a realm where nature and her secrets can be neither improved upon nor perverted, where we can listen but may not meddle."[58]

We see ourselves neither as unreasoning expressions of a hidden and incomprehensible grammar buried deep inside us, nor as Capekian robots[59] just carrying out a programme encoded in explicit rules belonging to the upper layers. We are reasoning individuals, or reflective practitioners in Schön's sense.

In our reasoning process, our reflection upon judgements and courses of action, our construction of what may sometimes seem to be rather elaborate models of the plausible emotional states of other individuals and of possible futures, we rely on what we have described as a social grammar. A grammar that neither determines the outcome of our reasoning, nor "allows" arbitrary or subjective outcomes.

We may use the arguments of Deacon: "Ideologies, religions, and just good explanations or stories thus exert a sort of inferential compulsion on us that is hard to resist because of their mutually reinforcing deductive and inductive links. Our end-directed behaviors are in this way often derived from such 'compulsions' as are implicit in the form that underlies the flow of inferences."[60]

GROßVATERS ZOPF

Writing about our virtues, Nietzsche looks to their origin. He asks "What does it mean to believe in one's virtue?" and whether this "nicht im Grunde dasselbe, was man ehedem sein 'gutes Gewissen' nannte, jener ehrwürdige langschwänzige Begriffs-Zopf, den sich unsre Großväter hinter ihren Kopf, oft genug auch hinter ihren Verstand hängten?"[61]

He believes that we still carry our grandfather's pigtail of virtue on and especially in our heads. One may wonder whether Nietzsche already had a notion about the importance of amygdala for emotions that we cannot explain and now perhaps even virtues.

We are looking for the origin of the social grammar. Perhaps this pigtail of history shows where the social grammar originates, in the history of man's development, in the evolution of man and of community. Parts of our social grammar may consist of remnants of values that evolved in periods during the evolution of communities that we have either no evidence or only very circumstantial evidence of.

The deepest and most durable elements of our social grammar may very well be a result of this evolution, all of it. Some of our fundamental notions of and feelings about morality will have origins hidden so deep in our evolution that we can only transmit them from generation to generation as habits and inclinations we are not even aware of, and if we are, then we cannot give any explanation for them. We may of course guess as to their possible purpose and function, but in fact it might be even more difficult to explain why we should have certain moral dispositions than it would be to explain why we have the morphology that most human beings have today. Why this relation among the different parts of our bodies and not another? Why this number of fingers, this placement of the eyes, the larynx and so on. Such a question might even sound curious, but a similar question with regard to our basic moral dispositions would sound even curiouser.

Might we not be fairly confident in assuming that, although many other configurations might have been possible, the configuration that we have is consistent and important to a degree that we may only begin to comprehend. It is not arbitrary; there is a "reason" but we may never be able to comprehend it. The "reason" has been produced and reproduced during man's evolution, transmitted from generation to generation, leaving an echo in somatic markers, deeply held convictions and in cultural habits. Perhaps we may even anchor Hegel's Geist der Geschichte in this process.[62]

This reason is not transcendental, is not given a priori and it does not represent a decree from God. It is located on the earth, in man. Like God and the transcendental this reason has been produced by man, but we can have no recollection of the process; we may only carry the faint imprint in our feelings and reactions. This does mean that this reason is innate; it may be imprinted in other ways, and if it is hardwired in any sense it might be in the neural network of our brain. This reason acts as the field of an invisible magnet on iron particles, orientating us into patterns or into grooves that we cannot comprehend.

These patterns, grooves or imprints are ineffable and tacit, in the same way that a part of our knowledge is. We only experience the feelings, not the reasons, not the explanations. These imprints may be so much part of what it means to be human that we cannot really think about them or question them; they make themselves felt in the way they influence our thoughts. The elements of the grammar we become aware of may likewise be regarded as "natural" intuitions, natural in the sense that we suppose they are shared by other human beings.

Cosmides and Tooby tell us that the tacit linguistic grammar "structures our thought so powerfully that alternative grammars are difficult to imagine."[63] We may be able to learn an infinite number of grammars, but the one we learn as a child is contained in our native language. It is neither arbitrary nor subjective, although many other forms of grammars may be consistent with our speech and language capabilities.

We assume that we may likewise be able to learn an infinite number of social grammars, but the one we learn is the one characterising our community. In this way social and ethical grammar come to be shared among the members of a community. Like the linguistic grammar it is neither freely chosen nor arbitrary, but the result is that "human thoughts ... run along pre-ordained grooves."

Richardson's view is that "Tacit exemplars resist rational deliberation because it is difficult to become fully aware of them. Their influence in giving life to terms we use and the views we hold is so pervasive that it is very difficult to bring them at all to consciousness, let alone to obtain a critical perspective on them."[64]

"Very difficult" would certainly be an understatement; in our view it would be impossible at least when we talk about the most deeply seated "natural" intuitions. In a way they define natural, and there is not much we can do about that, at least as long we have not met extraterrrestials, with different imprints, in which case we may realise that ours is not the only natural world.

It is in these "natural" imprints we locate the roots of those intuitions that philosophers have grappled with and attempted to anchor in first principles; attempts that we have to regard as rather futile in the light of our theses.

If the imprints are not a result of transcendental a priori categories, or God-given commands, or innate dispositions, they have to stem from somewhere else. The imprints we are talking about seem to exist independent of any specific individual, but where do they originate, and what has kept them alive during the evolution, if they are not located in the genes?

The answer is of course *Großvater's Zopf*, the values instilled and transmitted from grandfathers to fathers, to sons and to their sons; the values instilled by a community of grandfathers – and grandmothers.

This points to the importance of symbolic representations, of rituals, of religious convictions and of ideologies. To Deacon rituals are still an important component of what he calls symbolic education in modern societies "though we are seldom aware of its modern role because of the subtle way it is woven into the fabric of society. The problem for symbol discovery is to shift attention from the concrete to the abstract; from separate indexical links between signs and objects to an organized set of relations between signs."[65]

This would mean that repetition of rituals, the meaning of which might elude us, would by the sheer repetition lead an individual subject to these repetitions to absorb the general aspects of the social grammar, without being able to explain what they are. This represents once again a parallel to the first acquisition of linguistic grammar. In a sense it can be said that we learn the grammar by repetitive use of a language based upon this grammar. We seem able to generalise from this repetition, but we may never have understood explicitly any of the fundamental rules underlying our use of the language. We do not learn the grammar directly by being taught social grammatical rules; we learn it indirectly from people who use it, by imitating, by approval and disapproval, expectations, praise, and so on.[66]

"Repetition can render the individual details of some performance automatic and minimally conscious." Deacon continues: "This aspect of many ritual activities is often explicitly recognized as a means to help participants discover the 'higher meaning' of the otherwise mundane, while at the same time promoting group solidarity ..."[67]

The importance of ritual is also underlined in Bourdieu's writings. His concept of habitus represents a set of dispositions that disposes an individual member of a community to judge, act and react in certain way. "Symbols are the instruments *par excellence* of 'social integration': as instruments of knowledge and communication ..., they make it possible for there to be a *consensus* on the meaning of the social world, a consensus which contributes fundamentally to the reproduction of the social order. 'Logical' integration is the precondition of 'moral' integration."[68]

Social inculcation through participation in a collective practice produces habitus "that are capable of generating practices regulated without express regulation or any institutionalized call to order."[69]

Practices showing up in social habits, habitus, rituals and so on are all part of *Großvater's Zopf*, the imprints left in us of the evolution of man and community.

NOTES

[1] Kleist (1808/1976). Apparently the story uses material from an old chronicle.

[2] Ibid., p. 148.

[3] Thomas Mann used it to criticise the lax attitude that would accept injustice as just one of those things that happens. The Kohlhaas theme also seems to have been used in a fairly recent Western movie directed by John Badham and called the *The Jack Bull*.

[4] Hume's ideas are mainly found in *A Treatise of Human Nature* "being an attempt to introduce the experimental method of reasoning into moral subjects." From 1740. Hutcheson's ideas are found in *Inquiry into the Original of Our Ideas of Beauty and Virtue* from 1725.

[5] Hume (1740/1969), p. 509.

[6] Ibid., passim.

[7] Kant (1785/1962), p. 48.

[8] Paton (1986), p. 65. Paton's work represents an analysis and translation of Kant's *Metaphysik der Sitten*.

9   Kant quoted in Paton (1986, pp. 84–91). The universal imperative is: "Act as if the maxim of your action were to become through your will a universal law of nature." Ibid., p. 84.

10   Baron (1996), p. 197.

11   Mill (1863/1977) p. 6.

12   Hare (1981).

13   Rawls (1971), p. 11.

14   Ibid., p. 11.

15   Richardson (1994). See also the critical discussion of Rawls' position in Petersen (1985).

16   Nietzsche (1886a/1968), p. 154.

17   See the following: Nietzsche (1886a/1968), Ross (1930/1950), Ayer (1936/1964), Sartre (1993 ed.), Sartre (1992), Finnis (1980), Jonas (1984), Aristotle (1956 ed.), Wilson (1978) and Wilson (1998).

18   Brandt (1997), p. 137.

19   Ibid., p. 138.

20   Mill (1863/1977), p. 10.

21   Nietzsche (1886a/1968), p. 120.

22   This idea can be found in modern rule-utilitarianism. It is enough to calculate that a general rule against stealing would be advantageous. Once this is done, one does not have to calculate the consequences of individual acts of stealing; a view that has been criticised by Smart, who is an advocate of act-utilitarianism. See for instance Smart (1990).

23   Later there have been changes in the Rawlsian position, see for instance Rawls (1985), Rawls (1988) and Rawls (1993).

24   See for instance Russell & Fernández-Dols (1997b).

25   Damasio (1994). Damasio draws upon Darwin and Duchenne.

26   Baudelaire (1857/1993), p. 341.

27   Damasio (1994), p. 171.

28i   Ibid., p. 173.

29   Fodor (1983), p. 59.

30   Richardson (1994), p. 186.

31   Damasio (1994), p. 180.

32   It has to be said that Damasio discerns strictly between emotions and feelings, stating that all emotions generate feeling while the opposite is not always the case. Emotions would make your heart beat faster, cause it to make a jolt, make you blush. Emotions are divided into primary and secondary emotions. The primary being dependent on the limbic system of the brain, the amygdala and outside conscious control, while the

secondary emotions are related to the experience of feelings, connecting situations and primary emotions. Here prefrontal and somasensory cortices are apparently involved.

33 Deacon (1997), p. 430.

34 Damasio (1994), p. 179.

35 Wittgenstein (1953). Here quoted from Haller (1981), p. 59. Norman Malcolm in his memoirs tells us that Wittgenstein first got to the idea of "Sprachspiel" by watching a football game.

36 Cosmides & Toby (1994), p. 67.

37 Ibid.

38 Cawell (1976), p. 52.

39 Rules are here understood to mean ethical norms that have an explicit expression in laws, guidelines and so on. While norms, following Richardson, are principles – with propositional content which has at least potential normative significance.

40 Cosmides & Toby (1994), pp. 68–69.

41 Petersen (1998).

42 Black (1990), p. 108.

43 Sidgwick (1907/1962).

44 Quoted in Richardson (1994), pp. 128–29.

45 McIntyre (1981).

46 See also Richardson's attempts to find a decentralised alternative to Sidgwick's first principles. Richardson (1994).

47 Angell (1958), p. 9.

48 Durkheim (1933).

49 Jung (1953/78b), *Collected Works* 8, p. 436.

50 Ibid, p. 185.

51 James quoted in Moser and Nat (1987), p. 211.

52 Ibid. p. 211.

53 Wittgenstein (1953) quoted in Morscher (1981), p. 121.

54 McIntyre (1981) and Etzioni (1994).

55 See for instance the discussion in Richardson (1994).

56 Weber (1930/1989).

57 Discussions on generativity in general can be found in Hofstadter (1987). It is this general generativity we are using, not the special generativity that for instance Chomsky has been advocating. The difference between generativity and non-generativity has been shown in a small example by Bloom (1994):

a

$x \rightarrow yz$

z→a(x)

y→ "Y"

a→ "A"

This system of relations is generative because it can produce strings of symbols like YA, YAYA, YAYAA and so forth.

b

x→y(z)

y→ "Y"

z→ "Z"

This system is non-generative, because it can only produce two strings of symbols, Y and YZ.

58 Jung (1953/78a), *Collected Works* 12, p. 51.

59 Karel Capek's *R. U. R.* or *Rossum's Universal Robots* (1958).

60 Deacon (1997), p. 435. Actually this leads Deacon to conclude that "thinking in symbols is a means whereby formal causes can determine final causes. The abstract nature of this source makes for a top-down causality, even if implemented on a bottom-up biological machine" (Ibid., p. 435).

61 Nietzsche (1886a/1968), p. 110.

62 Hegel asserts that "Die Entwicklung ist auf diese Weise nicht das harm-und kampflose bloße Hervorgehen ... sondern die harte, unwillige Arbeit gegen sich selbst, und ferner ist nicht bloß das Formelle des Entwickelns überhaupt, sondern das Hervorbringen eines Zwecks von bestimmtem Inhalte. Diesen Zweck haben wir von Anfang festgestellt: es ist der Geist ..." G. W. F. Hegel in "Vorlesungen über die Philosophie der Weltgeschichte."

63 Cosmides & Toby (1994), p. 70.

64 Richardson (1994), p. 292.

65 Deacon (1997) p. 402.

66 Wittgenstein has given a description of what it means to be taught and of education in *Philosophische Untersuchungen*, for instance in paragraph 208, which seems to support our conception. Wittgenstein (1953).

67 Deacon (1997), p. 403.

68 Bourdieu (1983/1991), p. 166.

69 Bourdieu (1977), p. 17.

6 Weaving the moral fabric

Wahrlich, die Menschen gaben sich alles ihr Gutes und Böses. Wahrlich, sie nahmen es nicht, sie fanden es nicht, nicht fiel es ihnen als Stimme vom Himmel.

...

Wandel der Werthe, – das ist Wandel der Schaffenden. Immer vernichtet, wer ein Schöpfer sein muss.
Schaffende waren erst Völker und spät erst Einzelne; wahrlich, der Einzelne selber ist noch die jüngste Schöpfung.

Friedrich Nietzsche

PERHAPS WE ONLY SEE IT WHEN WE DON'T

What I am talking about is the moral fabric of society. It may be difficult to see what it is, because it is so much part of our daily lives that we usually do not see it or think about it, unless it is torn, leaving unexpected gaps or holes or perhaps when we run into a fabric of a different hue than ours.

That we only see it when we don't may be characteristic of many of our social habits, conventions and norms. Here is a beastly illustration in an excerpt from an interview made by Swedish television with a former doctor and SS-Untersturmführer, Hans Münch, who once belonged to the Auschwitz camp personnel.[1]

Swedish Television: Did you see the crematories yourself?
Münch: Yes, of course. It wasn't part of my daily routine, but it was impossible to avoid it, even if I hadn't known what it was. Everybody active in the SS in Auschwitz knew of course what the crematories were, and it was impossible not to notice the smoke and the chimneys and feel the smell. In the SS the use of gas was discussed quite openly.

ST: Were doctors present at the gassings?

M: They had to be present. According to strict regulations they had to be present, as in civilized states at every normal individual execution for legal reasons. In the same way there was a military order that at least one doctor had to be present at exterminations by gas in Auschwitz, for two reasons. Firstly, the whole thing had to be under medical supervision. And the gas wasn't thrown in by the regular camp personnel but by the camp doctors' medical orderlies.

ST: What objections did your colleagues have who were for it?

M: "Is it necessary to do this in the middle of the war? There will be time for it later." "One should try to get as big a work force as possible. It would be better if the people were fed better." That was one view. Then there was the opposite view. "It has to be done at once. If we wait any longer there will be objections, and there are those who are against it."

ST: From a purely technical point of view, people were against it? And economically?

M: That was the main problem.

ST: But ideologically?

M: Ideologically...

ST: The majority was for it?

M: The majority of the doctors were against it from a purely technical point of view, and also because of economic reasons.

ST: But ideologically in favour?

M: Ideologically nobody differed.

The striking thing about Hans Münch's statement is that it is nothing special. What he describes was some everyday, humdrum activity that had to be carried out. There is a strange sense of almost normalcy about the whole description. The orderly way to exterminate people, the necessity of legal reasons, the medical supervision, "this is the way it must be done, you see," the economic and technical arguments against the extermination. There is disturbing reasonableness of reasons, as if not having done what one did would have been odd, like not having the right table manners. At the time the activities of Dr Münch were almost normal daily activities. The camp personnel presumably drove on the right side of the road, greeted or rather saluted each other in a courteous way, made promises, kept promises, took deliverance of Zyklon B.

Now perhaps we see it, because we do not see it in Dr Munch's description – the moral fabric that we may have taken for granted. The reasonableness of his arguments may scare us, we may see them as pseudo-scientific, pseudo-legal and pseudo-economic and not the least moral. This must surely represent the views of a man lacking the most basic moral sense mustn't it? He cannot have been like you and me? Or – can he? Is that the really scary part about this story?

Now for something that may seem less scary. Listening to the NATO spokesman Jamie Shea every day during the bombing of Serbia, Montenegro and Kosovo, we were treated to another kind of strange normalcy: numbers, maps, counts of destruction, surgical strikes, estimates of collateral damage and pictures of destructive precision made from aircraft 15 000 feet above sea level, or perhaps even from the noses of the smart bombs. We are punishing the veiled enemy at no danger to ourselves. This is just a technical description of our competence, expressed in a tone of destructive normalcy, almost like the one we saw in Dr Münch's statement.

But wait a minute, this is a just war, a moral war, fought for humanitarian reasons, not for instance for territorial gains or to exterminate a race. This at least is what Prime Minister Blair was declaring very loudly, although one may wonder about constitutional problems, legal grounds, the role of the UN and other slight irrelevancies.

Still these descriptions of precision destruction and the normalcy of it may make us slightly uneasy, even after performing the implicit cost–benefit analysis that shows that they, not *we*, had to do all this in order to save someone else, in this case the Albanians living in Kosovo.

Being suddenly confronted with big tears in the moral fabric, we may become aware of the importance of this fabric, and perhaps start wondering about its nature. How solid and dependable are the values we believe we hold today? Are they robust enough to guard against the sort of tears that Dr Hans Münch represented?

What may have been the process that created the fabric we believe in? What are the basic strands of the weave, its pattern and its texture? How do values get transmitted and inculcated from generation to generation? And perhaps most important, in what way do we contribute to the reweaving of parts of the fabric, when wear and tear is discovered, or when there is a need to weave additions, changing the pattern, texture, colour and feel of the fabric to fit changes in society?

A FABRIC WEAVING ITSELF

In Hofstadter's book *Gödel, Escher, Bach* we find a fascinating story called the Ant Fugue.[2] The story is illustrated with a picture of a colony of ants building a living bridge with their own bodies. Does that mean that the ants practise a kind of cooperation as we understand it, or that they have knowledge of what they are doing?

According to Hofstadter and others the answer is a resounding "no!"[3] It would seem that ants primarily perceive the outside world through the antennae and presumably the behaviour of individual ants is pretty chaotic. But ants happening to discover food apparently become active, and through their antennae stimulate other ants in turn, thereby generating a certain collective rhythm, resulting in what might look to all intents and purposes like a purposeful activity, for instance food-gathering, nursing or bridge-building.

Scientists have built computer models of this kind of ant activity and found that this collective rhythmic activity emerges suddenly above a critical density. They found that this transition had the sudden character of a phase change, as in the sudden appearance of magnetic properties in hot iron when it cools below a certain temperature.[4]

What the ants do is of course not equivalent to a physical phase change in iron. This phase change represents only a sort of analogy for describing something that we are just beginning to understand. Hot iron has not gone through the rigours of natural selection like the ants.

From what we know it would seem that the cooperative behaviour of ants does not really represent cooperation in the sense we usually talk about. As human beings we may at least believe that we have some sense of purpose and that our behaviour stems from "mind-full" activity.

To understand the "mindlessness" of the ant level one may think of an experiment in which a couple of robots, looking remarkably like ants, are milling around on a level playing field surrounded by an immovable barrier. A round cylinder is placed on its side somewhere on this playing field. The robot ants are programmed to move forward, unless they meet an immovable barrier, in which case they wait for a while and then back off to continue their aimless activity in a random direction. Two robots hitting the rolling surface of the cylinder at right angles within the same short time interval and from the same direction will be able to move the cylinder. Often one hits the cylinder, often more than one from different directions, but the cylinder does not budge. Now waiting for some time we may see that by chance two robots happen to hit the cylinder from the same direction at right angles, and it moves. Because it moves, the robots continue to push. Now imagine that an outside observer comes along. To this observer it may look as if the two robot ants are cooperating in rolling the cylinder along.

What we have is a kind of statistical cooperation coupled with a simple programmed response. Perhaps this is the cooperation we find with ants too. And perhaps this is also a characteristic of some of our human efforts, for instance in situations where we have no idea of how to solve a problem that we do not really understand.

In some cases it would seem that spontaneous coordination is possible to achieve even with large numbers of individuals involved. Some of you will have seen football games and maybe even have taken part in one of those giant human waves sweeping around a stadium, made up of spectators alternately rising from their seats and sitting down. How are they synchronised? Like a flight of birds?[5]

Another example is recounted by Schön. It involves musical improvisation. "As the musicians feel the direction of the music that is developing out of their interwoven contributions, they make new sense of it and adjust their performance to the new sense they have made."[6]

Now let us shift to another thought experiment with human players, an experiment involving two men, with no knowledge of rowing boats or rowing. They are placed side by side in a small rowing boat and given an oar each. They are then asked to row across a small lake to a point on the other side of the lake. In the beginning it may look as if they would never get anywhere; their unsynchronised moves make the boat move erratically this way and that. Then by some tacit process the rowers by and by fall into sync and when they have synchronised their movements the boat moves along in the intended direction. Slower or faster, as strength, wind and water permits, or according to the urgency they feel, but at least with less erratic gyrations.[7]

Hume apparently had the idea that the utility of cooperation in such a case could be felt directly, instead of being a result of deliberations and conscious reflection. "Two men who pull the oars of a boat do it by agreement or convention, though they have never given promises to each other."[8] They can feel, for want of a better word, the advantages of cooperation directly. This again leads us back to the idea of the two robot ants happening to push in the same direction at the same time.

No compact was expressed for general discussion and mutual consent. This to Hume would have been far beyond the mental abilities of the individual members of early societies. Instead a tacit cooperation on concrete problems, like oar-pulling, showed itself to be advantageous, and this made it become more frequent, until its frequency gradually produced a habitual, voluntary and therefore precarious acquiescence in the people. In the oar-pulling process the cooperation may become better and better every time one has to row together with others. In other forms of cooperation stable patterns more important to morality may have emerged, in reciprocal exchange of favours, in trade arrangements and so on. Slowly this may have led to changes in expectations with regard to other individuals, and in emerging dependence on each other.

In other words, certain forms of behaviour may have coagulated in conventions, habits or norms, that by and by may have lost their close ties to the problems that brought them about, just leaving impressions in the tacit strands of an invisible moral fabric.

Jumping to a conclusion we may get the idea that the habitual responses produced, what Hume called additional force, ability and security of men acting together in society,[9] and the first embryonic forms of a moral fabric. But it did not necessarily change man's natural inclination, his self-love, "But when men have observ'd, that tho' the rules of justice be sufficient to maintain any society, yet 'tis impossible for them, of themselves, to observe those rules, in large and polish'd societies; they establish government, as a new invention to attain their ends, and preserve the old, or procure new advantages, by a more strict execution of justice."[10]

Larger boats with many rowers would thus need some sort of external direction in order to synchronise the movements of rowers, perhaps the beating of a large drum, like in Hollywood movies showing galley slaves rowing a trireme or something like that. This would represent an example of explicit coordination, based upon a commanding beat and the whip of an overseer.

What we get from these examples is the idea of a slow progression from what might be seen as spontaneous communities to highly structured societies, with explicit regulation of behaviour and institutionalisation of responsibility.[11]

Other very popular attempts to explain the evolution of cooperation and social order are based on game theory and simulations based on this theory. In some of Axelrod's game simulations, cooperation results from the interplay of very simple and single-minded individual players consisting of nothing more than small programs representing different behaviours, running through a number of iterations or repeated games. Axelrod builds a whole theory of cooperation on these simulations, although it would seem that the end results are very sensitive to the initial parameters of the players and the game.[12]

Continuing the tradition of studying cooperation through games, van Huyck, Battalio and others have used simple games with human players to study tacit coordination, and cooperation, apparently with limited success, as some of their experiments resulted in glaring coordination failures.[13]

Much more comprehensive and convincing is Sugden's attempt to account for the emergence of rights, cooperation and welfare, through a game theoretical analysis.[14]

The examples and experiments recounted here may indicate that given certain rather primitive conditions, virtual societies can be created that foster cooperation and a certain group coherence. The experiments even show that this could happen as a result of the actions of individuals acting in their own interest. In this way the experiments support some of the more basic tenets of modern economic theory.

What is happening here? Are these examples of spontaneous self-regulation, or self-production, as described by the ever so popular term autopoiesis?[15] We do not know the answer; we just note that some forms of coordination and cooperation apparently emerge without a conscious conductor as it were. This may be due neither to some property of the individuals making up the group or society, nor something in the environment, but perhaps something that "lies neither in the organism nor in the environment, but at some emergent level between the two."[16]

THE MORAL FABRIC OF COMMUNITIES

Traditional approaches to the problem of social order would focus on the social contract. Here one might refer to the answers presented for instance by Hobbes, Locke and Hume or Rousseau.[17] We shall use a somewhat different approach, starting with an attempt to find some of the basic strands of the moral fabric.

The basic strands. "Social behaviour isn't unique to human societies. Patterned interaction between individuals over extended periods of time is a characteristic of anthropoid primates going back millions of years, ... other social animals besides ourselves [are] well able to perceive each other as acquaintance or stranger, friend or foe, owner or intruder and behave accordingly."[18]

De Waal makes an attempt to find the origins of right and wrong in a study of the behaviour of primates. He attempts to find out whether animals show behaviour "that parallels the benevolence as well as the rules and regulations of human moral conduct."[19] He wants to make an attempt to understand what may motivate such behaviour, whether animals realise in some way how their behaviour affects others.

Now why would animals like primates and humans need something like moral strands? The answer sounds simple. Animals living in groups need each other to find and get at food; they may live in constant conflict with other animals and need the group for defence. To hold the group together internal strife and conflict has to be contained. De Waal talks of conditions for the evolution of morality. Some of these reasons for the evolution of morality may be found in Darwin too, and one may also be reminded of Hobbes' brutish war of all against all.[20]

There is a need for what looks like protoforms of moral behaviour. De Waal talks of the need for two levels of such behaviour: a dyadic level (individual to individual) with reciprocity and potential for making up with one's enemies; and a higher level. On the higher level de Waal places mediated reconciliation after fights, peaceful arbitration of disputes, altruistic behaviour towards the group, exemplified for instance by an individual helping another individual in distress, without any expectation of direct reward. This represents what he calls indirect reciprocity. Finally he talks of contributions to the quality of the social environment, letting it stand for a kind of general community concern.

Using his own and other studies he finds evidence of emerging strands of moral behaviour. He notes how groups of primates may show cooperation in getting food, and in the sharing of food. He also finds a kind of reciprocity between males and females, in food for sex exchanges for instance. Although of course this kind of reciprocity might be seen as sexual harassment in our societies.

He even finds evidence of a kind of moralistic aggression, of punitive actions against cheats for instance, evidently comparing this to moral indignation and the demands for retribution that we find in our societies whenever tacit or explicit behavioural norms are transgressed or broken. Some form of moral aggression seems to be necessary to preserve the arrangements of reciprocity, sharing and so on.

Other studies show reconciliation between former combatants, and also forms of conciliation or peace-making within the group through intermediaries. To de Waal this is a sign that "In so far as the interests of different individuals overlap, community concern is a collective matter."[21]

It might be possible to explain this seemingly moral behaviour of primates by a process without an inkling of a conscious intention. While milling around doing this and that, they are suddenly reinforced in a certain kind of behaviour, because it helps them achieve goals programmed into their genes. We saw how this might work when playing with our imaginary robot ants.

Of course I do not know if this is a plausible explanation; I am just questioning the tendency to read our own intentions and comprehension back into the behaviour of animals. Instead we may have to think back to the idea of emergence as being neither located in the individual nor its environment, but at some emergent level between the two.

Thus it would be problematic to assume that human morality is just an outgrowth of the morality strands we find in the behaviour of primates. After all *we* are doing the analysing and *we* are judging the behaviour of the primates; it is not the other way round.

Deacon seems to agree. He does not think that our moral stance "is directly rooted in the 'simpler' social behaviors of other species. Sophisticated predispositions for cooperative behaviour or for caring for other individuals have evolved in many social species, and need not depend on symbolic reflection to anticipate the social consequences of one's actions."[22]

To Deacon the really important ability of human beings that made possible the evolution of language and a moral stance is the ability to perform symbolic reflection and manipulation. He believes that there is a kind of symbolic jump from the abilities of the primates to the human

ability to form mental representations. Representations with no immediate reference to physical stimuli and events.

It is the ability to put oneself into the shoes of another person, of
holding other views in one's mind, of thinking: what if? Of being able to
use analogies, of being able to make abstractions and of utilising widely
separated experiences to create new representations. It is the ability to
write words, make sense of them and calculate with reasonable certainty
how they might be interpreted by a potential reader. It is the ability to
anticipate, and much much more. Bruner talks of the ability to understand the minds of others, "whether through language, gesture, or other
means."[23]

The ability to perform symbolic reflection is something that requires
a prefrontal cortex development that is unique to human beings. This is
equivalent to saying that apes may make sounds, sounds with a certain
meaning, but they do not have language like ours, and their physical
make-up would also prevent them from getting very far in relation to language development, notwithstanding the experiments showing the ability of primates to learn a kind of sign language. Through language, symbolic reflections may be shared between two or more individuals, making
possible a shared collective experience.[24]

"Ethical considerations are something in addition to the complex set
of socio-emotional responses we have inherited. The symbolic constructions of others' plausible emotional states, and their likely emotional
responses to our future actions, are analogous to a whole new sensory
modality feeding into our ancient social-emotional response systems."[25]
This virtual representation of the emotional state of others and their reactions "makes us the only species where there can be a genuine conflict of
simultaneous emotional states."

This is a human quandary, and absolutely necessary for landing in an
ethical dilemma. This idea receives support from the philosophical work
of Frankfurt, who declares: "Neben wünschen und wählen und bewegt
werden, dies oder das zu tun, können Menschen außerdem wünschen,
bestimmte Wünsche und Motive zu haben (oder nicht zu haben). Sie
können was ihre Vorlieben und Zwecken angeht, gern anders sein wollen,
als sie sind."[26]

We conclude this section by listing what would presumably characterise every human system of morality. This list is based upon what de
Waal believes are the general tendencies and capacities that would char-

acterise every system of (human) morality.[27] The list represents some of the moral strands that make up the basic structure of the moral fabric. This list may include sympathy-related traits, norm-related characteristics, reciprocity and finally some mechanism for getting along in a group. We have rearranged his list a bit and added the abilities that we see as absolutely necessary for taking an ethical stance, for instance symbolic reflection and the ability to get oneself into a quandary of states. Implicitly included are abilities related to self-monitoring, self-reference, and self-reflection.[28]

Sympathy includes:

- some kind of attachment, and succour and emotional contagiousness;
- some showing of consideration for the disabled and injured.

Norm characteristics include:

- some evidence of prescriptive social norms;
- some internalisation of these norms;
- some anticipation of punishment.

Reciprocity includes:

- behaviour that includes consistency in giving and receiving and, according to de Waal, revenge;
- some form of punishment or moral aggression guaranteeing compliance.

Getting along includes:

- reconciliatory behaviour;
- peaceful conflict resolution.

Symbolic reflection includes:

- the ability to put oneself into the place of another;

- the ability to see oneself or others as the cause of harm, help, pleasure and so on, or in other words consciousness of being the agent of something;
- the ability to discern between intended and unintended consequences;
- the possibility of having conflicting emotional states towards other beings at the same time, resulting in a kind of what now dilemma;
- the ability to communicate through a language.

Evolution has apparently provided us with what we call the basic strands of the moral fabric, the strands that all systems of morality have to build upon. Still there is long way to go in order to understand how the patterns found in the moral fabric may have come about.

The faded patterns.   Durkheim had the idea that in order to understand and explain social phenomena at any given moment, whether religion, moral behaviour, social contracts or economic relations, one had to begin by studying the most primitive and simple forms, and then try to understand how they evolved and got more complex through time, finally understanding the social phenomena one is trying to explain.

His view was that in primitive societies morality was essentially religious, in the sense that the important moral duties were anchored in duties towards the Gods of those societies. "Eine Religion ist ein solidarisches System von Überzeugungen und Praktiken, die sich auf heilige, das heißt abgesonderte und verbotene Dinge, Überzeugungen und Praktiken beziehen, die in einer und derselben moralischen Gemeinschaft, die man Kirche nennt, alle vereinen, die ihr angehören."[29]

In *Professional Ethics and Civic Morals*[30] Durkheim sees these practices and convictions as necessary for the coherence of the group, and its continuing evolution. From his study of what might be termed historical social facts he derives, perhaps not unsurprisingly, the function of morality. Almost like Hobbes' study he argues that the interests of the individual are not those of the group of which he is a member. There may exist a real antagonism between the interests of the individual and the interests of the group. What is significant is that the interests of the group as a group may only be perceived dimly by the individual, if at all. In a way the interests of the group are the interests of no one. "It seems, then, that there should be some system which brings them to mind, which obliges him to respect them, and this system can be no other than a moral discipline."[31]

Durkheim points to the way the guild might help a member who has fallen into misfortune, or to the rules governing the activities of the members of a guild. Other kinds of regulation were aimed at preventing deception and cheating. "The butchers were forbidden to inflate the meat, to mix tallow with lard, to sell dog's flesh, and so on."[32] Today the deceptions and tricks disclosed in recent food scandals may be somewhat more sophisticated, but one gets the idea.

Durkheim believes that he can find evidence to show that in primitive organisations and societies the binding collective framework of religion and morality was defined in a very concrete way. This means that duties were very concrete and did not leave much to the deliberation and initiative of the individual.

With the evolution of more primitive societies, the duties became more abstract, losing their tight relation to certain given practices, thereby also becoming more difficult to explain. What had once been very concrete and explicit evolved into abstract tacit norms and practices, which would influence concrete behaviour in a very circumspect way, so circumspect in fact that it would become impossible to unravel.

What might once have governed behaviour in a very strict way, allowing little individual latitude, became less of a strait-jacket on individual behaviour, thereby paving the way for individualism. "And if the collective type or ideal becomes that of humanity in general, it is so abstract and general that there is plenty of room for the development of the individual personality. The area of personal freedom thus tends to grow as society becomes more advanced."[33] This was seen by Durkheim as important for the development of modern individualistic societies and the idea of the sovereign individual.

Such ideas have become part of our collective consciousness, a consciousness upheld in the minds of every one of us, without anyone being aware of it. This may be part of the invisible moral fabric that we are looking for.

"Within every one of us ... there is at all times a host of ideas, tendencies and habits, that act upon us without our knowing exactly how or wherefore. To us they are hardly perceptible and we are unable to make out their differences properly. They lie in the subconscious. They do however affect our conduct and there are even individuals who are moved solely by these motives."[34]

By living and participating in society and by using a common language learned by mimicking others, every individual member of society comes to share in this whole "system of categories, beliefs and value-judgements," that Durkheim called collective consciousness.

What is important though is that we are not just passive reflections of past practices and moral norms; we have the ability to act on our own. With changing material and social circumstances this may slowly change the tacit collective consciousness without anyone being aware.

Durkheim asserted that the increasing division of work and the modern economic system would have to lead to changes in the collective consciousness. As long as this has not happened we live in state of anomie,[35] which we interpret as kind of mismatch between the material conditions of life and the collective consciousness transmitted from the past.

The moral fabric is anchored in a social consciousness. "Morality, in other words, does not originate in the individual considered precisely as such. It originates in society and is a social phenomenon; and it bears upon the individual. In the sense of obligation, for example, it is the voice of society which speaks. It is a society which imposes obligatory rules of conduct, their obligatory character being marked by the attachment of sanctions to the infringement of such rules. For the individual as such the voice of society, speaking through the sense of obligation, comes, as it were, from without."[36] It is a disembodied voice; the voice of conscience or of God.

This voice may manifest itself only in the inclination to think and act in a certain way under certain circumstances. According to this explanation it is easy to understand that we do not usually see the moral fabric. Instead of seeing the moral fabric, we may use the moral fabric to see – or not to see, as the case may be. We may use it to see that in some instances primates may act in a way that we see as indicative of moral behaviour. Or to see that there are large tears in the moral fabric of Dr Hans Münch.

Perhaps we may refer to Nietzsche's ideas in his *Zur Genealogie der Moral*[37] to explain how this morally biased seeing may have come about. He attempts to give us a glimpse of a moral "wie auf Erden Ideal fabriziert."[38] To Nietzsche this is a story of creating a moral fitting one's intentions, a kind of sophisticated cover-up or sham, presenting things differently from what they are.

Weber did not agree with Nietzsche's negative interpretation. He regarded the moral weave as representing a deep need of human beings to be able to interpret and justify their thoughts and actions as being moral, and their "Glück" as being well-deserved and just.[39] In *Die Protestantische Ethik* he tried to explain this interpretation and justification for a whole cultural area and time, and the profound influence that it had on the development of entire societies. Weber's thesis is often seen as expressing the thesis that the Protestant ethic was in some way responsible for the spirit that led to the development of modern capitalism,[40] but he was not really saying that the protestant ethic was *the* cause of capitalism.

The trick, if one may pardon the expression, was to let capitalistic accumulation, or good results of mundane work, be seen as a sign of grace. In the words of MacKinnon "ideal interest are best served by ignoring antimammonistic doctrines and following instead those injunctions calling for earthly accumulation."[41]

More recent attempts to explain social order may be found for instance in the works of Talcott Parsons, Rawls, Elster and others.[42] Talcott Parsons seemed to find that the society he lived in was structured in an almost Panglossian way as "the best of all worlds" with morality being important for upholding this world. Anything that would tend to disturb the equilibrium would have to be regarded as dysfunctional by Parsons, and so we get a moral fabric, containing values and attitudes that were seen as supportive of the existing social and economic structure. This view has been, to my mind, rightly criticised for being too harmonious. Gouldner and Dahrendorf [43] also criticise Parsons for not seeing that the existing order may not be the best of all worlds to all members of society.

We may be overstating our case a little, but it would seem that such a functionalist colouring is present in all the attempts to give an explanation of the moral fabric that we have encountered. This leads to the idea that the attempts to explain the creation, pattern and texture of the moral fabric can be seen as interpretations and justification of our actual behaviour and can be seen as the reflections on and of behaviour that we practise under the tacit influence of an otherwise invisible moral fabric. In this sense the theories are reflections of the existing values, attitudes and practices of the societies they were written for.

They are seen through the moral fabric they are trying to explain, delivering the collective self-confirmation we need for what we are doing. If one made the thought experiment of thinking up an explanation and an explicit moral fabric that would contradict the collective consciousness represented in our daily practices, then I guess that this would be seen as representing something having either nothing to do with the moral fabric or even as something that would be regarded as immoral.

Absolute or relative – the layers of the fabric.   Our discussion until now leaves open a serious question: can the moral fabric be seen as relativistic, something that could take many different forms?

Our interim answer would be that the brightest spots of tuft on the surface of the moral fabric might turn out to be relative in more than one sense. They may be relative in the sense that we could have used other colours, that what we see is just some of many possible colours and they may be relativistic in the sense that they fit into a particular context.

For the more basic and almost invisible strands we turn to the discussion in the preceding section, which established some of the basic conditions for morality, and to the previous chapter. From this discussion we argue that there are some universal and absolute strands in our moral fabric, even when seen through the moral fabric of our time and place.

These basic and very general strands may represent attachment, succour, emotional contagiousness, conciliatory behaviour, the ability to put oneself into the place of another and so on. Like the strong supporting strands holding the surface tufts of a carpet together, they are the most basic strands that are necessary to hold groups of human beings together.

These strands which, according to our view and that of Durkheim, are the most abstract, and least connected to concrete practices, represent the most tacit part of the collective consciousness. This is where we find the part of the moral fabric that to all intents and purposes can be regarded as absolute and universal.

Further up towards the surface of the fabric, in its faded patterns, we may find abstract values that carry notions of universalism, but are interpreted in certain contexts. Perhaps such a notion would be the notion of justice or fairness. Justice is neither fully relative or it would lose its meaning, nor is it absolute and universal. It is at this intermediate level that we locate most of the collective self-confirmation we need for what we are doing; the contract theories, the Protestant ethic, the Panglossian views of Talcott Parsons.

In contrast to this, the coloured tufts on the surface of the fabric seem to be more relative. Here it is possible to weave many different colours on the same substratum of basic moral strands. This is the only place where we believe that one can find a relevant place for what has today been called the many morals, or moral pluralism.[44]

We would have a layering of the fabric, like the layering we found in the discussion of the importance of an ineffable, social grammar. The layering is illustrated in Table 6.1.

Table 6.1 The layers of the moral fabric

Surface Time and culture dependent relativistic moral codes	Group specific morals Explicit ethical codes
Intermediate level Context sensitive general notions of morality	General social norms: the notion of justice or fairness, mechanisms for conflict resolution Collective self-confirmation
Substratum Universal tacit strands of morality	The conditions belonging to every system of morality: sympathy and mutual aid reciprocity getting along symbolic reflection

Interestingly Hayek[45] seems to have held similar notions, albeit in a slightly different context, writing of the need for "deep rules" to be located in a kind of "supraconscious" that we would never be able to make explicit.

The moral fabric has a substratum of universal strands of morality, and an intermediate level which connects the basic level and the multi-coloured surface. Although this analogy would allow for many different versions of morality on the surface, there is a limit to the diversity, and these limits are given by the deeper layers. If the surface tufts lose the connection to the deeper strands of morality we can no longer talk of morality. The weave would become loose and disintegrated; it would certainly no longer be a fabric, just lumps of moral fibres.

Perhaps it is the deep unconscious connection to tacitly held moral values that makes us aware that something is frightfully wrong with the views of Dr Hans Münch. There is no doubt that something resembling a strong moral code could be found in Nazi Germany, like the absurd idea of preserving a certain legality in the midst of it all. The strange moral code must have been imposed on the existing fabric, tearing holes in it, and loosening the surface layers from the basic layers, thereby making possible the kind of insane moral logic found in Dr Münch's statements.

Even if we still cannot see the moral fabric clearly, and ultimately I suppose that this will prove to be impossible, we may at least have a notion of its structure, some of its more basic elements and of its function in society. Now we need to understand how this collective consciousness may be upheld and transmitted from generation to generation.

THE TRANSMISSION AND INCULCATION OF BASIC HUMAN VALUES

How can values and moral norms that cannot be expressed explicitly, like the social consciousness of Durkheim, be adopted and internalised by the individuals of a society? How can they become deeply held convictions? How are they transmitted from generation to generation? And how do they become shared by a group, a society or even a whole culture?

By studying the behaviour of small children in a family setting Dunn has attempted to show the beginnings of social understanding and moral behaviour. Children very early on have an idea of harm to others, as shown by the case of a two-year old child, retold by Dunn:[46]

> Child accidentally knocks baby sibling (Thomas), who cries.
> Mother enters room.
> Child: Poor Thomas.
> Mother: What happened?
> Child: I banged him.
> Mother: Well, you'd better kiss him better.

To Dunn this can be seen as evidence that children have an early idea of agency, of seeing that they are the cause of something else, in this case of causing pain. Perhaps what we see here is that children show some of the abilities that belong to the basic structure of morality. Dunn certainly does, she regards the principle of agency and causing harm as an essential condition for the development of a moral sensibility.

In a series of small observations like these Dunn attempts to demonstrate that children develop an early understanding of some of the basic conditions for morality we touched on in earlier sections. The notion of responsibility, coupled with the agency idea from above and the ability to see who is to blame, enters early into the minds of children.

In relation to the mother, to other siblings and to family members Dunn believes that one can see how children develop an early understanding of the view of other persons together with notions of helping, of justice and fairness, of claims, of feeling perception and inner states, of self and self-interest, and a host of other notions. Four features of this understanding stand out: understanding others' feelings, understanding others' goals, understanding social norms and understanding others' minds.[47] This would seem to be closely related to Deacon's more speculative idea about the conditions for morality, such as the ability to put oneself into the shoes of another, or even indications of the ability to do symbolic reflection. This reflection must necessarily include the ability to compare, to calculate, to assign weight with regard to relevance, seriousness and so on. It would seem that without these abilities it would be impossible to get to a sense of justice, for instance when deciding what a fair share would be.

The driving force is found in the self-concern of the child, not in the self-interest which is opposed to everyone else's, but in the notion of developing a sense of oneself as cause and agent. This includes helping others and vying for the approval of others. "Children's interest in the realm of what is approved and disapproved by others is wide and persistent by their third year."[48]

Children show an early interest in social comparisons, in getting what the adult would term a fair share and an equal or better treatment, in comparisons with other children, for instance when sharing a cake. This self-interest and efficacy in social matters is important for the development of a growing self-awareness. But it is self-interest and social efficacy in a social setting, where the approval of others is important and where the self-interest and efficacy involves pleasure in cooperation and becoming as it were effective family members.

The child is not just told what to do and what not to do, it actively seeks the limits, vague and unstated though they might be, and it makes its own interpretation and mental representation. It is not just passively imprinted with the stamp of an explicit moral fabric. This might turn out to be really important in relation to our ideas about the nature of the moral fabric. It would mean that it is in the interplay between the child and the world surrounding it that a sense of the moral fabric is developed.

By such an interactive process the child may unknowingly come to hold the vague and difficult to define responsibilities, which we have discussed elsewhere. Because they are learned in this way, they cannot easily be shed. Perhaps they have even become part of the neural architecture of the brain. Reber talks of an interplay in which a requisite neuroanatomy and proper social relations are necessary to permit appropriate development.[49] This is just a suggestion though, but a responsibility anchored in this way, and not even understood by its holder, might presumably be really difficult to ignore later, although it would be impossible to explain just what this responsibility consisted in.

Interaction takes place not only with the mother or the rest of the immediate family. It involves other children as well. In *The Moral Judgment of the Child* Piaget[50] differentiates between the role of the parents and that of the peers, that is to say, other children. He sees morality as being almost prescribed by the parents, making it a moral of restraint, of the "good boy, naughty boy" characterisations. In their interaction with other children a morality of cooperation is developed. Here they learn to cooperate and from this interaction they learn to argue, persuade and negotiate, for instance when playing games with each other, learning for instance the basic notion of fairness. One is reminded of Hume's talk about how one may feel cooperation to be advantageous to oneself, without really being able to state this explicitly.

But how do children learn about and adopt values that none of them possess in advance? The answer might be analogous to the way our robots "learned" to push the cylinder, or to the way that two rowers synchronised their movements so that the boat could move smoothly in a certain direction In other words the solution reveals itself in the interaction between children.[51]

Let us say that the children of one generation learned to push the cylinder consistently and by concerted efforts, and further that they forgot about this when growing up, like they might have forgotten the games they played as children. Now how would this behaviour be transmitted to the next generation of children? It would not be through the parents or other adults, as they no longer play this game and may even have forgotten all about it. How then? The answer might be that children learn from other children;[52] from their peers, from mimicking certain behaviour, from socialisation in groups of children.[53]

Perhaps certain behaviours, values and attitudes are kept alive by children, by children being taught by children, cohort by cohort as it were. If a new generation of children grew up only with their parents and other adults they might never be able to learn this behaviour and these values.[54]

What we get from this discussion on the development of strands of a moral fabric in children is some important tentative conclusions, hunches and ideas.

We see that parents do not have to have any clear conception of the moral fabric themselves. Still, through their interaction with their children they seem to contribute to the development of a moral fabric in the children. Apparently they do not have to talk about morality; they just have to express their sense of morality in their actions, and in their behaviour *vis-à-vis* each other and *vis-à-vis* the children.

Arguments and reasons are disclosed by and by, for instance through the questions and arguments of the children in their interaction with the parents and other children. This means that the parents cannot have an explicit set of ethical codes to impress on the child. They release their views of the moral fabric in bits and pieces, not in any comprehensive model of explicit codes. They do it by acting and reacting in day-to-day situations, by tacitly using and expressing in their behaviour the collective and personal values, often in an unconscious way. Chan once summarised the process thus: "They [the children] learn group standards from the tone their parents use to say 'liar' or 'thief' and the excited whispers their playmates receive for gutter-talk about obscene occupations and supposedly shameful natural functions. They are taught impressively when wrong conduct is followed by some group gesture of rejection."[55]

Now we may perhaps have the first inkling of how the most basic strands of an invisible moral fabric with accompanying values, attitudes and behaviour may be transmitted from generation to generation, without ever being stated in explicit rules and algorithms on how to behave.

This supports the former attempts to show that we think with our hands, in the discussion of tacit knowledge, and judge with our guts, in the discussion of a silent social grammar. The silent social grammar may owe its continuing existence to some of the processes we have just described.

We may furthermore entertain the notion that even if we wanted to make these basic strands of the moral fabric explicit and explain why we held them we would not be able to get much further than we have here. We would just, like Hobbes, Hume, Durkheim or Weber help paint a picture showing that the values we hold are the values we value.

Turning now from an attempt to understand the silent mechanism of transmission of basic moral values from generation to generation to an attempt to understand how knowledge, values and attitudes spread within a society or an organisation, we shall see whether this is also a silent process.

MIMICRY AND SITUATED LEARNING

We have already seen how the most basic and tacit strands of the moral fabric may be transmitted to and developed in children, without their parents and peers needing to have much idea of what these moral strands are. It seems to be an interactive process, which is an important role played by an active and "trying" child, with its own hidden agenda.

Perhaps this may indicate where we have to look in order to understand how we all become inculcated with values and norms, while doing everything else but learning about ethics. We believe it may happen through a process similar to the one by means of which children internalise basic moral strands. They do not learn them by heart or rote from textbooks and through a formal education isolated from a concrete context. They learn indirectly in a situated context.

This leads to the idea of situated learning or legitimate peripheral participation.[56] Brown et al. assert that knowing "is inextricably *situated* in the physical and social context of its acquisition and use. It cannot be extracted from these without being irretrievably transformed."[57] In language we often use what are termed indexical words, like: this, here, there, above, since and so on; words that only have meaning in a context. Here is an example showing the shift in meaning depending on the context: "*This* is where I want to be;" "Now *this* book;" "*This* is not what I mean."

Perhaps situatedness is important also for ethical proficiency. Restating the view of Brown et al. in terms of ethics instead of knowledge, we may say that all constituent parts of the moral fabric are inextricably a product of the activity and situations in which they are produced and used. Because new situations, negotiations and activities are recast in a new, more densely textured form, concepts continually evolve with each new occasion of use.[58]

Vygotsky[59] has pointed to the importance of language and culture for development of mind. His work has influenced theories of mental development and of learning, underlining the importance of situatedness. Bruner does the same when he states that culture though formed by men also forms man. According to this view "learning and thinking are always *situated* in a cultural setting and always dependent upon the utilization of cultural resources."[60]

Reber talks of the need for immersion in the subject matter. Inspired by Dewey he finds that "maximal learning takes place when there is some direction provided at the outset about the underlying nature of the environment. However, this explicit element has little or no educational effect without the extended immersion ... We do not learn about the underlying structure of complex environments by explicit instruction; we must experience the patterns of covariation for ourselves."[61]

Interestingly this would indicate that the environment must have some structure or coherence, or there would be nothing to internalise. It is also tantamount to saying that moral integration tends to perpetuate itself.[62] A chaotic or multistructured environment may thus presumably make it impossible to get a coherent sense of the moral fabric. Somewhat flippantly one may say that it would be equivalent to using many different objects to imprint on at the same time in one of Konrad Lorenz's experiments with imprinting.

We assume that the need for immersion and situatedness is at least as pronounced for ethics as for knowledge. If we are right, it might be very problematic to attempt to pull out, analyse and explicate the moral strands from the overall moral fabric, in an attempt to teach ethics. Should we attempt to do this anyway, people who were taught ethics in this way may soon show abilities in common with those suffering from the Williams syndrome. Apparently people suffering from this syndrome can become very good at learning words, even from other languages, but they do not know what they mean. The equivalent with regard to ethics would be a person learning ethical terms by heart and somehow apart from their everyday practice. Perhaps we could call such an approach "dictionary ethics." Having access to a dictionary does not mean that you know the language.[63]

Situated learning is often illustrated with examples involving a master–apprentice relation. Kvale[64] even seems to argue for a rehabilitation of the master–apprentice aspects in learning theory. A simple variant of situated learning might argue that the apprentice learns the craft by observing and imitating the master, not by reading a book about the craft, or following a set of written instructions.

Observing and imitating may not be enough, because to see one has somehow to know, or one might not really be able to mimic the actions. If it was that easy to extract what a master does, then knowledge engineers might have an easier time. To Lave and Wenger apprenticeship involves "*participation* as a way of learning – of both absorbing and being absorbed in – the 'culture of practice' ... From a broadly peripheral perspective, apprentices gradually assemble a general idea of what constitutes the practice of the community."[65]

The interaction of a parent and a child, and a child and its peers, leads to the formation of notions of more and more finely tuned morality in the child. In a similar way the master–apprentice interaction may gradually lead the apprentice to become more and proficient, without ever being able to state his or her newly acquired knowledge explicitly.

The apprentice may even have got more than he or she bargained for; he or she may not only have learned a skill, he or she may also have learned certain values and norms. Seemingly peripheral activities like sweeping the floor, getting materials for the master craftsman or woman, and doing other chores may be important for getting an implicit sense of the importance of certain forms of cooperation for instance. Lave and Wenger see such activities as first approximations to forming a conception of the structure of the community of practices.

Situated learning includes both interaction in relation to the concrete activities that are the explicit goal, but also interaction that transfers cultural knowledge. Lave and Wenger call this talk *within* and *about* a shared practice and conclude: "Inside the shared practice, both forms of talk fulfil specific functions, engaging, focusing, and shifting attention, bringing about coordination etc., on the one hand; and supporting communal forms of memory and reflection, as well as signalling membership, on the other."[66]

What we notice here is the indirectness and interactiveness of the process of learning, the telling without telling, the slow dialogue with more than words. This indirectness may also be very important for the development of individual morality. If one is taught to follow a very precise and strict set of moral rules, demanding only a modicum of knowledge and thought, then by acting according to those rules and prescriptions one may act as if one possessed a morality, but it would be a kind of exterior or imposed morality, a morality that could be changed by any rule-giving authority, not a morality that was anchored in the individual.

The indirect form makes for ambiguity and openness, an ambiguity and openness the apprentice has to cope with. In such a learning environment the learner must not only find the concrete solution to his or her problems through an effort involving analogies and so on, but must also be able to generalise from the examples, thereby constructing what will become general moral strands anchored in his or her own mind. In some way this means that everyone must perform some kind of hermeneutic effort in order to act on concrete problems and in order to evolve the kind of generalisation that manifests itself in certain coherent inclinations and attitudes. Knowledge is most useful to the learner "when it is 'discovered' through the learner's own cognitive efforts, for it is then related to and used in reference to what one has known before."[67]

It has to be added that this interpretation may also be shared among individuals. When I see what an example means, this may also be a result of interaction with others, and furthermore this hermeneutic effort may take place tacitly, somewhat analogous to the "learning" of an artificial neural network. Weights and neural connections may quietly shift in the mind of the learner, with the learner being only dimly aware of the result of these changes. A connectionist system may not have the rule-like properties of a rule-based system, but as Reber mentions such systems "have sets of connections and associative links that make them 'act like' they have rules."[68] The importance here is that we may show rule-like behaviour even though we are not aware of any rules and even though a close examination of our arguments would not reveal any rules.

Perhaps we may show this by using looking at another example. A child learning a language may learn to pluralise certain words and extend this to other words, generalising as it were from a few examples. Sooner or later exceptions crop up. Others will correct the child until the child without thinking consciously about it has somehow learned to attach the right weight to the right neural connections, like in an artificial neural network, and it then 'knows' the rule without being able to explain it. A few exceptions may be learned by heart or by rote, without any further sense of meaning. In this way the child has become able, not only to pluralise a few well-known words, but through generalisation and explicit knowledge of exceptions able to pluralise new words. In the same way a child may generalise and make exceptions in relation to moral norms like: "Never tell a lie."[69] We might say that the norm cannot be expressed in propositional language and cannot be made into an algorithm of the kind "if x then y."

This view seems to fit with Bruner's emphasis on the narrative in transmitting culture from generation to generation. "The importance of narrative for the cohesion of a culture is as great, very likely, as it is in structuring an individual life. Take law as an illustration. Without a sense of the common trouble narratives that the law translates into its common laws writs, it becomes arid."[70] Narratives provide identity, narratives show us what we are.

Narratives are found in myth, history, fiction, in cartoons, in folk stories, in films and in art. Everywhere we find reflections that somehow help confirm us in what we already are, what we believe, what we hope, what we expect, and as a result of that, they may also show us what we want to become, or should be, ought to become. This seems almost Parsons-like in its functionality, in the sense that it would seem to integrate everyone into society. This is too much though. There are different narratives for different cultures, and different narratives within cultures.

Through the transmission processes discussed here we actively become inculcated with strands of the moral fabric. This is the indirect and tacit process that imperceptibly transmits values, norms and behavioural habits from one generation to another.

CHANGING VALUES

Some years ago a funny South African movie showed how behaviour and values may rather suddenly get out of sync and create a potential for change. I believe the movie was called *The Gods Must be Crazy* or something to that effect. In the movie an empty coke bottle is thrown out of an aircraft and found by members of what is presumably a merry band of Kalahari bushmen. In this band of bushmen the idea of individual possessions had hitherto been unknown. The coke bottle is seen as a gift of the Gods. Everyone wants to touch and keep this magic thing. They become selfish, and fights develop between individual members of the band of bushmen.

To our hero, the gift becomes something that destroys the band – and the most basic values – and he realises that it may represent the wrath of the Gods. He gets hold of the bottle and steals away with it, apparently believing that if he can just give it back to the Gods the problems of the band will be solved. He throws the bottle high into the air in order to give it back to the Gods, but has to realise that this does not work, as it keeps coming back. Other attempts turn out to be just as futile. Not giving up he travels far and wide in order to get rid of the bottle.

The story shows how some external event, the coke bottle falling out of the sky, may influence the behaviour of a band of bushmen and lead to changes in behaviour, which clash with some of the most centrally held values of this band.

New scientific and technological developments may thus lead to new modes of behaviour, resulting in conflicts with existing ethical norms. New problems created by such development may be handled in a more or less *ad hoc* way within existing values, but that does not solve the problem. Often the *ad hoc* suggestions for solving the dilemmas vary wildly, from condoning the new modes of behaviour to total rejection, where one attempts to cling to old modes of behaviour, for instance by attempting to throw the proverbial bottle up into the air.[71] This may lead to an increased awareness of something being wrong and contribute to a feeling of a latent need for change. Attempts to solve the conflict may lead to a series of changes or amendments to the more superficial rules and values, accompanied by changes in behaviour. This may not be enough though; the *ad hoc* changes may sooner or later lead to clashes with deeply held values and beliefs.

On a grander scale Marx tried to show change as being caused by the development of productive forces, leading to class struggles and fundamental social changes. He was not alone in emphasising the changes in the material circumstances of production as being the cause of value clashes and deep value conflicts. Durkheim attempted to explain the fits and starts in the growth of individualism and the state as being related to changes in material conditions, although he also emphasised the importance of shifts in values for changes in material conditions. Ogburn[72] talked of a cultural lag with values lagging material changes and creating a potential for conflict and upheaval. Mannheim had almost the same hypothesis, arguing that shifts in values and culture were made necessary by technological changes.[73] Thomas said it like this: "The very disharmony of the social world is largely due to the disproportionate rate of advance in the mechanical world."[74]

It would seem that there is a kind of interplay between material conditions and values. The important aspect in our context though is the possibility of a mismatch, not only between material developments, behavioural changes and values, but also between different values, or between more explicit superficial values and deeply held beliefs, giving rise to conflicts and a potential for change.

Over time far-reaching changes in behaviour and in the more superficial value layers may accumulate and lead to an erosion of some of the traditional norms and values, belonging to the deeper layers. This may be a slow process, with no change apparent on the surface. At some point in time the steady trickling down of changes in more superficial ethical rules and norms may cause fundamental changes in deeply rooted values and inclinations. These changes may accumulate like the tension in regions prone to earthquakes, resulting most of the time in only small tremors on the more superficial level, but at times leading to large-scale changes, the big quakes, which might represent times of social upheaval.

Time and time again we land ourselves in a kind of value quagmire, out of which we somehow have to pull ourselves by our own hair – or is it the bootstraps – repeating one of von Münchhausen's more improbable feats, readjusting our own behaviour and beliefs in ways that neither of us could have foreseen.

In order to understand how these processes may actually lead to changes in our tacitly held, self-evident values, we have to look for an explanation of such changes. Elsewhere I have tried to create a general model that might help us understand the process of change.[75] The model operates with a series of stages coupled with what might be visualised as a kind of spiral repeated again and again through time. These steps are:

1. gap between expectations and experiences, latent conflict;
2. catalysis, voice and open value crisis;
3. instability with rivalling attempts to explain and create solutions;
4. convergence around new solutions;
5. new stability, characterised by stereotyped behaviour.

Gap between expectations and experiences, latent conflict. The model asserts that there might be long periods and subject areas with no big value problems. Existing values are taken for granted, as tacit habits, not to be thought about and discussed too much. Perhaps we may see the period that Bell and others saw as representing the end of ideology as such a quiet period.[76] With almost stereotyped behaviour, with the focus on technological and material advancement, the big issues were seen as settled and what remained were just questions to be solved by application of modern technology and economics.

Then a coke bottle drops out of the blue sky and suddenly we experience clashes between what we tacitly believe in and the results we experience. New possibilities are opened, new conflicts arise and it is as if the existing moral weave is torn up in places. In a study of social organisation and change it is argued that the equilibrium of a social organisation is disturbed "when processes of disorganisation can no longer be checked by any attempts to reinforce existing rules."[77]

More or less suddenly we realise that there is a gap between our deeply held values and for instance the physical and biological possibilities we now face. In a sense a gap opens up between our collective expectations, based on deeply held values, and the behaviour we witness, which does not fit the expectations any more. This may not matter much as long as only a few isolated individuals feel the discrepancy. Only if there is a general feeling that there is something wrong will there be a potential for change.

Newer theories of social revolution, which use the notion of relative deprivation, seem to have some affinity to our model. This goes especially for those theories that see these upheavals in terms of people's psychological motivations for stirring up trouble and what Skocpol has called systems/values consensus theories.[78]

In the view of Gurr and others,[79] discontent arises from what is called relative deprivation. To Gurr relative deprivation is defined "as actors' perception of discrepancy between their value expectations and their value capabilities. Value expectations are the goods and conditions of life to which people believe they are rightfully entitled. Value capabilities are the goods and conditions they think they are capable of getting and keeping."[80] Here it has to be remembered that Gurr talks of values in a slightly different sense than we do. Gurr's values seem very instrumental. They include well-being, access to goods, but also needs, goals, power and values in our sense, all something that a group of people may be relatively deprived of, and this deprivation may cause unrest. Gurr also mentions that this relative deprivation has to be felt by many in order to cause upheavals. Individual deprivation doesn't count for much. The potential for social unrest and social change is coupled to deprivation. We have to be at least relatively deprived of something.

Note that in our examples it might be wrong to talk of relative deprivation. Our concept is more general and coupled to the sudden vague realisation that there is gap between what we expect and what we experience in relation to values and behaviour. This gap may show up first with people who in Gurr's sense are not the most deprived. To put it succinctly, slavery does not seem to have been abolished by those who were deprived, but actually by those who weren't.

Maybe there is not more to it than the widespread uneasiness resulting from many sensing individually that something is wrong, many individuals feeling that there is a gap between the values they hold and the behaviour and possibilities they are experiencing. Individually they may not feel able to do anything about it; it may just be something that leads to frustration and a vague uneasiness. They may not even know what this uneasiness is caused by. Remember for instance the uneasiness one may have felt, reading the transcript of the interview of Dr Hans Münch, our concentration camp doctor. Actually he may have felt an uneasiness himself, but perhaps also felt that it was an uneasiness only he could feel. This uneasiness means that the value clashes may exist only in a latent form.

Catalysis, voice and open value crisis. What is needed to go from a latent to an open crisis is discovering that others have the same feeling. Until then it is a personal affair, like in the case of the dirty coffee cups, where many thought that the existing behaviour was problematic, but felt that it was their own problem.

What is needed is a catalyst in the shape of a voice, which makes the latent and individually felt value clashes explicit, and makes everyone suddenly realise that many others have felt the same way. In other words voicing the problem, whether verbally, or in other ways, seems to be necessary for individually felt latent value clashes to coalesce into a collective expression of a value crisis.

Someone voicing only his or her own individual misgivings will not lead to any sense of value crisis if there is no widespread latency already. It might be expected that such voices will yell into an empty void, if the timing is not right or if they are the only ones to see a problem. Presumably there will be many cases where there is no latency and the voice will be lost in the cacophony of voices heard all the time.

In relation to social upheavals Gurr asserts: "When men have experienced disruption they are susceptible to conversion, to ideologies justifying new and intensified expectations. When their circumstances of life are relatively static and coherent they are unlikely to be attracted by new ideologies even if, in the observer's perspective, they are in a condition of objective deprivation."[81]

Runciman argues that some external influence is necessary to set the chain of events to break a vicious circle. "In the absence of external stimulus, the limited reference groups by which relative deprivation is kept low ... tend to be self-perpetuating."[82]

Voicing may in itself depend on someone having the independence of mind and the courage to dare voice their suspicions. It may mean that individuals or groups put their jobs, their reputation and even their sanity at stake, without being sure of having any effect whatsoever. Perhaps they are the whistle-blowers, not only of faulty O-rings, of old documentation showing a bank's dealings with Nazi Germany, or of corruption in the EU Commission, but of more widespread problems in organisations and societies. Like the first grassroots movements waging battle against the dominating opinions and existing laws for the sake of something bigger, the environment or the future of humanity.

The process of adoption and diffusion of a new sense of crisis in a population of individuals in latent readiness may be compared to the phase change that a glass of supercooled water undergoes, when the glass is stirred or a lump of ice is thrown into the water. One of the aspects that is difficult to understand is the rapidity with which the phase change may happen.

Instability with rivalling attempts to explain and create solutions. Thomas asserts that processes of social disorganisation may be stopped not by reinforcing the existing institutions, but by a "production of new schemes of behaviour and new institutions."[83] He does not really explain how this production takes place although he talks about "creative man."

We believe that many may initiate trial-and-error attempts to solve the crisis. This book may represent such an attempt based upon the awareness explicated in the preceding chapters.

A period with many different trial-and-error attempts will be a confusing period, where awareness is raised, explanations and suggestions abound and solutions are sought in many different directions. Inspired by divergent values systems, by comparisons with others and presumably also by a process like the one through which our robot ants happened to stumble upon what outside observers may see as a solution.

Some may try to solve the problem or the dilemma without actually attempting to find the causes, just attempting to alleviate the problem. Elsewhere I have discussed how in the area of economics Keynesian solutions were practised without the Keynesian theory. In fact this may have been an example, where one chooses a theory to suit what is already being done in practice.[84]

The correction may take many forms, but it may be initiated by a single or a few individuals feeling the problem acutely and having stronger values than most. The problem may loom larger, because they are experiencing a bigger gap, forcing them to act. The hero of the coke bottle movie took it upon himself to get rid of the problem. Many attempts may turn out to be erroneous, like throwing the bottle into the air.

One may well ask whether change could be a result of a majority decision, based on careful consideration and a free discussion, or whether change is a result of actions carried out by determined individuals or very motivated, small, coherent groups. Some views favour the careful consideration and free discussion approach, like the discourse ethics and the notions of ethics as defined by consensus, but they run counter to the layer model that we have established. And in our view the discourse models are in a way self-defeating because in order to carry out a discourse we already have to share fundamental notions, knowledge and cultural skills. This means that a discourse on a certain concept demands at least a "prior, partial agreement upon one use of the concept."[85]

Convergence around new solutions. How is "the right solution" then chosen? And what is a right solution? Does it happen according to some Spencerian "survival of the fittest principle," according to which the behaviour and norms we adopt will be the ones that fit the problem best? Or does the selection of changed behaviour and norms involve a rational choice?

Again the layers model may be invoked, the suggestion being that in order to become accepted new rules and norms must fulfil a few conditions related to these layers of our minds.

First and foremost the suggested solutions have to be seen as an answer to a latent conflict.

Secondly the new solutions must in some way connect to the corpus of deeper norms and values that prevail in our minds, in ways that we cannot fully explain. This is presumably a condition that will only be fulfilled after several trial-and-error attempts, because we cannot see all the connections between the new and the old before we attempt to practise the solutions, and then they may have to be revised again and again.

Finally, some of the responses may seem to solve the problem, that is it satisfies other expectations, and the solutions converge around these responses. Perhaps we may compare this convergence process with the circular woozle hunt of Winnie the Pooh. The first time round Winnie follows a pair of footsteps, the next time the number of footsteps has doubled and next time there are even more. Perhaps we confirm ourselves in our beliefs by running the same circle again and again, seeing from the number of footsteps that more and more people are doing the same, thereby confirming us in the values we believe in.

Or we may liken the process of adopting to and converging on new values and changed behaviour to what is termed gradient search.[86] Let us assume that we are left to our own devices in an unknown landscape in the middle of the night. We have to find the highest point in this landscape. By the simple expedient of feeling for the gradient and moving in an upwards direction (perpendicular to the height contours) we may end up on a hill of sorts, not necessarily the highest point though, if there are many hills. Now let us assume that the deep values and inclinations help us to understand the difference between up and down in the moral land-scape, then the comparable gradient method may help us find high moral ground, where we will meet others, who from different starting points have reached the same high ground. No one will of course end up in a trough, if they have this basic sense of the moral gradient. Large scale trial-and-error experiments may be likened to large random steps, en-abling some to choose different starting points, thereby some may reach even higher moral ground. We cannot be sure that this is the highest point, but then we never can, not through reflection and not through experience.

The whole process may be ergodic. No one would be able to design the new values in advance, using existing knowledge. The solution emerges as a result of the process.

Changes are not brought about by design or as a result of long delib-erations. Several rivalling alternative solutions may be spreading at the same time with their own accompanying bandwagon effects. Through the bandwagon effects the bigger and faster alternatives get even bigger and even faster, and the smaller and slower alternative processes get smaller and slower.

Some of the reasons for the bandwagon effects are seen by Hargreaves-Heap et al. in the following: "First individuals may desire the approval of the group to which they belong. ... Second, individuals may value an action when others are expected to do it simply because the action has become a coordinating device ..."[87] A supporting argument may be found in Machiavelli: "Men almost always walk in the path beat-en by others and carry up their affairs by imitating."[88] In this way new values are adopted, not as a result of individual deep reflections and long discussions, but perhaps because they seem to satisfy almost everyone.

Many people may not even note that there was a value clash, and that the new behaviour is seen as a solution. They just take up the practices adopted by the people they know, in the same way that they adopt new expressions or new ways of dressing up, without thinking about it. For most of us many of the new practices may seem like fads.

This may explain how new solutions, consisting of changed behav-iour, and new norms select themselves. The process does not demand that there is a lot of pondering and discussion, it does not demand a long process of deliberation and some rational consideration involving every-body. It does not demand a pronounced discourse about ineffable things.

New stability, characterised by stereotyped behaviour. After a while aware-ness of the changes may wane. The changed values and changed behav-iour may have become generally accepted and adopted. They may become codified in the form of a law or more commonly perhaps, just a new habit, a habit whose origin is soon to be forgotten, but also a habit that may influence us and through the learning process also the next genera-tion, on a far deeper level than we shall ever be able to understand or explain. That means the circle is closed and we are again responding to value problems in a fairly stereotyped fashion, without ever thinking about decisions as representing value problems.

As an example think perhaps of the interest in the environment. When the importance of the environment was first expressed by grassroot groups and popular movements, the values were not taken for granted. Now we do not usually question them. When this happened, not only our more explicit values changed, but deeper values changed impercepti-bly too, and after a while the new values have become part and parcel of those tacit values that are transmitted from generation to generation with-out explicit arguments or reasons. We are certainly not there yet with environmental values, but what I am asserting here is that the whole process described in the preceding paragraphs may be the process through which we have come to hold the deep tacit values that we hold, values we can no longer hope to explain, but which may have had their reason in the history of human development. Now they can only be experienced in the stereotypes of behaviour we all take for granted, until the next time a gap opens, that is.

REFLECTIONS OF A COLLECTIVE CONSCIENCE ...

Even if one accepts the attempt to explain the way we reweave and add to the moral fabric, one might still ask whether the new values and the behaviour we adopt may not actually lead us down an incline, into a spi-ral of increasingly poor behaviour, while still seemingly keeping the values consistent. What is to assure us that the values we adopt are better in any way than the old? There seems to be an abundance of historical examples showing that changes are not always for the best. Just recall Dr Hans Münch's arguments. Perhaps we are living with a precarious balance between up and downwards spirals?

The somewhat evasive answer may be that there is no one else but us to judge whether the new values are better or worse than some alternative values. In that sense all values are human made, like Nietzsche asserted: "Wahrlich, die Menschen gaben sich alles ihr Gutes und Böses. Wahrlich, sie nahmen es nicht, sie fanden es nicht, nicht fiel es ihnen als Stimme vom Himmel."[89]

Taken at face value this view may lead us into a kind of relativism in which strange things might be valued or robbed of all value. Would that not be an argument for a kind of Nazi ideology, robbing certain people of all their human value, degrading them to things, like the view found in the interview with Dr Hans Münch?

Might those who propagate the many morals version not be right after all, when they assert that we choose the values that suit us? As long as they are consistent to us, who is to say that they are wrong?

From the discussion in this chapter it ought to be evident that I believe such an argument would be wrong. Here some of the most important reasons are restated.

First of all when we looked for the emergence of the moral fabric, we discovered what might be termed universal conditions for morality, universal conditions that may be presumed to be important for the survival of not least the human species.

Secondly we must remember the discussion showing that our most basic values may only be seen when we don't see them, meaning that they are out of reach of everyone. They are to be found in what we earlier called Großvater's Zopf, the collective experience and conscience generated through all human and maybe even prehuman history, and preserved as inclinations and deep values that are transmitted through generations. We will have difficulty in substituting these inclinations and values with some arbitrary ones freshly made.

In fact the moral landscape and our inclinations may constrain our solutions to the high points found through a kind of moral gradient search as sketched in the section above.

Thirdly these basic values act as an anchor on attempts to move values beyond certain limits. Indeed they are the basic values that new values and behaviours have to fit into, more or less consistently. They are the basis for the uneasiness, the bad conscience, the somatic reactions and so on and it would be difficult to outrun these collectively.

And so to conclude there may perhaps be a very a solid, but invisible basis, enabling us to judge that Dr Hans Münch and many others with him, even today, have lost that anchor.

NOTES

1   Swedish Television interview made in 1981 with Hans Münch, a former doctor and SS-Untersturmführer in the Auschwitz camp. The excerpts are taken from Internet pages found at:
http://www.nizkor.org/hweb/people/m/mu…hans/swedish-television-interview.html.
Another example can be found in the transcripts of the Nuremberg trials, for instance the statements by the former camp commander at Auschwitz, Rudolf Franz Ferdinand Höss, or in some of the German laws of that period, for instance the law against mixed marriages (Aryans and Jews): Gesetz zum Schutze des deutschen Blutes und der deutschen Ehre. Gesetz vom 15 September 1935 (Reichsgesetzblatt I S. 1146).

2   Hofstadter (1987).

3   Goodwin (1998).

4   See Goodwin (1998). Another example of phase change can be seen when heating an iron wire suspended between two poles with an electric current. At 1000 K the wire suddenly sags, on cooling down again the wire will suddenly tighten.

5   According to a description found on the Internet a group of several thousand people at a conference in Las Vegas played a game of computer Pong, by waving small wands and watching a big screen showing the result of their combined efforts. "The audience roars in delight. Without a moment's hesitation, 5000 people are playing a reasonably good game of Pong. Each move of the paddle is the average of several thousand players' intentions. The sensation is unnerving. The paddle usually does what you intend, but not always. When it doesn't you find yourself spending as much time trying to anticipate the paddle as the incoming ball. One is aware of a another intelligence online: it's a hollering mob." The game was apparently made by one Loren Carpenter in the early 1990s, but I haven't been able to find the original Internet address. According to the description of the event he even made the audience land a virtual airplane on the screen in the same way, with hundreds of hands synchronising the movement of the rudder.

6   Schön (1983), p. 55.

7   The example is based upon an example found in Hume (1740/1969).

8   Hume quoted in Copleston (1994b), p. 344.

9   Hume said it like this: "By the conjunction of forces our power is augmented: By the partition of employments, our ability encreases: And by mutual succour we are less expos'd to fortune and accidents. 'Tis by this additional *force*, *ability* and *security*, that society becomes advantageous" Hume (1740/1969), p. 537.

10   Hume (1740/1969), pp. 594–595.

11   See also the discussion in Turner (1969/1982).

12   Axelrod (1984), Axelrod (1986). See also Rapoport (1970).

13   Huyck et al. (1990).

14   Sugden (1986).

15   Examples are: Varela et al. (1991), Luhmann (1985), Maturana & Varela (1980) and Mingers (1995).

16   Bates (1984), p. 189.

17   Hobbes (1651/1982), p. 225. One may wonder about this common source of inspiration from insect societies found in Mandeville, Hobbes and Hofstadter. See also Locke (1690/1976), Hume (1740/1969) and Rousseau (1755–58/1994).

18   Runciman (1998), p. 5.

19   Waal (1996), p. 3.

20   Hobbes (1651/1982).

21   Waal (1996), p. 205.

22   Deacon (1997), p. 431.

23   Bruner (1996), p. 20.

24   Here it may be interesting to note that Harris does not see language as necessary for the transmission of culture: "Language is not necessary for the successful rearing of children. The children of deaf couples sometimes do not learn sign language and thus cannot communicate with their parents except in the most rudimentary way, but they turn out just fine." (Harris 1998, pp. 118–19). What she forgets is that a few deaf individuals in a society of hearing people do not mean that language is un-important, or that centres of the brain where language resides are unimportant, and so her objection is not really serious.

25   Deacon (1997), p. 431.

26   Frankfurt (1971), p. 288.

27   Waal (1996), p. 211.

28   See for instance Reber (1989).

29   From *Die Elementaren Formen des Religiösen Lebens* (Durkheim 1981). Here quoted from Joas (1997), p. 90.

30   Durkheim (1957).

31   Ibid., p. 14.

32   A quote without reference found in Durkheim (1957), p. 23.

33 Copleston (1994a), p. 124.

34 Durkheim (1957), p. 80.

35 See for instance Durkheim (1933) and Durkheim (1973).

36 Copleston (1994a), p. 123.

37 Nietzsche (1969), Vol. 2.

38 Ibid., p. 791.

39 See the discussion in Joas (1997). See also Weber (1920).

40 Weber (1905/1969–72).

41 MacKinnon (1993), p. 212.

42 See for instance Durkheim (1957), Elster (1986), Elster (1989), Parsons (1951), Parsons (1960) and Rawls (1971). Joas gives a comprehensive overview of thoughts and theories on the emergence of values in his *Entstehung der Werte*, among these the thoughts of Nietzsche, William James, Durkheim, Simmel and Dewey (Joas 1997).

43 See for instance the critique in Dahrendorf (1959) and Gouldner (1971).

44 For discussion of moral pluralism see for instance Moon (1994) and Stone (1988).

45 Hayek (1962).

46 Dunn (1988), pp. 27–28.

47 Dunn is apparently somewhat in doubt about the last feature. She notes that children in their third year begin to talk about the mental states in themselves and others (Dunn 1988).

48 Ibid., p. 178.

49 Reber (1993), p. 139 ff.

50 Piaget (1965).

51 See also Bates (1984) and Bates (1992).

52 This is an assertion found explicitly in Harris (1998).

53 See also Miller & Dollard (1969).

54 Harris shows in a persuasive way how the child may be the father to the man, by using the example of a famous English public school. The children are often not very close to their parents, instead they are made into a new generation of English upper class through the public schools. Harris (1998), pp. 202–205.

55 Cahn (1955), p. 23.

56 Lave & Wenger (1991).

57 Brown et al. (1988), p. 1.

58 Ibid. p. 4.

59 Vygotsky (1978).

60 Bruner (1996), p. 4.

61 Reber (1993), p. 159.

62 Angell (1958).

63 As a matter of fact dictionaries of ethics exist, see for instance: *Blackwell Encyclopedic Dictionary of Business Ethics* (Werhane & Freeman 1998), *Lexikon der Wirtschaftsethik* (Enderle et al. 1993) and *A Dictionary of Ethics and Moral Philosophy* (Canto-Sperber 1996).

64 Kvale (1993).

65 Lave & Wenger (1991), p. 95.

66 Ibid., p. 109.

67 Bruner (1996), p. xii.

68 Reber (1993), p. 119.

69 The example may be found in Piaget (1965).

70 Bruner (1996), p. 40.

71 Just think of the parallel explanation found in Kuhn's theories of paradigm shifts or Lakatos' to my mind more sophisticated attempts to explain why central theorems of a theory are very resistant to change. See for instance Kuhn (1996) and Lakatos & Musgrave (1975).

72 Ogburn (1964).

73 Mannheim (1940/1950).

74 Thomas (1966), p. 181.

75 See Petersen (1985) and Petersen (1998).

76 See for instance Bell (1962), Tingsten (1966) and Waxman (1969). Later Bell realises that the idyl is breaking up. For instance in Bell (1979).

77 Thomas (1966) p. 5.

78 Skocpol (1979), p. 9.

79 Gurr (1970), p. 13. See also Runciman (1966) and Tilly (1978).

80 Gurr (1970), p 24.

81 Ibid., p. 105.

82 Runciman (1966), p. 23.

83 Thomas (1966), p. 5.

84 Petersen (1985), vol. 1.

85 Platts (1991), p. 157.

86 For an explanation of gradient search see for instance Petersen (1975).

87 Hargreaves-Heap et al. (1992), p. 292.

88 Machiavelli (1513/1975), p. 70.

89 Nietzsche (1886a/1983).

PART THREE

EXPRESSIVE ACTIONS

7 Containing the logic

When a man commits himself to anything, fully realising that he is not only choosing what he will be, but is thereby at the same time a legislator deciding for the whole of mankind – in such a moment a man cannot escape from the sense of complete and profound responsibility.

...

Certainly, many people think that in what they are doing they commit no one but themselves to anything: and if you ask them, "What would happen if everyone did so?" they shrug their shoulders and reply, "Everyone does not do so."

Jean-Paul Sartre

ONE MUST KNOW IT!

"Answer me this! Please, one more moment! A platoon of soldiers are walking down a road toward the enemy. Every one of them is convinced he is on the right road, the safe road. But two miles ahead stands one lonely man, the outpost. He sees that this road is dangerous, that his comrades are walking into a trap ... Isn't it clear that this man must have the right to warn the majority, to argue with majority, to fight with the majority if he believes he holds the truth? Before many can know something, *one* must know it!"[1]

The words are Dr Stockman's, spoken when defending himself at a tumultuous town meeting. He is the lonely soldier, and he is not pemitted to warn people about the Kirsten Spring, which has become a source of wealth to the town, not the least thanks to his own earlier efforts in discovering and publishing the spring's positive qualities.

In the play Dr Stockman discovers that the water of the Kirsten Spring is polluted by a tannery above the spring. This explains cases of skin disease found among the guests visiting the spring. He wants to have the intake of water moved in order to get rid of the pollution, and believes in the beginning that he is doing everyone in the town a favour, by attempting to make public that there is problem with the water of the spring.

It does not take long before the picture looks different. The mayor, his brother, represents the interest of the health institute running the spring and the town. He argues from a logic that is almost irrefutable. If Dr Stockman had his way, the spring would have to be closed for a long time, meaning that there would be no income from guests visiting the spring. The health institute would not have the money to pay for the changes that Dr Stockman proposes, as they are bound to cost several hundred thousand kroner. It will therefore be necessary to raise taxes to pay for the changes, and this will incense the townspeople.

Thus, the mayor soon succeeds in preventing the publication of the doctor's warning in the liberal local newspaper, and as he takes further action to discredit his brother, even former friends of Dr Stockman are converted. The publisher of the liberal newspaper declares that Dr Stockman is an enemy of the people.

The doctor, possessed by what one might call a ruthless ethic, will not budge, and does not listen to the anxieties of his wife, but declares: "You are fighting for the truth, and that's why you're alone. And that makes you strong. We're the strongest people in the world … and the strong must learn to be lonely!"[2]

And the curtain falls.

In a way the Dr Stockmans of this world may remind one of the very first people arguing the dangers of environmental pollution, the founders of Greenpeace or whatever movement we care to think of. In the play they do not seem to succeed, but outside the theatre, we have already seen that the truthtellers, or the futuretellers may represent the first stage of a cascading process, leading to changes not only in the behaviour of the majority of people but also in the attitude of the majority. But a beginning has to be made: "*one* must know it!"

Thus even given the tragic figure of Dr Stockman, *the ones* who know and who have a majority of established opinion against them, must be the ones to start the process of change and must become the catalysts of change and renewal. Without them it is difficult to see how concerns are to be voiced and represented. Without them it is difficult to see how the first attempts to do things differently are made. We have to remember that their "truth" is not always evident or pleasant. Let us see what kind of logic they are up against.

THE RUNAWAY LOGIC AND ITS CRITICS

With the aim of furthering trade, economic growth and general prosperity,[3] members of the Organization for Economic Co-operation and Development (OECD), the World Trade Organization (WTO) and the European Union (EU) actively promote a market-based economy. Many of the traditional harnesses on an unbridled market economy have been removed, for instance controls on capital movements, trade across the border or regulation of sectors like transport, telecommunication, energy, utilities and so on.[4] The removal of traditional regulation leads to a strengthening of the logic that belongs to the basic driving forces in Western societies.

It is a logic that necessitates lean and mean production, the substitution of labour with capital, relocation of production to places with low labour costs, also known as social dumping, or to places with less stringent environmental demands and/or less costly safety regulations.

In the case of the lean and mean production of pigs, farmers with many thousands of pigs, raised under the dictate of an extreme production efficiency that leaves no room for natural pig behaviour, defend their production conditions by pointing to the logic of competition: "I have to become more efficient or I will be the one to leave the market," and so say all of them while attempting to squeeze in a little extra efficiency, the clinching argument of course being that the consumers are not willing to pay for a production that would be a little more "piggish" for the pigs.

It must be emphasised that both the pig farmer and the seller of the products made by children may have their own doubts concerning the activities they are involved in. Personally they might wish that things could be different. It is strictly the logic of the market that demands that they act as they do. The logic of pig production and of footballs sewn by children seems irresistible. Every single producer is contributing to this logic, even though he or she may not like it. Even worse, they may feel that they have no alternative but to carry the logic even further, by looking for possibilities that may raise their efficiency compared to other producers or sellers.

Baumol and Blackman[5] have shown that it is impossible to introduce views, moral and ethical considerations into this logic. A perfect market may lead to allocative efficiency, but it is difficult to see how it could lead to virtuous behaviour. According to this view a single manager of a company can do nothing, whatever his own attitude and values. If a company tries to raise the standards on its own, it will soon find itself at a severe competitive disadvantage. According to Baumol and Blackman "[the company's] good behavior will terminate rapidly, either because it is abandoned by management as a matter of self-preservation, or, if management holds out because of its moral convictions, because the ethical firm is driven out of the market altogether, succumbing to the competitive prowess of its less fastidious rivals."[6]

The voluntary pursuit of socially acceptable goals in general is doomed to fail: "To put the matter bluntly, the market automatically interprets any expenditure by the firm that is undertaken only as a matter of good works as an act of unmitigated wastefulness."[7] In a competitive market building upon a Smithian self-interest there is no room for this kind of expenditure. Whatever the attitude of the owners, managers and employees, they would be forced to behave like all of their competitors.

We may draw the provisional conclusion that the market by itself cannot solve the problems related to externalities, exploitation of market power and violation of non-economic norms. It also seems evident that there are narrow limits to what a single company operating in this market can do in relation to issues like potential dangers of products and their use, resource utilisation and protection of the environment, improvement of working conditions, human rights and social responsibility.

With this in mind it is perhaps no wonder that businesses often are shortsighted and bottom line oriented, with the exception of those businesses that seem to be able to contradict the peer pressures of the market, by finding the right niche with sufficient latent customer susceptibility to leave the competition behind.

Soros asserts that "in today's global capitalist system, there has been a pronounced shift in favor of profit-maximizing behavior and a corresponding heightening of competitive pressures."[8]

The logic may bring us strange fruits, as for instance in the joint attempt of the U.S. Department of Agriculture and the Monsanto subsidiary, Delta & Pine, to create genetically modified (GM) seeds, that would result in plants that would have sterile seeds, meaning that farmers would not be able to use the seeds from this year's harvest for next year's seeds, but would have to buy new seeds from the company with the patent on the new GM seeds. No wonder these were nicknamed terminator seeds.[9]

Large companies transgress the borders of the nation states, pushed by this logic and contributing to it at the same time. Just witness the recent surge in mergers and acquisitions in banking, in telecommunications, in car manufacturing and in the air and space industries. Drucker asserts that the transnational company is "not totally beyond the control of national governments. It must adapt to them. But these adaptations are exceptions to policies and practices decided on for worldwide markets and technologies. Successful transnational companies see themselves as separate, nonnational entities."[10]

With the removal of barriers to capital movements virtual "world money" has been created. "This money has no existence outside the global economy and its main money markets. It is not being created by economic activity like investment, production, consumption, or trade." The influence of the gigantic movements of this world money is far-reaching, because the "volume of world money is so gigantic that its movements in and out of a currency have far greater impact than the flows of financing, trade, or investment. In one day, as much of this virtual money may be traded as the entire world needs to finance trade and investment for a year."[11]

This logic overwhelms every nation state, and in most cases they submit willingly to it, because this is also the logic that is believed to promote growth and better living standards.

For Forrester this leads to a very pessimistic outlook: "Die Privatwirtschaft ist nun freier als je zuvor – sie verfügt über jene Freiheit, die sie mit solchem Nachdruck gefordert hat und die sich in legaler Deregulierung, in offizieller Anarchie äußert. In einer Freiheit, die mit allen Rechten und größter Freizügigkeit ausgestattet ist. Ungezügelt durchdringt sie eine zugrunde gehende Zivilisation, deren Untergang sie noch beschleunigt."[12]

It has become a runaway logic. "We live in a world of infinite potential where we are masters of our destiny, yet are utterly dependent on the unpredictable outcome of forces over which we have no control."[13] This runaway logic is the main concern of critical books like Soros' *The Crisis of Global Capitalism*, Forrester's *Terror der Ökonomie*, and former German chancellor Helmut Schmidt's *Auf der Suche nach einer öffentlichen Moral.*[14]

In a more narrow vein the economic logic and its consequences have also been discussed in Yergin and Stanislaw's *Staat oder Markt*, Sen's *The Moral Standing of the Market* and *On Ethics and Economics*, Paul et al.'s *Ethics and Economics*, Lunati's *Ethical Issues in Economics*, Griffith-Jones' *Global Capital Flows: Should they be regulated?* and others,[15] often with a emphasis on the ambiguous nature of this logic.

A groundswell of dissent and protest is becoming noticeable, and the first waves are lapping at the foundations of institutions symbolising the logic. Grassroots movements have begun to fight it, in tumultuous and attention-drawing actions against high-level meetings furthering this logic, like the WTO negotiations in Seattle 1999, or the recent World Economic Forum in Davos 2001.

A petition currently being circulated among students of economics in France may be seen as part of the protest. The petition argues in favour of economic theory relevant for the big questions in economics like unemployment, inequalities, the place of financial markets, the advantages and disadvantages of free-trade, globalisation, economic development and so on.[16] Even representatives of trade and industry have begun to realise that the runaway logic cannot be left alone, that destructive tendencies have to be curbed.

According to the Prince of Wales Business Leaders Forum more than three billion people joined economies characterised by market principles in the past decade. In the opinion of the Forum this has brought unparalleled opportunities to these people, "but there is also rising inequality both within nations and between them." Other problems brought about by the new logic are "Growing levels of unemployment and economic insecurity, environmental degradation, social dislocation and a break down of traditional communities ..."[17] In the view of the Forum business has a responsibility for contributing to the solution of all these problems.

In a paper on globalisation the International Chamber of Commerce asks: "Can – or should – it be stopped? Is it pushing governments to the sidelines? Does it have a human face? Is it a threat to jobs? What are the benefits and what is the downside?"[18]

The market in itself is not a stable construction; every player pursuing a profit goal only wants to eradicate competition for his or her own products and services. In a policy paper by the International Chamber of

Commerce (ICC) the view is expressed "that as trade is liberalized, businesses seek other measures to protect their market position, and the problem of international cartels is too important to ignore."[19] Monopolies and cartels might be the way to protect one's market position. In this case the end result of the workings of the logic is not more competition, but less or no competition.

The way to prevent this happening has traditionally been to use state intervention, in other words regulation to curb the worst cases, and this is still important. One such example is the article against collusive behaviour found already in Article 85 of the Rome Treaty: "The following shall be prohibited as incompatible with the common market: all agreements between undertakings, decisions by associations of undertakings and concerted practices which may affect trade between Member States and which have as their object or effect the prevention, restriction or distortion of competition within the common market ..."[20]

Although this regulation may sound far-reaching one might in fact question the extent to which the competition rules and accompanying regulation really assure competition, especially in the light of the attempts to make European companies large and strong enough to be able to compete in the global market against American and Japanese companies. To compete in the global markets the logic demands creation of large transnational or global players, and this is actively promoted by the same Commission. A certain ambivalence therefore seems to prevail in the activities of the European Commission.[21]

The runaway logic is the driving mechanism of the economy, and how would we be able to account for the material living standards of the economically most developed countries of the world without something like this mechanism? The logic seems to represent something akin to Nietzsche's *Wille zur Macht*, it may be destructive and dangerous, but it is also a prime mover in economic development. This is the positive, progressive potential of this logic.

We have seen examples of the blindness, dangerousness and potential destructiveness of this prime mover. This represents its negative potential, the processes of decay and destruction. The logic is not a self-sustaining mechanism. If it is not embedded in some external framework consisting perhaps of some extended version of Adam Smith's general rules of conduct and a state apparatus, it might destroy itself.

Somehow the forces of this fierce mechanism must be harnessed. But this harness can either be too tight, threatening the logic like a command economy or too loose, letting it run amok. Too much regulation of market or even creation of a command economy, and material progress is threatened. Too much market and the market destroys itself.

The logic is the most efficient driver of economic development, but it cannot provide us with a direction in which to drive. *We* must do that, and thus we may conclude with the former German Chancellor, Helmut Schmidt: "Märkte, nationale wie internationale, sind zweckmäßige Veranstaltungen, man muß sie deshalb bejahen. Aber Märkte sind keine moralische Instanz, sie können weder auf soziale Gerechtigkeit und auf Beseitigung der Arbeitslosigkeit noch auf monetäre oder fiskalische Vernunft hinwirken ... Der Markt an sich erzeugt weder individuellen noch kollektiven Anstand; eben deshalb müssen Anstand und Moral von allen Teilnehmerm des Marktes verlangt werden."[22]

Let us see how this may come about.

THE POTEMKIN STAGE OF SOCIAL RESPONSIBILITY

Arrow holds that: "There are a number of circumstances under which the economic agent should forgo profit or other benefits to himself in order to achieve some social goal, especially to avoid a disservice to other individuals."[23] Of course Arrow recognises the driving force of the market economy as the motor of the growth and innovation that we all depend upon, but at the same time he realises that this logic is not self-limiting, which means that the limitations or bridles must come from somewhere outside.

Arrow regards the state-induced regulation and the forms of legal liability as insufficient, which leads him to consider ethical codes as a way to achieve social responsibility in business, arguing that purely selfish behaviour is "incompatible with any kind of settled economic life." Here he actually argues in a way that supports our arguments that something outside the rules must constrain us in our behaviour or we would not even obey the rules.

"Every contract depends for its observance on a mass of unspecified conditions which suggest that the performance will be carried out in good faith without insistence on sticking literally to its wording."[24] The gist of the exposition is that business as business carries a social responsibility outside of the economic logic. How this responsibility is carried out in practice Arrow cannot really tell us.

There have been many attempts to make the demands of this social responsibility more concrete, in order to implement the idea in the practices of business. One example is found in a fairly recent Danish attempt to drive home to individual businesses the notion of social responsibility. This drive represents a co-effort of the Ministry of Social Affairs and some Danish companies or rather the managers of these companies. A campaign called "It concerns us all" in 1994 marked the beginning of this effort, which was also part of the Social Summit held in Copenhagen in 1995.[25]

Businesses practising social responsibility are seen as an alternative to detailed public regulation. This fits well with our more basic notions, but does it work?

In "It concerns us all" the aim is to convince businesses that they have to act in a socially responsible way towards their own employees, unemployed persons and the local community. Already here one may see the lopsidedness of the drive. It is aimed towards fairly specific problems, like unemployment, and especially unemployed persons with handicaps that make them difficult to employ under normal conditions.

Elements of the drive are sweetened by special incentives aimed at reducing certain types of unemployment. Here the semi-submerged reasons for initiating such a drive may show themselves. The nation state and local governments are no longer able to correct all the social ills that are a result of the workings of the logic we have discussed before. That is why there is a demand for social responsibility in the private sector. Business has to share the burden with the public interventionist policies.

It seems strange that businesses, which may contribute to a growth in unemployment as a result of being subject to the logic of the market, should be able to reduce this unemployment to any substantial degree. It is rather evident that this would be difficult to achieve, although businesses certainly seem to accept that they have to become more socially responsible. Not because of any logic in the market, but because times seem to demand it. But they also state that conditions make it more and more difficult for instance to employ people who cannot deliver a peak effort.[26] This is a result of the logic we touched upon so many times now.

Businesses feel that they simply cannot afford to reduce their competitiveness.

A report[27] aimed at mapping the social responsibility of Danish businesses showed that companies were in favour of showing social responsibility on the abstract level. When asked whether they would be willing to employ persons who have been unemployed for a long time or whether they actually employed such persons, they showed less willingness. In reality the motives for showing social responsibility may be more dubious than that. Companies are also asked to state their motives for contributing towards employment of persons outside the normal labour market. Social responsibility is reported to be the main motive, but some companies state openly that it pays to employ these people.

The survey on which this report, as well as other reports,[28] is based, seems to have a fairly superficial conception of social responsibility. Not only is it very limited, it also accepts social responsibility at face value. Companies with written personnel policies covering these areas are classified as being more responsible than companies without written policies.[29] In other words if one can show some Potemkin villages[30] in the distance the report will state that it has found evidence of social responsibility.

It is admitted that this handicaps small companies with no written policies, even though they may take good or even better care of their employees than large companies with written policies. They just do not have the resources to brag about it.

In a paper on Corporate Social Responsibility the World Business Council for Sustainable Development seems to regard such activities as belonging to a more traditional view of social responsibility, a view in which "companies run their business successfully and ethically while making charitable contributions and engaging in elements of social or philanthropic investment in the community."[31]

This is a social responsibility that seems to reach back to the social philanthropy activities of an earlier phase of industrialism, to a period where "success" and "ethics" were weighed somewhat differently than today, to the days of the industrial barons, the captains of industry, or to use the Swedish expression to the "*brukspatron*", where the second part of the term says it all.

Evidently the modern version of this represents a very limited kind of social responsibility. In our typology of responsibilities it would seem to fall under the heading of special specific responsibility, aimed at narrow sections of the population. Some of the elements of this narrow conception of a presumably preventive social responsibility are formal policies concerning employees in general, like training, education, health and working hours. Other elements include employee clubs, athletics clubs, cultural activities for employees, company kindergartens, canteens or even the possibility of borrowing a company summer cottage.

To these specific schemes may be added remedial efforts directed towards employees with special problems: for employees with children it is a question of having special leave policies; for older employees it is a question of having a senior policy; for employees with a drinking problem, it is drinking policies; for employees who have contracted an illness it is a question of having policies of caring and offers of jobs with reduced demands.

The detailed list of schemes goes on and on, but I expect that one has already caught the idea. Most, if not all, of the schemes presented here as part of genuine social responsibility might be regarded as being in reality remedial, not in the sense used in the report, but in relation to the logic that we have discussed, and some of them may in fact be supportive of the logic. It might not be easy to say whether the activities show social responsibility or whether they are in fact part of an extensive and clever remuneration scheme, designed to attract employees and keep them loyal to the company, especially in sectors where there is universal demand for the skills of these employees.

The CEO of a Danish subsidiary of an American computer company acted according to many modern textbooks by carrying out a survey of employee satisfaction in the company.[32] It turned out that employees were rather dissatisfied, although well paid. They complained that often they would not have time to go to a supermarket to buy ingredients for supper, because they worked long hours on projects that had to be finished on time. And not only that, when they got home they would have to spend time preparing supper, with the result that they had very little time left for their family.

The CEO's solution to this problem was to introduce a scheme allowing employees to order a take-away supper from the company canteen at lunchtime. A company cook would then prepare it and they would collect it before leaving for home, where they would just have to put it into the microwave oven for a few minutes and presto, supper would be ready. Afterwards there would be plenty of time for the family.

A later survey showed that employee satisfaction had not improved a lot, and now the CEO was wondering what to do next, because according to the general definition of social responsibility his company was absolutely in the forefront.

What did the CEO do wrong? According to the wisdom presented here, apparently nothing. What one might suspect is that neither he nor the social responsibility drive may have understood that what led to dissatisfaction might have been the working conditions, the overtime work and the pressures of the projects that had to be finished on time. The CEO's solution may have done nothing to alleviate this situation. The complaining employees may actually wish to be able to spend time to go to the supermarket and prepare their own and their family's supper, instead of staying at work longer and be treated to the bliss of carrying home a prepared supper.

Only very peripherally does such a responsibility touch upon the logic that may have been a contributing factor to the problems that these social responsibility schemes are aimed at alleviating. In part this also seems to be the view of Waddock and Graves, who argue that so-called corporate social performance should not be confined to "a set of discretionary activities undertaken when there are sufficient slack resources."[33] Instead they argue that corporate social performance must be part of a company's ongoing routine operations.

In the light of such considerations the social responsibility promoted in the schemes we have referred to may seem almost asocial. On the other hand one might regard the more vague central responsibilities as being impossible to implement against the all encompassing logic we have discussed.[34]

Although there is no lack of principles and declarations it would seem that the application of these principles in practice, at least when judged from the above examples, would certainly leave something to be desired.

THE ILLUSION OF CORPORATE CITIZENSHIP

In Soros' view of the global capitalist system,[35] publicly owned companies have come to dominate the scene. This renews the focus on stockholders, or shareholders. And the logic of this type of diffuse ownership demands that the managers of these companies focus exclusively on profits and on maximising shareholder value, thus emphasising the short term. Managers may even be bound explicitly to this logic by all sorts of stock option plans rewarding them handsomely for increases in share values.[36]

This view of business is supported by theories emphasising the importance of shareholder value[37] and some of the theories of agency,[38] views that play along with the logic that we have discussed in the previous section, views ignoring the problems created by this kind of logic. Kay mentions that this may even include disposing of an entire collection of businesses and buying a new one; as long as this results in higher share values, it would seem perfectly in accordance with the basic logic.[39]

An alternative to these views is found in the theories of stakeholding and trusteeship. Instead of focusing exclusively on the shareholders, the stakeholder concept tries to incorporate the interests of all those who are influenced by the actions of a company. Freeman, who must be seen as one of the early proponents for a stakeholder view of the company, in 1984 defined a stakeholder as "any group or individual who can affect or is affected by the achievement of the organisation's objectives."[40] According to Donaldson, stakeholders "are persons or groups with legitimate interest in procedural and/or substantive aspects of corporate activity. Stakeholders are identified by *their* interest in the corporation, whether or not the corporation has any corresponding interest in *them*."[41] Freeman also urges that the stakeholder groups "must participate in determining the future direction of the firm in which they have a stake."[42]

Newer theories on stakeholders have taken an even broader view, talking in general terms of a stakeholder capitalism.[43] In most of these the basic notion is inclusion, meaning that one somehow has a say in decisions of companies and organisations. To Hutton "a stakeholder society and a stakeholder economy exist where there is a mutuality of rights and obligations constructed around the notion of economic, social and political inclusion."[44] He wants to apply these principles to "the operation of free market capital," thereby harnessing the operation of "the unfettered markets."[45]

In a simple version of the stakeholder theory the idea is to involve employees in decisions concerning the future of the company, in order to have a workforce that is committed *to*, and identify *with* the company. "The importance of securing participation by the workforce, by providing proper motivation to get improved performance, and therefore success, is a major part of the philosophy of stakeholding."[46] In this version stakeholding is a way to enhance productivity, while reducing the potential for adverse reactions from the workforce.

Kay[47] has a more sophisticated answer. According to his proposal the purpose of the stakeholder corporation would of course still include paying the shareholder what is seen as a return "sufficient to remunerate past investments and encourage future investments." The purpose would also include development of the competencies and capabilities of employees and suppliers of the company; stability and security in employment and business relations; the production of goods and services of good quality at fair prices; and of course high standards in the general conduct of business. Somehow one gets the impression that these general suggestions are no more than what a prudent company might observe anyhow.

While accepting that much of stakeholding is common sense, already practised by all successful companies, Kay demands that public policy should force every company to heed these notions. Thus we are back again with a solution based on public regulation being necessary in order to make companies behave sensibly.

It would seem that the stakeholder proponents must have a rather simple view of business, perhaps more suited to businesses belonging to another era than ours. If we think of the transnational and global businesses that dominate the economy today, or the financial institutions involved in the global capital flows, or the diverse and extremely far-reaching relations that even simple forms of production may depend upon today, the idea of involving all the stakeholders in decision making would seem rather far-fetched and impossible to implement in any kind of consistent praxis. A global company may operate in many countries, assembling finished products in one country, producing special parts in other countries, having their product development in a third country and corporate headquarters in a fourth. To such a company "national boundaries have largely become irrelevant."[48]

It is difficult to see how the more involved stakeholder ideas could ever be practised in any serious way in such a company, let alone the idea of conducting dialogues with representatives from all their stakeholders. Who are the stakeholders by the way? Many groups may be influenced in different ways by the decisions and actions in a company, but may not even know about it. Where do we set the limit on involvement in this case?

There are other problems with a stakeholder view going beyond the banal version, Willets[49] points to some of them. He argues that there is no reason why the interest of different stakeholders should coincide. The shareholders might not mind that a company relocates or closes down business in order to enhance profitability, while the employees involved would presumably argue differently, the local community would have their interests, the suppliers theirs and so on. If we take into account the point made above that we may be dealing with a company operating across the borders, it certainly becomes very difficult to envisage a scheme that could somehow lead to a common stand among the stakeholders.

To this might be added that there are potential stakeholders who are only indirectly influenced by the actions of the company in question. These potential groups may include the unemployed, the handicapped, people below the official poverty line, minorities, people in underdeveloped countries, future generations and in order to make the whole concept seem really inconceivable one may even think of animals. It looks as if stakeholders suddenly become a very diffuse concept, where it will prove to be impractical to involve more than a few stakeholders and even so it might prove impossible to reconcile their views on any important topics.

Our assumption would be that a prudent company might very well take into account the views, the voice and especially the potential harmful actions of groups who possess the potential to create problems for the company. This is prudent, but it presupposes that only those groups who possess this potential will be listened to and somehow accommodated, without needing any form of stakeholder theory.

In a policy statement from the International Chamber of Commerce (ICC) we find support for this view: "Public interest groups and individual consumers exert pressure through their behaviour and attitudes. Therefore, industry appreciates the need to seek out these concerns and to include them in its development of policy."[50] This was certainly the case in relation to corporate activity in the former South Africa. Global and transnational companies "have had the idea thrust upon them, as the result of public outcry over corporate activity in South Africa, that their moral sensitivity must sometimes range beyond the narrow confines of commercial endeavor."[51]

This may be contrasted with the views of some of the more idealistic conceptions of stakeholder involvement, involving what is called a democratic dialogue[52], based on the idea of a dialogue not influenced by power, a rather naïve attempt to implement some of Habermas' theories of communicative action.[53] This totally ignores the various strong asymmetries in power and knowledge, and this alone would tend to make the attempt invalid.

It would thus seem that only the simpler ideas of stakeholder involvement really mean something in practical terms, for instance the idea of involving employees, in order to create amicable relations, commitment and loyalty, and of course to raise productivity and efficiency. Perhaps some local groups could be included as well, but it may be feared that this will also be used to create amicable relations, in fact taking the representatives hostage to the necessities brought about by the logics of the market.

At the moment the interest may actually be shifting from stakeholder models to corporate governance, where the main focus quite clearly will be on shareholders, but with prudent regard for the interests of stakeholders. According to preamble of the recently published *Principles of Corporate Governance* by the OECD "Good corporate governance should provide proper incentives for the board and management to pursue objectives that are in the interests of the company and shareholders and should facilitate effective monitoring, thereby encouraging firms to use resources more efficiently."[54] This may in fact represent a more realistic view of what stakeholder management is all about, but then of course, if this is the case, it may lose some of its appealing flavour.

Once more we return to the impersonal logic of the market. If there is any question of choosing between the values of one group of stakeholders and the future of the company, logic will prevail, for instance leading the company to move production abroad, whatever the consequences on the local community. Attempts to create a kind of pseudo-corporate citizenship, based on stakeholder involvement, seem doomed to failure. Only the simple models may have any meaning at all, but then they only fulfil a very limited purpose, in some cases perhaps the same purpose as declarations and visions. This would tend to make implementations of stakeholder theories limited to innocent pastimes, with stakeholder representatives having dialogues with representatives from a company's PR department and agreeing on the same kind of airy values that one would find in all value statements. This would do no harm and may even during quiet periods further the image of the company. Thus stakeholder models seem to represent more of a placebo than an active cure against the runaway logic and its consequences.

CONTAINING THE LOGIC WITHOUT STRANGLING IT

In an article dating from 1978 Sommers foresaw a collision between ethics and economics. Ethics is the democratic ethic that is concerned with issues of participation, just distribution, creation of egalitarity and oriented towards the consumption of goods. The free market is cumulative, organised on dominance and leadership; it is a logic driven by incentive and reward, anti-egalitarian, and darkly suspicious of altruism. To Sommers "Democracy legislates values, arrays priorities, praises and condemns" and thus sets the goals, while the logic of market contains no priorities, no values, no end, no purpose, ... but "liberates the enormous energies contained within self-interest."[55]

The market will produce anti-personnel mines as well as the crutches that will be used by the victims of those mines, cigarettes as well as the hospital equipment and medicine to treat the lung cancer caused by the smoking of cigarettes and nuclear power stations as well as nuclear waste treatment plants and storage techniques.

Although Sommers' view may look rather simple, this is basically the issue we are discussing here. The question is how do we gain some measure of control over the runaway logic of the market? In the preceding section we have scorned a whole series of efforts as being incapable of harnessing the logic; instead they may have helped to put a kind of gloss upon it, or they hid it beneath the heady words of high-minded declarations, or they have argued for remedial action to be taken where the logic grinds too loud against the values found in declarations or public opinion. What then is the alternative?

We shall see if we can get around to an alternative answer utilising ideas and theories presented in previous chapters. Our starting point is the model of change we constructed earlier in order to help us understand changes in the moral fabric.

Perhaps the coke bottle out of the sky example shows where we have to look to find alternatives to the measures discussed above. As shown in Chapter 6 on the weaving of the moral fabric, the important starting point for the emergence of new values, attitudes and changed behaviour is the experience of a problem in relation to values we already hold, what we have variously called a gap or a discrepancy.

In the beginning we thus have, not darkness, but a problem, a gap or a discrepancy. In other words somebody must feel concerned. But what comes next?

CONCERN OR AWARENESS THAT SOMETHING IS "WRONG"

The closest parallel to our coke bottle out of the sky example might be the discovery of large holes in the protective ozone layer. A thin layer of ozone is formed in the stratosphere through the influence of sunlight on oxygen. The ozone is in a constant process of creation and destruction, which makes the delicate balance between creation and destruction very important.

The ozone layer filters out excessive ultraviolet radiation, meaning that it protects life on earth from the effects of this radiation. Depletion of the ozone layer leading to the so-called holes would lead to increases in skin cancer, less productivity in plants and other adverse effects.

The discovery of the depletion of the ozone layer and the causes of this depletion was not as easy or evident as the coke bottle out of the sky example. It was not something that could easily be registered and observed. Only indirectly and through the apparatus of science and scientific insight was it possible to register the depletion and the probable causes.

In the early 1970s Crutzen pointed out that it was probable that nitrogen oxides from fertilisers and from the fuel used by the engines of supersonic aircraft like Concorde might have a negative influence on the ozone layer.[56] In 1974 Rowland and Molina found that CFC gases played a major role in the destruction of the ozone layer.[57] CFC gases were not something esoteric; they were the gases used for instance in everyday appliances like refrigerators, air-conditioning equipment and aerosol cans.

The discovery certainly did raise eyebrows and gave cause for grave concern, for obvious reasons, not least among scientists, although it must be said that the findings were not uncontested. The concern for the ozone layer and for the terrible long-term effects of its depletion was first felt by a group of specialists. Since then the concern has more or less become a concern shared by everyone.

There has also been a growing concern over the so-called greenhouse effects, with global temperature increases seen as being caused partly by the increasing consumption of fossil fuels in cars. Although there are different opinions as to the significance of these findings, concern about the future of the planet has been voiced very loudly by many groups.

Many of the concerns raised here concern the environment, and many areas of concern today can be said to relate to a general concern for the environment. In fact we assume that the many concrete environmental concerns in themselves have contributed to raising general awareness, the implication being that many people in all sorts of professions have a heightened sensibility in relation to the environment. To many this sensibility may even have become self-evident, "but of course the environment *is* important." In fact the value put on certain parts of the environment may have become part of the semi-submerged, almost ineffable, set of values that many hold and show in relation to for instance the next generation, in effect making these values an integral part of the weave of the moral fabric.

Nowhere may this be more clear than in Beck's description of the Modern Risk society[58], as a society in which we may have a vague feeling that the product of all our industrious activities is threatening the society we are living in, that the coke bottle did not fall out of the sky, that it was made by us and that many types of coke bottles are raining down upon us. In a diffuse way we may have become aware that the problems we see are caused by us.

Concern is concern in relation to something, or else there would be no gap, no discrepancy, nothing to worry about. Concern is concern in relation to some of the values we already believe in, without necessarily being able to state exactly what they are. Concern may arise in many ways. Concern may be felt by people without having any exact knowledge or even in some cases with no apparent reason at all. Based upon the nature of the concerns it might be possible to separate out different types of concerns.

For the present it is possible to discern three different types:

1. Concerns caused by the revelation of transgressions of existing value boundaries;

2. Concerns caused by large-scale accidents and the discovery of acute danger;
3. Concerns caused by the discovery of (slowly) emerging problems and potential problems.

Concerns caused by the revelation of transgressions of existing boundaries
These might be concerns in relation to the revelation of large-scale corruption: problematic arms deals, like Swedish Bofors selling weapons to India; evasion of embargoes, as found for instance in the attempted construction of a giant gun in Iraq, with British companies apparently delivering parts for the weapon to Iran; or the involvement of German companies in the building of chemical plants in Iraq and Libya, plants that could be switched to the production of nerve gases.

All activities that either violate international and national laws or are so blatantly against the values we hold dear, that the revelation that such activities are taking place is enough to create scandals, with shaming and condemnation, and with outcries for more control, more rules and more stringent regulation. In this case concern and the voicing of the concern seem to be contained in one step. The revelations may be brought about by the voices and actions of whistle-blowers, or be based on "deep throat" sources using the media to reveal the dubious activities.

Other kinds of concern may arise as a result of reports on the use of child labour or forced labour, or of terrible working conditions suffered in the sweatshops in some far-off country, where our shoes, T-shirts and footballs are produced.

Then there are all the concerns related to the social and political sphere, like concerns voiced over the human rights violations in Burma, China and not too long ago South Africa.

Other concerns have been raised with different degrees of awareness, but in fact following the same development, beginning with a few pressing issues in relation to values we already hold and by and by leading to changes in these.

All this seems to represent aspects of a more general concern found for instance in our discussion of the probable adverse effects of the logics of the market and of competition, and in the popular books lamenting the effects that this logic may have.

Concerns caused by large-scale accidents and the discovery of acute danger.
These have some of the characteristics of a coke bottle falling suddenly out of the blue sky among a band of bushmen: the coke bottle in this case being a Bhopal catastrophe, a Seveso tragedy, an Exxon Valdez pollution, an O-ring disaster, or some new catastrophe lurking in the wings of the stage on which we are playing in the future. Often it seems that it is this type of concern that is discussed in textbooks on business ethics.

One may point to the turning-around of public opinion in relation to nuclear power: from the PR efforts in relation to "our friend the atom" of the Eisenhower area to the concern shown by many in the aftermath of the Three Mile Island incident, the Chernobyl catastrophe or the recent Japanese nuclear fuel accident and rumours of possible risks in connection with a similar kind of operation carried out by Rolls-Royce in Derby in Great Britain; or the evidence of leakages from the German Castor containers used for transporting spent nuclear fuel. It is as though the accidents seem to deepen the concern that has already been voiced, voiced by the anti-nuclear movement, a movement with beginnings in the first large-scale protest against nuclear power plants, for instance in Wyhl in Germany in the early 1970s.[59]

The accidents serve as gigantic reminders, accompanied by loud voices shouting: "What did we say!" Birkland[60] talks of focusing events, seeing for instance the nuclear power plant accidents as examples of focusing events.

Concerns caused by the discovery of (slowly) emerging problems and potential problems. Discovering emerging problems is much more interesting, because in this case boundaries do not exist beforehand, instead the problems must somehow be discovered or revealed, in other words must be seen to be problems. Then the issues of boundaries can be discussed, and we can make up our minds as to what should be done about the problems and by whom. Here we actually have to make up our values as we go along.

The discovery of the ozone layer depletion may be an example of such a concern, and so may the concern for the greenhouse effects of the use of fossil fuel, or the raised awareness concerning the dangers of smoking.

Concern may arise as a result of changes in science and technology. Just watch the recent concern over the GMOs (genetically modified organisms) or GE (genetic engineering).

Changes in medicine may lead to concerns, as for instance when one realises that one can now design babies with specific qualities or "produce" children from unborn mothers, or realises other potential aspects of genetic modification or engineering, or discovers the possibility of transplanting organs from transgenic animals to human beings, or achieves the ability to make head transplants, or more mundanely realises that it is now possible to save a foetus born so early in a pregnancy that abortion would still have been allowed. The list has become very long and very complicated.

Concern may arise because of new knowledge or discoveries, as in the case of the depletion of the ozone layer, or the probable effects of CO_2 on the increase in global warming with all its attendant threatening effects.

Concern may arise when we are told that more people could be saved by installing safety equipment in cars, in the shape of safety belts and airbags. With the result that the number of airbags in some cars now has reached a count of 8, without necessarily reducing the number of accidents, but certainly cushioning the impact.

That we feel concerned about certain things, whether as scientists or as laypeople may not in itself lead to change; we may not even be able to express our concerns in any articulate way, and even if we could, they may mean nothing to those who hear what we have to say. More is needed for concerns to become issues that we take seriously and are prepared to act upon.

VOICES OF CONCERN

Without giving voice, structure and some kind of coherence to our concern, it may never become more than a vague personal uneasiness, based upon the tacit awareness that something might be wrong, without really being able to put one's finger on it.

The general raising of awareness that something is wrong and has to be taken seriously may be easy to achieve in a situation where expressions of concern are followed by accidents that seem to demonstrate the correctness of the concern, as in the case of accidents with nuclear power stations or the handling of nuclear fuels. The focus provided by accidents really seems to show that fears are well founded.

It also seemed to work quite well in the case of the ozone layer, where scary projections of the horrible consequences that would result from the depletion of the ozone layer also helped bring home the message. Even so part of the industry claimed that the findings of the scientists were mere speculation, and should not be taken seriously. It is to be presumed that the contra voices were from those who would be hit by a ban on the use of CFC gases, while other voices came from the developing countries, maybe not questioning the finding, but the consequences.

Still the findings of the scientists were taken up by other groups and by UNEP (United Nations Environment Programme) and the loud voicing of concern of these various groups led to a pressure to ban the gasses that were believed to be responsible for the destruction of the ozone layer. UNEP provided recognition and the channel for voicing this concern on a global scale and for promoting international action.

The voicing of this concern, and the cascading of the concern and awareness of it in ever widening circles, from a few scientists, to special groups, to politicians, to the general public and not least to business, is of fundamental importance for the recognition of the concern as a problem that has to be taken seriously and acted upon.

In some cases the first concern and voicing of it seem to be very much an affair of special groups, not really involving the populace in their findings and discussions. Perhaps this may be indicative of many of the concerns that are raised or will be raised in our societies. The issues have become so technical and complex, and they may only concern a very limited slice of life, that the populace will have to stand on the sidelines and limit its activities to applauding one or the other voice. This might also indicate that concerns are brought forward rather haphazardly, and not selected according to any obvious criteria of importance. Still we have to remember what was said in the former section, concern for a single issue may be a result of general changes in the values one holds. With more concern about the environment, scientists may actually become more active in relation to these issues, pointing to new problems in relation to this general concern.

The next step in the cascading process is that special interest groups may take up the concerns of the scientists, or they may employ their own scientists. This is where voicing really takes place, now we have the first crusaders, raising banners, designing campaigns, shouting slogans and collecting followers. With banners and slogans and colourful actions there is a good chance that the media will jump on the bandwagon, remembering though that the interest of the media may again be partly caused by changes in the general focus that we discussed in the previous section. At this stage it becomes a battle for public opinion, for the attention of us, of politicians and decision makers everywhere.

In other cases we do not need scientists to make us aware that something is wrong. In relation to the question of human rights the first voices may be the voices of the people who fight oppression and terrible working conditions, groups actually experiencing the conditions, or the first light may be shed on the conditions by organisations like Human Rights Watch or Amnesty International. They are the ones that make us see the gaping holes in the fabric of the human rights, as well as in working conditions.

It is evident that special issue groups, social movements and NGOs[61] in general play a very big role in the cascading process that puts the issues and concerns voiced on the agenda of everyone – consumers as well as businesses. Making everyday decisions to buy or not to buy certain products, or to behave or not to behave in certain ways, becomes a matter of serious moral judgement.

The general form is not new. Groups and movements have been fighting for independence, freedom from oppression, better living conditions, more equality, using methods ranging from the non-violent civil disobedience of a Mahatma Gandhi to outright acts of terrorism. Such movements were important in making us aware of racial issues, discrimination and lack of civil rights. They have long roots, in fact they may be found everywhere, being instrumental in challenging and changing the basic structures and institutions of society. In fact our conceptions of human rights and good working conditions are a result of the activities of such groupings.

What is new is the proliferation of single-issue organisations. This is recognised by Carr: "The rise of non-profit organisations, on a worldwide scale ... could be as significant a movement at the end of the 20th century as the rise of the nation state at the end of the 19th ... due to this explosion of do-it yourself the future of relationships between state and individual citizen could be forever altered."[62]

Today concerns are often voiced by single-issue groups made up by people who have coalesced in the belief that their concerns and the concerns they may have adopted from scientists are to be taken seriously. We showed in a previous chapter that this coalescence, which might be seen as a form of self-organisation with very little overall guidance in the beginning, might be a result of the workings of some sort of catalyst, making many people recognise that theirs is a shared problem, thereby creating a kind of collective awareness that something is wrong, perhaps even some sense of what it is wrong in relation to.

The self-organised entity that is held together by the conviction that they share a genuine concern may lead to all sorts of voicing and actions, from banner-waving to "action directe." In fact some of the groups show how serious the issues are and they are, by breaking existing laws or attempting in other ways to stop the practices that have given them cause for concern.

A good example would be the activities of Greenpeace. Greenpeace was founded in 1971 in Canada, by activists carrying out actions against American nuclear tests in the Pacific. Since then they have taken up a series of issues that can be grouped under the heading of concern for the environment. I have no idea how they choose the issues, but the methods they use would seem to result in a very good media coverage. Many people will have got their first inkling that there might be something called environmental issues, from watching footage of people in inflatable rubber boats darting around whale catchers armed with harpoon guns, literally spoiling their aim.

Sometimes the pictures were very dramatic with inflatables overturning and the orange-clad warriors being spilled into the sea, fighting to avoid the drums of chemicals being dumped over the sides of the ship they were acting against, or the almost "St George-against-the-dragon"-like qualities of the footage from the fight against the dumping of Brent Spar, with the St Georges of course in orange survival suits and the dragons in the shape of the yellow-red leviathan called Brent Spar.

One of their more recent activities has been directed against GMOs. They have acted by tramping through or uprooting fields with GM organisms; they have tried to block shiploads of GMOs; often without any direct success, and often resulting in their arrest.

In Europe at least a result of activities of Greenpeace and other groups[63] and organisations has been that people are generally weary of GMOs. They cannot point to any concrete danger, but they have become very weary of having GMOs in their food anyway.[64]

The efforts of Greenpeace have in several cases been carried one stage further in the cascading process by more or less established consumer groups all over the world. Large and small issues have been taken up by these loose organisations, often with direct repercussions for the companies and industrial branches that the searchlight of these organisations has been directed at.

In the cascading process often begun when Greenpeace has taken up an issue, consumer organisations may thus play an important role, an example being the National Federation of Consumer Groups in Great Britain, which represent the views of grass roots members to government, and to business, and organise campaigns to promote "awareness of and affect changes in a wide range of consumer issues."

The list of issues taken up by special interest groups is long: environmental justice; the rights of indigenous people; working conditions with campaigns against sweatshops; renewable energy; health care; pharmaceuticals; food safety; GMOs, tobacco; and Internet regulation.

In the story of the emperor's new clothes by Hans Christian Andersen, two tailors weave an invisible cloth for the emperor. The cloth is so special that only those loyal to the emperor can actually see it; to the disloyal it is invisible. Accordingly all members of the court can see the cloth, where there is none. All goes well until the emperor shows off the new clothes in the public and a small boy yells: "but he has got no clothes on."

What we usually forget in this story is that the yell of the innocent may not mean a lot, if the rest of the public is not willing to listen. As long as they want to stay loyal they may see the invisible cloth and so the boy is just a naughty, ignorant little boy, who is told to shut up. So much for the importance of receptivity for all kinds of whistle-blowers, from small innocent boys, engineers in O-ring cases, to major social movements.

Still it is important that the small boy, in the shape of the first individual who acts as a condensation point for the coalescence of a group of concerned scientists, a pressure group, or larger social movements, actually yells: "But he has got no clothes on!" Or whatever may be appropriate in the separate instances. Without the little boy's yelling there will no recognition of a shared problem.

The picture we see slowly emerging from the hinterground clutter of all the concrete examples is that the voices we hear in these cases may in fact represent individuals acting from a conviction and with a sense of responsibility of the more vague and universal character. We no longer talk about the passive and irresponsible bystanders. Instead we see individuals acting, doing what is within their means to voice a problem that they may feel very deeply about, voicing their concern in ways that demand our attention, thereby sometimes endangering their jobs, or even their lives in order to make us believe that they are serious and that the concern they are voicing is a serious one.

They seem to take upon themselves the kind of responsibility that shows some of the characteristics of the universal responsibility, a responsibility that is owed to everyone, in some cases even every living being. They are not only concerned about their own future, their own material well-being, or even their own families. They seem to show responsibility towards everyone, humankind, animals and even inanimate nature and future generations as yet unborn.

The universal responsibility is not universal in the sense that these groups see responsibilities everywhere, instead they seem to concentrate on certain aspects where they may demonstrate a universal responsibility,. like voicing their concern in relation to the ozone layer depletion, or whale catching or some esoteric issue that is deemed to be important to all of us.

This raises the tricky issue we have already touched upon of whether the more or less haphazardly chosen issues, and the groups coalescing about these single issues, do not in fact represent new problems. Because of the narrow focus on these issues, they, and we, may lose a more general sense of purpose. Here we may refer back to our discussion of what we called the society of masks, where we asserted that the mask we were carrying at any given moment was the only important one, meaning that we would lose sight of the other masks that we might be carrying at other times, not realising of course that the mask we carried was just a mask. The result would be that we sometimes would be acting against ourselves in our different roles.

There is an important difference between the examples used in the discussion of the mask society, and the activities of the groups described here. The actions of the groups we see here do seem to demonstrate aspects of a universal responsibility absent in the society of masks. In other words the groups we observe here cry out for the sake of someone or something outside of themselves. This is important to remember, even though that does not solve the problem of incoherence and inconsistency in the voices of different groups.

There are other differences between the excuses we have discussed before and the actions we see here. We see that individuals or groups of people act as if they don't care whether they are acting alone or not. Even the successful social movements have had their beginnings in the individuals coalescing about something apparently without any explicit direction from the outside and certainly without having any assurance that their efforts would be successful. They act as if they do not care whether their act of joining the group has any decisive influence or not. Although to be sure each and everyone of them may feel that they help save the earth. They break the kind of logic that makes Tom with his child labour problem and the rest of us wait for some governing body or institution to prescribe the way and the solution. They break the logic that tells them that their joining the cause does not matter as long as most people believe their cause is lost or esoteric. They seem to want to set better examples no matter what.

We see them in strange situations, locking themselves to the gates of a plant emitting dioxin from its chimney, as lone and loony-looking protesters when decision makers assemble to decide what is the right thing to do, now that these rabid people have raised issues that no one had thought about before. Seen from the outside they may look like masochists willing their dire plight with the intense glow of something greater shining in their eyes.

They seem to thrive on opposition from established authority and power. The more authority attempts to submit them to more traditional ways, the more they shine, also in the media. Without some kind of conflict with established authority they might have been invisible. They break the law and the traditions in order to further the one cause they hold to be bigger than almost everything else.[65]

They show civil disobedience in the manner of a Henry David Thoreau,[66] although he certainly did not stay long in prison, or more seriously perhaps like a Gandhi, or any civil liberty movement acting against discrimination or nuclear power.

The basis for civil disobedience can be none other than the deep values we attach so much importance to. What else can give reasons for rule transgressions? Here is one instance where we seem to be able to count on the support of Habermas. "Mit dieser Idee eines nichtinstitutionalisierbaren Mißtrauens gegen sich selbst ragt der Rechtsstaat über das Ensemble seiner jeweils positiv gesetzten Ordnungen hinaus. Das Paradox findet seine Auflösung in einer politischen Kultur, die die Bürgerinnen und Bürger mit der Sensibilität, mit dem Maß an Urteilskraft und Risikobereitschaft ausstattet, welches in Übergangs- und Ausnahmesituationen nötig ist, um legale Verletzungen der Legitimität zu erkennen und um notfalls aus moralischer Einsicht auch ungesetzlich zu handeln."[67] "Sensibilität, Urteilskraft and Risikobereitschaft" are terms that seem to refer to the same complex of tacit values that we regard as absolutely fundamental for acting responsibly.

Is that why we are listening and perhaps even supporting or joining their cause, because they ring true to our deeply held values, while their opponents with their interest in keeping and consolidating what they have, their influence and their power for instance, ring less true? Is that it, or is there something more to it?

I believe that more is necessary to explain the success of some of these causes. The latency we talked about elsewhere for instance, the feeling that they have hit upon something which has been felt as a problem by others, in the shape of a vague uneasiness. Finally someone voices the uneasiness, an uneasiness that may not have been very specific, an uneasiness that only got its shape from the voices heard from these groups.

The uneasiness or latency may in itself be a result of former fears and beliefs, in a kind of positive feedback loop, where earlier beliefs reinforce new concerns in ever widening spirals, like we discussed with regard to environmental considerations.

Finally we have to take into account processes of social convergence, of peer pressure, of mimicry. Somehow we want to believe what everyone else believes, we want to imitate success, we want to be on the bandwagon. This stage is not that interesting, because at this stage we know or presume we know what the bandwagon is and where it is going. It is the earlier stages, where the issue is still undecided and open that is important. It is the stage where the activists have not yet become the heroes, where they still may be seen as fighting, perhaps not for Dulcinea and against windmills like Don Quixote,[68] but for causes and against developments that seem at the outset just as lost and sad and hopeless. Or even as tragic as the story of Michael Kohlhaas.[69]

Even taking into account our attempts to explain why we may listen to the voicing of certain concerns and not others, we do not have reason to believe that we are home scot-free. We really do not have a very precise idea of the reasons for adopting some of the new concerns and causes and rejecting others.

Elsewhere we have tried to compare this whole process to a search in the dark for the hilltops of an unknown landscape, groping and stumbling in the dark, trying to avoid walking downwards by using the gradient to lead one upwards, being guided only by this sense of up and down. What we are saying is in fact that the process is self-organising, self-regulating and unpremeditated. There is no overall design for change. Behaviour, rules and norms that are not accepted and adopted by large parts of society will not be seen as part of the value structure, and so the process may be a result of a what we have already termed a gigantic error-trial-error-trial-success process involving all of us.

AMBIGUOUS RESPONSE: MORE REGULATION

The voices of concern are not just yelling into empty space, they are directed towards someone, and that someone is in most cases the state, in the shape of the political system and the state organs. The voices demand that the state listens and responds to the concerns raised.

To see how an example of the new form of regulation might come about we take a look at what happened in relation to the ozone layer problem. Evidently the problem concerned the whole world and most of the world seems to have listened to the loud voicing of concern by scientists, by the UNEP, by Greenpeace and others. The dissenting voices were apparently not believed, perhaps because they were seen as having too much at stake, in relation to the existing state of affairs. Perhaps this represents a case where we should not listen too much to the stakeholders, in the shape of produces and users of CFC gases.

As a result a convention for the protection of the ozone layer was adopted in Vienna 1985, followed by later protocols and amendments as more became known about the causes of depletion. Pressures from outside the industry thus prevailed, perhaps the life-threatening aspect of the depletion of the ozone layer was used in persuading governments to agree to a solution which converged around international protocols ratified by an overwhelming number of countries, and banning CFC and other gases, with important repercussions for the production of refrigerators, air-conditioning equipment and aerosol cans, and adding measures to remove the gases from equipment to be scrapped. Exceptions were granted for the developing countries, because they would not be able to make a fast shift to new techniques. In addition assistance was promised.

Apparently the loophole granted for the developing countries has been used by unscrupulous companies to produce more of the gases destroying the ozone layer and selling them to other countries, although this is not allowed in the ban on these gases. The logic of a market containing no priorities, no values, no end, no purpose, is functioning beneath the regulative measures and controls, meaning that traders are "illegally exporting new CFCs to the industrialized countries either in the guise of recycled substances or in the guise of export to developing countries. The profits are said to be higher than those obtained by exporting cocaine."[70]

Regulation may thus lead to new problems because a rational bottom-line calculation may include the computation of the risk of being discovered. It would therefore seem that ignoring the questions of attitude raises the costs of controlling and of assuring compliance.

Incentive schemes have been used to promote environmentally friendly production, for instance energy production using renewable resources, by paying a higher price for electricity produced by windmills. Such schemes may work in relation to the more physical concerns, resulting in changes in production and consumption patterns, but they would seem difficult to use in relation to some of the other issues raised, like human rights violations, animal rights or the concern over GMOs. Here the demand is for direct regulation, regulation in the shape of embargoes towards certain countries or certain products, establishment of certain minimum standards of worker protection, a ban on the use of test animals in the production of pharmaceuticals or cosmetics, or the introduction of schemes for labelling products containing GMOs.[71]

Even representatives of business have argued for certain kinds of regulation. Competition left to itself is too destructive, and so we find that among others the International Chamber of Commerce argues that "the main lesson of the recent crisis in emerging markets is that a globalized economy requires more efficient rules and supervisory mechanisms at both the national and international level."[72] The rules are seen as necessary to prevent sudden collapses of investor confidence.

Similar observations lead Drucker to conclude that there is a "need for moral, legal, and economic rules that are accepted and enforced throughout the global economy. A central challenge, therefore, is the development of international law and supranational organizations that can make and enforce rules for the global economy."[73] And Drucker is certainly not alone. Griffith Jones has similar arguments.[74]

Combining deregulation with re-regulation.   It seems evident that there is some ambiguity concerning regulation. We see that traditional regulation is being removed in order to further growth in the global economy. Now we hear voices raised in favour of some kind of regulation, a new regulation, but presumably one that repeats the arguments of earlier national regulation, now at a transnational or global level. Here we have to remember the aim of *de*regulation has been to promote trade, economic growth and general prosperity.

In contrast the clamour for new regulation has been directed at topics like the containment of the economic logic, international capital movements, product safety, the environment, working conditions, human rights, questions of democracy and of course social responsibility.

While there are many forms of overlap, it would also seem that the clamour for regulation represents something new, something that may not hitherto have been regulated, realising of course that there may be a connection between increased growth, trade, productivity rises and the new concerns that have led to the voicing of demands for new regulation.

In some instances it would seem that we are talking about the re-regulation of areas that have been deregulated in recent years. Capital movements that have been nationally regulated are now deregulated or in the process of deregulation. Here the demand is for re-regulation on a supranational level, a regulation that will supposedly level the playing field for the global players and establish boundaries to this field.

On a more detailed level the demand is for regulation that will improve the right kind of competition. Thus the Trade and Competition Policy Forum of the International Chamber of Commerce reluctantly reaches the conclusion that for instance antidumping laws are "the only instrument available to counteract unfair trade practices ..."[75]

The demands for regulation or even prohibition of products with GMOs represents something new, something that has not been regulated, and could not have been regulated because it was non-existent until advances in genetic research made such products available.

This also goes for the regulation and prohibition of gases like CFC or the attempt to find ways to curb the growth in CO_2 in order to reduce the emission of greenhouse gases into the atmosphere. The knowledge that CFCs and CO_2 might contribute to disastrous changes in the environment is new, and so is this regulation, although of course it may seem to remind one of the more local ordinances demanding higher chimneys in order to reduce local pollution.

Charters, declarations and regulation in relation to human rights and working conditions are not in the same way a result of new knowledge, but the topics may be new in the sense that we act on the basis of changed values. We are more concerned about human rights and working conditions on a global basis than we have ever been, and this is new, and so is the demand for public intervention in the cases where human rights are violated.

In the end it turns out that arguments for combining deregulation of certain areas with regulation and re-regulation of others may not seem inconsistent, or be the result of the activities of a vacillating brain.

Extending regulation while avoiding an erosion of responsibility? In earlier chapters we emphasised that the focus on public regulation of behaviour has led to all sorts of problems. We have argued very emphatically that regulation in particular would tend to reduce what we termed the vague and undefined part of both universal and special responsibilities, in effect eroding individual responsibility, substituting instead a very specific institutional responsibility, a responsibility only owed in specific, rule-bound circumstances, in other words a responsibility defined by public regulation in the shape of laws or other kinds of rules.

Smart schemes using prices to influence behaviour leaving the rest to the economic logic and individual utility calculations may not be subject to quite the same criticism. They seem to leave more room for market forces and for individual inventiveness. Still, whatever their merits, the smart schemes do very little to change the attitudes of the people whose behaviour is influenced. If the price of petrol is doubled or even trebled within a short time span, it may certainly lead to changes in behaviour, reduction in the amount of kilometres driven and a reduction in the sales of "gas-guzzling" cars. The results would seem fine to someone concerned

about the consumption of fossil fuels, as individual consumers and industry probably would change their behaviour. Such schemes would not
strangle the logic we have talked about, it would just alter the direction
this logic is moving in. The bottom line would still be important, no
other considerations have to creep in, one does not have to change one's
attitude.

This is stated quite clearly: "Rather than seeking to affect the psyche
of the business person, it seeks to change the entries in her payoff matrix
in such a way that when she pursues her own goals, she unwittingly and
automatically is led – by a strengthened invisible hand – to work towards
those of society ..."[76]

And, Heureka, once more the almost invisible hand does the job.
Recent recommendations can be found in the field of resource and
environmental economics, where one may find schemes like markets for
pollution – or perhaps more euphemistically – emission rights.[77]

This would also seem to be the problem with these smart schemes.
They do not really make us more responsible, we act as if we have become
more responsible, but we have not. We are in a way forced to behave
responsibly. In fact it may be presumed that the problems of individual
irresponsibility may become larger.

In conclusion we have to say that the new forms of regulation do not
avoid the criticism levelled at traditional regulation. Regulation will still
lead to the problematic effects we saw in the first chapters and so with a
solution mainly based on public intervention we will have painted ourselves into a corner. To avoid the problems related to regulation we have
to look for alternative ways of responding to the concerns and the raised
voices. We see the problem, but at the moment we only have a vague idea
of how to get out of this corner without waiting for the paint to dry.

The responsibilities of political decision makers.   Political decision makers
are the arbiters of many different demands, they cannot just represent the
single-issue view of some interest group. They owe a universal responsibility to everyone in society. One is reminded of Sartre's existentialist
demand: "When a man commits himself to anything, fully realising that
he is not only choosing what he will be, but is thereby at the same time a
legislator deciding for the whole of mankind – in such a moment a man
cannot escape from the sense of complete and profound responsibility"
(italics added).

If political decision makers cannot take up this responsibility, they certainly cannot demand that we, the public, must show a responsibility reaching further than the tip of our noses. That is to say we look for the same extended sense of responsibility that we have discussed earlier. Schmidt[78] talks of politicians with "Leidenschaft, Augenmaß, und Verantvortungsbewußtsein." To Schmidt this means that the aims and actions of a politician must rest upon certain basic values. "Eine Politik ohne Grundwerte is zwangsläufig gewissenlos, sie ist eine Politik der moralischen Beliebigkeit und tendiert zum Verbrechen."[79]

A political decision maker who is just reflecting public opinion cannot act as a voice for deeper more latent concerns, and cannot act as a catalyst for changes in society made necessary by these concerns.

Discerning the voices showing characteristics of universal responsibility and representing the long waves of change. Even though I am sure that no politician can afford to ignore a strong public opinion, especially not in the modern democracies, where the mass media play an important role, I agree with Etzioni that public opinion is suspicious as a criterion for listening and acting, for the reasons already given. Instead one might look for the concerns and voices that seem to represent a genuine universal responsibility. At least these voices do not just act in their own interest; they may want influence to carry their views through, but they do not represent established and entrenched interests guarding what power and influence they already have.

It may also be important to listen to what I, for want of a better expression, call the long waves of change. Instead of listening to and acting upon day-to-day issues raised in the media, political decision makers may in fact adjust to the same forces of change that make every one of us aware, sooner or later, that certain issues are expressions of major shifts in society, whether they are caused by scientific and technological development or social and cultural changes. Examples of long waves of change may be found among issues that have been discussed earlier, like the concern for the runaway logic, the concern for the environment, the concern for human rights and so on.

Other issues representing long-term changes may be globalisation of the economies, the reduced influence of nation states, the problems of modern welfare states and of course our own concerns as they were discussed in earlier chapters.

In a somewhat vague way one might reflect that these fundamental changes show themselves to be important through the sheer number and intensity of problems that they give rise to. Although we may have been the cause of these waves, we cannot really see them before we observe and experience the multitude of problems and dilemmas that all seem related to these basic issues.

The task for politicians would be to discuss ways and means to tackle these more fundamental changes, and perhaps devise possible solutions, involving of course new types of regulation, for instance like the international climate protocols which seem to represent a new type of worldwide regulation. There is one caveat though, detailed regulation is subject to the criticism voiced earlier. What is needed is a regulation that would leave more to individual responsibility.

Encouraging self-organisation and self-regulation.   What may be important is to reflect the demands raised by the many interest groups back onto them, in effect seeing that one of the major tasks before us is to change the mindset of all those who have lost their sense of universal responsibility and perhaps also of their own abilities. This would mean that political decision makers should become very wary of making all sorts of *ad hoc* regulations satisfying perhaps this or that interest group or solving a small problem.

Instead the efforts of government might be directed at encouraging self-organisation and self-regulation of individuals, of local communities and of businesses. This would encourage and demand that individuals and organisations show a universal and vague responsibility, instead of giving in to requests to create ever more areas with a limited, special and specific responsibility, or, in other words, institutional solutions.

The idea would be that we should change our mindset, reduce the demands on a state more and more incapable of solving problems caused by the logic we have described. Instead we should take responsibility for alleviating and solving the problems where we stand. In fact this might help liberate our own minds. Instead of thinking that someone else must do something to solve a given problem, even problems caused by us, it might after all be possible to find an alternative in self-regulation, a self-regulation not based upon a detailed public statute, but based upon our own deep values and a reawakened sense of universal and vague responsibility.

RESPONSIBLE ENTREPRENEURSHIP

In our opening play Dr Stockman was the one who had discovered the qualities of the water originally, and now he was the one to warn against it and propose costly changes to get rid of the pollution. Without stating it he was in fact attempting to break with the logic and the result was that the logic broke him.

With this in mind we may ask whether there is a possibility for breaking, containing or changing the direction of the logic from within the logic itself. In other words, is it possible for a single or a few entrepreneurs to change the logic in such a way that external regulation is avoided or reduced, while finding answers to the concerns that have been raised? Is it possible to get around the reaction of all the Toms of this world selling leather footballs made by children, or all the Joe Kellers of this world installing faulty aircraft engines,[80]while arguing "it makes no difference whether I do or don't?" Without, that is, getting windows smashed by the stone-throwing youth of the town, or being voted an enemy of the people by a majority, or losing a business, or job and reputation.

In order to discuss this possibility we have to look at different, but possibly related aspects of the issue. The aspects to be discussed may range from the activities of the individual Dr Stockmans of this world, to responsible entrepreneurs, and to self-organising and self-regulating in certain business sectors, from "*one* must know it!" to a more general change in attitude and practice.

Fundamental changes in attitudes towards the environment in smaller or larger sections of the population open up a space for responsible entrepreneurship. When crusaders and preachers of the rights of animals turn the attitudes of large sections of the population against using animals for testing cosmetics, entrepreneurs experimenting with alternative products may see their chance and seize the opportunity to produce and sell products that may at least go part of the way towards satisfying the new demands of these sections of the population.

Is this not the only way to explain the success of concepts like Bodyshop and smaller contemporaries?[81] These companies show that they have understood some of the longer waves of change in the values and attitudes of people, and they react with what is within their means to come up with as a solution. It may not be much but it opens up a new vista of possibilities and it shows the way that one has to think in the future, if one wants to continue doing business.

Of course we have to realise that not all businesses show responsible entrepreneurship. Some may only show exploitative entrepreneurship by riding on a wave of environmental concern and offering the strange Potemkin-like answers to the clamour for environmental concern. This might be called cause-related marketing in that the company relates itself to a good cause.

The alternative would be to grab this genuine concern and use one's expertise in a certain field of production, to experiment and develop better and better answers to this concern, giving a concrete form to emerging values, and raising the expectations of all those having this general concern. No one else but those with this special knowledge will presumably be able to create the new alternatives to existing practices. The crusaders and preachers may neither have the means nor the knowledge to do it.

An example might be the development of the 3-litre car. Although Greenpeace had expert help in developing a very fuel-efficient showcar based on a well-known small car, it did not seem to represent a palatable alternative to existing cars. What was important was instead that many car manufacturers and engineers apparently became convinced that they had to devote considerable energy to the development of very fuel-efficient cars, one result of these efforts being Volkswagen's 3-litre per 100 km Lupo.[82] Without the effort of engineers possessed by an attitude that reflected some of the emerging values, it might be difficult to see how the new and more efficient technologies could ever evolve.

The appeal for state regulation may represent a very clumsy attempt to force through changes in production processes and products. Neither the crusaders, nor the state need possess the knowledge and technological possibilities that for instance a whole car industry possesses. This is the crux of the matter; the crusaders may voice the problem, and the state might attempt to regulate by limiting the amount of dangerous emissions, but it does not possess the ability to create alternatives. Now why should it not be possible to create new solutions through state regulation instead? The state might set goals for the achievement of certain emission limits for instance and demand that industry lives up to these limits. It may initiate and finance new solutions, helping bring about solutions to the problems voiced.

To see why this might not work very well, one might compare state regulation to an algorithmic program running on a von Neuman-type of computer, while the manifold individual search guided by changes in values and attitudes might be compared to an artificial neural network running on a massive parallel computer. In one case we would have to guide the whole effort from above; someone would have to state the problem and indicate the direction, in a research programme for instance, while the solution based on individual businesses picking up the changes in values and attitudes divides the work of creating new solutions among many nodes, many more than a state apparatus would ever possess. This argument is in fact similar to the old arguments against command economies, as found in the works of say von Mises or Hayek.

What is advocated here is in fact that the creation of solutions to environmental problems and even problems of human rights violations demands the active creation of new solutions by myriads of people experimenting with new approaches, thereby gaining new knowledge, and competing for support for their alternative attempts. To get going they would somehow have to reflect the concerns of the crusaders in their own fields of expertise, letting the changes in attitudes guide their own work. In fact they would become crusaders in their own right within their field of expertise. What I am emphasising here is the importance of reflecting the new values in their own practice, because this is what will drive and guide them in their search for alternatives.

The textbook assertion that business should just cater to the demands of the consumers might turn out to be rather too simplistic here. Consumers may of course be influenced by the crusaders and preachers. They may change their attitudes and values, and become dissatisfied with existing solutions, but they may not have the knowledge necessary to see how the new values and attitudes might influence the products and services that they are buying. In a certain way one might say that consumers do not know what their demands are in relation to the changes in values and to what degree they may be fulfilled.

Business may have this possibility. This means that business has to persuade the consumer that the new products might be the answer to the concerns and worries voiced. Business itself must help create new concrete expectations, thereby turning the simplistic version according to which one should just listen to the consumers upside down.

To see what this means we may even use the difficult issues of human rights or more specifically children's rights. As a result of activities of social movements consumers may come to know that some of the products they are buying may be based on child labour. The short-circuit solution to this is to have the state ban the import of such products, with the result that the children may be worse off than before. Or even simpler, to have businesses bring forth certificates from their suppliers, guaranteeing that no child or forced labour has been involved. A more considerate approach may involve attempts by responsible entrepreneurs to create changes in working conditions for the children, and guaranteeing this by involving themselves in all stages of the process.[83]

Instead of bans and attempts to regulate the logics we have talked about, this might represent a solution working with the logic. This is a solution where the logic is redirected and contained in practice, by business itself. By business putting the ear to the ground and listening for the long waves of change, not the fluctuating attention of so-called political consumers, in their vacillating vogues.[84]

The first to put their ear to the ground will presumably be those who have some of the mentality of the crusaders. They see the need for a change of direction, and instead of waiting for public regulation to make changes mandatorily they somehow see the opportunities opening up before them, when new values are spreading through the population, and begin their own attempts to do things in a different way.

They may be represented by the first ecological farmers, the first zealots believing that they represent the future, and insisting that traditional non-ecological farming will have to change. They may come up against the logic we have talked about so many times now, the "force" that a single individual supposedly cannot hope to cope with, the argument that it does not matter whether I do or I don't. These people are trying to prove that it is possible and that one does matter. Invariably some of the early crusaders will fail, or will have to depend on a small niche production, but they represent the first trials and errors of the error-trial-error-trial-success model of change.

Perhaps one might venture to say that they are not different in this sense from the early pioneers of personal computing, with many falling by the wayside and latecomers exploiting the market that they helped create. It may be a similar kind of zealousness that drives them, a zealousness derived from the conviction that this is right, that this is the direction we have to move in. Without this zealousness it is hardly to be expected that the first trials will ever be made.

Even the most driven responsible entrepreneurs will not know where the quest will end, they just have the drive to begin the journey. The process may turn out to represent a tortuous trial-and-error process, where one has to learn as one goes along, experimenting, rejecting, improving, discovering.

The experience of Patagonia, producing outdoor clothing, mountain equipment and so on, may be typical. In the 1980s Patagonia was an early advocate and manufacturer of clean climbing equipment. Then their attention was turned inward. In the words of the company: "We realized how our own business was contributing to the destruction of ecosystems. Although we long had an office recycling program and made early forays into improving energy efficiency, we gave little attention to the impacts associated with the products themselves. In 1990, we set out to learn more about the impacts that our products had on the environment."[85] As a result of this inward looking the company began to improve what they were doing, "switching to organic cotton, incorporating fiber from recycled plastic bottles in almost all of our fleece products, and adopting a wide variety of green building techniques for our stores and facilities."

According to company statements this was not enough: "We have come to understand much about the ways in which our business practices and our products harm the environment (more research and analysis are continually required) but we must now give specific attention to reducing the impacts of our products."

One of their findings was that conventionally grown cotton was destructive: "One of many reasons why: 25% of the world's synthetic insecticide used is used on cotton, even though cotton production uses up a tiny fraction of arable lands." The solution was to use only organic cotton and PCR (post consumer recycled) material, like plastic bottles.

This small example is intended to show that the development of new manufacturing processes and products seems to be guided by the certain values, and beliefs, here evidently a concern for the environment. In a way it is to be assumed that Patagonia did not wait for the consumers' demands. Instead they were catering to latent concerns about the environment and showing possible solutions, thereby presumably creating their own demand.

Other companies seem to have followed a similar evolution, getting deeper and deeper into the matter, giving values and attitudes a very concrete form in the shape of production processes and products, business philosophies and employee relations.

The Danish Company Novotex, with the product called "Green Cotton", seems to have followed a similar development, with the founder and CEO becoming more and more smitten by what he was doing, in fact becoming a crusader in his own right.[86]

Other often used examples might be found in Reder's book *In Pursuit of Principle and Profit*.[87] Many of his cases seem to demonstrate the searching and stumbling way that pioneer businesses develop new production processes and products from a few basic ideas and values.

In a policy statement on responsible entrepreneurship the International Chamber of Commerce talks of the need for responsive and responsible entrepreneurship as "a driving force for sustainable economic development" emphasising that responsible entrepreneurship "speaks to a more flexible, market driven and innovative response."[88] This seems to fit reasonably well with the viewpoint presented here.

SELF-ORGANISED AND SELF-REGULATED CHANGE

The efforts of those who succeed will soon be mimicked by others with less zeal but with more sense of the financial opportunities, by large established companies seeing an opportunity opening, for instance a market evolving as a result of new production methods and new products. Perhaps even a market for leather footballs made by children, but under a programme with schooling and good working conditions.

When an idea spreads it creates the opportunity for a kind of collective action, for self-organisation of the like-minded businesses, and for self-regulation. Although we still have to discern between business organisations that promote certain values in a more peripheral way and organisations that somehow signify that they want to build their businesses on certain core principles. From the more general version that may be found in the shape of Rotary and various round tables to the more dedicated groups that organise for instance groups of ecological producers.

It seems significant though that several new organisations recently have been created around values that seem to reflect the concerns, voices and responsible entrepreneurs we have just discussed. This would indicate that at least some groups of business leaders have seen the light and want to do something to further the emerging values.

One such example is the Caux Round Table started in 1986. In an executive summary it is stated that this round table "exists to promote principled business leadership and responsible corporate practice on the basis of jointly held values reflected in the CRT [Caux Round Table] *Principles for Business*. It believes that business, which provides three-fourths of the world's employment and possesses enormous resources, must play a key role in solving the problems that impede the development of a global society that is more prosperous, sustainable and equitable."[89]In the principles it is also recognised that "Law and market forces are necessary, but insufficient guides for conduct."[90] We can only agree.

A glimpse of the core beliefs of the Caux Round Table shows that they reflect the concerns voiced earlier, even when stating the obvious, that the primary responsibility in a corporation is to conduct its operations proficiently. More interesting are the following excerpts from the core beliefs:"

- Corporations must be increasingly responsive to issues affecting the physical, social and economic environments not only because of their impact on business performance but also out of a proactive sense of responsibility to all constituencies served.
- Corporations need to consider the balance between the short-term interests of shareholders and the longer-term interests of the enterprise and its stakeholders.
- Meeting the traditional objectives and performance criteria is not sufficient. Voluntary standards which exceed the requirements of prevailing law and regulations are necessary to the development of sustainable practices. Society's "licence or franchise to operate" has to be earned.
- Corporations should lead by example through business practices that are ethical and transparent, and that reflect a commitment to human dignity, political and economic freedoms, and preservation of the planet.
- Corporations cannot act alone but should seek to address key global issues through cooperative efforts with governments, other institutions and local communities.[91]

Here we find most of the concerns voiced in the former sections. In the *Principles for Business* they are elaborated even further. As we see them they are only on paper and on the Internet of course, and so at the moment the only interesting thing about them is that they are made by representatives of big business on a global basis. In fact they represent nothing more than business' own reflection of the concerns voiced, not answers, not collective experiences that can act as models for the rest of business. Although it certainly seems to be self-organised, we do not really see the self-regulating part.

What is missing here is therefore the action part, and perhaps also some decisions as to what has the highest priority. A less sympathetic reading might show that there is a belief in exactly the logic that has caused at least part of the problems that ought to be alleviated. But of course paper as a material is patient and very tolerant towards inconsistent statements.

The attempt to combine the efficiency of the market forces with an extended sense of social responsibility of business also seems to be the goal of the royally protected Prince of Wales Business Leaders Forum. In a millennium campaign they will explore the theme of "Human Capitalism: Values in Leadership for the 21st Century." The Leaders Forum "campaigns globally and locally to promote social responsibility and cross-sector partnerships for business, the public sector and civil society." The forum participates in partnership programmes involving the World Bank, organisations under the United Nations and local organisations to promote its goals. Apart from that they are actively engaged in furthering specific themes and local activities in regions around the world.

Here we see some action, but also the media-related efforts with the intention of emphasising "the values and inspirations" that are the foundation for "Human Capitalism,"[92] or is it capitalism with a human face?

The International Chamber of Commerce argues: "An important aspect of voluntary initiatives by industry has been the transformation of EHS [Environmental Health and Safety] management from an individual company activity to the responsibility of a group of like-minded companies representing significant segments of a nation's industrial production."[93]

With like-minded companies joining the effort to exercise responsible entrepreneurship, the containment of the traditional logic and radical changes in the direction of the logic become possible.

In the area of Environmental Health and Safety management the ICC believes the following factors will support collective and voluntary self-organisation and regulation:

- Agreement among participating companies that successful EHS management can be shared to promote collective performance improvement.
- Peer pressure among companies driven by an understanding that the failure of one company to deliver on its commitment threatens the entire group's licence to operate.
- Input from interested parties or stakeholders both within and outside the industry which continually emphasises their expectations and raises industry performance.
- Belief that given the opportunity to innovate and introduce flexibility into their response to regulation, companies can meet or exceed regulatory and stakeholder expectations.[94]

What is interesting to note in relation to the ICC factors is that they seem to assume that direction originates outside the market mechanism, and that the market mechanism is somehow to be guided by these considerations.

To illustrate the importance of the point on peer pressure one may just think of the effects that disclosure of instances where ecological producers have cheated the consumers have had on the credibility of the rest. Such attempts by individual businesses to exploit the changes in values through Potemkin-like faked responsibility may be averted through a kind of self-control and self-regulation among the businesses involved. When self-control and self-regulation are lacking or are not working, it will lead to demands for public intervention making use of labels, standards, rules, controls and sanctions to make compliance credible. This would paint us back into the corner of the earlier discussion.

The neutral term "input from interested parties or stakeholders" would include exactly the kind of pressure discussed in the previous sections; we would not expect the more idealistic and unrealistic version of stakeholder involvement to play a big role, except on paper that is.

As regards the last point, we agree that this is in fact the only way to prevent a more or less solid iron cage of public regulation being introduced, with the attendant problems we have touched upon earlier.

While the attempts of the Caux Round Table, the PWBLF, the ICC and other organisations[95] may be regarded as conscious collective efforts of self-organisation and self-regulation, a different kind of unpremeditated and unconscious self-organisation and self-regulation may be much more important in containing and changing the direction of the logic. What I am talking about is the kind of mechanism that we discussed in Chapter 6 on the weaving of the moral fabric; the adjustment we all perform, when we conform to fashion vogues, the adjustment we perform when being part of a social group. In other words the mutual mimicking process that does not demand that we meet and create committees or business round tables in order to make our views conform.

It would be too simplistic to say that this is the same as adjusting to the market, although it may work partly through the market. If a company does not adjust, it will lose business. But the process works outside the market too. Several companies may react to the voicing of concerns, and converge in their attempts to find ways to answer these concerns, without any attempt to coordinate efforts. Their activities may be imitated or even taken over by others, and suddenly business has changed. The logic has changed direction and has been contained. Considerations hitherto ignored become important in the decision processes of the company and in production processes and products.

Processes outside the economic logic are important in giving direction to the whole logic. The logic in itself does not contain any sense or direction. The processes we have described may be important in legislating values, arraying priorities, praising and condemning and thus be goal-setting, while the logic of the market contains no priorities, no values, no end, no purpose, … but "liberates the enormous energies contained within self-interest."

Managers must realise that they are legislators "deciding for the whole of mankind," and that they are not only "doers and commanders, but catalysts and cultivators of a self-organizing system in an evolving context."[96]

NOTES

[1]   Arthur Miller (1994), *An Enemy of the People,* p. 71. Adapted from Henrik Ibsen's En Folkefiende.

[2]   Ibid., p. 98.

3   This of course is an important aim in the EU. Witness for instance the EU Commission's white paper: *Completing the Internal Market* from 1985. A comprehensive discussion of these issues can also be found in Tsoukalis (1997).

4   The internal market in the EU has the aim of deregulating a long series of branches and abolishing all non-tariff barriers to the movement of capital goods, people and services.

5   Baumol & Blackman (1991).

6   Ibid., p 5.

7   Ibid., p. 13.

8   Soros (1998), p. 114, passim. Notice the reference to Popper's "The Open Society and its Enemies."

9   In October 1999 chairman Robert Shapiro of Monsanto announced that the company would no longer experiment with terminator technologies. Apparently this decision was a result of widespread protests against terminator seeds.

10 Drucker (1997), p. 168.

11 Ibid., p. 162. See also Griffith-Jones (1999).

12 Forrester (1997), p. 42.

13 Judt (1997), p. 109.

14 Soros (1998), Forrester (1997) and Schmidt (1998).

15 Paul et al. (1993), Paul et al. (1985), Sen (1985), Sen (1987), Lunati (1997), Griffith-Jones (1999) and Yergin & Stanislaw (1999).
    Others are: Buchanan (1985), Buchanan (1978), Brittan & Hamlin (1995), Crouch & Marquand (1993), Blau (1993), Blumberg (1989), Shand (1990) and Sufrin (1989).

16 The protesting French students have created a post-autistic economics network (paecon) on the Internet. It can be found at http://www.btinternet.com/~pae_news/index.htm.

17 Statement by the Prince of Wales Business Leaders Forum: "Why we do it."

18 "The Case for a Global Economy." The International Chamber of Commerce. Found at http://iccwbo.org/home/menu_case_for _the_global_economy.

19 Overview of issues discussed at the Consultative Forum, Trade and Policy Forum, The International Chamber of Commerce.

20 See Treaty of Rome, Article 85.

21 This is also a view found in Bennett (1997). See also Vogel (1998).

22 Schmidt (1998), p. 109.

23 Arrow (1973b), p. 303.

24 Ibid., p. 314.

25 *"Det angår os alle", om virksomhedernes sociale medansvar* (1999). København: Socialministeriet.

26 Holt (1998), pp. 24–26.

27 Ibid., pp. 36–37.

28 See for instance Kylling (1994), *Sociale Regnskaber – et værktøj til virksomhedens udvikling* (1998).

29 This is indirectly admitted in the report. See for instance Holt (1998), p. 48 and passim.

30 This refers to the story of General Grigori Aleksandrovich Potemkin's Hollywood-like sham villages, built to impress Empress Catherine on her inspection tour of the Crimea 1787. I suspect the story is apocryphal, but the trick is not.

31 *Corporate Social Responsibility* (1998), p. 5.

32 The story was told by the CEO of Hewlett Packard Denmark at a Business confere-nce about attracting and keeping employees, arranged by Junior Chamber Odense (29 October 1998).

33 Waddock & Graves (1997), p. 2.

34 The necessity of focusing on some of the core issues is recognised by the World Business Council for Sustainable Development. As a result of discussions in this forum they have drawn up a loose list of priority issues for social responsibility, involving: Human rights, Worker rights, Environment, Community involvement, Supplier relations, Monitoring and other Stakeholder rights (*Corporate Social Responsibility* 1998).

35 Soros (1998).

36 On this subject see for instance Bok (1993), Kay, I.T. (1997) and Jensen & Murphy. (1990).

37 Recently there have been a spate of publications on the subject of shareholder values. Here are just some examples, with Rappaport's book apparently being in widespread use as a reference: Rappaport (1997), Charkham & Simpson (1999), Black et al. (1998), Knight (1997) and Kay, I. T. (1997). Knight's book is interesting from another viewpoint. It shows that value-based management is a somewhat ambiguous term, meaning both management with emphasis on pecuniary values and the opposite, and management with a focus on for instance ethical values.

38 The theory of agency in relation to economics and business is explained in Pratt & Zeckhauser (1985). In Freeman and Bowie one finds a serious attempt to combine and enlarge the theories of agency to include the stakeholders, in effect combining theories of agency and stakeholding (Freeman & Bowie 1992).

39 Kay, J. (1997).

40 Freeman (1984), p. 46.

41 Donaldson & Preston (1995).

42 Freeman (1984) quoted in Donaldson & Preston (1995), p. 11.

43 See for instance Kelly et al. (1997). Prime Minister Tony Blair is one of the more eloquent proponents of this all encompassing view of stakeholding.

44 Hutton (1997), p. 3.

45 Stakeholder concepts are also popping up in the public sector. Thus Alstott and Ackerman in a recent book talk about the stakeholder society (Alstott & Ackerman 1999) McCormick uses the same notion to describe the agenda for New Labour in Great Britain, with talk of corporate governance the dispersion of opportunities, and the creation of an enabling welfare state, succeeding one that may have been more disabling (McCormick 1997).

46 Darling (1997), p. 18.

47 Kay, J. (1997).

48 Drucker (1997), p. 168

49 Willetts (1997).

50 *Responsible Entrepeneurship* (1998) International Chamber of Commerce at http://www.iccwbo.org/home/statements_.../statements/1998/final_responsible.as.

51 Elfstrom (1991), p. 7.

52 See for example Meyer and Arentz (1997).

53 Habermas (1981).

54 *OECD Principles of Corporate Governance* (1998). Paris: OECD. Preamble.
    A strange example of "stakeholder involvement" is offered by the software giant SAP AG. In their effort to create software to help bring about what they call value-based management, where it must be emphasised that the value they talk about is shareholder value, SAP have designed solutions that will help a company to manage stakeholder relationships. This subsystem can help the company to communicate enterprise strategy, plans and initiatives to the different stakeholder groups, and also serve to collect data on stakeholder expectations. In this way the company can manage the expectations of its stakeholders. It would seem that at least in this case stakeholders are more or less equal to shareholders and customers. (SAP SEM – Enabling Value Based Management 1999). Somewhat in the same vein, but stating the purpose more brazenly, is the so-called Stakeholder grassroots management system, "in the control of today's sophisticated Public Affairs professional, STAKEHOLDER provides tremendous leverage for moving opinions on public policy." (A description of the system is found at http://www.stakeholder.com/grassroots.html.).

55 Sommers (1978), p. 16.

56 This finding was of course very convenient to those criticising Concorde.

57 For their work the three scientists received the Nobel prize in Chemistry in 1995.

58   Beck (1986).

59   The anti-nuclear movement reaches back to the voicing of concerns about using the atomic bomb by scientists like Leo Szilard and others in the 1940s, and it is connected to later peace movements.

60   Birkland (1997).

61   Gordon and Miyake argue that voluntary efforts to create codes of conduct have involved significant contributions from NGOs (Gordon & Miyake 1999).

62   Carr (1998). See also Salamon (1994).

63   Like the rainforest group Nepenthes in Denmark.

64   During 1999 this seems to have had repercussions in America, with government and agriculture seeing possible problems for GMOs as a result of the European protests. See for instance the article by Michael Kläsgen in *Die Zeit*, 23 September 1999.

65   Petersen (1994).

66   Thoreau (1849/1866). *Resistance to Civil Government, or Civil Disobedience*. The text of the small treatise can be found at http://www.vcu.edu/engweb/transweb/civil/civildisobedience.htm.

67   Habermas (1996), p. 87.

68   Saavedra, Cervantes (1998).

69   Kleist (1808/1976).

70   Sarma (1998).

71   Fields with GM seeds pollinate adjacent fields, making it impossible to keep GMOs out of an ecological production. This together with other problems will apparently mean that only products containing more than 1 per cent GMOs will have to be labelled as containing GMOs.

72   Statement made by the International Chamber of Commerce, 26 April 1999, Washington DC.

73   Drucker (1997), p. 169.

74   Griffith-Jones (1999).

75   Overview of issues discussed at the Consultative Forum, Trade and Policy Forum of the International Chamber of Commerce, 5 June 1998.

76   Baumol & Blackman (1991), p. 47.

77   See for instance Hagem & Westskog (1998).

78   Schmidt (1998).

79   Ibid., p. 58.

80   Referring of course to Arthur Miller's play *All My Sons*.

81   An example being the Danish company Allison of Denmark, labelling at least some of its products "Uden dyreforsøg," or "Without animal testing."

82   Perhaps it is worth noting that Volkswagen also announced that they would produce a luxury car with a 12-cylinder engine to compete with the top segment of BMW and Mercedes, thus expanding at both ends so to speak.

83   According to the International Labor Organization (ILO) the number of working children is around 250 million. Here it is important to remember that most of these work in agriculture, not in the production of goods for export. To prohibit the import of footballs made by children might in fact just mean that we close our eyes to the problem. Also we have to remember that to some developing countries the efforts by developed countries to ban products made by children is seen as a way of banning the cheap products of these countries. This issue was apparently also discussed at the unsuccessful WTO meeting in Seattle in December 1999.

84   Noting of course the seeming contradiction in listening to long waves, while ignoring the vogues, which of course also have something to do with waves.

85   Statements found on the home pages of the Patagonia Company.

86   See for instance Dafolo Development (1992).

87   Reder (1995).

88   *Responsible Entrepeneurship* (1998) International Chamber of Commerce at http://www.iccwbo.org/home/statements_.../statements/1998/final_responsible.as.

89   *The Critical Role of the Corporation in a Global Society*. Position Paper, Caux Round Table. Found at www.cauxroundtable.org/ES_Role.htm.

90   Preamble of *Principles for Business*. Caux Round Table.

91   From *Core beliefs*. Caux Round Table. Found at www.cauxroundtable.org/CORE_BEL:HTM.

92   The Millennium Campaign of the Prince of Wales Business Leaders Forum.

93   *Responsible Entrepeneurship* (1998) International Chamber of Commerce at http://www.iccwbo.org/home/statements_.../statements/1998/final_responsible.as.

94   Ibid.

95   Like for instance: Business in the Community and Sustainable Business Network, or organisations like Transparency International, Corporate Watch and for instance Investors in Social economy (Les Investisseurs de l'Economie Sociale or INAISE). These types of organisations and corporations seem to proliferate at the moment.

96   Foerster (1984), p. 2.

8 Self-organising solutions

ORGANISATION AND LEADERSHIP – A BOY'S GAME?

In Golding's novel *Lord of the Flies*[1] a group of young British boys, who are the sole survivors of an air crash, land on an isolated and uninhabited island. They are left to their own devices, with no adults to help them, and like all survivors in such a situation they will have to find ways and means to support themselves, find something to eat and drink, find a place to sleep and soon they will also have to think about what they can do to enhance their chances of rescue.

In this instance they seem to see their predicament as some sort of game, for the moment content to be free of the adults and free to play as they like, although the fat boy Piggy is terrified of having no adults to take charge or to guide them. Piggy represents the voice of logic and reasoning found in the grown-up world they have left. He strives for some sort of law and order. He wants to hold a meeting, to make up a list of the survivors and so on.

Together with Ralph, the boy with fair hair, he finds a conch shell, and suggests that it can be used as a horn for calling the others from the jungle in order to hold a meeting. Among those emerging, when the sound of the conch is heard, are Jack and a gang of black-clad boys with badges, part of a choir in fact. At the meeting Ralph proposes that they should have a chief, who would then decide what they should do. Jack, who is already leader of the black gang, argues that he must be chief. In the end though Ralph is elected chief, in opposition to Jack.

It is soon evident that Jack does not want to submit to Ralph. This means that the boys separate into two groups because of disagreement about the way the game should be played.

Jack and the black-clad gang leave the others. At this stage it seems evident that we have the beginning of a conflict between a fat and ridiculed Piggy representing the voice of reason and civility, and a strong black Jack representing the beastly side cut loose from the voice of reason and the norms of the society they have left.

A new meeting is called. At the meeting rules are established, for instance that everyone respects the conch as a symbol of authority, meaning that everyone has to listen to the boy who holds the conch. Piggy makes the suggestion that they should build a fire to make smoke signals that could be seen by ships happening to pass by. They decide to build the fire in a concerted effort using Piggy's glasses to light the fire.

Later on some of the littl'uns, the small boys, are being harassed by members of Jack's gang. Nothing serious, but like in a good thriller one gets a sense of something sinister approaching. Perhaps the beast that one of the littl'uns has nightmares about is closing in.

A ship passes by but cannot observe any smoke signal, because Jack's gang has abandoned the fire to hunt for pigs. This leads to new strife between Jack the hunter and Ralph the chief, when Jack returns with the pig they have killed.

Ralph calls a new meeting because things are not working out too well. They make decisions in meeting, but the decisions are not carried out. Water ought to be fetched, but it is not being done and there are many other tasks that they have agreed upon, which no one does anything about. Then there is the matter of the beast they all, except Piggy, feel is closing in on them.

By and by the few rules that they had agreed upon are being ignored and Ralph seems to realise that their small society is unravelling; that the laws of their society are breaking down. Piggy is becoming scared, at home there was always an adult one could ask but here there is no one to ask, no one to take charge.

In a strange encounter with a head of a dead body crawling with flies, Simon realises that the beast is part of each and everyone of them, which it is found deep inside them. "Fancy thinking the Beast was something you could hunt and kill! You knew, didn't you? I'm part of you?"

Boys steal away from Ralph and Piggy to join Jack's gang, and with this Jack gains power, and quietly becomes the chief. Even Ralph and Piggy join the group around the fire where a pig is being cooked, while the gang is carrying out a pagan ritual pretending to kill a pig, shouting and chanting. In the darkness something staggers out of the darkness. The boys attack the beastly thing – and kill Simon.

In a later confrontation between the black gang and the remnants of Ralph's group Piggy screams: "Which is better – to have rules and agree, or to hunt and kill?" The answer is a boulder hurled down from Jack's fortress. Piggy is struck by the boulder, is carried over a ledge and falls to his death.

Ralph escapes, but he seems to be losing his sanity, and he is hunted by Jack's gang.

In a final scene Ralph runs out into the ocean, right into the arms of a naval officer.

It is obvious that something went awfully awry in this boy's game. This is the thrilling story of how an early attempt to recreate a kind of civil society disintegrated. Slowly and imperceptibly at first and then accelerating to a beastly end.

In their game the boys first made an attempt to reproduce some of the structure of civil society as they knew it, by electing a chief, making rules, deciding upon the necessary tasks and dividing the work to be done among them. One can almost see them following a textbook on management and organisation, in an early attempt to replicate the society they had left. Surely this must be the way to do it, if they are to survive and to have a chance of being rescued.

Then comes the accelerating decline in order, in behaviour and norms. Giving way to the beast, to the breaking of those invisible strings that made it impossible for Jack to kill the first pig. The order and authority of Ralph and the conch is substituted by the arbitrary actions, the power of the hunter, "the stick sharpened at both ends", and by the man of action, who is less and less bound by the moral conventions of the society left behind.[2] The order of a civil society is being substituted by the raw power of the dark beast inside the boys. Is this perhaps the overflowing strength of the beast of Nietzsche's rearing its head in the hunters?

What happened here, why did the boys not succeed in creating a miniature copy of society? Apparently they had the physical means to do so on the island. They were not forced to eat each other, unlike what is supposed to have happened in other more or less mythical air crashes and shipwrecks.[3] Still, in the fictional story, order breaks down and shades of Hobbes' "warre of every man against every man"[4] emerge, although, as we can see in a paradoxical move, the weak fearing the beast seek the comfort of the strong boy representing the selfsame beast. In part it is the same story we find in the breakdown of order in Orwell's *Animal Farm*.[5]

And it is not only in fiction we find parallels. The story was carried out in practice in the Third Reich, where the voices of reason and morality became the hunted where Jews, slaves, handicapped people and those of another opinion in general became "*Untermenschen*," to be hunted by the forces of dark, with their twin lightning SS badges and where the littl'uns and the big'uns likewise sought shelter with the strong, but very dark forces.

The story was also replayed in more recent conflicts in the Balkans and elsewhere, where an (un)civil war brought forth the selfsame beast as found in the *Lord of the Flies*. What we see in these and many other cases is a breakdown of order and morality and a giving-in to darker forces.

We also see the story repeat itself in a non-lethal form in organisations in trouble, organisations in which we work, organisations perhaps characterised by the breakdown of civility and of norms and symbols of order and authority, organisations being slowly worn down by the undermining and cunning behaviour of people lusting for power and influence, following the urgings of their beasts. We all know our local Piggys with their insistence on reasoning and order, the well-meaning and well-liked Ralphs, who do not really seem able to carry through their intentions, the Jacks representing the darker sides of the struggle for power, and all the littl'uns who seem to shift their allegiance to the strongest.

If we look to both *Lord of the Flies* and *Animal Farm*, there does not seem to have been any lack of reason, morality or rules in the beginning. In *Animal Farm* there was an abundance of slogans and plans and rules, but ever so slowly they were altered to fit the behaviour of those in power. The rules, slogans and plans did not prevent the whole construction from breaking up, meaning that something else apart from reason and rules is necessary to prevent this from happening and to guard against the disintegration.

We see two possible solutions. In the case of the boys' game, it seems clear that authority emanating from adults, external to them, might have prevented the disintegration. Piggy was right there. The alternative is that the norms of civil society must be so ingrained that the beast already bears an invisible leash, in the shape of the moral fabric we have discussed in earlier chapters, and of course the boys must have the courage to show it.

Now, it does not take much thought to see that the external control brought about by the presence of adults must in itself rest on the same kind of moral fabric that we have discussed earlier. Thus it turns out that those internal and ineffable bindings that we have discussed earlier might be the only real constraint on any urge to give in to the demands of the beast. In fact it might, as we have asserted time and time again, be the only solid basis on which to build any kind of organisation, from business organisations and public institutions to whole societies.

SPONTANEOUS COOPERATION VERSUS MANAGED COORDINATION

A very simple example of spontaneous synchronisation may be heard every time, when the unsynchronised clapping of many hands applauding a performance changes to a synchronised clapping of many hands. A small article in a recent issue of *Nature* sees this phenomenon as an expression of social self-organisation.[6]

We previously looked at the emergence of spontaneous cooperation and coordination. In one of the scenes we saw two inexperienced rowers in a rowing boat, each having one oar, and the goal of reaching a landing stage on the other side of a lake. We expected that these rowers by some kind of tacit process, which strangely enough might even involve shouting, would sooner or later learn how to move the oars so that they would move the boat in the direction of the landing stage, with constant adjustments to assure a synchronised movement.

Another example that indicates the possibilities for spontaneous coordination is Schelling's amusing story[7] of what one would do if one had arranged to meet someone in town at say 12 noon without actually arranging where to meet. Using the local example of Copenhagen, most people having just a minimal knowledge of the physical configuration of Copenhagen tell me that they would go to stand under a well-known clock in the main railway station or go to "*Rådhuspladsen*" (the city hall square) and hope that the other person would think of the same place to meet. According to this example there is an abundance of shared tacit knowledge that one can use in order to reflect upon what another person would do. Apart from trivial spontaneous cooperation it would mean that such shared partly tacit and partly explicit knowledge is important for spontaneous coordination to take place.

Simon uses the example of a group of house painters "each fitting in where he thinks his efforts will be most effective and will interfere least with the others."[8] He assumes that most of the mutual adjustments will take place silently and without discussion, which somehow seems to assume that the group has some form of previous experience in working together.

To get a sense of the direction in which we are moving we return to the boys' game, elaborating a little on the story. Some of the tasks most of the boys had agreed upon after the first meeting were tasks essential for survival. Building a shelter, finding or hunting for food, preparing food, collecting water, nothing too complicated on an island where there seemed to be enough resources.

We want to place a magnifying glass over these tasks. We know that there was overall agreement, but what could have happened next? Are we to expect that Ralph with a little prompting from Piggy drew up detailed plans and schedules for the building of shelters and all the other tasks? Or would every one of the boys know what to do without prompting by a Ralph? Neither of these possibilities would seem realistic, Ralph and Piggy would not know precisely what to do and in what sequence, and we would not expect the boys to carry a shelter-building programme hard-wired into their brains.

What one might imagine could have happened is that the meeting might have decided upon a division into groups, a group for building shelters, a group for collecting or hunting for food and so forth. Each of the boys might elect to join one of these task groups, or might be told to do so by the elected chief.

Then the same kind of question we just raised pops up again: how would the groups go about their different tasks? Let us look at the building of some kind of shelter. Would they know what is meant by a shelter? We may suppose that they have a vague notion, a notion of primitive houses perhaps, with some kind of roof, supports and with walls for protection. So there might be a vague idea in the heads of the boys, but there is no reason to suppose that their ideas would be similar or very detailed.

There are of course many ways they could proceed. They might get someone with knowledge of shelter-building as a leader, or they might proceed without a leader. Proceeding without a leader they might start by arguing about where the shelters should be built, and whether they should have one or several. Ideas might spring back and forth and be elaborated upon by the others, in a process that might be seen as a small example of a brainstorming session.

They might not get very far, having no clear idea of anything. Still they might somehow reach a decision on the spot to be used, perhaps deciding, on the basis of shared ideas, on the need for some kind of level area, free of obstructions, perhaps using some existing structure, a cave or a stone or tree as an anchor point. Vague ideas of what is important in a shelter and what is already found in the environment might be important in reaching this decision.

Next they might have some idea of collecting materials that could be used for a roof, thinking of course of something that would be impermeable, something that water would run off, something having a certain extension, and solidity, while not being too heavy. Likewise they would need something that could support and maybe anchor the roof, something that would hold up the roof material, and perhaps constitute walls.

Each one of the boys might act with only a vague idea of the whole thing. They might look for leaves as roofing material, testing them for the purpose with their fingers, and measuring them with their eyes, still with no clear idea of how they could be fitted together as a roof, whether they would need many layers to make water run off or what. Others might find driftwood in different shapes and return with that, seeing it as potentially useful for supporting the roof and making up walls, while others might have an idea of using broken-off branches of trees for the same purpose. Someone might even find something that could be used as a string to tie the different elements together.

Many minds would be active, see, probe and discard possibilities, carry material to the spot chosen, perhaps experimenting with the ability of the branches to support weight, or testing their flexibility or their brittleness and so on. Some might start placing driftwood sticks as if they were tent poles. Others might find driftwood pieces or branches that would seem to fit the construction already begun by the others, or they might suggest alterations, additions or substitutes, realising during the construction of the shelter contraption that something will not work, and that other things can be improved.

The result of the whole unplanned and unmanaged activity of the boys might in the end be one or more shelters fulfilling the demand for shelter against rain and high winds, and for protection against animals of a certain size. The shelters might not look like much, might lack overall consistency, symmetry and a clear concept, but they might just work.

The process of coordination and cooperation we see at work here might remind us of the way the two rowers went about their task. What we would see would be a kind of mutual adjustment to the task, thus realising an overall idea that none of the boys had any clear conception of beforehand. In fact the boys might be seen as a small anthill organisation.

For some tasks the way they act may perhaps also remind us more of the robotic ants that had no purpose, and no sense. Not that the boys do not have any purpose and sense. It is just that in some instances it might actually look as if the solution they "discover" is a result of the qualities of the materials and of the environment, just as the hexagonal cells of bees are not simply a purposeful result of the mental activities of the bees, but also of characteristics of the environment. The shape of the shelter may be partly determined by the supports they found, or the quality of the roofing material they got hold of. There is no clear foresight, no conception, no plan, there is only a vague idea of what a shelter is and of the purpose it has to fulfil.

Formal organisational structures may be almost nonexistent inasmuch as everyone just goes off in search of what he believes might be relevant for the shelter. Tasks are not consciously divided up by anyone. No single boy is in command, making a productive enterprise out of the boys' resources and the material resources.

Control seems to be distributed among all the boys, more or less to be sure, but they may correct and add to each other's proposals and solutions, sometimes even without speaking, seeing for instance that someone has a problem making ends meet, someone else substitutes one of the branches for a piece of driftwood in order to solve the problem, or corrects what shows itself to be weakness of construction, by adding more support, or whatever. The boys may urge each other on, shouting at those not contributing.

The construction emerges so to speak from the mutual activities of several boys having in the beginning only vague ideas of what they are constructing, but slowly, through mutual interaction, and interaction with their environment, seeing a shelter emerge, and an idea becoming more focused and concrete. It might be said that the organisation of the boys would have the characteristics of an all channel network[9] or with everyone having the possibility of conferring and acting together with anyone else without direction, although these more traditional communication based views of organisation seem somehow insufficient for catching the self-organising richness of the possible interaction between the boys of the group. Malik talks of a "polycentric system with reciprocal, anticipatory adaption and modification of behavior by the participating persons or groups ..."[10]

During the course of these activities it might turn out slowly and quietly that one of the boys may have a clearer idea of the overall construction and the efforts needed to achieve it than the rest. This might be recognised tacitly by the rest with the result that a leader emerges, at first slowly and imperceptibly, later perhaps a little more convincingly, one that seems to focus and catalyse their joint efforts.

He might be the one to focus their energies by being more eager, by urging, by prodding, by insisting; the one to have an answer, when a boy asks, "where am I going to put these leaves?"; the one to propose a solution in the case of a stalemate between the efforts of two of the boys; the one to jump for a solution to a construction question, seeing the need to weigh carefulness against urgency.

In a case where the simultaneous coordinated effort of several individuals is necessary, "the various members of the group may merely accept one member as the 'leader' and adjust their movements to his – a group of men heaving a heavy load, for example."[11]

The strange thing here is that the spontaneous self-organisation might also create its own kind of leadership. To the mutual directedness of the boys may thus be added the other directedness of a leader focusing and unifying their efforts. He may not be a manager in the traditional sense, but he may be an expression of some of the aspects that are an integral part of leadership. He embodies focus and tacit coordination; he shows the direction they have to go without pointing. Perhaps somewhat in the same way that Jack embodied the forces of the beast. It was in this that he was a leader. Nowhere do we see him as a manager; coordination is achieved in a similar way to the coordination of the rowers in our rowing boat exercise.

Not only shelters and leadership may emerge from the activities of the boys. In the neural network of their brains new and shared knowledge of shelter-building will emerge as a result of the self-organising efforts of the brain. What this means is that the next time the boys have to build a shelter, they could draw upon their previous experience. It is to be assumed that such a situated learning experience will be important for raising the group's standards from bungling efforts to more and more purposeful and coordinated efforts, and new standards of construction.

Of course this is only a hypothetical solution to the boys' task of constructing some kind of shelter. An alternative might follow more closely along the lines of "prevoyance, organisation, commandment, controle." A boy might have been appointed by Ralph to oversee the building of shelters. He might elicit ideas from all of them, decide upon a construction and make a detailed plan. He might organise the boys, give them different tasks and instruct them what to look for.

In this solution the hierarchy of traditional management can be seen. Plans, directions, supervision, control and correction would have to come from the boy in charge. He would become a bottleneck with other boys waiting in turn for directions and answers to their questions. They would not have to act very independently; they would just have to wait for the next command telling them what to do. Communication-wise this would represent the traditional simple hierarchy or the star configuration, in which everyone would have to communicate through the hub in the centre.[12]

This might result in a kind of Balaclava like leadership. Do as you are told even if you do not think it will work, because it is not your responsibility. If management makes a blunder it is not for the employees to voice their misgivings or to reason why, as it is described so well in Tennyson's poem *The Charge of the Light Brigade*.[13]

SELF-ORGANISING AND SELF-REFERENCING SYSTEMS

When looking at the construction of African termite towers with refined ventilation ducts and other systems for keeping the right temperature in the tower, one might be forgiven for thinking that this would have to be the result of conscious design and computation by some mastermind. But here too there is no mastermind and thus these towers represent complex structures created without a mastermind and master plan.

The same goes for human anthills. There is no mastermind behind the workings of large companies, large public institutions, cities, markets and whole societies. These complex phenomena seem to emerge from the interactions of many spontaneously interacting simpler elements, in the shape of human beings, almost like the boys' helter-skelter shelter construction. Could it be that we can only create and maintain such complex organisations and institutions through the complex interactions of individuals and their environment?

In their attempt to understand and describe *Self-organization and Management of Social Systems*[14] Ulrich and Probst turn, as many others have done, to the work on autopoiesis by Maturana and Varela,[15] although autopoiesis is mainly concerned with comparatively simple biological systems and with cognition, often on a very abstract level.

In the view of Varela "an autopoietic system is organized (defined as unity) as a network of processes of production (synthesis and destruction) of components such that these components: (i) continuously regenerate and realize the network that produces them, and (ii) constitute the system as a distinguishable unity in the domain in which they exist."[16] It might be difficult to get much practical sense out of this definition at least in relation to the subject we are discussing.

Varela has an example concerning vision. Vision is seen as a result of a cooperative exercise involving a patchwork of modalities such as form, surface properties, three-dimensional spatial relationships and three-dimensional movement. A flurry of signals between these different subsets of neural activity is exchanged until a kind of coherence is achieved, leading to what we call vision. There is no central projection of the scene on an internal mental screen for the benefit of a homunculus observer. There is no central coordinator, no manager centralising the task of seeing.[17]

The interesting aspect in relation to self-organising is thus that "(i) a system can have separate local components [in] which (ii) there is no center or localized self, and yet the whole behaves as a unit and for the observer as if there was a coordinating agent 'virtually' present at the center."[18]

Looking at more fanciful illustrations we may get some idea as to why this concept might be relevant to the study of self-organisation. The anthill or termite tower would be an example of an autopoietic system, inasmuch as it continuously regenerates and realises the anthill, and exists as a distinguishable unity, without any central planning and controlling function. Perhaps the penguins in one of the newer Batman and Robin movies may also be seen as such a system. I believe that after they were programmed they were left to their own devices, creating flocks of penguins hunting through the labyrinthine streets and underground canals of Gotham City. The same idea will apparently soon be realised in a military version in the shape of the so called LOCAAS (Low Cost Autonomous Attack System),[19] which will consist of flocks of autonomous killer robots loitering over an enemy-held area.

Still this concept of self-organising seems too simple; the boys are not robot ants without any consciousness and ability to think. They are human beings, with awareness, consciousness, with memories, with the ability to reflect, not the least on the behaviour of others, and with intentionality. Their behaviour is not the behaviour of ants in an anthill. This must somehow be taken into account.

The interaction between the boys and between the boys and the environment they found made it possible to transform very vague ideas into something very concrete and tangible like a shelter. The shelter may thus be a result not of isolated individual actions, nor unconscious antlike activities, but of the interactions of a group of boys with somewhat the same consciousness and intentions of building a shelter and with somewhat congruent conceptions of what a shelter is.

Interaction with the environment is important too; the objects they find limit their possibilities and make certain solutions and physical constructions more likely than others. Think of the different conditions for building a shelter when stranded in the arctic, with only snow and ice as materials, compared to the condition found here, where trees and driftwood and palm leaves might have been available. Varela says that "living beings and their worlds of meaning stand in relation to each other through mutual specification or *co-determination*."[20]

Groups of human beings have the ability to self-reflect, to think about the consequences of their actions, to think of the responses and actions of others, to anticipate the future by foreseeing possible outcomes, to compare contemporary incidents with the past using experience and memory. "To ignore the ability to reflect may be ignoring exactly the sorts of things that make human systems interesting. Systems without the ability to reflect or anticipate may be extremely interesting, after all evolution cannot look to the future, but it can build agents which can. But when we talk about human systems, it seems reasonable to leave open the possibility, as game theory does, that the agents think about their situation and what they are doing."[21]

We agree, and thus the theories of self-organisation found in the biological theories of Varela and Matura may give us a much too simple picture of self-organisation, when it concerns human beings.

Thus the analogy between Varela's vision example and the construction of shelters by the boys or any other human activity should not be carried too far. It would also be difficult to put some substance on the abstract skeleton theories of Varela, but at least his theory may help us to see the activities of boys building a shelter as an example of spontaneous cooperation without explicit coordination. There need be no centre, and still, to an outside observer, it would look as if the boys were either acting according to a master plan, or listening to the tacit commands of an unseen manager's mastermind.

In an attempt to use complexity theory in connection with strategic change processes Stacey elaborates on the importance of the interactions between individuals, the interactions we also discussed in relation to the boys' shelter construction. "Organizations are clearly feed back systems because every time two humans interact with each other the actions of one person have consequences for the other, leading that other to react in ways that have consequences for the first, requiring in turn a response from the first" and so on.

Complexity theory is not about any sort of complexity; it is not about the complicated structure of a complicated machine, like a fine Swiss mechanical watch. In fact it is not about any machine-like structure. Instead it is about the complexity of an interacting system of elements, each of which may be simple, but whose interaction produces complexity through complicated positive and negative feedback loops. It is about self-referential and self-replicating[22] systems. In relation to our discussion two interesting properties emphasised by McKergow are relevant:[23] "They are non-deterministic. Wholly accurate predictions of future states cannot be made, *however well the current and past states are known*" and "They show emergent properties – patterns which result from the overall action of all the elements of the system."

Complexity theory represents an attempt to understand "how the interaction of billions of individual entities can lead to something that appears designed or displaying an overall systems level pattern."[24] While not quite operating with billions of entities, we can see how this may fit an observation of the boys' spontaneous attempt to build a shelter, where accurate predictions of the future state were impossible, and where something complex and orderly, like a shelter or an organisation, emerges from the simple interactions of many individual agents.

This idea has already been used in connection with attempts to understand the emergence of complex human organisations. Axelrod's experiments with simple computer programs with a very limited repertoire of behaviours, playing against each other as robot ants in large-scale computer simulations, are just one example. These comparatively simple experiments were used in an attempt to explain large-scale political phenomena, like east–west relations during the cold war.[25] In fact there have been many attempts to use game theory to throw light on complex social phenomena, either following in the tracks of Axelrod or making tracks of their own.[26]

In *The Cement of Society* Elster uses game theory to discuss how two kinds of social order may have come about: that of stable, regular, predictable patterns of behaviour and that of cooperative behaviour, two kinds of order that must somehow be found in every kind of society. His problem is to a certain degree the same problem we are facing here, the problem of understanding how spontaneous order may come about. In his attempts Elster does not stop at the level with stupid individual players, with no senses and feelings. The simple programs of Axelrod cannot represent human beings. In fact he recurs to human motivation and uses envy, opportunism and self-interest with guile, and codes of honour, or what he calls "the ability to make credible threats and promises,"[27] in an endeavour to explain social order.

A more general and overreaching attempt to make a convincing argument for the spontaneous emergence of social order out of the activities of many individual interactions is of course found in Hayek's earlier attempts to present an alternative to every form of central planning and command economy.[28] In his arguments Hayek uses the free market to show how spontaneous order may emerge from the individual actions and the interactions of many individuals. He explains the institutions making up society as being a result of processes like the processes in the market.

A result of myriads of individual actions and interactions, a result that is unforeseeable even in principle, but is kept within bounds by already established norms and rules.[29]

According to this view, knowledge is distributed over all individuals making up society, nowhere can a central mastermind be found. We have seen in more detail how this might be possible in our own attempts to describe and explain tacit knowledge, and the moral fabric of society. In these explanations we saw how already existing tacit knowledge and silent values created in earlier generations made up the shared bounds.[30]

Ulrich finds that "the functional efficiency of free enterprise is based directly on the fact that the total available knowledge is distributed in an extremely diffuse manner throughout the system and cannot be concentrated at a single point. In other words, the distribution of knowledge to all system elements is the necessary prerequisite for the creation of a self-controlling system, whereas, contrariwise, the attempt to centrally control the economy is already doomed to failure because of the 'inability to know' in the sense that individual controlling agencies do not have at their disposal the necessary knowledge."[31]

Although the theories of self-organisation and self-reference presented here are not very specific and range from single-cell organisation in the case of Varela to the whole of society in Hayek's case, these theories show an alternative to a trivial machine view. Now we have at least a vague idea of how a large organisation in the shape of a company or an institution may be able to function and develop without having centralised management fulfilling in detail the functions of "foresight, organisation, instruction, control."

It is still only a vague idea for it is evident that not many companies and institutions would be able to work in the same way that a few boys might do, when self-organising the building of a shelter, with only a vague idea of what to produce for instance and no idea of how to organise and plan processes in advance. Companies might perhaps have single departments or work groups working more or less in accordance with the shelter-building of the boys for instance in research and development (R&D), but that is all.

What we generally find is that companies and institutions today contain highly specialised functions that somehow must fit together in an effective and efficient manner, according to detailed plans and procedures.

Where does that leave us? With no other alternative than to return to a trivial machine view, or will it be possible to find some in-between alternative?

BETWEEN MASTERMIND AND MANY MINDS

When the boys attempted to build a shelter we did not suppose that their minds were totally blank. They would have vague ideas of buildings and even shelters they could use to guide their endeavours in the direction of something that also would be seen as a shelter by an independent observer having more knowledge of buildings and shelters.

It was also assumed that the boys would be able to form some expectations with regard to the material objects they collected for the shelter, from concrete individual experiences with equivalent materials. They would have explicit and tacit knowledge resulting from earlier everyday activities. Thus they would already have experience with simple constructions, with houses and sheds, with materials like wood, stone, textiles, with concepts like permeability, gravity, solidity, flexibility and so on. In other words they certainly would not have to start from scratch. In order to see what is meant by this one might refer back to Chapter 4 on tacit knowledge.

Previous experience with physical materials, conceptions already formed and all the existing tacit and explicit knowledge the boys possess, would limit the outcomes we would find as a result of the boys' activities. They would presumably not just throw things together haphazardly. They would not work in the manner described by Gulliver in his tale of the students in the grand academy of Lagado, where the most ignorant persons with little bodily labour and essentially by chance would write books on philosophy, poetry and other subjects,[32] using a simple wooden contrivance to generate random words.

In a production company, the already existing structures, the knowledge, experience, and the physical and economical conditions and relations of the production process would limit the outcome further. Thus the employees would have to follow very detailed schedules, very detailed maintenance manuals and so on. Nothing much might actually be left to their discretion.

"Automatons and automatic assembly lines represent to a large degree self-controlling operating systems which, under normal circumstances, make personal control measures by managers unnecessary. Where human actions predominate at the operational level, we find them increasingly being controlled by computerized production systems which, by means of automatic data processing determine and initiate necessary executional actions."[33] An automatic assembly line using industrial robots would be such a system, where human activity is in a certain sense directed by technical work processes.

What happens is that physical processes, like a work process, to a large degree determine the behaviour of employees, at least in industries with a high degree of automation. There might be less and less overt direction from a supervisor or manager, and more and more predetermined actions, predetermined by the work process, and by the equipment used. In a sense it might be compared to a situation in which the boys had found a Lego-like kit for the construction of shelters on the island, where all the parts had knobs and holes that would only fit together in one way. Thus there would be less self-organisation and more pre-organisation.

All this seems to point to development in which the more management-like aspects of foresight and control are being depersonalised as it were and reified in structures, procedures, equipment, programmes and so on. This would not diminish the importance of management-like functions, on the contrary, but it would transform the management function, making certain aspects more important than others, emphasising for instance planning, design, implementation of structures and physical processes, and de-emphasising the direct and personal people management. "Consequently in industrial operations production planning and control systems, material procurement systems, quality control systems, etc., must be developed, realized and kept under control."[34]

Such tendencies would, if they were the only ones, tend to take the wind out of our sails, making our arguments in relation to self-organisation strangely irrelevant. Instead they would point in the direction of a mastermind-like management.

The recent spate of models, methods, instruments and technologies we discussed in relation to modern scientific management would tend to support such a conclusion. Instead of arguing from the position of complexity theory that would see complex modern organisations as a result of less complex individual interactions, which cannot really be modelled in detail, it would seem that modern scientific management believes that complexity can be overcome and the whole system can be modelled and designed in detail, almost as if it were a Swiss watch. Advances in modern information technology have not exactly reduced the belief in such possibilities.

In our view such views would be naïve for several reasons. We shall attempt to discuss them sequentially, although they are of course interrelated.

The impossibility of complete specification.   An example inspired by a story found in one of Borges' short, but fantastic pieces comes to mind. In an attempt to create a good map of a geographic area, one might construct a large scale map, say at a scale of 1:25 000. This would be a map that could be used for showing in detail the paths that could be used for walking, with enough detail to make it possible to orientate oneself in the area, at least if one possessed a minimum of knowledge about the correspondence between map symbols and real features. Still 1:25 000 will not show every feature of the landscape. We would still have to use some additional knowledge in order to orientate us. An attempt to make the map more precise, would normally mean that it would have to become bigger, and a lot more effort would be necessary to produce such a map. The ultimate map showing the landscape in 1:1 would be extremely unwieldy and costly, in fact it would cover, when unfolded, the whole area that it was supposed to represent.

In Borges' story "succeeding Generations came to judge a map of such Magnitude cumbersome, and, not without Irreverence they abandoned it to the Rigours of Sun and Rain.[35]"

Now, if we use this map metaphor to think of the level of detail that would be necessary if nothing had to be left to the discretion of employees, to their knowledge and their experience, then we would in fact need a very comprehensive description, and a description of the description explaining the different terms used. A long recursive process might be necessary. In the light of the discussion in earlier chapters we know that such an attempt would be futile. We would never be able to succeed.[36]

Thus we can conclude that it will neither be possible nor cost effective to specify all elements of even simple work processes in a mastermind scheme, although it may look as if this is being done in complicated technical procedures, for instance when constructing and launching space shuttles. Here it might be relevant to think back to the O-ring disaster, which may show that even attempting to plan technical aspects to the last detail, we cannot leave out human discretion. Thus there would still be scope for self-organisation, self-reference and self-control, albeit on another level than in the case with the boys constructing a shelter.

What we could do instead of making one-to-one maps of the work processes, and publishing written codes of behaviour, can in a way be compared to the way we use a steel spring when constructing the suspension of a car, seat of a chair or the thousands of other objects where steel springs are used. As far as I know we have difficulties describing precisely what goes on in a steel spring, when it is compressed and released. Luckily we do not need to know the internal workings, only some specifications of its external "behaviour." The steel spring forms a closed system with molecules keeping together and adjusting to external pressure and pressure release. It is identifiable and closed towards its environment, to all practical purposes at least.

Perhaps this can be seen as a primitive metaphor for the way we incorporate people, work groups and organisations within organisations. We do not need to specify or even understand their internal workings as outside observers, we just use the orderly external behaviour to fit into our purposes, almost like fitting a spring to a car. "Almost" is important here, because as we have said earlier, there is a difference. Individuals are conscious beings, not integrated circuits or steel springs. In a way we might say that a human "spring" has to be self-organising, knowing what to do when it is being "compressed" and when being "released", and conscious of the function it is supposed to fulfil, or it would not really work. Instead of the molecules of a spring there would be the many minds of the work group. Here we might see an analogy to our discussion of knowledge especially the section on what we have called lumpy or stratified knowledge.

Thus the work group might be a self-organised and well-defined entity that can be reckoned with in the larger picture, in the sense that it will show an order that will mean something in the larger organisation and can be taken as constant in planning work processes for instance. This might illustrate how self-organisation, self-reference and self-control has a large role to play even in companies and organisations that are planned in very great detail.

The preconditions for change and innovation. This part is a bit more speculative, but it concerns the importance of self-organisation for change and for innovation. The idea is that we have a situation somewhat like the one the boys on the island were in. We assumed that they had a vague idea of what they would need in order to survive and to have a chance of being rescued. The situation is unexpected, and even though they might have had some sort of survival kit, they would still have to adapt to suddenly changed conditions. In our shelter story we guessed how they might cope.

This story may serve to illustrate what happens when an organisation ends up in an unexpected situation, perhaps threatening its survival. There might be a goal of establishing some kind of normalcy, of counteracting the disturbance that may have brought about the situation, but only a vague idea of how this is to be achieved. No mastermind may have a solution. In such a situation one might expect to find some of the processes at work that we found in the boys' shelter-building. I am not saying that one might succeed, I am only saying that in order to succeed something like the self-organising process in the shelter-building case might be necessary for the organisation to survive.

Innovation might also represent a situation where self-organising and self-referencing are relevant. In the beginning there may only be a vague idea, somewhat in the sense that the boys may have had a vague idea of a shelter. In order to concretise and realise this idea the process we have described earlier may be necessary. The concrete product may slowly emerge from a self-organising process like the shelter-building. The crystallisation of an idea into a concrete product may thus be seen as a result of the self-organising.

Here we are in a sense talking about two things at the same time. The self-organising going on in the minds of single individuals and the self-organising going on in groups with a common, but vague purpose. Perhaps this self-organising could be compared to the "self-organising" of artificial neural networks.

From a somewhat different position Langlois and Everett argue that a vertically integrated organisation has inherent limits in its ability to deal with change, especially in situations characterised by uncertainty. Thus a "decentralised network of independent agents may have the advantage when uncertainty is greatest."[37] We take this to be an argument supporting the view presented here.

The shift in emphasis from traditional production to knowledge-intensive production. "Knowledge-intensive" is a loose term, denoting companies where knowledge is relatively important in relation to more traditional factors of production. Recent studies have pointed to the growing importance of intellectual capital and human capital,[38] of knowledge-creating companies and knowledge management[39] and what have been called continuous learning organisations.[40]

We touched upon these concepts earlier. Suffice it to say that according to Edvinsson and Malone[41] intellectual capital includes among other things inventions, techniques, processes, data, programs and publications.

Now if knowledge was only seen as consisting of existing inventions, techniques, processes, data, programs, and publications I suspect that knowledge management in the sense found for instance in *Information Technology for Knowledge Management*[42] and in attempts to benchmark and list knowledge would seem relevant, and with such a view of knowledge management the need for self-organisation might seem limited.

Of more interest to us is the knowledge residing in the heads of the individuals making up the organisation. Knowledge-intensive in this sense would seem to imply that processes cannot be reduced to algorithms, cannot be made into detailed plans and carried out mechanically in an automated process, whether that be an assembly line or a computer program. This would include all the elements of knowledge that we touched upon earlier, when discussing explicit and tacit knowledge, including: what we can say, the silent patron, lumpy knowledge, community and heritage, the cell walls of our minds and influence of the environment.

In the somewhat popsmart world of Tissen et al. "hot" new organisations must have these characteristics: "heavy on know-how, light on resources, decentralised decision-making, centralised knowledge management, sharing knowledge, processes and team-based organization, intellectual capital shared by knowledge professionals, unlimited access to explicit and tacit knowledge, smart sourcing."[43] Such a list is of course very accommodating; in our view some of the elements would seem contradictory or impossible, for instance the statement about unlimited access to explicit and tacit knowledge, or the somewhat optimistic view about knowledge sharing.

The more knowledge-intensive an organisation or company is in our sense, the more there will be a possibility and a need for self-organisation, all the way from the individual level, via work groups and task forces, to the level of the whole organisation.

Drucker asserts that in "information-based organizations, knowledge will lie primarily at the bottom, in the minds of specialists who do different work and direct themselves,"[44] and these specialists cannot be told in detail how to do their work. They will have to direct themselves to a very large degree. A former Apple Macintosh programmer describes how the original Macintosh Finder system was conceived and programmed by a group of people self-organising in the same way as the boys building a shelter.[45]

The efficiency of the modern organisation or company is dependent on knowledge being distributed in the heads and minds of the individual members of the organisation, and neither concentrated in a single manager nor in a collection of manuals or computer programs. In fact we are back to the boys and their attempts to construct a shelter without any clear idea of shelters', materials' and constructions' principles for shelters. Distributed and massive parallel computing as represented by the individual brains would presumably out-compute as it were the attempt to create what would amount to a traditional von Neuman non-parallel computer as represented by a single executive manager with an armoury of plans and guidelines.[46] The less intelligent knowledge management conceptions seem to ignore this in their endeavour to design system solutions using information technology to manage knowledge in a company.[47]

Thus it would seem that self-organisation will become more important with the emergence and growth of modern knowledge-intensive companies, such as companies producing non-tangible products, in the shape of new knowledge. Part of what has been termed the new economy, with focus on knowledge, information technology, networks, knowledge and of course globalisation.[48] All the traditional favourites of information technology like multimedia and Internet solutions belong here, but knowledge-based companies may also be found on the exciting frontier of genomics; just think of companies like Incyte, Human Genome Sciences or Celera.[49]

Team based organising. In *The Wisdom of Teams* Katzenback and Smith argue the case for team-based working processes. And teams or autonomous work groups have been catchwords for some time, especially of course for companies, where the work processes cannot be reduced to algorithms in the shape of detailed plans that can be carried out more or less mechanically in an automated process. Closely related to the idea of team-based organising we find ideas of democratisation of institutions and organisations and the concept of empowerment. Thus Freimuth and Straub talk of a "Demokratisierung der Verfügbarkeit von Informationen im Gefolge der modernen Informationstechnik,"[50] seeing a necessity for democratisation as a result of the more and more organisationally diffused character of knowledge.

When knowledge lies at the bottom and specialists will have to self-organise and self-reflect in a collaborative process, management and leadership will still be necessary, but cannot be exercised through plans, automated processes or personal management directives. In fact team-based organisation and the autonomous work groups may be seen as the only possible solutions.

We do not want to discuss the merits of team-based organisation here though. What we want to emphasise is that team-based organising must by necessity imply a large measure of self-organisation within the team. If one were to design the work processes for the individual members of the team we could no longer talk about team-based organisation.

Again we may be back with the boys and their shelter-building. As we saw leaders can emerge spontaneously and take upon them certain aspects of direction in the group, but this we consider to be part of the self-organising and self-reflecting activity of the team or group.

The right scale of the map. The attempt to construct a one-to-one map would seem to correspond to the idea of having a mastermind laying out a plan for all our actions, with goals and the precise algorithms to achieve each goal. The rejection of any map would seem to correspond to the idea of leaving it to every individual mind to start from scratch, with no sense of direction and no idea of where to go.

What we have to look for is something in between, the right scale where we know about the lie of the land from already existing bounds, but where self-organisation and self-reference are possible within these bounds. These shared bounds may have to be taken for granted at a given moment, but over time they may turn out to be neither immovable nor impenetrable.

Knowledge bounds would represent existing knowledge, meaning that we do not have to start from scratch. Remember even the boys were supposed to possess some general knowledge and previous experiences they could use for their shelter-building attempts. Physical bounds would represent the scientific laws, properties of physical objects and of biological elements, but may also include the bounds of physical processes, like a production process of an industry. Social and organisational bounds would be represented by existing structures, frameworks and coupling restrictions with other organisations, like work groups acting in a company. And finally there would be the bounds that we have a special interest in, the bounds representing values and moral attitudes, as represented by the moral weave.

Leaning on the theories developed during our discussion of the social grammar, we might say that the bounds may work somewhat like a non-determinative grammar. As we have said before, in a way it may be like playing according to well understood, but not always explicit general rules of a game. They define the game, but they do not define the individual actions. Team sports are played within certain bounds in space and time, according to certain rules and conventions defining the game, and within bounds of a more universal character. The rules and conventions make a game recognisable as a handball match, a football match or a cricket match, and not as a collaborative attempt of the human genome project or some more mundane cooperative activity, like shelter construction or bridge-building.

There will be other bounds. We all have limitations as to how many contacts we can maintain concurrently. Physical bounds, like communication channel capacity or distance, will limit the size of the self-organising organisation, although new information technologies may reduce the influence of this. It is not a simple limit on the number of people that we talk about. Large organisations may consist of lumps of self-organising units.

What we have to remember is that we are not talking about a simple two-tier system, with the bounds making up a single grammar and the sentences representing self-organisation. No, the grammar in itself must be seen as a result of self-organising, albeit on another level of self-organisation shaped by other bounds. In this way self-organisation and bounds form an intricate weave of recursion and self-reference.

A COARSE VIEW OF TRANSACTION COST AND SELF-ORGANISATION

Further support for self-organisation, self-reference and self-control by organisations in the shape of companies may perhaps be had from the theories of transaction cost. The term stems from Coase's 1937 work *The Nature of the Firm.*[51]

Coase argues that a reason for the creation of firms is a reduction in transaction costs. If one had to use the market mechanism every day to engage the resources of someone else, one would have to pay the cost of comparing the available offers in the market as to price and output. Added to these costs would be the cost of negotiation, the cost of making contracts and perhaps engaging the services of a lawyer. These costs Coase regards as the costs of carrying out market transactions.

If this process had to be repeated every day for the same kind of resources then it would be advantageous to create a more permanent arrangement in the shape of a company. By doing this many of these market "transaction costs" could be avoided or reduced. The manager would not have to engage in renewed transactions every day to engage the services of workers, and would thus avoid these cost, a fairly simple explanation for the existence of firms one would think.

An extension of Coase's rather simple theory is relevant to our discussion because it gives us another argument for self-organisation, which may also be applicable internally in an organisation or company. Instead of initiating a costly procedure of planning and negotiating in detail the tasks of employees, only an overall specification would be necessary; many of the more specific tasks could be left to self-organising efforts of a single individual and work group.

Williamson[52] argues that internal organisation in the shape of a company has the attractive property that "it permits the parties to deal with uncertainty/complexity in an adaptive, sequential fashion without incurring the same types of opportunism hazards that market contracting would pose."[53]

If we look to the first part of the argument, then we would argue that in order to realise the sequential adaptive approach some kind of self-organisation would be called for. It does not seem possible to solve uncertainty/complexity issues by precise planning and calculation on a managerial level. What is called for is the collective effort of say employees engaged in a common endeavour, without the opportunism hazards of a market-based relation. In fact we see this as an example of the myriads of individual actions and interactions which are unforeseeable even in principle, but are kept within bounds by already established norms and rules.[54]

Williamson also argues that internal organisation, that is to say a company, has several advantages over market-based contracts: "First, in relation to autonomous contractors, the parties to an internal exchange are less able to appropriate subgroup gains, at the expense of the overall organization (system) ... Second, and related, internal organization can be more effectively audited. Finally, when differences do arise, internal organization realizes an advantage over market mediated exchange in dispute settling respects."[55]

It is as if Williamson's arguments are based on the idea of a traditional hierarchical organisation. We would argue that the argument could be carried further. That self-organisation within this organisation might lead to further gains, because it could in a sense be self-monitoring and self-auditing to a very large degree, again of course given the existence of bounds of what Hayek called established norms and rules. It is as if the existence of these bounds is not really recognised by the advocates of transaction cost theory.

A third argument of Williamson concerns the inequality, or asymmetry, of information among participants entering into a transaction. Once more the argument is that "internal organisation (of the appropriate kind) serves to attenuate incentives to exploit information impactedness opportunistically."[56] And once more Williamson argues that attempts to exploit this information impactedness can be overcome more easily in an internal organisation.

We agree that an internal organisation might share information more easily than it would be possible in the market, again with the proviso that an all channel network of self-organising group might be more effective than a star-shaped network with a central hub as found in a traditional hierarchical organisation.

With regard to the opportunism argument, we would repeat that the existence of common values and morals, acting as bounds on the individuals making up the organisation, might do more to reduce opportunism than anything else. Such bounds may presumably be found in a self-organising group, where the bounds would be part of the tacit morals of everyone.

In fact this seems to be recognised in Williamson's fourth argument: "Distinctions between calculative and quasimoral 'involvements' are relevant. Market exchange tends predominantly to encourage calculative relations of a transaction-specific sort between the parties. ... Internal organization, by contrast, is often better able to make allowance for quasimoral involvements among the parties."[57]

What Williamson does not seem to realise is that the "atmosphere" is important in relation to all the points he makes, not the least in relation to his often repeated emphasis on opportunism, and the assertion that opportunism would be easier and less costly to curb in an internal organisation. His argument has to do with changes in motivations and possibilities for monitoring and control, within the structures and hierarchies of traditional organisations. We would argue that these types of bounds would lead to internal transaction costs, including costs of making written rules of conduct for instance, costs of monitoring compliance with the rules and costs of punishing transgressions.

Thus we argue that the atmosphere or what we call the moral weave, the internal bounds of every individual and the mutual bounds of groups of individuals, do in fact make up the most basic and in a certain sense also the most efficient barrier to opportunistic behaviour. We would argue that behind the efficiency arguments in favour of the internal organisation we would in each and every instance have to presume the existence of the moral bounds, and that the control and monitoring aspects would be less important in relation to that. The efficiency of Williamson's solution would in fact depend on the pre-existence of a moral weave, for reasons we have already discussed in earlier chapters.

This seems to be the case in relation to all of Williamson's points. It would seem that in a certain sense the most basic and presumably most efficient barrier to strategic manipulation of information or intentional misrepresentation of intentions, and against individuals acting only in their own interest, would be shared moral bounds, upheld not by any monitoring agency but by mutual recognition by the individuals making up the organisation.

The same argument could be used in connection with the problem of subgroup gains, at the expense of the overall organization, or the exploitation of information impactedness.

One might speculate whether it would be possible to turn part of Coase's and Williamson's argument chain against themselves. The idea would then be to look for the advantages of aspects of the market inside the organisation. Using the inspiration from Hayek, we see this as an argument for self-organisation within the company. Individual actions and interactions, as found in our discussion of self-organisation, kept within the bounds of already established norms and rules, and the confines and demands of the company as such, might do more for complexity reduction, sequential problem solving, and knowledge sharing than the non-market based internal hierarchical type of internal organisation Williamson apparently foresees.

Here we are in fact turning the argument that "Hierarchical organization and associated controls are traced to the limited capacities of human actors to cope with the complexity and uncertainty with which they are confronted"[58] on its head, arguing that the only way to cope with this complexity and uncertainty might be the kind of self-organisation we have discussed. This does not mean that we cannot have complicated hierarchical organisations, only that this cannot be masterminded; they have to consist of self-organising elements.

It might be argued that it would be impossible to test the statements made here, but so, we would argue, are the statements of Williamson. The idea that internal organisation instead of market transactions or one type of organisation and governance could be chosen over another as a result of precise cost breakdowns and calculation, would be naïve.

Taking just the bounded rationality argument of Williamson's one might already have a hunch that such calculations would be impossible. What might be happening instead is that the solution chosen is a result of a kind of natural selection, whereby successful solutions are imitated by others, without any calculation whatsoever of what this means for transaction costs. Practice would show whether one solution is better than another, not theoretical arguments.

An issue, which we would regard as being important in relation to the creation of companies and the internal organisation of these, is the issue of non-separability. Even when looking at a small and simple organisation, it might be impossible to determine precisely the contribution, and the marginal productivity of every employee and manager to the overall output or the results of the organisation. Alchian and Demsetz see this as a metering problem, their example concerning men jointly lifting cargo into trucks. "The output is yielded by a team, by definition, and it is not a sum of separable outputs of each of its members."[59]

This non-separability is an important reason for the existence of organisations like companies, perhaps more important than the transaction cost arguments. With knowledge-intensive companies and intangible products this non-separability might become more and more pronounced.[60] It might be seen indirectly as a further argument in favour of self-organisation, where there is no necessity for an outside designer/observer/mastermind, which will be able to separate out the different contributions of every cog in the machinery, or employee in the company. It will not be necessary to design detailed machinery with exactly meshing gears, and connecting rods, in fact that will to a large degree be left to the machine itself.

COHESION, DIRECTION AND DRIVE IN SELF-ORGANISING GROUPS

In our story of shelter-building by a group of boys we assumed that they all had agreed to the importance of this task for reasons having to do with their own survival and possible rescue. After that we assumed that they stayed together and contributed to the common goal of building a shelter without further ado, as a team, cooperatively, just guided by a vague conception of a shelter and its function. It seemed that nothing else was necessary to make them enter into this task together, although to be sure we thought of the possibility that someone might shirk, but assumed that shirking would be curbed by the urgings of the others actively participating in the shelter-building business.

Apart from that we did not see the introduction of anything like explicit rewards, monitoring, control or punishment to make sure that everyone stayed in the group, gave his best and cooperated with the others in ways that made the result of their efforts more than a simple collection of individual efforts.

In the discussion of transaction costs we saw that some of the important topics were the cost of curbing opportunistic behaviour, of attempts to achieve individual gains to the detriment of the common effort and of attempts to exploit information asymmetries. What could explain why these effects did not show up in the shelter-building exercise?

Or we could ask more generally: What keeps people together into an organisation? What makes them contribute to some shared goal? What makes them predictable in their interactions with each other? What assures a cooperative effort in self-organising groups?

Perhaps we may subsume these questions under the heading of cohesion and cooperation, with cohesion being "the act of or state of cohering, uniting, or sticking together," and cooperation being an "an act or instance of working or acting together willingly for a common purpose or benefit."

What we also presumed in the fictional example of shelter-building was that the boys were able to act in concert and in the same direction, that of building a shelter, without having anything like an explicit description to hand, or a detailed plan, or a manager directing their efforts. This raises another series of questions concerning the direction of common efforts. How do people in a self-organising organisation know what to do and where to direct their efforts? Does the goal have to be specified externally and in detail? What in fact guides their efforts in a mutually supporting direction? These might be seen as questions concerning the direction of efforts.

Finally we shall seek answers to questions like: What keeps a self-organising group going? What pushes or compels the individual members to exert efforts, to work for some shared goal? In the original boys' game we remember that not all joined in the concerted effort; some of the boys were just playing around. In the shelter-building exercise we assumed that they all contributed to the task. Part of the answer may be found in the answers to the cohesion and cooperation question, but understanding the framework and values that held the group together does not tell us what drove them to act within this confining framework.

We shall discuss these questions of the drive or the energising force that pushed or pulled the boys along.

Cohesion and cooperation.   Thinking about the first series of questions we may refer back to Elster's *The Cement of Society.*[61] He emphasised the importance of two kinds of social order: that of stable, regular, predictable patterns of behaviour and that of cooperative behaviour. Something like these kinds of order must have been present in the boys' exercise, and must be present in every collaborative effort. But what makes us behave predictably and cooperatively?

A convincing answer might be based upon the theories that we have developed in weaving the moral fabric: that of time and culture-dependent moral codes, of context-sensitive general notions of morality, and of tacit, basic and shared universal strands of morality, involving sympathy, reciprocity, getting along in a group, and symbolic reflection with the ability to put oneself into the shoes of another.

Time and culture-dependent codes of morality would have been internalised in the course of one's interactions with other members of a society, and would bring about behavioural bounds that would limit the modes of behaviour; not by predetermining behaviour completely, but by containing behaviour within certain bounds. Certain things are not to be done, while others must be done. If the boys share the same cultural upbringing they would presumably possess mutually supporting codes of this kind.

Unknown to themselves they would possess tacit strands of morality that would compel them to value general notions like fairness and justice, which presumably would go a long way to explain that they would not just shirk their responsibilities in relation to the shelter-building, even in the absence of a formal monitoring and sanctioning apparatus.

Finally, on an even deeper universal level, they might not even be aware of, they would appreciate the value of sympathy, of reciprocity, of getting along in a group and of reflection. And act accordingly.

These interlocking levels of moral bounds explain the cooperation of the boys, as well as acting as the hold-together-glue of a self-organising group of conscious human beings. In the boys' game we saw what happened when these bounds began to break down, and something else in the diffuse shape of the beast became stronger.

Our answer still sounds too simple, too cooperative and docile in fact, to be true. Where, for instance, is the competition we see as the engine of capitalist development? Is competition only something that can be found between organisations, something that can be switched off when joining an organisation?

To answer this we look at the characteristic differences between cooperative and competitive behaviour? In a series of experiments Deutsch studied the outcome of cooperative efforts of groups and of competitive effort. Tjosvold reports on some of the results.[62]

In relation to mutual assistance, cooperation would imply that individuals in a group would expect other individuals to help them "perform effectively to reach their goals and actually assist each other," while competition would imply that individuals would not expect help from each other, but rather attempts to obstruct and trip others, in an effort to come out on top.

With respect to communication and influence, individuals cooperating would be expected to believe that communication would be conducted in an atmosphere of trust, with no intent to furnish false information or misrepresent one's position. With competition there would be less trust, and more misinformation.

In relation to task orientation. "Persons in cooperation divide up tasks and encourage each other to complete them so that they can move toward their goals. Competitors must do these tasks themselves; they may try to undercut the others' efforts for these interfere with their own goals."[63]

Finally in relation to attitudes towards other individuals. In cooperation they would be friendly and positive, in competition less positive.

Tjosvold mentions that experiments with rather simple tasks give inconclusive evidence as to whether cooperation or competition is more effective. Here we are only interested in the more complicated and difficult to structure tasks, like the boys' shelter-building task. We presume that in such cases some form of cooperation increases efficiency.

Earlier we concluded that competition in a free market economy is a very effective logic for generating growth, but this conclusion is not necessarily applicable to intra-group competition. In the market no one cares about any kind of shared goal, only their own interests are in view, leading to benefits for all. Just remember the invisible hand argument of Adam Smith or the argument concerning the beneficial nature of vices found in Mandeville's writings. To cooperate in the market might actually lead to inefficiency, as for instance in the case of cartelisation.

In the self-organising organisation we are discussing here, there would always seem to be a shared goal, the goal for which the organisation was created. What does that mean for cooperation and competition? For a complicated task under the non-separability constraint discussed in a previous section, competition based only on individual actions would not work, perhaps not even for the comparatively simple task of building a shelter. Here some form of cooperation and collaboration is needed.

But does that rule out competition? I suppose not. What one might find in these cases is a kind of competition under a mutuality constraint.

The boys in the shelter-building business might well show a degree of competition. They might compete with each other with regard to ingenuity, smart solutions to unforeseen problems, speed in collection of materials for the shelter and so on. This competition would take place under a severe constraint though. Their competition must not lead them astray from the shared goal of building a shelter in accordance with a vague, but shared vision. Thus their individual goals would have to be interdependent, compliant and compatible, and subject to the shared goal.

Thus the overall goal of constructing a shelter has to guide the effort, when trying to solve the question of whether this or that piece of driftwood would make a better corner support. A majority may decide to use one support instead of another, or a clever boy might show that in relation to the next step one solution would be best, or …. How the conflict is solved we cannot say, but we would expect that the glue of moral bounds and the direction given by the vague idea of the end product are necessary for keeping the conflict within bounds. There might even be a need for something like Piggy's conch shell and a belief in its authority, in order to avoid the moral bounds of the boys becoming unglued, giving way the sinister chain of events that led to the killings.

Direction. In a certain sense the moral bounds give direction to the behaviour of individuals or perhaps we should say that they ought to. When observing a fellow human being in distress, moral bounds would direct one to help. But this would only give a certain sense of direction; something else is necessary, knowledge of what to do in certain situations, knowledge of what would be help and what would probably worsen the situation. Such a knowledge of causation, of states of things, of implicit goals and so on, also has to direct one's efforts.

Here we can draw upon the discussions in Chapter 4 on tacit knowledge. The ideas of explicit knowledge, the personal tacit knowledge, the lumpy knowledge we build upon, and the social, or should we say collective knowledge, limited and bounded by what we have called the cell walls of our minds and the environment. Without these forms of knowledge we would really be like the mindless robot ants we have played with a few times now.

Collective knowledge will be of special relevance for the coordination and the direction of efforts. Here we may also refer to Weick's idea of a collective mind. Somewhat like us he argues that a collective mind emerges in the practice of social interaction, at least where the interaction is conducted mindfully, unlike the mindless interaction of our robot ants. To Spender this view fits with the Durkheim's and Halbwach's theories,[64] thus "our understanding of not only the workplace but also the human experience is socially constructed and tightly contextualised."[65] This is in line with our earlier arguments about the situatedness of learning.

Direction and knowledge necessary for a coordinated effort must come from something outside the moral bounds. Many sources are thinkable: hardwired knowledge in the brain, experience, external factors delimiting choices, like production processes, the curb of the road we are driving on, management directives, shared ideas and visions, leadership, an inner drive, hunger, thirst, ambition, will-to-power, beastly or not. But perhaps we are not asking the right questions, perhaps direction is a product of self-organisation too?

Our attempt to answer this question will be very limited, and very tentative. We would assume that direction comes from all the above-mentioned sources. What is more interesting is in what proportion, and what that would mean for self-organisation within companies and institutions for instance.

In the boys' game we assumed that the sense of direction was partly based upon existing knowledge, in an attempt to reproduce as it were, the grown-up world they had left behind, with meetings, with tasks to be done, with appointment of a chief. Later something else seemed to take over, the sinister directives of the beast, representing some inner drive actually breaking down the moral bounds, making them redirect their efforts to hunting pigs and boys, and building a protected position.

In the shelter-building exercise we assumed that direction came from the goals of survival and rescue, the vague idea of shelter, all the previous experience which could be used to guide their efforts, and perhaps ideas of someone knowing in more detail what to do. Furthermore we argued that the direction might emerge from the self-organised efforts. The process of shelter-building itself, the experimentation with different solutions and the acknowledgement of the different possibilities and limitations of the objects used, might give the boys' efforts a certain direction.

Do we need more than that? Do we need all the precise directions of a manual or a set of precise guidelines telling us what to do? Do we need to follow an already established algorithm or is a vague idea of the goal sufficient?

For well-defined and clearly structured tasks where explicit knowledge already exists, direction might stem from a plan made by management, or from the work process itself, with only little involvement on behalf of the employees. Under such conditions it would seem that self-organisation would not mean a lot. If the work process is specified in detail with the different tasks allocated to single employees, the scope for self-organisation would be rather small, in fact self-organisation under such conditions would seem rather illusory. This might be a characteristic of the assembly line, of highly coupled technical systems, perhaps like a nuclear power station,[66] and of traditional bureaucracies, where either the specific demands of the work process must be obeyed or the detailed description of a comprehensive bureaucratic reulation must be followed.

If the goal is vague, and the tasks cannot be defined beforehand, it would seem that direction must somehow come from the experience and the knowledge of the group, must evolve from their interaction, from the loops of trying, reflecting, commenting, suggesting and must in a sense be self-directed and emerging from the interaction.

Even in situations where it can be clearly specified what is needed, for instance where an object is to be used to fulfil a certain function in a larger assembly of functions, such as a new wing for a windmill, there would be possibilities for self-organising. The process for making this object might be little known or not well understood, and this would leave latitude for self-organising. For instance in a group taking over the responsibility for designing and building a new wing that has to be used in the larger assembly of a windmill.

With the knowledge-intensive companies of the new economy, such tasks may become the exception rather than the rule, making our argument for self-organisation even more pertinent. Weick emphasises that "self-fulfilling prophecies, enactment, and committed interpretation should be most visible in young, small professional organizations that must make non-routine decisions turbulent environments."[67] We agree, but would like to add that small organisations may be found within the confines of all organisations characterising the new economy.

I do not know how far direction and sense-making go hand in hand, but might not self-direction be important in relation to sense-making? In a hierarchical system with highly detailed directives for action, it might be difficult to make sense of what one is doing. Sense-making under such conditions will perhaps consist in creating self-organising groups of like-minded people that are not necessarily interested in the directives they are given. The result of self-organisation might instead become subversive in relation to the overall goals, leading to the creation of groups interested in keeping their workload down, uninterested in quality of products and fostering attitudes that could almost be seen as sabotage.

There seems to be a growing understanding of the importance of sense-making in organisations, and quite possibly self-organisation would help bring about a sense-giving and sense-making environment, contravening the negative forms of sense-making just described. Ring and van de Ven are quoted for the following views: "Sensemaking processes derive from ... the need within individuals to have a sense of identity – that is, a general orientation to situations that maintain esteem and consistency of one's self-conceptions ... [O]rganisational participants come to appreciate the nature and purpose of a transaction with others by reshaping or clarifying the identity of their own organization. By projecting itself onto its environment, an organization develops a self-referential appreciation of its own identity, which in turn permits the organization to act in relation to its environment."[68]

Drive. In the original boys' game a simple answer to the question of what drove them might be that the urge to better their chances of surviving drove them to exert efforts. But not for long, as we remember they soon neglected some of the tasks they had agreed upon. On the other hand the activities of Jack's group seemed to continue, and they certainly could not be explained with reference to a quest for survival. Instead we are told that they were spurred on by the beast, of something inside them that acted as a strong force, somehow compelling them to chant and to kill and unite their efforts. It is as if Golding wants to tell us about a sinister force driving us along in the absence of strong bounds, moral and otherwise.

In the Michael Kohlhaas story it looked as if Kohlhaas was driven by a desire to right a wrong, with terrible consequences. He was urged on by what might be seen as in more than one way a burning desire for justice.

Psychology may tell yet another story of what drives us, recurring to deeper forces of which we may not really be aware, sexual drives for instance. Organisation theory has developed a whole series of motivation theories, from the somewhat doubtful Hawthorne experiments, Maslow's (in)famous pyramids, X, Y or even Z theories, the motivating effects of cognitive dissonance, the algorithm-like models of Vroom, the kick in the pants or KITA view, with managers believing in a simple and direct cause – effect relationship,[69] to the modern arsenal consisting of concrete attempts to bait, lure, tempt and attract people to exert effort in companies and public institutions.

This is an enormous topic that we do not want to go into in detail. What we want to question, it can be no more than that, are the effects of some of the last mentioned motivating factors. In relation to the deeper factors, the "beast" of the boys' game and the "burning desire for justice" of Michael Kohlhaas, some of these superficial baits may seem to be of lesser importance. One might therefore speculate whether the drive that is needed to propel successful self-organisation would not have to be based on something as strong as the beast or the burning desire for justice.

Potential candidates for such strong driving impulses might be, in no particular order: the search for power and influence; for domination of others: for status in the eyes of others; for being better, perhaps according to the Olympic ideals; for making a difference; for contributing (although that would seem to be a circular explanation). With these driving impulses the weight is on factors that might better the lot of a single individual.

Getting the inspiration from Michael Kohlhaas, other potential candidates might be: the fight for justice, for freedom, for a better world, for self-government, for partaking in decision making, for democracy, equality, or for ecology and against pollution; in this case factors that might better the lot of many, although, and this represents a problem, in the background one might find the individual factors popping up again. The fight against a world free from genetically modified organisms might also be a quest for personal power and influence. Less aggressive factors may perhaps be the desire to belong, to be seen as having done one's share, to been seen as important, as having worth.

Somewhere in the bundle of factors we have listed here, the social drivers that could be found in Durkheim's theory[70] or Weber's Protestant ethic[71] might also be at work.

We have no desire to unpack this jumble of possible explanations, and we do not know what myriad of factors are most important; we just want to emphasise the importance of "beast" and "desire for justice"-like factors that somehow seem to have been forgotten in the quest to design more simple mechanical lures, like individual performance-based pay, individual fringe benefits, individual stock options, often limited to managers, and the rest of the tricks that are supposed to better productivity and encourage creativity and performance.

These lures fit conveniently into the tool boxes of modern manager minds, as we shall see in the next chapter, but they may not be very contributive in relation to what we are looking for, the drivers in self-organising groups. In fact they may belong to a very narrow and mechanical view of organisations in which self-organisation is not seen as playing a very big role, a view that rates individualised contributions to the plan, and to predefined key success criteria, as the important thing worth striving for. As we have seen in our discussion on deceptive measures such lures may seem to work, inasmuch as people seem to strive for these rewards. What one tends to forget is that they may have become self-fulfilling prophecies, in situations where there is little emphasis on either "beast" and "desire for justice"-like factors.

When people are only rewarded for some metered individual contribution on a fairly simple scale, it is no wonder that they strive to achieve better grades on these scales. This may, as we have seen, represent a perversion of underlying drivers, in fact making for less cohesion and cooperation, and for disregard of moral bounds.[72] Pointing to individual success stories in which it would seem that a promise of rich rewards in the stock options have driven a manager to create a successful company might be misleading and one runs the risk of confusing cause and effect. It may not be these lures that have brought forth the drive that brought success; it may be the urge to create the best product that may have caused them to earn the reward, not the other way round.

What all these modern lures might do is thus to put a shiny pseudo-rational gloss upon some of the more basic drives, thereby ignoring that some of the lures are in fact beastly in character, and that many of them presumably would contravene the necessary cohesion and cooperation that is a precondition for self-organisation of conscious human beings. They may also be in conflict with the basic moral bounds, the importance of which we tried to demonstrate earlier.

Thus the modern lures that are supposed to bring forth individual efforts may necessitate the creation of external bounds in the shape of detailed behavioural rules and/or external direction in the shape of what we have termed modern scientific management, with the problematic consequences we have already discussed.

It will be necessary to look for alternatives to these schemes, if self-organisation is to succeed. In this endeavour we might be inspired by the organisations that have demonstrated self-organisation in practice. Such organisations played an important role in our attempt to show how the runaway logic of capital might be contained. We saw how organisations emerged that somehow seemed to voice and embody new concerns; organisations that generated and put forth suggestions for new solutions that transcended the self-interest of their members, examples like Greenpeace, and human rights movements. Perhaps the efforts of organisations like these can be seen as representing an enlarged attempt to build shelters, this time against some of the effects of the logic of capital; shelters representing ecologically sound production of food, preservation of species, upholding of human rights, bettering of working conditions, or in general, suggestions for new ways of living.

Of course within these organisations the same individual drivers may be at work that we have listed, but there is something else too, something positive that transcends the individual drives, a burning desire for justice perhaps. At the moment we do not seem to be able to get any closer to an explanation. What we want to conclude is that such drivers could fuel self-organisation efforts, while being compatible with cohesion, cooperation and common direction.

It is from the dynamism of self-organising initiatives and movements like these that we may learn what drivers are important for self-organisation to succeed: drivers that would represent the real alternative to the petty efforts that turn us into egotistical competing individuals and drivers that would have a much bigger potential for calling forth extraordinary efforts and enhanced creativity.

They may not fit traditionally managed businesses very well, but in all the sectors of the so-called new economy, where the knowledge, beliefs and values of the employees may be extraordinarily important, they may represent the only drivers that will realise the potential inherent in these employees. It is drivers like these that drive development and change in sectors such as information technology, nanotechnology, biotechnology and new service industries.

But, and this is important, it would necessitate the existence of the cohesion and direction-giving aspects we have just discussed, or the beast may win.

NOTES

1   Golding (1954/1978).
2   Although during the war these conventions may have broken down too.
3   One example being told in Hanson (1999).
4   Hobbes (1651/1982).
5   Orwell (1945/1995).
6   Néda et al. (2000).
7   Schelling (1980).
8   Simon (1945/1957), p. 104.
9   As discussed for instance in Williamson (1975), or in Foerster (1984).
10 Malik (1984), p. 109.
11 Simon (1945/1957), p. 104.
12 Malik (1984).
13 From the *The Charge of the Light Brigade* (Tennyson 1854/1908). The poem of course refers to the incredible blunder involved in the charge of Britain's light cavalry brigade on 20 September 1854, at Balaclava. For the full story, see Woodham-Smith (1953/1998).
14 Ulrich & Probst (1984).
15 See for instance Maturana & Varela (1980). Autopoiesis, meaning self-producing, is a term coined by Maturana and Varela.
16 Varela (no year).
17 This conception of vision would seem to fit the one found in Minsky (1986). See also Dennett's arguments against the brain being inhabited by central agents. Dennett (1991).
18 Varela (no year), p. 14.
19 The idea is to let a swarm of automous lethal flying objects loose over an enemy-held area, letting them act on their own as a swarm of killer bees. As far as I understand there has even been experimentation with programs replicating the behaviour of swarms of insects or flocks of birds. And at least some of it is for real. On 24 May 1999, a 36-month advanced technology demonstration of a LOCAAS was funded by the Munitions Directorate of the U.S. Air Force and Lockheed Martin Voughts.

20 Varela (no year), p. 19. This co-determination thesis harks back to an earlier discussion where we used the theories of Bates to describe co-determination, the creation of hexagonal bee cells being one of the simple examples. See also Bates (1984).

21 Goldberg & Makóczy (1998), p. 14.

22 For a discussion of self-referencing and self-replicating aspects, see for instance Hofstadter (1987). A simple illustration of self-reference in language would be: "This sentence contains five words." Thus in the context of language, a self-referencing statement refers to itself or contains its own referent. Self-reference would seem to imply a kind of circularity; in the case of self-organising groups it might for instance imply organising by the organised, leading by the led.

23 McKergow (1996), p. 722.

24 Goldberg & Makóczy (1998), p. 4. Goldberg and Makóczy mention that the terms complexity and chaos are often used synonymously. In their view chaos is about extremely simple non-linear systems leading to chaos, while complexity is about "the (simple) interaction of many things (often repeated) leading to higher level patterns."

25 See for instance Axelrod (1984), Axelrod (1986) and Axelrod (1997).

26 Some examples with relation to our subject: Binmore (1994), Brown & Eisenhardt (1997), Camerer (1991), Elster (1989), Hirshleifer & Coll (1988) and Ridley (1996).

27 Elster (1989), p. 251.

28 See for instance Hayek (1976), Hayek (1978) and Hayek (1964).

29 See also the discussion of the Hayek programme in Petersen (1985).

30 Hayek (1945).

31 Ulrich (1984), p. 86.

32 The reference is to the decription found in *Gulliver's Travels*, in the Voyage to Balnibarbi (Swift 1726/1992). The idea is essentially the same as letting a number of monkeys write poetry by letting them hammer the keyboards of computers running a word processing program. It is difficult to see how much might come of that. One may also refer to Borges' novel *The Library of Bable*, in which every combination of the letters of the alphabet is found, so somewhere the key to understanding the universe can be found, but most books will of course contain garbage, like "ioioio" or page after page of "z's" (Borges 1970a).

33 Ulrich (1984), p. 84.

34 Ibid., p. 85.

35 Borges (1954), p. 131.

36 Although it strikes me that in the Deep Blue chess contest, the Deep Blue computer may have contained what to all intent and purposes were complete descriptions of

chess draws, although even here there would be a limit as to how far ahead the computer might compute. See also Newborn (1997).
37   Langlois & Everett (1992), p. 67.
38   Stewart (1994), Stewart (1997) and Edvinsson & Malone (1997).
39   See Sveiby (1994), Sveiby (1997), Tissen et al. (1998), Nonaka (1991), Nonaka, (1994), Nonaka & Takeuchi (1995) and Prusak (1997).
40   One might expect Senge's *The Fifth Discipline* to show up here, but I have preferred less well-known references: Denton (1998), Garvin (1998), Probst & Büchel (1997).
41   Edvinsson & Malone (1997).
42   Borghoff & Pareschi (1998).
43   Tissen et al. (1998), p. 116.
44   Drucker (1989).
45   The programmer in question was Bruce Horn, who was responsible for the so-called Finder. The description stems from a lecture at the Apple Macintosh User Group at Aarhus University in the mid-1980s.
46   A similar idea is presented in Schmidt (1993). For a more throrough discussion of parallel architectures and the possibilities inherent in artificial neural networks one would have to turn to more specialised references.
47   The following may perhaps be seen as representative: Borghoff & Pareschi (1998) and Thierauf (1999).
48   Magretta (1999). The term new economy generally seems to be used as a hold-all for information economy, technology, networking, knowledge, virtual companies, e-commerce, globalisation and changed mindsets, emphasising for instance mobility, and flexibility. It has already got the attention of institutions like the OECD, as can be seen from the OECD Forum 2000 conference "Partnerships in the New Economy," Paris, 26–28 June 2000.
49   These companies represent front line companies in the bio-pharmaceutical industry, focusing on human genetics, especially in the form of genomic knowledge, which can be used to create drugs to treat and cure diseases.
50   Freimuth & Straub (1996), p. 14.
51   The argument is found in Coase (1990).
52   Williamson (1975). See also Williamson (1981) and Williamson (1995).
53   Williamson (1975), p. 25.
54   See also the discussion in Petersen (1985).
55   Williamson (1975), p. 29.
56   Ibid., p. 35. Information impactedness is not quite the same as information asymmetry, it exists in a situation "when true underlying circumstances relevant to

the transaction ... are known to one or more parties, but cannot be costlessly discerned by or displayed for others." ibid., p. 31.

57 Ibid., p. 38.
58 Williamson (1981), p. 551.
59 Alchian & Demsetz (1972), p. 779.
60 To use the word "distinct" instead of "pronounced" would seem strange in this connection, where distinctiveness certainly does not seem to be a characteristic.
61 Elster (1989).
62 Tjosvold (1984).
63i Ibid., p. 746.
64 Here we refer to Durkheim (1933) and Halbwachs (1950).
65 Spender (no year), p. 7.
66 Perrow once warned against such a simple view, believing that the attempt to create a tight coupling of activities under highly complex conditions can be dangerous. (Perrow 1984). Perhaps the Three Mile Island accident and the O-ring disaster attest to this dangerousness.
67 Weick (1995).
68 Ring & Ven (1989). Here quoted from Weick (1995), pp. 22–23.
69 Some of the classical references are: Roethlisberger (1941), Maslow (1996), McGregor (1957), Festinger (1958), Vroom (1996) and Herzberg (1968).
70 Durkheim (1957).
71 Weber (1930/1989).
72 We may refer to the examples discussed in Petersen (1996). Resultatløn og snavsede kaffekopper. *Berlingske Tidende* (9 November 1996).

9 Spirited and value-based leadership

Good spirit in a management organisation means that the energy turned out is larger than the sum of the efforts put in. It means the creation of energy. This, clearly, cannot be accomplished by mechanical means. A mechanical contrivance can at its theoretical best conserve energy intact; it cannot create it. To get out more than is being put in is possible only in the moral sphere.

What is necessary to produce the proper spirit in management must therefore be morality. It can only be emphasis on strength, stress on integrity, and high standards of justice and conduct.

Peter F. Drucker

WHAT MANAGEMENT IS ABOUT ...

In his now classic article Chester Barnard points out that the essential functions of the executive are: "[F]irst, to provide the system of communication; second, to promote the securing of essential efforts; and, third, to formulate and define purpose."[1]

This is interesting, because we are in fact quite close to Piggy and Ralph's first activities in the boys' game played in the previous chapter; their attempt to create order and structure, sense and direction of common efforts.

The first function makes it necessary first of all to select a manager of the system of units, or the organisation, since communication will only take place through the agency of a person. This must be followed by the creation of a system of positions. This is in fact the creation of the scheme of organisation, accompanied by organisational diagrams and all the other paraphernalia; the breaking-up into specialised functions and relations, or the boxes and the arrows of organisational diagrams so to speak.[2] Such a system is also what Ralph, in the boys' game, attempted to bring about with a little help from Piggy and the symbol of authority in the shape of the fragile conch.

To secure the essential efforts, the second executive function, people must be brought into a cooperative relationship and the contributions must be elicited from them, in order to survive every organisation "must deliberately attend to the maintenance and growth of its authority to do the things necessary for coordination, effectiveness, and efficiency."[3]

In this Ralph did not succeed very well. Indeed what we saw was a decline. Instead of growth in authority, coordination, effectiveness and efficiency, there was an almost total break-up of coordinated efforts, leading us to the conclusion that a cooperative and contributive relationship among members of an organisation is not something that can just be planned and implemented by a manager. Something else is necessary, something that we do not find in Barnard's description. In fact what Barnard is doing is to a large degree to describe some of the necessary mechanisms that *somehow* must be present and function in order to have a workable organisation. What he does not do is give an explanation of this "somehow."

Finally the third function of the executive is to "formulate and define the purposes, objectives, ends, of the organisation." Ralph and Piggy never got far with defining the purpose, but at least they had got the basics. To assure survival they had to collect water, hunt for food and build shelters; to attract the attention of passing ships they had to build a fire.

Barnard makes the interesting comment "that it is an entire executive organization that formulates, redefines, breaks into details, and decides on the innumerable simultaneous and progressive actions that are the stream of syntheses constituting purpose or action."[4] A single executive cannot take this task upon himself; he must share it with others in the organisation who know more about the part of the organisation they carry responsibility for than the executive. This again seems to demand a unity of efforts that cannot be brought about just by organisational diagrams.

Nothing like an entire executive organisation ever seemed to work in the boys' game, although certainly it may look as if Jack's black gang had succeeded in doing something like this, but apparently with less deliberation and more animal instinct than we find in the exposition by Barnard. In more or less "simultaneous and progressive actions" the members of the black gang actually seemed to carry out the tacit designs of the invisible beast, apparently without needing any plan. They found their own ways of carrying out their dark tasks. In a black and sinister way they demonstrated the strength and purposefulness of forces beyond the reach of the single individual. It does not seem that Jack had to force the members of his gang to do their evil things.

Barnard does not seem to take into account that a precondition for the synthesis to work is not a plan or some conscious effort, but something that might at first sight seem more vague and undefinable, an unspoken common sense or common purpose uniting their efforts, a brain programme that unites their efforts as surely as the efforts of individuals ants of an anthill, albeit in a more sophisticated version, with more latitude and openness in the programme.

The closest we get to such a conception in Barnard's work is his emphasis on the importance of "indoctrinating those at the lower levels with general purposes, the major decisions, so that they remain cohesive and able to make the ultimate detailed decisions coherent" adding a further comment on the need for the upper levels of management to understand the necessity of leaving the concrete and specific decisions to what he call the ultimate contributors, the people on the lower levels of the hierarchy.

Indoctrination is not what is found in Jack's leadership. In fact what we see is tacit coordination carried out by the individual members of his gang. This tacit coordination of evil, found for instance in the teasing of Piggy and the hunting of pigs, may perhaps represent the dark mirror image of something that is more important than the boxes and diagrams of the modern theories of organisation and management, something that is far more important than the descriptive prescriptions found in the work of Barnard and other lesser authorities on leadership.

Here we are of course preparing an opening for our own understanding, as found in our work on the tacit and ineffable aspects of knowledge and values. These theories might present us with the first inkling of an understanding of what actually assures a unity of purpose and a sense of direction and a coordination of efforts – stronger than all explicit attempts.

Let us see what another grand old man of management theory has to say about these things. In his discussion on the roles of management Drucker begins by emphasising the importance to advanced societies of the institution of management. To him "Management also expresses basic beliefs of modern Western society. It expresses the belief in the possibility of controlling man's livelihood through systematic organisation of economic resources. It expresses the belief that economic change can be made into the most powerful engine for human betterment and social justice …"[5] No wonder that for instance Burnham from a similar standpoint can talk of the managerial revolution of modern capitalism.[6]

Not to diminish the role of management we would not go as far as that. Indeed management must be seen as an important and necessary part of the way a modern economy is organised, with a more refined division of work, with more and more complex conditions for producing even simple products, but instead of being "the most powerful engine" management may just be one of the expressions of a far more complex engine.

Drucker and Burnham's ideas seem to belong to a time in the middle of the 20th century where there was an optimistic belief in the almost infinite possibilities in the management of not only organisations, but whole societies. There was a belief in the West that ideologies were dead and all that remained were mere technical questions.[7] Today this may seem to have been overly optimistic.

The first job of a manager is the management of business. For this to take place management has to manage, "and managing is not just passive, adaptive behaviour; it means taking action to make the desired results come to pass."[8]

The second job is to "make a productive enterprise out of human and material resources." This is the task of managing managers, the task of managing human resources. This means that Drucker regards many employees as having a managerial task that must be managed. In passing we note that the modern expression "management of human resources" has old roots.

Only through the management of human resources can a business organisation achieve the objective of generating "an output that is larger than the sum of its inputs." Organisational diagrams, boxes and arrows are not enough to do this job.

Other aspects are important to Drucker. Foremost is the necessity to create a sense of direction: "An effective management must direct the vision and efforts of all managers towards a common goal."[9] To Drucker this means the creation of sets of objectives for all levels in the organisation; objectives showing what must be done in order to achieve the overall objective of the organisation in question. Interestingly these objectives are not designed from above as the components of an overall strategy and plan. In fact it seems that Drucker finds it possible to generate objectives from below, in the sense that one generates objectives from below that fit into more encompassing objectives above.

In the boys' game this would have meant that Ralph with a little help from Piggy only saw to the overall objectives, survival and rescue, while each and every one of the boys would contribute with efforts that would help achieve this overall objective, by building a fire, by constructing a shelter, by collecting food and fetching water. The processes would have to have strong aspects of mutuality and cooperation; it would certainly not be a question of every boy for himself.

The objectives only point to the end product of one's endeavours. The construction and fulfilment of the objectives demands a large degree of self-organisation and self-control. "The greatest advantage of management by objectives is perhaps that it makes it possible for a manager to control his own performance. Self-control means stronger motivation: a desire to do the best rather than just enough to get by."[10]

Did we not find something like that with Barnard, when he asserted that it would be impossible for a single executive to break up the plan into details, and decide upon the innumerable simultaneous and progressive actions that would be necessary to achieve the objectives of the whole organisation?

Objectives and self-organisation are not enough though. Objectives tell a manager what he must aim for, and the proper organisation might enable him to achieve the objective. "But it is the spirit of the organisation that determines whether he will do it. It is the spirit that motivates, that calls upon a man's reserves of dedication and effort, that decides whether he will give his best or just enough to get by."[11]

What is needed is 'leadership' and 'spirit' shown by management. "Managing managers requires special efforts not only to establish common direction, but to eliminate misdirection. Mutual understanding can never be attained by 'communication down', can never be created by talking."

Perhaps this is what separates management and leadership. Management provides no spirit, while leadership might act as a catalyst on the energies of every member of the organisation. Although management can establish an explicit system consisting of objectives and organisation structures, this explicit system of management will not be enough. It will just be the shell, the enabling framework, the means. What is needed to fill out the shell is something else that calls forth the energies of managers and employees alike. In the boys' game this was apparently only found in the negative drive of the beast found inside the boys.

Again we come to the conclusion that a very important part of leadership is not and cannot be made explicit. Neither Barnard nor Drucker can tell exactly what this part really is. Barnard talks of the need for indoctrination, while Drucker talks of spirit, or is it spirits?

Does this in fact parallel Weber's talk of the "Geist" ('spirit') of capitalism as the driving force,[12] the force we cannot observe, in the manner that we can observe systems like bureaucracies or divisions of work, organisational diagrams and written objectives.

In order to get closer to those aspects of leadership that to Barnard, at least in part, fall under the heading of indoctrination and to Drucker under the almost Weberian heading of spirit, we turn to Bennis' polemic attempt to explain why managers can't lead. Although he deems it necessary for leaders to show both managerial ability and leadership ability, he discerns between the two roles by pointing out that "Leaders are people who do the right thing; managers are people who do things right,"[13] adding that he had often observed people in top positions doing "the wrong thing well."

According to Bennis' observation leaders seem to posses four essential competencies that one may presume set them apart from mere managers doing the wrong things in the right way.

The first leadership competency is the ability to communicate an extraordinary focus of commitment, to an outcome, a goal or a direction. One might object here that to Bennis it does not seem to matter in what direction one is committed. Leaders may to a greater or lesser extent also be the Jacks of the boys' game, or the despots of authoritarian regimes.

Hitler certainly understood how to command attention, just look at the eyes of people taking part in the Third Reich's mass rallies in Nuremberg or Berlin in the old newsreels. Watch the enthusiasm and fire in the eyes of the people attending, or listen to their chants, and their synchronised yelling and shouting. Is it not the powerful beast found in *Lord of the Flies* that we see in their eyes and hear from their throats?

The unity of spirit found in Jack's band or in the rallies is certainly not just a result of very elaborate design and planning. On the contrary, design and planning were a result of this spirit, just as in Jack's gang. We even seem to find the same kind of rituals, the atavistic rituals connected to "*Blut, Ehre, Boden, Vaterland*" and the ritualistic chanting and prancing.

It remains to be seen whether there exists a force that could be the positive mirror image of the beastly image we see here, a force that would be able to convey just as strong a focus of commitment, commitment to an outcome, to a goal or a direction, but would not kill boys, or build extermination camps, or commit other atrocities.

Bennis does not provide us with a clue; he only sees the need for the commitment, but cannot tell us what it is, how it comes about; and whether it is just some mysterious quality found in leaders.

This would certainly not be our view. Whether we talk of a positive force or the beast, it would never be sufficient to look only to the qualities of the leader. The explanation for the apparent success of leaders like Jack or Hitler cannot be found only in their personal leadership qualities.

In *Lord of the Flies* we found the beast was part of us. This is important, because it may mean that a leader can only be a leader if he or she is a catalyst for the forces found in each and every one of us. This would mean that a leader, whatever his or her charismatic qualities, must be seen in conjunction with the group that is being led. Leaders may thus represent the visible interpretation of something found latently in the group, something that people are not individually aware of, they just respond to it, like Jack's gang of choir boys. The "Hitlers" of this world would then be an answer to something that members of the group tacitly strive for, are inclined to, or want. It is difficult to find the right expression for this "something."

Bennis never gets further than saying that people do not embark on any old vision. "Some visions and concepts have more staying power and are rooted more deeply in our human needs than others."[14]

We have to realise, of course, that the story is more complicated, that there are bandwagon effects, with the timid ones following more hesitantly, as well as diverging opinions and all sorts of opposition. There may even be voices of reason as found for instance in the examples of Ralph and Piggy, and all the real Ralphs and Piggys of this world.

The second leadership competency that Bennis sees is the management of meaning. "To make dreams apparent to others and to align people with them, leaders must communicate their vision. Communication and alignment work together."[15]

The third competency that Bennis takes up is what he calls the "management of trust," arguing that the main determinant of trust is reliability, or "constancy." While agreeing to the importance of trust, I am not sure that constancy is enough. Would one have trust in a leader whose constancy contained beastly traits? Who was vindictive in a fairly constant way for instance? Although one might trust that such leaders would show this trait always, it is difficult to regard this as trust.

If the theories presented later in this chapter are right it would mean that the attempt to define leadership independently of the led might be a futile exercise, although this is exactly what Bennis and others attempt to do. This is certainly also the case with his fourth leadership competence, the management of self, "knowing one's skills and deploying them effectively." Bennis sees this as critical; if one does not see the limit of one's competency one might bring about disaster.

Again Bennis argues too glibly, using the example of incompetent doctors making life worse for their patients. Ralph apparently did not know the limits of his skills, but he somehow came to realise them during the boys' game, but did Jack? He was not elected leader, but he somehow ended up being the leader. What is the kind of knowledge of oneself he ought to have heeded, in order to avoid disaster?

I am afraid that there is no rational sense of self-command,[16] restraint or insight that could have stopped Jack. His self-command was given over to darker impulses. And by the way he did not seem to lack the skills for leading the group, and neither did Hitler for that matter.

What may have been missing is thus not the skills as a leader, but a better purpose. This by the way also goes for the doctor examples of Bennis'. Incompetence may be a problem, but even more problematic may be a competence used for dark purposes, also with doctors. We just have to think back to Dr Hans Münch, formerly of Auschwitz. He may, for all we know, have been a competent doctor with regard to medical skills, and thus with the competence Bennis is looking for. Still the result was disastrous, and perhaps even more so if he was a good doctor.[17]

The self-command or restraint that is needed is therefore quite different from what Bennis would have us believe. In fact we might be looking for something that carries the same force, or is even stronger, than the beast, which would in effect make it impossible for Jack to contribute to the killing of another person and that would have made it impossible for Hans Münch to have any part whatsoever in the extermination of Jews and others in the gas chambers of Auschwitz, and for other doctors to perform their experiments on the inmates of concentration camps.

This something must be bigger than the self-command Bennis is talking about, and we would further expect that it would have to be something that would be shared among leaders and the led. What we are looking for is something like the invisible moral weave we have spent so much energy on, in the attempt to explain how it came about.

What we see in all these expositions is a tendency to concentrate on the right man characteristics. Women do not really seem to have been part of the management and leadership equation. In fact I believe that this blind sight indicates one of the major problems with these attempts to elicit the important leadership characteristics. They are a product of the self-awareness of managers, and not only managers, but also social science at the time they were written.[18] They may in fact tell us more about implicit assumptions of their time than about leadership, about the focus on management, on males, on rational and scientific methods, on the belief in individual traits of character, on the necessity of having real managers and correspondingly people or resources that had to be managed.

They have also provided us with an idyllic, almost pastoral picture of management and leadership inasmuch as we are told of qualities that most would tend to give an appreciative nod, while qualities that may be more sinister have not been brought to light. In our attempt to show the importance of these darker qualities in relation to the boys' game we may have gone too far, but at least we have seen how we have to recur to something sinister in order to understand the conditions for leadership in something as simple as a boys' game. Several times we have seen how this included a dark force in the vague shape of the beast that is part of all of us. We have been looking for a positive reflection of these sinister forces, but have not found it in the classical views of management and leadership.

Perhaps one may ask whether ruthlessness is an inherent part of management and leadership: the ruthlessness found in the ability to act also in situations where there can be no advantage to all, or where one has to take risks on behalf of others; the ruthlessness necessary to stick to a course one believes is right even in the face of heavy costs. This might include persisting in situations, where the outlook is not very bright; the almost Churchillian ability to continue in the face of serious setbacks and mounting losses; still possessing a belief, a will, a tenacity to go on and be able to convince others.

But this might also include the ruthlessness shown when putting the axe to parts of an organisation that does not help to achieve the goals of the organisation. Or engaging in activities like: outmanoeuvring competition, making competitors go bankrupt, cutting back operations of a company, dismissing people, moving capital and plants, thereby creating unemployment, knowingly disregarding possible bad effects of the company's operations on employees, customers, society or the environment, for instance by producing both anti-personnel mines and crutches – all for the best of the company and its shareholders.

What I ask is: Is this also part of management and leadership?

It certainly looks like the Machiavellian part of leadership, remembering the way in which "The Prince" used deviousness, and every trick in the book to achieve his will. "How commendable in a Prince it is to keepe his word, and live with integrity, not making use of cunning and subtlety, every one knows well: yet wee see by experience in these our dayes, that those Princes have affected great matters, who have made small reckoning of keeping their words, and have known by their craft to turne and wind men about, and in the end have overcome those who have grounded upon the truth."[19]

How do we discern between what would be acceptable and what would not be acceptable? Where do we draw the line between the beast and the beauty, or the positive reflection of the beast? Or is beastliness always a part of leadership? Remembering of course the force of Nietzsche's blond beast and his concept of the "der leibhafte Wille zur Macht." This beast strives to grow, to reach out, attract, wants to achieve, to get the upper hand, not because of any kind of morality, but just because it lives, and this living is *Wille zur Macht*.[20] It may be destructive and dangerous, but it may also a prime mover in societal development. This is the positive, progressive potential of the beast.

I am sure that no fine line can be drawn between the positive and negative side of this. There is no sand to draw it in, and there do not seem to be any discerning features in the landscape that can help us in our attempts to elicit the secrets of management and leadership, behind the examples we have seen here.

THE LAYERS OF MANAGEMENT AND LEADERSHIP

Before continuing we might collect our wits by attempting to structure the following discussion of management and leadership, utilising, somewhat in contradiction to our views, boxes for grouping the descriptions. The overall idea of Table 9.1 is to show three important layers of management and leadership. The three layers are: (1) the mechanics of management and administration, or the boxes and arrows part; (2) the leading part of leadership, or the spirit part; (3) coalescence and self-organisation, representing the unspoken purposefulness, unpremeditated coordination, tacit drivers and the beastly force. In the boys' game Ralph would represent the first layer, Jack the second layer and the beast the third and lowest layer.

The first layer relates to the attempt to make management a scientific endeavour. It therefore seems fitting that aspects found here can be organised under the headings found in Fayol's *"Prevoyance, Organisation, Commandment, Controle."*[21] The aspects in this layer also carry the imprint of a whole body of administrative science exemplified for instance by the work of Gulick and Urwick, who seemed to regard organisation as a technical problem.[22] Further roots may be found in production management and in industrial engineering.[23]

What we see is the clear imprint of attempts to rationalise about human behaviour. Simon's *Models of Man*[24] comes to mind immediately together with other attempts to algorithmetise problem solving and decision making in general, like systems thinking, operations research, and more recently total quality management, balanced scorecards and knowledge management schemes, implicitly asserting that this is in essence what management is about.

The second layer connects to traditional definitions of leadership. Here we find the attempt to blow spirit into the inanimate clay of the organisation, to motivate and let people direct and control their own efforts. This in a way is what Bennis for instance regards as the essence of leadership. Perhaps the stories of what the great leaders did can be related to this layer. It does not seem to have mattered much, whether we are talking of religious leaders, political leaders, military leaders or leaders in business. This is where we find the hero, or the great man thesis, the belief in the Churchills and the Iacoccas of this world.[25]

Table 9.1 The layers of management and leadership

The mechanics of management and administration
(the boxes and arrows)

"Prevoyance:"   Plan, design and implement a system of communication
"Organisation:"   Bring people together into a cooperative relationship and
                       elicit contributions from them
"Commandment:" Make a productive enterprise out of human and mate-
                       rial resources
"Controle:"   Design and implement systems of control and correction

---

The leading part of leadership
(the spirit)

Provide sense of direction and communicate purposes, objectives and ends
Create a spirit "that motivates, that calls upon man's reserves of dedication"
Identify, amplify and communicate important values and beliefs
Possess a will to power (ruthlessness)

Coalescence and self-organisation
(the beastly force)

Coordinate without a plan, based upon an unspoken common purpose
and tacit drivers
Create a recombinant organisation
Decentralise responsibility and decision making
Synthesise knowledge and competence

Finally in the third layer we harp back to our own ideas and arguments, utilising arguments from former chapters in an effort to get closer to the hidden aspects of leadership and self-organisation.

In itself a taxonomy and a box like the one we have created here seem to belong to the activities of the first layer. In this layer we find it natural to categorise; this is the scientific approach.

It is extremely important to remember that although the different factors found in this taxonomy of leadership aspects may look as if they are of like importance, or on the same footing, the box-like appearance is deceptive. They are certainly not independent of each other and we cannot just select and choose as we like in order to practise management and leadership.

Perhaps what we have here is analogous to the layer models presented earlier, where the lower layers represented the tacit part of knowledge for instance, and the upper layer represented the explicit part of knowledge. By way of analogy the lower layer aspects would represent the tacit aspects of leadership and management, aspects that perhaps we can only "know" about in the tacit sense we talked about earlier. This would fit with the sense in which the boys in *Lord of the Flies* knew about the beast. They felt its presence, but they could not actually point to it or identify it. Some were having nightmares about it, but apart from that they could not get hold of it.

The middle layer would represent the aspects grasped more easily, they may still be implicit, but at least they can be talked about and perhaps even identified in a fairly intersubjective manner, almost in the same manner as if we tried to talk about and identify expressions like "fair" or "just."

The upper layer would be where we find the boxes and arrows, or the attempt to scientify the whole issue. This is the level of definitions and analysis, of explicit models, methods and measurements. What those who get carried away in an endeavour to create scientific models of management and leadership often forget is that that this layer rests on the murky, shifting depths of the other layers; it cannot be seen in isolation.

It strikes me that in a strange way we might even invoke Kierkegaard and see the upper layers as the aesthetic stage, the intermediate layer as the ethics stage and the bottom layer as a relating to faith, or the religious stage.[26]

Apparently such a view of the different aspects of management and leadership has not yet caught on. What seems to have happened is that the mode of thought that is found in the management layer, or the upper level, is crowding out attempts to understand aspects of leadership, and the deeper foundation of it, in the shape of the third layer representing the submerged level. When aspects of the intermediate and deeper layers are taken up, they are couched in a methodology belonging to the management layer. They are reduced to visible fragments and pseudo-algorithmic procedures. Today attempts to scientify, or should it be "scientologise," and to evolve rigorous methods with claims of rationality, are pouring forth in a never ending stream.

IMPOSSIBLE MANAGEMENT CONSTRUCTS

"Stream," this may remind us of something, a drawing by Escher[27] called "Waterfall." This drawing gives one the impression of a waterfall, where the water is streaming over a fall, runs all the way towards the back of the drawing and then forward towards the same fall, in a closed eternal loop. In the drawing at least this seems plausible. We are led to see the water as running downhill all the time. It is difficult to see what is wrong with the drawing, but then we cannot see gravity.

Perhaps that is also the case with some of the models and methods of modern scientific management. Many modern approaches to management and leadership seem to share this superficial plausibility with "the waterfall." A first look at the models show some recognisable ingredients and the details of the models seem to convey the impression that they are built using the well-known and established elements of knowledge connected in a way that fits with well-established principles. But like the waterfall the approaches would not work if we tried them in practice. Gravity represented by the forces loosely described by the aspects of the second and third layer would see to that, although we have to remember that the models and tools of modern management theory are more difficult to unravel than Escher's drawings.

In order to demonstrate that working with these models and tools may be seen as adventures with impossible constructs, we cannot use the same pseudo-scientific approach that we are criticising. That would be self-contradictory. What we are appealing to is instead the insight we hope to have brought forth in our attempts to show the deep tacit foundations of leadership.

In our critical analysis of topics related to the attempt to measure everything that counts, we looked at topics like the ISO 9000 complex, total quality, intellectual capital and attempts to scale leadership and to create individual incentives. Now we begin to see how these attempts and many others found in modern management theory relate to the first layer, to the mechanics of management. Certainly some of the attempts postulate that leadership aspects are included, for instance in the attempts to scale leadership and create individual incentives. It seems evident though that they cannot be seen as covering the aspects of the second and third layers.

Perhaps many managers identify their position as managers with the ability to work with quantitative information, with models and schemes. Perhaps they fear that without these tools they would never be seen as real managers. Perhaps this might also explain why we sometimes experience a large gap between the unconscious processes and the attempts to create formal and rational procedures.

In Patching's discussion of "Managers as people"[28] he refers to the divergence between the strange activities of their minds and the formal procedures they attempt to implement. Using observations and reflections from management meetings, he argues that during these meetings the unconscious parts of the minds constellate archetypes, forming attitudes, projecting aspects of the shadow, and forging metonymic links between individuals and archetypal leaders, fools, warriors and amazons. Yet people persist in "attempting to 'teambuild' by providing clearer terms of reference, allocating roles, and in hundreds of other ways engage only the rational, cognitive, and intellectual parts of team members' personalities."[29]

Hirschhorn describes an interesting case where it turned out that a manager used knowledge of quantitative information, of models and schemes, just to appear to be in control. The manager in question "was projecting a defensive fantasy that made him feel more in control of his situation than he actually was. In doing so, however, ... [he] also distanced himself psychologically from the very people on whom he had to depend in order to do his work successfully."[30] In other words he clung to a view belonging to the first layer, presumably like so many others that do not possess that ability to act like leaders.

New waterfall-like management theories and models seem to ignore the important aspects found in the intermediate and third layer. Perhaps it is no wonder that Astley and Zammuto talk of language games, where organisational scientists should be viewed "not as engineers offering technical advice to managers but as providers of conceptual and symbolic language for use in organizational discourse."[31]

A close and pensive look at these waterfalls might reveal that they also collapse upon the first layer. They are not the same models as found in traditional management theory, but they represent a continuation of the belief in the strict rationalistic and scientific version of management. In their attempt to show explicit models of how to act, they ignore the deeper and less explicit questions of leadership, not to mention the forces of the third layer, which might be regarded as the forces of gravity in management and leadership.

What about the more disjointed models and tools that are used in practice then? What are the answers in practice to the questions of how a leader may: provide sense of direction and communicate purposes, objectives and ends; create a spirit "that motivates, that calls upon man's reserves of dedication;" identify, amplify and communicate important values and beliefs?

What we are looking for is not management of objects and financial and physical resources, but leadership. We do not expect to find any one-to-one correspondence between the aspects listed in our layer model and what is found in practice. Practice may be too messy for that, not nicely divided into a meccano set of management bricks.

THE LEADING PART

Most people in business will have heard of Steve Jobs, one of the charismatic founders of Apple, who in the early 1980s was possessed by the idea of creating a computer for the rest of us in the shape of the Macintosh computer. In Sculley's book *Odyssey* about his involvement with Apple, he writes of the awesome Mac and the group who created it: "Steve was their inspirational leader, and they idolized him. In a story on Silicon Valley, Tom Wolfe once wrote about what psychologists call 'the halo effect.' 'People with the halo effect seem to know exactly what they're doing and, moreover, make you want to admire them for it. They make you see the halos over their heads.' That was Steve's power – to make people believe in him."[32]

Later of course Steve Jobs had to leave Apple, where he was succeeded by a series of rather short-lived CEOs. A few years ago Steve Jobs returned to a company in crisis. Now, sitting in front of a new Macintosh computer with its extraordinary shape and colour scheme, with almost see-through panels of strange colours like tangerine and blueberry, I came to wonder whether one man could really make such a difference. Apple no longer seem to be in crisis as they have once more created a consistent line of new computers, which are universally admired, and imitated, at least with regard to their see-through design.

Steve Jobs may not be a brilliant scientist or engineer, or a man of ideas, nor does he appear to be a great manager, but somehow his influence seems absolutely decisive in the creation of a series of trend-setting computers. His influence is seen in everything, in the consistent graphical user interface, as well as the shape and colour of the first Macintosh. Steve wanted it to look friendly and human, and so the computer for the rest of us came to look like a small stooping friendly guy.[33] Today one automatically assumes that he has had a decisive influence in the new line-up of attractive personal computers that have made Apple a prosperous company once more.

Perhaps what we see here are small glittering reflections of spirited leadership that Drucker is talking about, where the energy turned out is larger than the sum of efforts put in, where energy is created, where something more than mechanical means are involved and something that energises and focuses the efforts of an organisation more effectively than any manager will ever be able to do, whatever the amount of vision statements, strategies and plans for action.

It is something that seems to characterise all great leaders. They all have the ability to energise and focus the efforts of fellow human beings, whether we are talking about a Mahatma Gandhi, a Winston Churchill, a John F. Kennedy and to a lesser degree maybe even a Tony Blair.

Still spirit is a rather vague concept. To Drucker "Good spirit requires that there be full scope for individual excellence. Whenever excellence appears, it must be recognised, encouraged and rewarded, and must be made productive for all other members of the organisation. ... Altogether the test of good spirit is not that 'people get along together'; it is performance, not conformance."[34]

What spirited leadership seem to bring forth is more than just individual excellence, somehow it is instrumental in bringing about a synergised effort of people in an organisation. This is where energy is created in the sense of Drucker.

This may sound as if spirited leaders are just natural born manipulators that can make any group of people jump through loops and perform other tricks because they possess the ability to energise and focus the individual energies. This would be a great man thesis and represents a simple view of spirited leadership.

Spirited leadership in our sense is not only defined by the characteristics of a leader-individual, but also by something that characterises the group to be led. A simple example of that is the beastly force felt by the boys who became members of Jack's group in the boys' game. This somehow was essential in turning Jack into a leader, his own ruthlessness and aspirations were certainly not enough, and he did not seem to persuade or force the others to join.

Our conception of spirited leadership must thus rest upon all the aspects found in the middle and lower layer of Table 9.1. This is important in relation to our other topic, that of self-organisation. Self-organisation would seem to preclude any kind of "arrows and boxes" management, but it might be compatible with, and necessitate, some kind of spirited leadership in our sense of the term, although initially it may perhaps sound strange to introduce leadership into a self-organised group.

No leadership is found in an anthill, nor in the case of two rowers adjusting their movements to each other, and leadership may not be necessary for the small group of boys involved in shelter-building, or for Simon's group of house painters, quietly adjusting to each other in their daily work. Where then is leadership of self-organising entities necessary and in what sense can leadership and self-organisation be combined?

Perhaps an analogy with a human mind can provide us with an idea. Somehow the "I" resides in the neural network of our brain, and the I can think consciously, but when I want to do something intentional, like writing these sentences, I do not have to do a lot, most of the task seems to be taken care of automatically. Somehow the parallelism of my brain self-organises the task, sending messages to arms and fingers and so on. The "I" does not have to do all the detailed work. In a sense then one might say that the "I" directs the activities of self-organising networks of neurons, without really knowing how they perform their act. Perhaps this may be used to illustrate how a simple combination of leadership and self-organisation may work, although it must be noted that the "I" is in itself a result of self-organisation of the human mind.

In a more concrete example one might think of a person having the idea, perhaps from a study of aerodynamics, that it must be possible to construct a new type of windmill with wings of a new shape. This person may have no more than this idea, but he or she may engage others in his or her efforts to construct such a wing; others with more knowledge of technology issues and the different components making up a wing. These people may only have a vague idea of the whole windmill, but may be able to self-organise the different tasks of building a wing. Still their efforts have somehow to be guided by an idea of what they are to achieve, in effect combining self-organisation and leadership. In this example the innovator and leader are combined in the person of an entrepreneur-leader. It does not have to be like that, the innovator may not be a leader, and the leader may try to realise an idea originating with someone else. What he does is unite and drive people with this idea.

If one substitutes windmill with new type of personal computer and windmill wings with a new graphical interface, one might perhaps see this example as a simple illustration of the way the Macintosh computer was created, remembering that it represented something that no one had any clear idea of in advance.[35]

These examples do not really show how self-organisation and spirited leadership may fit together in any concrete detail; they may just provide us with the beginnings of an understanding. We cannot yet demonstrate how the different aspects of leadership fit in here. What we want to do therefore is to take a closer look at the importance of the different leadership aspects in relation to self-organisation.

According to Purser and Cabana "Strategic-level managers are the stewards of the corporate vision, the arbitrators of resource allocation conflicts, and the guardians of the operational philosophy ... Another important role the strategic level plays is to create cooperative synergies among business units with complementary skill sets ..."[36] Although they talk only of management, we see the activities of such strategic level managers as belonging to the leading part of leadership.

In an earlier discussion on self-organisation and direction we saw that to a certain extent the organisation may be self-directed, in the sense that direction may evolve from the interaction of members of the group, from their knowledge and their reflection. It may emerge from the process they are carrying out. In the attempt to construct something like a new windmill wing they may discover that certain processes or materials make it easier to progress towards the shared goal, almost in the sense that valleys and passes of mountain make for easier progress.

But any organisation of a certain complexity has a need for more direction than that. Something like a compass and course is needed too, or the self-organising groups might just follow the easiest routes, the valleys, in whatever the direction they are leading.

The role of a leader may be to provide this direction. Purser and Cabana see the role of strategic management primarily as being that of managing the relation between an organisation and its environment, and "understanding changes and opportunities in the industry, changing and aligning the enterprise to delight the customers, and championing innovations that will bolster the firm's competitive advantage."[37] Nothing new in here though; this might already be done by managers publishing company visions, strategic and operational plans, leaving only the details to be taken care of by self-organised groups. Somehow this would seem to be too limited in scope in relation to our concept of self-organising groups.

Once more it may prove more profitable to look to leaders who provide direction and focus without prescribing the exact route to take. They stand for and communicate the big idea, they do not specify what activities every member of the organisation has to perform in order to realise the idea. The leader's direction-giving activities may compared to the "I have a dream" directions. I have a dream of a new type of computer, a new type of windmill, a new service on the Internet, or something much bigger, like a new kind of society.

The visions of these leaders do not spring only from their own minds, but stem from their interactions with the environment, or from activities within the organisation. The important thing is that leaders represent the dream or the vision, they keep it alive, they communicate it and they inspire.

It is striking how often examples of leadership involve activities in relation to the creation of something new that one has never seen before, like changes in society, in social structure, in the minds of people, or the creation of new products, services and ways to produce them that no one had thought possible or even been aware of.

Thus the movement, the change and the creation may be an essential aspect of leadership, while management may be more about repetition and fixation of existing structures, processes and procedures.

Leadership by inspiration demands the skills of a great communicator. To inspire others through rhetoric, leaders must possess two skills: "The first is the process of defining the purpose of the organization in a meaningful way. ... This process is called 'framing.' The second skill is the leader's ability to use symbolic language to give emotional power to his or her message. This is a process of 'rhetorical crafting'."[38]

Framing means that a leader is able to communicate an engaging vision, the dream so to speak. Gandhi's dream of a non-violent achievement of Indian independence may show how compelling these visions may be. What seems to be characteristic is that the vision is more than a product or service. It may have more of the ring of an organisation like Greenpeace or Amnesty International. Instead of having a vision of building a computer that is a few per cent faster than existing computers, the vision is to build another type of computer, a computer that can be used by the rest of us, for a price we can afford. The vision is to make something revolutionary, to transcend existing limitations.

This is the stuff that myths are made of, myths that may be extremely powerful in engaging people, as part of narratives that are told, and retold, until they become a part of the fixtures of one's mind.[39] This the really powerful stuff, but it often seems to carry the seeds of destruction between the lines. Myths and narratives may become a powerful weapon against an enemy in a war, but if the myths and the narratives are believed they deliver the reasons for committing even the most abominable atrocities, as experience have shown.

Thus one should perhaps be wary of myths, but then again this is part of the ambiguity we already saw in the case of the beast. It represents the force, but it does not discern between good and evil. That is something that must decided outside the myth and the narratives.

A spirit that calls upon man's reserves of dedication cannot be had by a goal like a 20 per cent increase in sales. It must something more, something that touches deeper values and beliefs of the members of the organisation, confirming them, and giving them a more concrete shape. What seems to be happening here is that the leader becomes an evangelist for ideas that amplify values shared by the whole organisation and perhaps even the society the organisation is acting in. Members of the organisation are not told what to do in detail, they are shown a value that they can believe in, they are shown a meaning, a sense and a purpose, not technical details, stepwise description of procedures and measurements.

In a more limited sense Conger talks of value and belief amplification. "Value amplification is simply the process of identifying and elevating certain values as basic to the overall mission," while belief amplification amplifies beliefs about "which factors support or impede actions taken to achieve those desired values."[40] This includes the well-known and often used trick of painting images of enemies that will try to hinder us in achieving our goals. Such images help unite the efforts of the organisation, making the members close ranks against "the enemy."

The rhetorical crafting has to do with the way the dream is articulated. Publishing a list of organisational goals in the shape of a list may not stir many people, but Kennedy's *"Ich bin ein Berliner"* from the Town Hall of Schöneberg in Berlin after the Berlin Wall had gone up certainly stirred the minds of many people.

The rhetorical crafting may of course reside in something else other than the speeches of a great communicator, in symbols, ways of doing things and so on. From the poster showing Kitchener's gigantic forefinger pointing and shouting "Britons [Picture of Kitchener] "Wants You" Join Your Country's Army! God Save the King"[41] to the subdued "No loss should hit us which can be avoided with constant care" voiced by the founder of the Danish Maersk company.[42]

In these discussions it may look as if the leading part of leadership rests on a bag of "framing" and rhetorical tricks that can be used to give direction, unity and sense to the efforts of self-organising groups.

We strongly disagree. Such tricks have an effect, but if we return for a moment to our former arguments concerning the complementarity of the drive that the leader represents and the latent drive of the individuals making up a self-organising group, we may conclude that the personal qualities of the leader would have only a limited effect, if they did not represent condensation points for already existing latent drives.

This is important also in relation to the present discussion. Somehow the amplified values and beliefs must be genuine, must reflect or express the values and beliefs of the people making up the organisation, or it would just be rhetoric and myth.

Thus the leading part of leadership must include the ability to identify, amplify and make concrete some of the important values and beliefs of the members of the organisations. Again we postulate a complementary relationship. If this complementarity is lacking it is doubtful whether one could talk of self-organising groups. Groups manipulated through framing or rhetorical tricks would certainly in a very basic sense be organised and steered from the outside.

"I have a dream leadership", goal-setting, framing and rhetorical crafting is not enough. If self-organisation is to work, further conditions must be fulfilled. The leading part of leadership must help bring about a spirit that motivates and promotes independent input from members of the organisation, must encourage certain organisation characteristics, frameworks and bounds that will allow self-organisation to unfold.

"Self-managing organizations redistribute power to make decisions to people who have the strategic know-how, or to groups who are responsible for a whole work process. Under such new arrangements, the traditional tasks of management – planning, controlling, organizing, and coordinating the work of others – no longer make sense. Rather, it is management's responsibility to create the conditions that allow people to plan, control and organize, and coordinate their own work."[43]

To illustrate what this means, Purser and Cabana use the experience of the manufacturer of Gore-Tex fabrics. Here empowerment has replaced a traditional hierarchy of decision making. In the Gore scheme "there are no fixed positions of formal authority (people have sponsors not bosses), lines of communication are direct, objectives are set by those who make them happen, teams are formed when the need arises, tasks and functions are organized through commitments, not compliance."[44]

Even in traditionally strongly hierarchical and regulated organisations like banks such principles may work, as shown by CREDO's research into Jyske Bank's attempt to introduce elements of value-based leadership and management in the whole organisation.

According to Jensen[45] the basic idea in this reorientation is that detailed regulation, control and sanctioning are reduced and substituted by a strong reliance on the integrity and ability of local units and individual decision makers to act rationally in relation to the stated goals, policies and values of the organisation.

In practice this has meant that all decisions are in principle made according to a two-tier system, called by the German term the "*Vier Augen*" principle. Credit approval decisions made according to this principle demand that one person makes the recommendation and another approves, or disapproves as the case may be. No more than two persons are involved, and the approver may be another employee, not necessarily a manager. In this way a certain kind of reciprocity is possible.

"Designed to cut red tape, speed up customer-related decisions, and unambiguously place responsibility, this system has made it nearly inescapable for individual managers to delegate real authority to their staff. Authority, e.g. for credit granting, is assigned on the basis of an evaluation of the professional competence of the individual staff member combined with an assessment of the needs, e.g. typical size of credit lines, of his or her customer portfolio. Compared with earlier, and with the distribution of authority of most competitors, this has considerably enhanced the local decision-making capabilities of the bank."[46]

Other examples of delegation of authority resulting from the attempt to introduce value-based leadership and management in the bank can be found in Nielsen and in Jensen.[47] Although it has proved difficult to get a comprehensive view of all the changes that have taken place in the bank during the attempt to implement value-based leadership and management. The process seem to have taken on a life of its own, with managers everywhere in the organisation interpreting value-based leadership and management in their own way and implementing it in their own concrete instances.

As a small example one might refer to the initiative of a local manager, who by the way had recently been on a course in value-based leadership. He decided to introduce a new style of job advertisement putting the emphasis squarely on the qualities that would have to characterise an employee in a value-based leadership and management scheme, not mentioning salary at all. The CEO of the bank first noticed the totally new style when his wife made him aware of it, having seen the job advertisement in one of the major Danish newspapers.[48] The example inspired others in the bank to come up with something similar, in effect creating a new style.

One might fear that a scheme that allows such distributed decision making might lead to overall inconsistency and inefficiency. This does not seem to happen, on the contrary. What it means is that the spirit of value-based leadership and management seems to pervade parts of the organisation, bringing forth initiatives that would never have been possible in a centrally directed system, where consistency between overall goals and concrete initiatives may be guaranteed, but where there is no latitude for new local initiatives, meaning that all activity has to be guided by directives from higher up in the hierarchy.

It is difficult to get a concrete quantitative measure of what the attempt to introduce value-based leadership and management in the bank has meant.[49] Of course it is possible to refer to individual examples of what may have happened as a consequence of the introduction of value-based leadership and management, but not necessarily only because of that. What seems evident though is that a kind of spirit has caught on in a large part of the organisation, making top management and local management behave differently from how they would have without this spirit; initiating their own drives towards value-based leadership within their respective areas of responsibility.

In order to make it possible for value-based leadership and self-organisation to take hold, it is evident that something more than changes in the ever popular written value and mission statements are necessary. It is also evident that the spirit we have just discussed cannot take hold in an organisation based on hierarchical decision making, detailed job descriptions, detailed rules and personnel policies. This would be incompatible with such a spirit.

COALESCENCE AND SELF-ORGANISATION

In the boys' game the boys feeling the beast at work somehow felt drawn to Jack's group. Why Jack? The answer might be that Jack very early on in his actions showed what the others had just begun to feel. Jack was the catalyst in bringing forth the actions of the beast, making the other boys exclaim: "Look, he killed a pig!"

What we see here is that Jack attracts others who are beginning to feel the urge to break the ties of convention, the urge to go killing pigs, to carry out atavistic rituals, to rant and chant and finally to hunt Ralph. It is important to note that it was not only a question of what Jack was doing or saying; the attraction was a result of something that all the boys of his black gang felt. The boys coalesced around him and his actions, almost as if he was a condensation point.

This coalescence depended on two things: the latent urge felt by the boys joining, almost as if they were supercooled water droplets in a cloud; and the early realisation of this latent urge in Jack, as if he was a physical condensation point, a small ice particle upon which the supercooled droplets froze to ice, that is to say altered their physical state. Later other boys felt they had no alternative but to join his group, but now fear was at work, fear of the beast.

Earlier we talked of the need to look for less sinister forces that might give rise to a similar kind of attraction. Where then can we find examples of positive condensation points? Perhaps it may help to think back to the discussion in Chapter 7 on the condensation points in the shape of persons voicing concerns over the environment or human rights or a myriad of other problems and to "coalescence, which might be seen as a form of self-organisation with very little overall guidance in the beginning, might be a result of the workings of some sort of catalyst, making many people recognise that theirs is a shared problem, thereby creating a kind collective awareness that something is wrong, perhaps even some sense of what it is wrong in relation to."

Now in this case the people who coalesce around an environmental or human rights issue seem to be driven by something as strong as the beast in the boys' game, but it would be a stretch of one's imagination to call this drive beastly. Here in fact we find what we are looking for, a positive force, a force to believe in. It is of course possible that the individuals joining such groups may have ulterior motives of their own, but the group as such represents a belief that reaches further than personal motives, as we concluded earlier; something that is greater than any of them.

Even so the whole cascading process of such movements may have a lot in common with the mechanism that we saw at work in relation to the boys, for instance that of a latent urgency, this time not related to any beast, but perhaps to a feeling that something is wrong with the environment or with human rights. Individuals may feel the urge to do something, but nothing happens until they can coalesce around some condensation point. Someone must show a possible way, a vision to believe in, an action to imitate and follow.

In the section on driving forces of self-organising groups we talked about latent shared social drivers like the fight for justice, for freedom, for a better world, for self-government, for partaking in decision making, for democracy, equality, or for ecology and against pollution. But we also talked about individual ones like power and influence, domination of others, status in the eyes of others, the urge to make a difference and perhaps even curiosity. These and other drivers were seen as absolutely necessary for the development of self-organisation.

The shared social drivers are the ones we are looking for. They are the ones we found in environmental movements, human rights movements and perhaps they also represent some of the strongest drivers of organisations, especially those belonging to the new economy. They may be the foundation for the enthusiasm found in the group creating the first Macintosh. They may be the drivers of people who want to work for organisations whose goals and activities fit their own values, whether they realise it or not.

This is where values and beliefs enter the picture, and no stronger drivers may be found. These drivers may be latent, people feel or believe in them almost like they feel and believe in the beast. Then along comes a person who shows them in his actions, and then we have a condensation point. Might not a Steve Jobs be such person, attracting those seeing the new world emerging with the growth of information technology, and looking for a chance to realise it, to become part of it.

Somehow we expect that such a person will be able also to energise his surroundings. "That was Steve's power – to make people believe in him." The energising properties mean that such a leader not only adds up the existing capabilities of his fellow workers, but fuels their capabilities, provokes, cajoles, persuades, makes them want to do more, makes them transcend existing capabilities, in order to realise shared and valued objectives, which may look impossible to achieve at the present; like a new type of personal computer or more intangible objectives related to a better environment, human rights or independence and self-government.

The leaders we see here are those leaders that drive the creation of new organisations and changes in the existing organisations; not on their own and not because of their individual qualities, but because they are condensation points and energisers of the latent striving that can be found in the people wanting to join the effort. This fits well with our earlier attempt to explain the process of change.

The traditional simple models of change found in management books[50] barely touch upon these important points, focusing instead on the management of a change that is somehow forced upon the organisation, and acting according to the recipe-like instructions for managing change, as if planned recipe-like change is just something that can be imposed upon the people making up an organisation.[51] What we see here is different, for instance in emphasising the complementarity between leadership and self-organisation.

The driving part of leadership we have just discussed is of course important, but drive is not enough. There is also a need for a recombinant organisation, for distributed responsibility and decision making, and for synthesised knowledge and competence.

The alternative to a rigid structure is recombinant[52] organisations that would be able to recombine on their own initiative, recombine people and resources according to necessity, and although it may sound frivolous, according to fancy. What is meant is that recombination according to necessity may not be enough in a competitive market, whereas recombination according to fancy would mean that self-organising task forces could and would be created on the basis of independent inputs, new ideas, suggestions and possibilities coming from potentially any member of the organisation, or from outside the organisation.

Although it may sound heretic this would also help to reduce the need for detailed strategies from top management. Instead of a fixed strategy, including blinkers that no one would be aware of, a general organisation-wide attention to internal and external developments, with ability to grab potentially promising developments and turn them into new products or services might be much more important. This fits well with Hirschhorn's comment: "Strategy work cannot be located in one division, one location, or one work station. Instead, as business theorists suggest, strategy is *enacted*. It takes place as influential executives throughout the organization test new ideas, invest in projects, and compete for development money."[53]

This would only be possible with self-organising groups, and open-ended decision making. What is needed from management is thus more the idea of direction than a detailed strategy, and the creation of acceptance of and support for what we have termed a recombinant organisation structure, with lower level management and with employees.

To illustrate the idea we might use the previously mentioned LOCAAS (Low Cost Autonomous Attack System) concept. Think if you will of a group of loitering airplane-like autonomous weapons flying over an enemy territory. All the units communicate with their neighbours, sharing information about enemy whereabouts and details of their own position. When a unit discovers an enemy object, it may attack on its own, or it may call for specialised units, or even the whole pack of available units, depending on the type of target. When a unit is destroyed during the attack a new unit takes its place. The LOCAAS concept may even include a kind of complementarity between specialised units working together. They are all programmed to react to certain enemy characteristics, and then let loose over enemy-held area. What happens from there on is not planned. The units are ready for many different eventualities, almost like a swarm of killer bees.

Now, perhaps the concept could be used on a recombinant organisation where the units, or rather the members of the group, can act semi-autonomously, where they know each other's general capabilities, where they can combine and split according the most pressing tasks they see. Not unthinkingly and according to a few lines of computer program, but consciously and according to vague, general, and perhaps even ambiguous ideas represented by a leader. The ambiguousness here means that they would be open to interpretation. The recombinant organisation will find its own way to reduce ambiguousness without limiting the search and solution space beforehand.

Such a structure would also mean that a leader/manager cannot sit at the hub of the organisation like a giant spider and channel all information, incoming and outgoing, through the centre. Instead an amoeba-like organisation of information may be more relevant. Using the LOCAAS analogy once more it may be important that members of the organisation share information on a many-to-many basis, in order to make sure that information is distributed among the members of the organisation, perhaps somewhat like the collective consciousness of the organisation or the culture of an organisation.

What we would find is not that everyone would communicate with everyone else, but amoeba-like structures of communication, where information is passed freely within the amoeba, that is to all the units that cluster around a given problem or topic. This would also mean distributed decision making, decisions being taken where the information and knowledge relevant for the decision resided, in the amoeba-like recombinant groupings of self-organising individuals.

A relevant analogy may perhaps be the brain or even a simple artificial neural network. Nowhere do we find a decisive node through which all information has to pass, realising of course that such a node would soon be become equal to the von Neuman bottleneck of traditional non-parallel computers. What we would need instead would be massive parallelism, and precisely such parallelism would be important for an organisation that wants to stay alive and grow in the new economy where it has to cope with a wealth of information of a very diverse nature. Recombinant organisation can only exist where there is open-ended and distributed decision making and decentralised responsibility.

Purser and Cabana state that a key feature of what they call self-managing organizations is "an underlying *design principle*, which requires restructuring work so that the responsibility for control and coordination is located at the level where the work is actually done." Thus individuals and groups control and coordinate their own effort.

Thinking back to the example concerning credit recommendation and approval, one would thus presume that the two persons making up a small decision-making group have the sole responsibility for the work they are doing and for making sure that they take into account all that is necessary to write the recommendation and to decide whether to approve or not approve. In practice the situation will of course be more complicated because of explicit and implicit bounds, legal restrictions and the procedures that must be followed.

Part of the responsibility formerly belonging to management must now rest with the individual or the small group actually doing the evaluation, writing the recommendation and making the approval. Only when the concrete process and the power to make decisions has been put in their hands can we expect people to show an independent initiative.

We call this open-ended decision making because it would represent an organisational framework in which decisions are not pre-empted, either by very detailed directives from someone above in the hierarchy, or by the work process. Even in a flat organisation it would not really be possible to motivate and promote independent input, if the work process left no latitude for independent thought and decision making. If an employee just had to follow a given algorithm, say a detailed assembly instruction, or a manual for treating customer complaints or for taking care of old persons in a nursing home, independent input would not be necessary, called for or possible. The employee would not be much more than a competent robot, soon to be replaced by the algorithms of a real robot.

In a discussion of how IBM entered the microcomputer market, Langlois and Everett assert that IBM was hindered by its corporate culture and rigid hierarchical structure, procedures and controls. To make it possible to design a microcomputer IBM spun off a semi-autonomous unit, "exempting it from internal procedures and isolating it from the dominant corporate culture ... suggesting that its corporate culture was incapable of producing such a new product – a competence-destroying innovation."[54]

Self-organisation demands a high level of insight and competence from every individual member of the organisation. The pre-programmed autonomy of LOCAAS robots would not be enough; that would just represent the anthill stage, an anthill designed by engineers.

In the shelter example we did not expect too much from the boys, we did not presume that they had much knowledge of, or competence in shelter-building, instead we presumed that they had a distributed general knowledge of houses and sheds, and materials. Using this general knowledge in a mutual trial-and-error process we expected them to be able to make some kind of shelter.

In a counter-example we might presume that an appointed chief had all the necessary knowledge of shelter-building, in this case the rest would just have to follow the detailed instructions of the chief; they would not need to know a lot and would not have to reflect on their own efforts, the chief would know what to do. Such an organisation might only be efficient under well-structured routine production conditions, when replicating existing designs. It would also mean that someone had to hold almost all the necessary knowledge and be able to use it for detailed instructions. Once more we see the traditional management aspects pop up.

In situations characterised by less replication and more creation and development this would not work very well. What might work instead is a kind of parallel processing by all the individuals in the organisation, where knowledge and competencies are distributed over the whole self-organising organisation, not in the manner that the members would just possess some specialised knowledge and competencies that could be fitted together according to some plan. That would be like making pins in Adam Smith's famous example of division of work.[55] No, in a manner so that their mutual interaction could bring forth something new, like the shelter in the boys' game. In a manner that would allow and encourage suggestions for changes in the process and for alternative solutions coming from any of them. This means that each member of the organisation would have to understand what they were trying to do as an organisation. Presumably this would mean that they would have to possess both specialised knowledge and competencies and more general knowledge and abilities.

What a group of individuals would bring forth in ideas and products, for instance a new concept for a chair, would be a result of their mutual interaction, as was the case in the boys' game, not a result of competent people working in isolation and under strict guidance on their separate part of a common project, a project they would have no idea of.

Nonaka talks of the need to create a field of interaction. "The inter-action between knowledge of experience and rationality enables individ-uals to build their own perspectives on the world. Yet these perspectives remain personal unless they are articulated and amplified through social interaction. One way to implement the management of organizational knowledge is to create a 'field' or 'self-organising team' in which individ-ual members collaborate to create a new concept."[56]

Interaction may of course be designed by a leader/manager but it might also be a result of individuals actively looking for others that are interested in the same problems or who might possess supplementary knowledge that might be important. This would fit the idea of an amoeba-like recombinant organisation better, perhaps somewhat like Brown and Duguid's concept of "evolving communities of practice."[57]

The evolving communities are not specified in advance, but may grow and retract according to the perceived need, although it is to be expected that often activated connections may persist, even though they may no longer help generate new knowledge. This would lead to a certain fixation and rigidity even of amoeba-like structures over time, perhaps like a brain growing old, and relying on often activated connections, in essence falling into already trodden tracks.

Given the importance of distributed knowledge and competence for organisational development, especially in knowledge-intensive companies of the new economy, it is no wonder that there has been a recent prolif-eration of publications on what has been called knowledge manage-ment.[58]

Knowledge management generally represents an attempt to present ways and means of optimising the management of knowledge in organi-sations, emphasising of course knowledge-intensive companies. This includes theories and models of knowledge generation, distribution and sharing of knowledge, and the utilisation of knowledge, often accompa-nied by a presentation of methods or information technology tools to be used in knowledge management.

Davenport and Prusak present a whole list of conditions related to the implementation of knowledge-based management, including knowledge-orientated culture, a necessary technological and organisational infrastructure, the support of senior management and so on.[59]

Others have a more reductionist view of knowledge management, seeing it essentially as concerned with knowledge storing and sharing, utilising the most advanced form of information technology.[60] Such a view runs the danger of substituting technology for organisation and information for knowledge, and it certainly leads to a reduced emphasis on the tacit aspects of knowledge that cannot be stored and distributed in a computer network.[61]

In itself the idea of using information technology to facilitate the sharing of knowledge may be misguided. What we have tried to emphasise in this discussion of leadership and self-organisation is not so much the sharing of existing knowledge by distributing it on a network, as the generation of new knowledge in a self-organising group. When building a shelter the boys contributed, not so much by sharing knowledge as by assembling or synthesising knowledge in the sense that during the construction process they mutually contributed to solving successive problems, thereby creating new knowledge and a construction that none of them had ever seen or known before.

KEEPING THE ORGANISATION UPRIGHT

What kind of bounds would prevent or curb the beastly versions of leadership and morally corrupt organisations? The answer to this question would be especially important in relation to the arguments for self-organisation.

From the discussion in the first chapter we know that solutions depending on the creation of more and more detailed behavioural regulation are counter-productive inasmuch as they exacerbate the problems they are supposed to help alleviate or solve. Something else is needed and this has to be something that builds upon the understanding we gained in the chapters on the social grammar and the weaving of the moral fabric.

Modern bureaucratic management with a strong orientation towards boxes and arrows might find that the bounds on behaviour would have to consist in what Paine calls a compliance strategy. The emphasis would be on conformity with externally imposed standards in the shape of public regulation. Management would have to "develop compliance standards, train and communicate, handle reports of misconduct, conduct investigations, oversee compliance audits, enforce standards."[62] Paine does not advocate such a position but characterises it as a compliance strategy.

Such a strategy could have been found in the Third Reich. Just think back to the strange normalcy in the activities of Dr Hans Münch formerly of Auschwitz. There one would surely find all kinds of written standards, and the necessary apparatus to assure compliance.

This would not be compatible with the view of self-organisation and leadership presented here. Instead we must look for more fundamental bounds that may be observed, but cannot necessarily be seen like rules and regulations. What we refer to is of course what we have called "General social norms like the notion of justice or fairness, mechanisms for conflict resolution and so on." and the tacit basic and universal strands of morality like: "The conditions belonging to every system of morality: sympathy and mutual aid; reciprocity; getting along; symbolic reflection such as the ability to put oneself into the place of another." Tacit values like these must be part of the most basic conditions of the self-organising organisations, and must be observed by leaders of organisations employing principles of self-organisation.

The restatement of these basic conditions would not bring us very far though. What is also needed are more specific bounds and values that can prevent leadership and self-organisation from sliding down the incline of moral aberrations that we have seen so many examples of.

Guiding values that have a more specific content may be found in our discussion of responsible entrepreneurship. These values were derived from existing and evolving general values found in the society of which the organisation is a part. When values concerning the environment, human rights, anti-discrimination and working conditions become important, companies and organisations will have to incorporate these values, letting them act as guides for and bounds on their own more specific activities; not waiting for these values to have a concrete expression in law and regulation, but acting on emerging values.

This also seems to be the idea behind the core beliefs found in the Caux Round Table referred to in a previous chapter. These principles show how business may interpret emerging values, and how values like these might lie behind the drivers we have discussed in relation to self-organisation and leadership. These values may be the positive drivers that have the force of the beast in the boys' game or the enthusiasm of the Third Reich with the thousand-year perspective, without becoming beastly.

Emerging values like the ones found in these principles have the additional quality that they can point to a direction, although rather vaguely, with a wagging forefinger perhaps, and they can act as bounds that implicitly declare certain objectives and activities to be out of bounds.

What we would be looking for in value-based leadership would thus be elements from responsible entrepreneurship. A leader would have to express his or her beliefs and commitment to these values, not so much by writing statements or publishing credos copied perhaps from the Caux principles, as demonstrating the commitment in his or her concrete activities, reflections, decisions and actions.

Inside the company or organisation such values would also be important in guiding the activities of the individual members and the self-organising groups. But this could in effect only happen if the leader stood for these values, demonstrating them in practice and encouraging initiatives supporting such values.

Being guided and bound by such values would not be enough though. Some of the moral ailments we discussed earlier would be able to emerge and multiply nicely in organisations committed to the promotion of ecological production methods or any other good cause. The good cause might be undermined by corruption in the organisation, by mistrust, bad management practices or even bad working conditions, and by almost any other organisational ailment.

To discourage such ailments the leader must at least be committed to and encourage:

- individual responsibility;
- consequence and consistency;
- transparency;
- trust, sincerity and honesty;
- the other opinion and the social grammar;
- subsidiarity.

Individual responsibility might be encouraged by delegating responsibility to individuals. This sounds self-evident, but here we must remember that such delegation may very easily become illusory, if accompanied by detailed written rules and instructions. This would be the case if for instance a specific employee was to be responsible only for one specific duty, under some very specific conditions. We have characterised that as a special, specific responsibility, and somewhat derogatively called it the 9 to 5 responsibility, where the responsibility is specified so finely that the individual does not have to use his or her own judgement, and where they can easily decline responsibility for anything not falling within their specified area of responsibility. In fact demarcating areas of responsibility that would leave open large unforeseen white spaces, where no one would have any responsibility.

The individual responsibility that a leader would have to encourage would have to be a more universal responsibility that could not be specified very clearly, but would leave the specifics to the responsibility of the individual or to the self-organising group.

What must be encouraged is the ability, willingness and courage to act so as to uphold the implicit moral values, in all positions and on all levels of the organisation. Without this even the most comprehensive rules and regulations could not prevent the bad spirals of moral decay, unless an equally strong and very costly system of control and punishment was put into place, and then it would not be a question of upholding values, it would be a question of avoiding punishment.

In his analysis of the origins of value-based leadership and management in Jyske Bank, Jensen[63] describes how the bank lost in the region of 500 million Danish kroner through the illegal activities of the managing director of the Gibraltar subsidiary in the early 1990s. This was a very large loss to the bank coming at the time of an economic crisis. It was to be expected that the reaction of top management would be to introduce stringent control measures, in order to prevent further losses caused by such activities. Jensen describes how responsibilities and processes were in fact stipulated in detail for employees and managers.

Surprisingly the CEO at that time soon realised that this would not prevent further incidents like the Gibraltar loss. Accordingly he initiated a process which soon led in the opposite direction of the stringent regulation and control approach, emphasising instead more individual responsibility and less reliance on clear-cut rules and procedures. In an interview with representatives of CREDO he emphasised that the bank does not specify values and attitudes that have the character of fixed rules, instead the values are general and perhaps even ambiguous.[64] They have to guide the employees of the bank, not direct them like precise rules. The present CEO expresses the thought like this: "We wish to work with attitudes and values that every employee has to interpret and make sense of on his own."[65]

What this means in relation to an incident like the one in Gibraltar, is that employees should not look only to their own 9 to 5 responsibilities, and ignore observations and suspicions that would indicate that a local branch manager might be engaged in problematic activities. They should no longer be innocent bystanders with no responsibility to act if rules and value are transgressed, or just employees following the directions they are given, even if they can see that this would be contrary to the values promulgated by the bank. They must become responsible employees, who act according to the values of the bank.

They cannot just say "this is no concern of mine" or something like "it would not matter whether I did something or I didn't." Neither would it be enough with verbatim compliance, a strict adherence to written rules and procedures. Hirschhorn gives an example from a nuclear power station showing that such verbatim compliance can never work. A manager suggested that "The next major accident in the nuclear power industry [after Three Mile Island] will be caused by operators' following procedures."[66]

This does mean that individual responsibility will automatically follow from the introduction of less precise rules and procedures, consisting of vague and perhaps even ambiguous values. Nor will it be brought about because a CEO talks about it in public speeches, or publishes it in value statement like "Min Bank" in the case of Jyske Bank. Much more is needed, not the least if it is to be combined with self-organisation.

What is needed is *consequence and consistency* on behalf of leadership and management; consequence pointing to the importance of showing in practice the values and attitudes of the organisation. Employees and managers not living up to these values and attitudes must be castigated, while those who live up to the values must be shown to stand for the values of the organisation. After all it is upon their acts that we shall judge them.

Earlier we saw how a manager with a singular orientation towards the bottom line could easily corrupt a whole branch of a bank. This is where management must show that the bottom line is only important if certain other values are observed. It is by establishing such examples that members of an organisation can see that management really means business.

Paper statements are certainly not enough, and excuses make employees cynical. Only by acting consequently according to the values commonly expressed can leaders deepen the belief that these values are to be upheld by everyone.

Consistency is important too, for evident reasons, but also in relation to the overall activities of leadership and management. If a CEO introduces a strict orientation towards the simple-minded concept of shareholder value, or introduces individual incentive schemes rewarding those who contribute most to the bottom line result.[67] the whole organisation might soon be on the wrong track. Single-minded orientation of this kind would pervert the attitudes of members of the organisation to the detriment of the whole organisation in the long run.

Other measures will have to be compatible with and not contrary to the basic values, or these values might soon decline in importance, with most individuals choosing the "loyalty" option, and only a few individuals here and there voicing their misgivings, soon to be followed by their dismissal or their own "exit" choice[68] – loyalty here of course meaning loyalty towards management, not towards the values and attitudes believed in.

As seen in the trivial dilemmas in Chapter 2 on ambiguous spirals of decay, management must take its own medicine, or it will contribute to corruption of the organisation, with anyone feeling free to ignore the values ignored by management, unless kept on a tight leash by supervision, controls and threats of punishment.

Thus management carries a special responsibility for demonstrating in practice those values they want the organisation to believe in. This certainly does not bode well for the extreme difference in the salaries and share option schemes for management and employees especially found in America. To an up-and-coming manager such incentives might be seen as the only thing worth striving for. Individual incentives of this kind may act as a driver, but they also make for bought loyalty and disregard of other values necessary for a cooperative effort.[69]

By *transparency* we are thinking of openness in the decision-making process and certain see-through qualities related to the result of this process. If decisions concerning all members of an organisation are made in semi-secrecy and/or members of the organisation are held in ignorance of, or misled with regard to the decisions made, it may be difficult to realise the combination of spirited leadership and self-organisation aimed for in this chapter. The value of transparency might perhaps be inferred from a couple of examples.

In seminars on value-based leadership for managers in Jyske Bank, conducted by members of CREDO, the question of pay often pops up in the discussion, for instance in relation to transparency of pay scales. Individual managers and employees do not in principle know what pay their colleagues get. It turns out that female managers have a suspicion that male managers in equal positions are paid more than they are. They know cases where individual male managers have told them in private what they get, and from this the female managers infer that there is a consistent gap. If this was the case they would find it very unfair and not at all in accord with the values espoused by the bank, where fair and equal treatment is expected.

From discussion in the seminars it is evident that the majority of the male managers do not want to have their individual pay brought out into the open, one argument being that employees and colleagues would not understand the reason for the apparent differences, which implies of course that there may be real differences and that they may be difficult to explain publicly. It is not said, but one gets the impression that understanding follows the pay scale, the higher one is placed the more one understands why.

In relation to this example one may ask whether it would not be more fair and in accordance with the espoused values to have a greater degree of transparency with regard to pay. Transparency would demand that the reasoning behind the decisions made with regard to pay would somehow have to be understandable and found fair by employees and managers alike, and these explanations would have to be in accord with openly held values. They would not necessarily have to be explained, if they were implicitly understood and accepted as being fair with regard to these values. Without such transparency it might be difficult to close a gap that female managers perceive, and it might be impossible to achieve congruence between the values openly held and the decisions actually made.

This is important not only in relation to pay but also in relation to the whole decision-making structure. When setting examples, or in this case making an example, transparency may also be important. In Jyske Bank it had until recently been common, when dismissing a manager or moving someone to a new position, to be deliberately vague about the reasons, especially in the case of problems. This of course always led to a lot of speculative gossip and it certainly did not help make clear-cut examples out of these cases.

Recently there has been a marked change in the explanation given publicly. Now a more telling explanation is given. This small change got a very mixed reception. Many managers voiced their disagreement. When this example was presented by members of CREDO during a course on value-based leadership and management at an international summer school, this new practice was compared by the majority of participants to putting people in a pillory.

We would argue that there is no alternative if one wants to demonstrate congruence between values held, decisions made and actions taken. If congruence is non-existent or not to be seen, such an approach could lead to disagreement and conflict.

Not all decisions can be made transparent. Transparency with regard to competitors would not be such a good idea. What then could be transparent and what has be opaque? An answer might be had from a transparent decision-making process itself. If it would be transparent to all why some decisions had to be opaque, and still be in accordance with deeply held values, then perhaps everyone would be able to see some sense in the opaqueness. If not, transparency ought to be chosen.

Trust carries with it connotations of integrity, confidence, reliability, responsibility and belief.[70] To Ciulla "Trust has taken over from authority as the modern foundation of leadership"[71] and to Seligman trust is indispensable in modern societies, but like us he contends that it is being eroded.[72]

To trust someone means that one would entrust them with one's possessions, meanings, ideas, tangible and intangible things, without fearing that one would lose them, or that one's confidences would be betrayed, or ideas stolen. Thus trust may be an important aspect of leadership, and we may begin to see the faint outline of a leadership quality that would not be found in the leadership of a Jack or a Hitler. Although an inner circle might expect some constancy in their behaviour, for instance with regard to what and who would be rewarded. But then we are not speaking of trust, are we?

Leadership would have to include some kind of mutual trust. While it may be important that the leader is trusted, the leader must also trust the members of the group. In fact it might be doubtful whether there can ever be something like single-sided trust. It would sound curious to say: I have trust in you, but you do not have trust in me. At least it would mean that if I confided something to you, you might not trust that I actually did confide anything, somehow there might be another motive. Could one trust a leader, who did not trust the group, but relied on surveillance, control and threats of sanctions? Would it not be a curious kind of trust that a member of the group showed a leader, who would find it necessary to use all these instruments? And vice versa of course, could trust only reside in the members of the group, while no one trusted the leader?[73]

Trust is not only a condition brought about by a leader, but is a kind of mutuality condition pervading the group or organisation. In *Cases in Leadership, Ethics, and Organizational Integrity* Paine[74] talks of the need for organisational integrity. Maybe this is something that can only exist in an atmosphere of mutual trust. Whenever the mutuality condition is not fulfilled, organisational integrity would leak out.

Trust would come to nought if there was no *sincerity and honesty* in the relations among people of an organisation. Sincerity and honesty may not be enough to create trust. Jack for all his faults may have been sincere and honest, at least in the beginning of the boys' game, but that does not mean that he was trusted.

Trust may be built upon bogus sincerity and honesty, but this trust would be punctured by the slightest revelation that it was not sincere and honest. Perhaps this is the sincerity and honesty we find with someone who has been trained to evoke a mock kind of trust, while being in reality insincere and dishonest. The stereotype of the used car salesman immediately comes to mind.

What we have here is perhaps a presentiment that the expectation of trust, sincerity and honesty does not only depend on the individuals involved, but on whole classes of individuals and on previous experiences with representatives from these classes. We may still have some trust in our doctor, and a priest perhaps and see them as being sincere and honest, at least to a certain degree. But we also know that revelation of breaches of trust, insincerity and dishonesty will have repercussions for all others of this class.

From this we can see that many-sided trust, sincerity and honesty will be extremely important in an organisation based upon the principles we espouse in relation to self-organisation and leadership.

With a focus on individual responsibility, with fewer rules and controls, with open-ended and distributed decision making, with recombinant organisation, trust, built on sincerity and honesty that is at least so genuine that it would not matter if one forgot one's explicit part of the play, is extremely important. No one is more important in upholding this than the leader, not only by acting with the integrity emphasised by Paine, but also by setting examples.

In an example with a CEO voicing integrity but acting in a way that did not show integrity Ciulla touches upon this problem. "What the CEO failed to realize was that he was espousing the value of integrity, but in effect saying that employees would be punished if they did not act with integrity (with firing) *and* punished if they did act with integrity (with reduced compensation)."[75]

Trust cannot be the naïve trust in everyone. Sincerity and honesty cannot be expected of everyone and should perhaps not be honoured on every occasion. But if not, may we not be back with Carr's poker game management, or even the deviousness of Machiavelli? The answer to that is in my mind a resounding NO! There are several things to remember. Carr accepted that the rules of the game had to be obeyed, or it would be difficult to know what one was doing, and so cheating is only allowed within a playful framework. The methods of the Prince would not be acceptable today, at least not in a democracy, and even at the time when Machiavelli wrote *The Prince*, deviousness may have been enacted as part of a complicated power game with rules (perhaps rules of chivalry and valour) that we just cannot discern today.

What is left is the ambiguousness we touched upon earlier that can only be resolved within the framework of a social grammar. Trust, sincerity and honesty are trust, sincerity and honesty as expected within this social grammar, not absolute trust, sincerity and honesty.

We may still expect to be led behind the light by our competitors and we may still have our own ulterior purposes, may still be less than honest, where it is expected. Here we are not talking about expected in the sense that certain individuals are not to be trusted, we are talking about "the rules of the game," the social grammar we share; a grammar that may in its concrete manifestations be historically relative, but which still represents the most objective yardstick for what we are to expect of trust, sincerity and honesty. What we cannot do is convert that yardstick into a concrete measure, as it is part of our tacit knowledge and ineffable values.

When discussing cohesion and cooperation in self-organising groups, we reached the conclusion that not only might we find competition within such groups, but that competition under the mutuality constraint of having a shared goal could be seen as an advantage.

Looking at the same issue from the view of the leader it would mean that a leader would have to encourage this kind of competition. This would mean that a leader would encourage what we have called *the other opinion,* meaning the differences of opinion that would help to open up the spectrum of possibilities, the search space, as well as the spectrum of possible solutions, or the solution space. The result would be multiple reflections of all the members of an organisation, not just a few individuals appointed to think and reflect.

Leadership must encourage the other opinion of every member of the organisation, allow for a degree of conflict, under the mutuality constraint of the shared goal. It would be naïve to expect that everyone would agree to every new step taking for instance the boys' shelter-building effort. Based on different previous experience, differences in knowledge and insight, and probably other differences, we would expect disagreement here and there. Stacey and Parker talk of creative tension as something that drives renewal and change.[76] Organisations that attempt to block tension and eliminate conflict cannot be sufficiently flexible to adapt to changing circumstances.

Somewhat in the same vein Langlois talks of the importance of variation: "The variation that drives an evolutionary system depends on people being on different wavelengths – it depends, in effect, on outbreeding."[77]

It strikes me that even individual problem-solving creativity and development might depend upon something like this. When confronted with a new non-routine task demanding a trial-and-error approach, a wide spectrum of conflicting views may be an advantage, although this might also lead to an impasse characterised by conflict.

Perhaps one of Dennett's attempts to explain the conflict resolution of the mind might come in handy here. Mentioning that any parallel architecture of the mind encounters "impasses," these impasses are seen not as problems but as opportunities for the system in question, in this case the mind. "Impasses are basic building opportunities in the system. Conflicts are not automatically dealt with by a presciently fixed set of conflict-resolution principles (an authoritative traffic-cop homunculus already in place) but rather are dealt with *non*automatically. An impasse creates a *new* 'problem space' ... in which the problem to be solved is precisely the impasse."[78]

This would probably mean that a moral bound as tight fitting as a straitjacket would be counter-productive; it might assure cooperation, but it would lack ingenuity and competition within bounds. This would not lead us very far. The moral weave must have the qualities of the moral grammar. It must be open-ended and generative. It must allow self-organising groups to make up their own new solutions under the general constraint of the moral weave. It must allow them to compete, to persuade, to cajole each other, to circumvent blockheads, in other words it must allow for competition.

The other opinion and competition must be contained within the bounds of a moral grammar, and perhaps we also need to have something like Piggy's conch shell and a belief in its authority.

Even so, encouraging the other opinion might presumably lead to deadlocks and conflicts, where diverging views are holding up the self-organising process. It would be naïve to think that such deadlocks and conflicts could easily be solved within the self-organising group.

A bureaucratic-minded manager might choose to ignore the conflict as long as it did not formally endanger the organisational structure, even though he or she might be aware that it endangered the work carried out by the self-governing part of the organisation. Or he or she might rely on formal procedures to solve conflicts. As long as every external procedure is followed to the letter, there simply is no problem to this manager, who limits his or her view with paper-blinders made up of bureaucratic rules.

No wonder that Hirschhorn[79] sees certain forms of bureaucracy as regressed forms of hierarchy, not possessing the qualities of leadership in our sense of the term, management regresses, or even takes flight, to schematic forms of bureaucracy.

This is simply not good enough; awareness of the problem would seem to demand that a leader with insight and authority looked into the problem as soon as it came to his or her knowledge. The impasse would have to be solved, whether it touched upon the formal structure or not, and the solution would have to take into account the shared moral grammar, which means that a leader must encourage and if necessary enforce a solution that would be seen as representing an acceptable expression of this grammar.

Thus more must be expected from a leader possessing the kind of authority respected by most members of the organisation, and based for instance upon great insight in the organisation, a belief in the shared goals and a strict observance of the shared *social grammar*. Only such an authority would be accepted by the members of the organisation. In a discussion of practical reasoning Paine[80] argues that three dimensions "purpose, principles, and people" must be taken into account. Although her scheme does not quite fit with our argument here, certain parts of her argument may be equated with ours.

Leaving the decision to a single leader is not good enough though; it might ultimately lead to authoritarianism, to the kind of leadership practised by Jack in *Lord of the Flies* or a Hitler. What is needed are thus structures and procedures that allow for different instances of appeal, a system of checks and balances like the one woven into every democratic constitution. "Rival and opposing interests are best controlled if purpose and power are separated and negotiations, trade-offs, and exchanges produce compromises acceptable to all concerned."[81] Ultimately this would only work if it involves all the members of the organisation, and is based upon a shared social grammar.

Thus organisational decision-making structures and processes would in essence have to contain a concrete expression of some fundamental aspects of the shared social grammar so that the decisions and actions that are a result of this structure and process will be seen as following from the shared social grammar.

In the sense we tried to illustrate this earlier with a reference to Wittgenstein. "Es kann nicht ein einziges Mal nur ein Mensch einer Regel gefolgt sein. Es kann nicht ein einziges Mal nur eine Mitteilung gemacht, ein Befehl gegeben, oder verstanden worden sein, etc. – Einer Regel folgen, eine Mitteilung machen, einen Befehl geben, eine Schachpartie spielen sind *Gepflogenheiten* (Gebrauche, Institutionen)."[82]

These "*Gepflogenheiten*" have to be observed by leaders and by the institutions, and used for deciding among the different "other views" in case of conflict.

If these "*Gepflogenheiten*" are not observed, any member of the organisation will have the individual responsibility of voicing this. This is an important consequence of our concept of the shared social grammar.

Thus the responsibility of observing the "*Gepflogenheiten*" of the grammar is not just the responsibility of a leader or a manager entrusted with very specific formal responsibilities. It is a responsibility that belongs to every individual. If a leader does not observe this shared grammar, it is the responsibility of the individuals who observe this to point out the transgression and to voice it to the leader doing the transgression, and if that does not stop the transgression, to a wider audience.

As we argued earlier responsibility and the necessary authority must be distributed among all members of the organisation, and must be demanded by every member. In the context of business organisations Hirschhorn talks of a new authority relationship, where upward identification with some authority is no longer sufficient. What is needed and what he sees as emerging is a kind of personal authority. When individuals possess this personal authority "they bring more of themselves – their skills, ideas, feelings, and values – to their work. They are more psychologically present. It is not uncommon today to find a subordinate heading a task force of which his or her boss is a member. The subordinate must bring greater courage to such a role."[83]

We would enlarge upon this personal authority to include the personal authority to show and demand adherence to the shared social grammar by everyone in the organisation, whether a formal superior or not. This form of personal authority may represent the ultimate checks and balances in any organisation; it would not hinge on the ability and responsibility of any appointed person, be that a manager or ombudsman, to ensure that the organisation adhered to the social grammar.

Nothing else, absolutely nothing else, can be more effective in curbing tendencies of those in power to become authoritarian or corrupt. No written rules and no controls would work if no one felt responsible for pointing out rule transgressions, or were afraid to do so because no one else might understand.

We repeat: "A social organism of any sort whatever, large or small, is what it is because each member proceeds to his own duty with a trust that the other members will simultaneously do theirs."[84] In fact it is the tacit belief that others will do their part that will help create the fact that will desired by all. Or as James would have said: "There are, then, cases where a fact cannot come about at all unless a preliminary faith exists in its coming. *And where faith in a fact can help create the fact ...*"

Subsidiarity: we use a term that has been brought into common use by the EU, meaning "gesellschaftspolitisches Prinzip, nach dem übergeordnete gesellschaftliche Einheiten (bes. Der Staat) nur solche Aufgaben an sich ziehen dürfen, zu deren Wahrnehmung untergeordnete Einheiten (bes. die Familie) nicht in der Lage sind."[85] This is an issue that touches upon empowerment and decentralisation.

Worker participation and later empowerment does not sound like a new rallying cry, the first having been on the agenda for many years and the latter also getting cold as a term. This cooling off of empowerment has been described and explained very well in Ciulla's *Leadership and the Problem of Bogus Empowerment*,[86] the major reason being the insincerity with which it has been attempted in practice.

Self-organisation, independent decision making and responsibility demand some form of subsidiarity, some latitude, some vagueness and ambiguity of direction that leave the concrete filling out to the group and the individual. As previously indicated that latitude may be limited, not by managerial directives or human supervision and control, but by the work process itself. Again this is to be avoided if we want to assure self-organisation and self-responsibility.

A case in the point may be the new tendencies in the Danish public sector to create self-governing units, based upon a detailed written contract between a local council, and for instance a department of health of the local council. On the surface this might seem to fulfil the subsidiarity condition, and allow the local department of health to manage the affairs falling within its responsibility on its own.

In practice very detailed contracts specifying the services to be performed in very great detail would seem to severely limit the degree of self-governing. Care may be specified with regard to processes like "taking a bath, help with personal hygiene, dressing and undressing, tending catheter and stoma bags, visits to toilet, skin care, help with personal aids borne on the body."[87] This is presumably further specified with regard to frequencies, content, level and so on.

One may get the feeling that care somehow evaporates during this process of specification, and that the willed openness and ambiguity that for instance both the present and the previous CEO of Jyske Bank emphasised, disappears, turning in fact all the employees of so-called institutions of care into unthinking and uncaring human resources that are to be used efficiently according to a well thought out scheme.[88] Thereby losing that latitude of organisation, of interpretation of care, of decision-making and of individual insight and responsibility that we sought to establish. It is almost as if one is introducing a kind of miniature command economy, with a high degree of specification of every single activity to be performed.

Perhaps some iron filings and a magnet may help us see the problem. Let a small amount of iron filings represent the organisation to enter into the contract with the local council. The individual iron filings are the individuals making up the organisation. Now the contract could be seen as analogous to an attempt to specify explicitly the orientation and activity of every single iron particle.

The alternative would be to use a magnet to orientate every single iron particle simultaneously without actually touching and directing them. Could this not be seen as analogous to an attempt to orientate every single member of an organisation through common values and attitudes? Not quite like iron particles of course; more as if individuals were provided with the kind of compass we talked about earlier, making it possible for everyone to orientate himself or herself in the same general direction, without explicit direction of every single move.

The magnetic field would be the values and attitudes that would guide the individual member without detailed instruction and leave the concrete tasks to be performed to the individual.

BREAKING WITH MODERN SCIENTIFIC MANAGEMENT

The arguments, theories and proposals presented here lead to the demand for a new kind of management with more emphasis on leadership, on *value-based* leadership, building upon the theories we presented in the chapters on tacit knowledge, social grammar and moral weave. In other words resting upon a foundation that may at first glance seem arbitrary and vague, unscientific even, but which may, as we have seen in the previous chapters, in fact represent a more consistent and solid basis than much of the postulated rational scientific basis of the modern management theories.

To adopt these ideas a manager-cum-leader will have to move beyond the teachings of traditional textbooks on management, leaving behind the pseudo-scientific approach found there and make an almost Kierkegaardian leap of faith[89] into another stage of management and leadership; a leap into the unknown that cannot be reduced to the pseudo-rational arguments and algorithmic methods of the traditional view. A leap that also represents a major shift of emphasis: from management to leadership.[90]

We are still at the trial-and-error stage, even though a major Danish bank[91] is trying out the ideas in practice, in collaboration with CREDO. As yet we cannot specify in detail what the right approach is, but at least we can show where to begin the trials. We have attempted to show a glimpse of the leap and the vista from there, but we cannot of course present a fully fledged alternative. In a way that would also be contrary to the idea of the leap of faith, a leap that must be carried out by every single one of us on our own.

What we have done in this chapter is more a question of creating an awareness, of voicing the problem, and of showing possible approaches, and proposals, thereby opening the minds of managers and leaders to something they may already have felt themselves.

It is my hope though that those who have seen the cracks in the lofty, traditional structure of organisation and management theory will feel inspired to embark upon their own attempts to elaborate on these proposals, and perhaps even try out some of these proposals in practice without waiting for someone to else to make sure that they will work. Such waiting would in itself be contrary to the idea of making a leap of faith.

Waiting for some pseudo-scientific proof of the value of self-organisation and value-based leadership would of course mean a relapse into the kind of organisation and management thinking that we are trying to supersede here.

NOTES

[1] Here quoted from Barnard (1938/1996), p. 181.
[2] For critical reflection on the boxes and arrows management, see Patching (1999).
[3] Barnard (1938/1996), p. 187.
[4] Ibid., p. 187.
[5] Drucker (1955/1959), pp. 1–2
[6] Burnham (1962).
[7] This topic has been analysed extensively in the second volume of *Planlægning og Samfundsudvikling* (Petersen 1985). See also Bell (1962).
[8] Drucker (1955/1959), p. 8.
[9] Ibid., p. 108
[10] Ibid., p. 112.
[11] Ibid., p. 124.

12 We are not talking about spiritual leadership, but leadership with a spirit.

13 Bennis (1996), p. 224. See also Bennis (1989).

14 Bennis (1996), p. 227.

15 Ibid., p. 225.

16 For a discussion of some of the possible meanings of self-command, see Schelling (1984).

17 A whole series of examples showing how competent doctors were involved in terrible experiments with human beings are described in "Augen aus Auschwitz." *Die Zeit* (27 January 2000), p. 88.

18 This also goes for classics like: Taylor (1911), Follett (1926), Fayol (1930) and Mayo (1933).

19 Machiavelli (1513/1929), p. 78.

20 Nietzsche (1886a/1968).

21 Fayol (1930).

22 Gulick & Urwick (1937/1969).

23 Newer examples might include: Magee & Boodman (1967), Dilworth (1992).

24 Simon (1956) and Simon & Newell (1958).

25 See for instance Iacocca & Novak (1986).

26 See for instance Kierkegaard (1843/1983).

27 "Waterfall" by the Dutch artist M. C. Escher.

28 Patching (1999).

29 Ibid., p. 334.

30 Hirschhorn (1997), p. 20.

31 Astley & Zammuto (1992), p. 443.

32 Sculley (1987), p. 160. For another view see Young (1988).

33 This of course refers to the original 1984 Macintosh 128K and 512K grey-beige models. For a discussion of how the Macintosh evolved see the Internet discussions of Jeff Raskin and Bruce Horn. They were both members of the original team.

34 Drucker (1955), pp. 124–125.

35 For those who rember the Apple Lisa, it might be possible to point to a precursor, but the Macintosh was not just a scaled-down Lisa or a cheap version of a Xerox work station.

36 Purser & Cabana (1998), p. 313.

37 Ibid., p. 312.

38 Conger (1991), p. 32. See also Snow et al. (1986).

39 See for instance Bertaux & Thompson (1993).

40 Conger (1991), pp. 34 and 36.

41 From a famous recruiting poster used during the First World War.

42 A. P. Møller in a letter to Mærsk McKinney-Møller, dated 2 December 1946. Somehow the original Danish verion seems slightly different, as it uses the expression "*rettidig omhu.*"

43 Purser & Cabana (1998), p. 7.

44 Ibid., p. 8.

45 Jensen (1999).

46 Ibid., p. 14. An evaluation of this empowerment scheme can be found in Jensen (2000).

47 Nielsen (1999) and Jensen (2000).

48 Verbal communication from Anders Dam, CEO of Jyske Bank A/S in connection with a course on value-based leadership. The job advertisement can be found in Morgenavisen Jyllands-Posten, Sunday, 5 September 1999. p. 3, section 1.

49 An attempt to measure what the new spirit has meant is made by Poul B. Jensen in Jensen (2000).

50 For instance in models belonging to what has been termed change management (which strangely enough is not about changing management). A recent example is found in Jørgensen et al. (1998).

51 See for instance Dutta & Manzoni (1999), Manganelli & Klein (1996), Storey (1996).

52 The term recombinant is taken from genetics meaning "of or resulting from new combinations of genetic material", according to *Webster's Encyclopedic Unabridged Dictionary of the English Language* (1989).

53 Hirschhorn (1997), p. 122.

54 Langlois & Everett (1992). Actually Apple did something similar when developing the Macintosh, isolating the first small development group in a building separated from the main effort at the time.

55 Smith (1776/1974).

56 Nonaka (1994), p. 22. We prefer not to use the remaining parts of Nonaka's theories, because they seem to establish a too structured and fixed view of knowledge creation. An example would be the so-called "modes of knowledge creation." Instead we prefer the view we developed in earlier chapters.

57 Brown & Duguid (1991).

58 See for instance Alvesson (1995), Davenport & Prusak (1998), Thierauf (1999) and Tissen et al. (1998).

59 Davenport & Prusak (1998), p. 153.

60 Borghoff & Pareschi (1998), Thierauf (1999).

61 Sternberg and Wagner emphasise the tacit aspects though (Sternberg & Wagner 1992).

62 Paine (1996), p. 94.

63 Jensen (2000).

64 Interview with Kaj Steenkjær, CEO of Jyske Bank, 17 March 1997. The interview was carried out by members of CREDO (Centre for Research in Ethics and Decision-making in Organisations).

65 Interview with Anders Dam as quoted in Petersen & Lassen (1997), p. 90.

66 Hirschhorn (1997), p. 61.

67 It might also be relevant to ask what the shareholder value concept means at a time when the share values of certain companies in the information technology or biotech sector are still rising steeply, on account of a potential that is difficult to ascertain, and perhaps because they are popular, which makes them even more popular. Here tra-ditional ideas of shareholder value come to nothing. Perhaps we may even say that the rise in share prices reflects more a belief in the potential of a few entrepreneurs with the right drive and spirit than trust in their ability to manage efficiently, in fact showing the value of the spirited leadership ideal presented here, also with regard to share prices.

68 Referring to Hirschman (1970).

69 See for instance Bok's analysis of this topic (Bok 1993).

70 See also Hwang & Burgers (1997).

71 Ciulla (1998), p. 82.

72 Seligman (1998).

73 The emphasis here is on trust as a condition of a relationship.

74 Paine (1996).

75 Ciulla (1999), p. 170.

76 Stacey & Parker (1994).

77 Quoted in Langlois & Everett (1992), p. 74.

78 Dennett (1991), p. 267.

79 Hirschhorn (1997).

80 See for instance the list of topics related to the three dimensions (Paine 1996, p. 233).

81 Bass (1998), p. 175.

82 Wittgenstein (1953) quoted in Morscher (1981), p. 121.

83 Hirschhorn (1997), p. 9.

84 James (1896/1987), p. 211.

85 *Duden: Deutsches Universal Wörterbuch A – Z* (1996).

86 Ciulla (1998).

87 Based upon material from a contract used in Vallø Kommune 2000, but equivalent contracts and specifications can be found in many of the local councils in Denmark in these years.

88 See for instance Dyer & Reeves (1995) and Huselid et al. (1996).

89 The expression "Leap of faith" is attributed to Søren Kierkegaard, where it is supposed to stand for the leap beyond the aesthetic and the ethical stages. Here the expression is used to bring home the idea that we somehow have to make a leap beyond the modern scientific management theory, beyond the pseudo-rationalism of it, and beyond the traditional views of business ethics, for the reasons given in our discussion.

Evidently Søren Kierkegaard never used precisely the expresssion "leap of faith" not even in the Danish translation. See for instance McKinnon (1993). We might get close to it through the Abraham paradox discussed in *Fear and Trembling* (Kierkegaard 1843/1983) or in "Springets qualitative Overgang fra Ikke-troende til Troende" as found in his "Concluding Unscientific Postscript."

90 Here it might be worth remembering that according to the *Encyclopedia Britannica*'s online edition, management is: 1: the act or art of managing: the conducting or supervising of something (as a business); 2: judicious use of means to accomplish an end; 3: the collective body of those who manage or direct an enterprise.

Leadership on the other hand is defined as 1: the office or position of a leader; 2: the capacity to lead; 3: the act or instance of leading. We may all recognise common usage in these definitions, and yet they are insufficient. In our own discussion we hope to have reached a deeper understanding of management and leadership without attempting to convey all the meaning in a single definition.

91 Since 1995 the management of Jyske bank in collaboration with CREDO has been moving in the direction indicated here.

References

Aitchison, J. (1996). *The Seeds of Speech – Language Origin and Evolution.* Cambridge: Cambridge University Press.

Alchian, A. A. & Demsetz, H. (1972). Production, Information Costs, and Economic Organization. *American Economic Review,* 62(December), 777–795.

Alstott, A. & Ackerman, B. A. (1999). *The Stakeholder Society.* New Haven, CT: Yale University Press.

Alvesson, M. (1995). *Management of Knowledge-intensive Companies.* Berlin: Walter de Gruyter.

Andersen, L. L. & Møgelvang-Hansen, P. (1997). *Finansiel Rådgivning: Et Debatoplæg om Pengeinstitutternes Rådgivningsansvar.* København: Thomson Information.

Angell, R. C. (1958). *Free Society and Moral Crisis.* Ann Arbor: University of Michigan Press.

Aristotle (1956). *The Ethics of Aristotle – The Nicomachean Ethics* (1988 ed.). London: Penguin.

Arrow, K. J. (1973a). *Information and Economic Behavior.* Stockholm: Federation of Swedish Industries.

Arrow, K. J. (1973b). Social Responsibility and Economic Efficiency. *Public Policy,* XXI(3), 303–317.

Asch, S. E. (1969). Änderung und Verzerrung von Urteilen durch Gruppendruck. In M. Irle (ed.), *Texte aus der Experimentellen Sozialpsychologie.* Neuwied: Luchterhand.

Astley, W. G. & Zammuto, R. F. (1992). Organization Science, Managers, and Language Games. *Organization Science,* 3(4), 443–460.

Austin, J. L. (1957). A Plea for Excuses. *Proceedings of the Aristotelian Society,* 57, 1–30.

Axelrod, R. (1984). *The Evolution of Cooperation.* New York: Basic Books.

Axelrod, R. (1986). An Evolutionary Approach to Norms. *American Political Science Review,* 80(4), 1095–1111.

Axelrod, R. M. (1997). *The Complexity of Cooperation: Agent-based models of competition and collaboration.* Princeton, NJ: Princeton Studies on Complexity, Princeton University Press.

Ayer, A. J. (1936). *Language, Truth and Logic* (1964 ed.). London: Golancz.

Barnard, C. I. (1938). The Functions of the Executive. In S. J. Ott (1996), *Classic Readings in Organizational Behaviour*. Cambridge, MA: Harvard University Press.

Baron, M. W. (1996). *Kantian Ethics Almost Without a Thought*. Ithaca, NY: Cornell University Press.

Bass, B. M. (1998). The Ethics of Transformational Leadership. In J. B. Ciulla (ed.), *Ethics, the Heart of Leadership*. Westport, CT: Quorum Books.

Bates, E. (1984). Biograms and the Innateness Hypothesis. *The Behavioral and Brain Sciences,* 7(2), 188–190.

Bates, E. (1992). Language Development. *Current Opinion in Neurobiology,* 2, 180–185.

Baudelaire, C. (1857). *The Flowers of Evil* (1993 ed.). Oxford: Oxford University Press.

Baumol, W. J. & Blackman, A. B. (1991). *Perfect Markets and Easy Virtue*. Oxford: Blackwell.

Beach, L. R., Chi, M., Klein, G. et al. (1997). Naturalistic Decision Making and Related Research Lines. In C. Zsambok & G. Klein (eds.), *Naturalistic Decision Making*. Mahwah, NJ: Lawrence Erlbaum.

Beck, U. (1986). *Risikogesellschaft – Auf dem Weg in einer andere Moderne*. Frankfurt/M: Suhrkamp.

Bell, D. (1962). *The End of Ideology – On the Exhaustion of Political Ideas in the Fifties*. New York: The Free Press.

Bell, D. (1979). *The Cultural Contradictions of Capitalism*. New York: Basic Books.

Bennett, G. S. (1991). *The Quest for Value: The Eva Tm management guide*. New York: Harper Business.

Bennett, R. (1997). *European Business*. London: Pitman.

Bennis, W. G. (1989). *Why Leaders Can't Lead: The unconscious conspiracy continues*. San Francisco, CA: Jossey-Bass.

Bennis, W. G. (1996). Why Leaders Can't Lead. In J. S. Ott (ed.), *Classic Readings in Organizational Behavior*. Orlando, FL: Harcourt Brace.

Bento, R. F. & Ferreira, L. D. (1992). Incentive Pay and Organizational Culture. In W. J. Bruns (ed.), *Performance Measurement, Evaluation, and Incentives*. Boston, MA: Harvard Business School Press.

Bereiter, C. & Scardamalia, M. (1993). *Surpassing Ourselves: An inquiry into the nature and implications of expertise*. Chicago: Open Court.

Berofsky, B. (1995). *Liberation from Self: A theory of personal autonomy*. Cambridge: Cambridge University Press.

Bertaux, D. & Thompson, P. (1993). *Between Generations – Models, Myths and Memories*. Oxford: Oxford University Press.

Binmore, K. (1994). *Game Theory and the Social Contract, vol. 1: Playing fair*. Cambridge, MA: The MIT Press.

Birkland, T. A. (1997). *After Disaster: Agenda setting, public policy and focusing events.* Washington, DC: Georgetown University Press.

Black, A., Wright, P., Bachman, J. et al. (1998). *In Search of Shareholder Value: Managing the drivers of performance.* London: Pitman.

Black, M. (1990). *Perplexities – Rational Choice, the Prisoners Dilemma, Metaphor, Poetic Ambiguity, and other Puzzles.* Ithaca, NY: Cornell University Press.

Blau, J. R. (1993). *Social Contracts and Economic Markets.* London: Plenum.

Bloom, P. (1994). Generativity within Language and other Cognitive Domains. *Cognition,* 51, 177–189.

Blumberg, P. (1989). *The Predatory Society – Deception in the American Marketplace.* New York: Oxford University Press.

Bok, D. (1993). *The Cost of Talent: How executives and professionals are paid and how it affects America.* New York: The Free Press.

Borges, J. L. (1954). Of Exactitude in Science. In *A Universal History of Infamy.* London: Penguin.

Borges, J. L. (1970a). The Library of Babel. In *Labyrinths – Selected Stories and Other Writings.* Harmondsworth: Penguin.

Borges, J. L. (1970b). Funes the Memorious. In *Labyrinths – Selected Stories and Other Writings.* Harmondsworth: Penguin.

Borghoff, U. M. & Pareschi, R. (1998). *Information Technology for Knowledge Management.* Berlin: Springer Verlag.

Børsetiske Regler (1997). København: Københavns Fondsbørs.

Bourdieu, P. (1977). *Outline of a Theory of Practice* (1992 ed.). Cambridge: Cambridge University Press.

Bourdieu, P. (1983). *Language and Symbolic Power* (1991 ed.). Cambridge: Polity Press.

Brandt, R. B. (1997). *Facts, Values, and Morality.* Cambridge: Cambridge University Press.

Brittan, S. & Hamlin, A. (1995). *Market Capitalism and Moral Values.* Cheltenham: Edward Elgar.

Brown, J. S., Collins, A. & Duguid, P. (1988). *Situated Cognition and the Culture of Learning.* Palo Alto: Institute for Research on Learning, 2550 Hanover Street, Palo Alto, CA 94304.

Brown, J. S. & Duguid, P. (1991). Organizational Learning and Communities of Practice: Towards a unified view of working, learning and organization. *Organization Science,* 2(1), 40–57.

Brown, S. L. & Eisenhardt, K. M. (1997). The Art of Continous Change: Linking complexity theory and time-paced evolution in relentless shifting organizations. *Administrative Science Quarterly,* 42(1), 1–34.

Brown, T. (1993). *Understanding BS 5750 and Other Quality Systems.* London: Gower.

Bruner, J. (1996). *The Culture of Education.* Cambridge, MA: Harvard University Press.

Buchanan, A. (1985). *Ethics, Efficiency, and the Market.* Totowa, NJ: Rowman and Allanheld.

Buchanan, J. M. (1978). Markets, States and the Extent of Morals. *American Economic Review,* 68(2), 364–368.

Burnham, J. (1962). *The Managerial Revolution.* Bloomington, IN: Indiana University Press.

Byrnes, M. A., Cornesky, R. A. & Byrnes, L. W. (1994). *The Quality Teacher: Implementing total quality management in the classroom.* Port Orange, FL: Cornesky & Associates.

Cahn, E. (1955). *The Moral Decision: Right or Wrong in the light of American law. Bloomington,* IN: Indiana University Press.

Camerer, C. E. (1991). Does Strategy Research Need Game Theory? *Strategic Management Journal,* 12, 137–152.

Canto-Sperber, M. (1996). *A Dictionary of Ethics and Moral Philosophy.* Paris: Presses Universitaire de France (PUF).

Capek, K. (1958). *R. U. R. Rossum's Universal Robots* (1990 ed.). Aarhus: Aravna.

Carr, J. (1998). *Civil Society and Civil Society Organisations.* London: The British Council.

Cawell, S. (1976). *Must we Mean what we Say?* Cambridge: Cambridge University Press.

Charkham, J. & Simpson, A. (1999). *Fair Shares – The Future of Shareholder Power and Responsibility.* Oxford: Oxford University Press.

Chi, M. T. H., Galser, R. & Farr, M. J. (1988). *The Nature of Expertise.* Hillsdale, NJ: Erlbaum.

Christiansen, E., Knudsen, P. S., Larsen, F. et al. (1980). *Måleteori, Dataindsamling, Databehandling i Adfærdsanalyser.* Århus: Aarhus Universitet.

Ciulla, J. B. (1998). Leadership and the Problem of Bogus Empowerment. In J. B. Ciulla (ed.), *Ethics, the Heart of Leadership.* Westport, CT: Quorum Books.

Ciulla, J. B. (1999). The Importance of Leadership in Shaping Business Values. *Long Range Planning,* 32(2), 166–172.

Clausewitz, C. v. (1812). *Vom Kriege* (1966 ed.). Bonn: Fred. Dümmlers Verlag.

Coase, R. H. (1990). *The Firm, the Market, and the Law.* Chicago: University of Chicago Press.

Collins, H. M. (1990). *Artificial Experts: Social knowledge and intelligent machines.* Cambridge, MA: The MIT Press.

Conger, J. A. (1991). Inspiring Others: The language of leadership. *Academy of Management Executive,* 5(1), 31–45.

Copleston, F. (1994a). *A History of Philosophy, vol. ix.* New York: Doubleday.

Copleston, F. (1994b). *A History of Philosophy, vol. v.* New York: Doubleday.

Corporate Social Reponsibility – A Dialogue on Dilemmas, Challenges, Risks, and Opportunities (1998). Conches-Geneva: World Business Council for Sustainable Development.

Cosmides, L. & Toby, J. (1994). Beyond Intuition and Instinct Blindness: Toward an evolutionary rigorous cognitive science. *Cognition,* (50), 41–77.

Crenson, M. A. (1971). *The Un-politics of Air Pollution: A study of decisionmaking in the cities.* Baltimore: Johns Hopkins Press.

Crouch, C. & Marquand, D. (1993). *Ethics and Markets – Co-operation and Competition within Capitalist Economies.* Oxford: Blackwell.

Dafolo Development (1992). *Environmental Audit – Novotex.*

Dahl, R. A. (1957). The Concept of Power. *Behavioral Science,* 2, 201–215.

Dahl, R. A. (1961). *Who Governs? Democracy and Power in an American City.* New Haven, CT: Yale University Press.

Dahrendorf, R. (1959). *Class and Class Conflict in Industrial Society.* London: Routledge.

Damasio, A. R. (1994). *Descartes' Error.* New York: Grosset/Putnam.

Darling, A. (1997). A Political Perspective. In G. Kelly, D. Kelly & A. Gamble (eds.), *Stakeholder Capitalism.* London: Macmillan.

Davenport, T. H. & Prusak, L. (1998). *Working Knowledge.* Cambridge, MA: Harvard Business School Press.

Davis, L. (1997). *Quality Asssurance: ISO 9000 as a management tool.* Copenhagen: Handelshøjskolens Forlag.

Davis, R. (1993). *Beyond the BS 5750/ISO 9000 Certificate: The bureaucracy buster's guide to quality assurance.* Letchworth, Hertfordshire: Technical Communications Ltd.

Deacon, T. W. (1997). *The Symbolic Species – The Co-evolution of Language and the Brain.* New York: W.W. Norton.

Deci, E. L. & Ryan, R. M. (1985). *Intrinsic Motivation and Self-determination in Human Behavior.* New York: Plenum Press.

DeLillo, D. (1984). *White Noise* (1986 ed.). London: Picador.

Deming, W. E. (1982). *Quality, Productivity, and Competitive Position.* Cambridge, MA: The MIT Press.

Deming, W. E. (1986). *Out of the Crisis.* Cambridge, MA: Massachusetts Institute of Technology.

Dennett, D. C. (1991). *Consciousness Explained.* Harmondsworth: Penguin.

Denton, J. (1998). *Organisational Learning and Effectiveness.* London: Routledge.

Det angår os alle, om virksomhedernes sociale medansvar (1999). København: Socialministeriet.

Dickens, C. (1854). *Hard Times* (1995 ed.). Ware: Wordsworth.

Die Zeit (2000). Augen aus Auschwitz. 27 January, p. 88.

Dilworth, J. B. (1992). *Operations Management: Design, planning, and control for manufacturing and services.* London: McGraw-Hill.

Donaldson, T. & Preston, L. E. (1995). The Stakeholder Theory of the Corporation: Concepts, evidence, implications. *Academy of Management Review,* 20, 65–91.

Dostoevsky, F. (1880). *The Karamazov Brothers* (1994 ed.). Oxford: Oxford University Press.

Dreyfus, H. L. (1987). Misrepresenting Human Intelligence. In R. Born (ed.), *Artificial Intelligence – The Case Against.* London: Croom Helm.

Dreyfus, H. L. (1997). Intuitive, Deliberative, and Calculative Models of Expert Performance. In C. Zsambok & G. Klein (eds.), *Naturalistic Decision Making.* Mahwah, NJ: Lawrence Erlbaum.

Drucker, P. (1955). *The Practice of Management* (1959 ed.). London: Heinemann.

Drucker, P. (1989). *The New Realities: In government and politics/in economics and business/in society and world view.* New York: Harper & Row.

Drucker, P. F. (1997). The Global Economy and the Nation-State. *Foreign Affairs,* 75(September/October), 159–171.

Duden: Deutsches Universal Wörterbuch A–Z (1996). Mannhein: Dudenverlag.

Dunn, J. (1988). *The Beginnings of Social Understanding.* Cambridge: Blackwell.

Durkheim, E. (1933). *Émile Durkheim on The Division of Labor in Society; being a Translation of his De la Division du Travail Social, with an Estimate of his Work by George Simpson.* New York: Macmillan.

Durkheim, E. (1957). *Professional Ethics and Civic Morals.* London: Routledge & Paul.

Durkheim, E. (1973). *Der Selbstmord.* Neuwied: Luchterhand.

Durkheim, E. (1981). *Die Elementaren Formen des Religiösen Lebens.* Frankfurt am Main: Suhrkamp.

Dutta, S. & Manzoni, J.-F. (1999). *Process Reengineering, Organizational Change and Performance Improvement.* New York: McGraw-Hill/Institut Européen d'Administration des Affaires.

Dyer, L. & Reeves, T. (1995). Human Resource Strategies and Firm Performance. *The International Journal of Human Resource Management,* 6, 656–670.

Edvinsson, L. & Malone, M. S. (1997). *Intellectual Capital.* New York: Harper.

Elfstrom, G. (1991). *Moral Issues and Multinational Corporations.* London: Macmillan.

Ellis, B. (1968). *Basic Concepts of Measurement.* Cambridge: Cambridge University Press.

Elman, J., Bates, E., Johnson, M. et al. (1996). *Rethinking Innateness: A connectionist perspective on development.* Cambridge, MA: The MIT Press.

Elster, J. (1986). *Ulysses and the Sirens – Studies in Rationality and Irrationality.* Cambridge: Cambridge University Press.

Elster, J. (1989). *The Cement of Society – A Study of Social Order.* Cambridge: Cambridge University Press.

Enderle, G., Homann, K. & Honecker, M. (1993). *Lexikon der Wirtschaftsethik.* Freiburg: Herder.

Estes, R. W. (1996). *Tyranny of the Bottom Line: Why corporations make good people do bad things.* San Francisco: Berrett-Kohler.

Etzioni, A. (1988). *The Moral Dimension – Toward a New Economics.* New York: The Free Press.

Etzioni, A. (1994). *The Spirit of Community – Rights, Responsibilities and the Communitarian Agenda.* New York: Crown.

Fayol, H. (1930). *Industrial and General Administration* (English ed. 1930 ed.). London: Pitman.

Festinger, L. (1958). The Motivating Effect of Cognitive Dissonance. In G. Lindzey (ed.), *Assessment of Human Motives.* New York: Holt, Rinehart & Winston.

Feuerbach, A. R. v. (1996) *Lost Prince: The Unsolved Mystery of Kaspar Hauser.* New York: The Free Press.

Finnis, J. (1980). *Natural Law and Natural Rights.* Oxford: Clarendon Press.

Fodor, J. A. (1983). *The Modularity of Mind – An Essay on Faculty Psychology.* Cambridge, MA: The MIT Press.

Foerster, H. v. (1984). Principles of Self-organization – In a Socio-managerial Context. In H. Ulrich & G. B. J. Probst (eds.), *Self-organisation and Management of Social Systems.* Berlin: Springer.

Follett, M. P. (1926). *Scientific Foundations of Business Administration.* Baltimore: Williams & Wilkins Co.

Forbrugerombudsmanden (1995). *Retningslinier om Etik i Realkreditinstitutioner* (6 September 1995 ed.). København: Forbrugerstyrelsen.

Forbrugerstyrelsen (1998). *Rapport fra Erhvervsministeriets Turnuspanel om Regelforenkling på Forbrugerstyrelsens Område.* København: Forbrugerstyrelsen.

Forrester, V. (1997). *Der Terror der Ökonomie.* Wien: Zsolnay.

Foucault, M. (1977). *Overvågning og Straf.* København: Rhodos.

Frankfurt, H. (1971). Willensfreiheit und er Begriff der Person. In P. Bieri (ed.), *Analytische Philosophie des Geistes.* Bodenheim: Athenäum.

Freeman, R. E. (1984). *Strategic Management – A Stakeholder Approach.* Boston: Pitman/Ballinger.

Freeman, R. E. & Bowie, N. E. (1992). *Ethics and Agency Theory: An introduction.* New York: Oxford University Press.

Freimuth, J. & Straub, F. (1996). *Demokratisierung von Organisationen. Philosophie, Ursprünge und Perspektiven der Metaplan Idee.* Wiesbaden: Gabler Verlag.

French, P. A. (1972). *Individual and Collective Responsibility.* Cambridge, MA: Schenkman.

French, P. A. (1984). *Collective and Corporate Responsibility.* New York: Columbia University Press.

Friedman, M. (1962). *Capitalism and Freedom.* Chicago: The University of Chicago Press.

Friedman, M. (1970). The Social Responsibility of Business Is to Increase Its Profits. *The New York Times Magazine,* 126.

Frijda, N. H. & Tcherkassof, A. (1997). Facial Expressions as Modes of Action Readiness. In J. A. Russell & J.-M. Fernández-Dols (eds.), *The Psychology of Facial Expression.* Cambridge: Cambridge University Press.

Garvin, D. A. (1988). *Managing Quality.* London: Collier Macmillan.

Garvin, D. A. (1998). Building a Learning Organisation. In *Harvard Business Review on Knowledge Management.* Boston: Harvard Business School.

Gaschke, S. (1997). Und Keiner Schaut Hin. *Die Zeit* (17, 18 April 1997), 1.

Ginet, C. (1990). *On Action.* Cambridge: Cambridge University Press.

Gjørup, H. (1996). Vi ønsker ikke at leve af børns arbejde. *Ledelse i Dag* (23), 47.

Glover, J. (1975). It Makes no Difference Whether or Not I Do it. *Proceedings of the Aristotelian Society,* XLIX, 171–90.

God rådgivning – Forbrugerombudsmandens Retningslinier om Etik i Pengeinstitutternes Rådgivning (1997). København: Finansrådet.

Goldberg, J. & Makóczy, L. (1998). *Complex Rhetoric and Simple Games.* Cranfield, Bedford: Computer Centre and School of Management, Cranfield University.

Golding, W. (1954). *Lord of the Flies* (1978 ed.). London: Faber and Faber.

Goldsmith, M. M. (1985). *Private Vices Public Benefits – Bernard Mandeville's Social and Political Thought.* Cambridge: Cambridge University Press.

Goodin, R. E. (1996). *Utilitarianism as a Public Philosophy.* Cambridge: Cambridge University Press.

Goodwin, B. (1998). All for One... One for All. *New Scientist,* 158(2138), 32–35.

Gordon, K. & Miyake, M. (1999). *Deciphering Codes of Corporate Conduct: A review of their contents.* Paris: Working Papers on International Investment, OECD.

Gorlin, R. A. (1990). *Codes of Professional Responsibility.* Washington, DC: The Bureau of National Affairs.

Gouldner, A. (1971). *The Coming Crises in Western Sociology.* London: Heinemann.

Green, D. (1996). *The Complete ISO 9000 Manual: A practical guide to a quality system policy manual, core procedures and forms.* London: Kogan Page.

Griffith-Jones, S. (1999). *Global Capital Flows: Should they be regulated?* London: Macmillan.

Gulick, L. & Urwick, L. (1937). *Papers on the Science of Administration* (1969). New York: A. M. Kelly.

Gurr, T. R. (1970). *Why Men Rebel.* Princeton, NJ: Princeton University Press.

Gyatso, P. (1997). *Fire under the Snow.* London: Harvill.

Habermas, J. (1981). *Theorie des Kommunikativen Handelns, Bd 1.–2.* Frankfurt am Main: Suhrkamp.

Habermas, J. (1996). Ziviler Ungehorsam – Testfall für den demokratischen Rechtsstaat. In J. Habermas, *Die Neue Unübersichtlichkeit,* Kleine Politischen Schriften V. Frankfurt am Main: Suhrkamp.

Hagem, C. & Westskog, H. (1998). The Design of a Dynamic Tradeable Quota System under Market Imperfections. *Journal of Environmental Economics and Management,* 36(1), 89–107.

Halbwachs, M. (1950). *On Collective Memory* (1992 ed.). Chicago: University of Chicago Press.

Haller, R. (1981). *Sprache und Erkenntnis als soziale Tatsache.* Wien: Hölder-Pichler-Tempsky.

Handberg, S. (1990). *Asbest: det kriminelle tidsrum?* Aalborg: Cementarbejdernes Fagforening i Aalborg.

Haney, C., Banks, C. & Zimbardo, P. (1973). Interpersonal Dynamics in a Simulated Prison. *International Journal of Criminology and Penology,* 1, 69–97.

Hanson, N. (1999). *The Custom of the Sea.* London: Doubleday.

Hare, R. M. (1981). *Moral Thinking – Its Levels, Methods, and Point.* Oxford: Clarendon Press.

Hargreaves-Heap, S., Hollis, M., Lyons, B. et al. (1992). *The Theory of Choice – A Critical Guide.* Oxford: Blackwell.

Harrington, H. J. & Mathers, D. D. (1997). *ISO 9000 and Beyond: From compliance to performance improvement.* New York: McGraw-Hill.

Harris, J. R. (1998). *The Nurture Assumption: Why children turn out the way they do.* London: Bloomsbury.

Haugeland, J. (1985). *Artificial Intelligence: The very idea.* Cambridge, MA: The MIT Press.

Hayek, F. A. (1945). The Use of Knowledge in Society. *American Economic Review,* 35(September 4), 519–530.

Hayek, F. A. (1963). *The Theory of Complex Phenomena. In M. Bunge (ed.), The Critical Approach to Science and Philosophy, Essays in Honor of Karl R. Popper,* pp. 332–349. London: Collier Macmillan.

Hayek, F. A. (1976). *Individualism and Economic Order.* London: Routledge and Kegan.

Hayek, F. A. (1978). *Law, legislation and Liberty, vols. 1–3.* Chicago: University of Chicago Press.

Hayek, F. A. v. (1962). Rules, Perception, and Intelligibility. *Proceedings of the British Academy,* 48, 321–344.

Hegel, G. W. F. (1807) *Phenomenologie des Geistes* (1973 ed.). Frankfurt am Main: Ullstein.

Held, V. (1970). Can Random Collections of Individuals be Morally Responsible? *Journal of Philosophy,* 67, 471–481.

Herzberg, F. (1968). One More Time: How do you motivate employes? – Not by improving work conditions, raising salaries, or shuffling tasks. *Harvard Business Review,* (January/February), 53–62.

Hillestrøm, K. (1998). Rådgiveransvar – Bruger-/forbrugerbeskyttelse. *Revisorbladet,* 59(6), 50.

Hirschhorn, L. (1997). *Reworking Authority – Leading and Following in the Post-modern Organization.* Cambridge, MA: MIT Press.

Hirschman, A. O. (1970). *Exit, Voice and Loyalty.* Cambridge, MA: Harvard University Press.

Hirshleifer, J. & Coll, J. C. M. (1988). What Strategies Can Support the Evolutionary Emergence of Cooperation? *Journal of Conflict Resolution,* 32(2), 367–398.

Hobbes, T. (1651). *Leviathan* (1982 ed.). Harmondsworth: Penguin.

Hodges, A. (1987). *Alan Turing, The Enigma of Intelligence.* London: Unwin.

Hoffman, P. (1998). *The Man Who Loved Only Numbers.* London: Fourth Estate.

Hofstadter, D. R. (1987). *Gödel, Escher, Bach: An Eternal Golden Braid.* Harmondsworth: Penguin.

Holmes, B. (1998). Irresistible Illusions. *New Scientist* (5 September), 32–37.

Holt, H. (1998). *En kortlægning af danske virksomheders sociale ansvar.* København: Socialforskningsinstituttet 98:1.

Holtzman, S. & Leach, C. (1981). *Wittgenstein: To Follow a Rule.* London: Routledge.

Hume, D. (1740). *A Treatise of Human Nature* (1969 ed.). Harmondsworth: Penguin.

Hummeltenberg, W. (1995). Bewertungsmodelle für TQM. In D. B. Preßmar (ed.), *Total Quality* I. Wiesbaden: Gabler.

Huselid, M. A., Jackson, S. E. & Schuler, R. S. (1996). Technical and Strategic Human Resource Management Effectiveness as Determinants of Firm Performance. *Academy of Management Journal,* 40, 171–188.

Huston, T. & Korte, C. (1976). The Reponsive Bystander: Why he helps. In T. Lickona (ed.), *Moral Development and Behaviour.* New York: Holt Rinehart & Winston.

Hutton, W. (1997). An Overview of Stakeholding. In G. Kelly, D. Kelly & A. Gamble (eds.), *Stakeholder Capitalism.* London: Macmillan.

Huyck, J. B. v., Battalio, R. C. & Beil, R. O. (1990). Tacit Coordination Games, Strategic Uncertainty, and Coordination Failure. *American Economic Review* (March).

Hwang, P. & Burgers, W. P. (1997). Properties of Trust: An analytical view. *Organizational Behavior and Human Decision Processes,* 69(1), 67–73.

Iacocca, L. & Novak, W. (1986). *Iacocca: An Autobiography.* New York: Bantam Books.

Intellectual Capital Report 2000 (2000). Aarhus: Systematics Software Engineering.

Jackendorff, R. (1987). *Consciousness and Computational Mind.* Cambridge, MA: The MIT Press.

Jackendorff, R. (1994). *Patterns in the Mind: Language and human nature.* New York: Basic Books.

James, W. (1896). The Will to Believe. In P. K. Moser & A. v. Nat (1987), *Human Knowledge: Classical and Contemporary Approaches.* New York: Oxford University Press.

Jensen M. C. & Murphy K. J. (1990). Performance Pay and Top Management Incentives. *Journal of Political Economy,* 98(2), 225, 250–251.

Jensen, P. B. (1999). *A Value- and Integrity-based Strategy to Consolidate Organisation, Marketing, and Communication – the Case of Jyske Bank.* Aarhus: CREDO Working Paper, The Department of Organisation and Management, The Aarhus School of Business.

Jensen, P. B. (2000). *Fra Afhængighed til Individualitet og Differentiering – Om Værdibaseret ledelse af bankvirksomhed.* Aarhus: PhD Thesis, The Aarhus School of Business.

Joas, H. (1997). *Die Entstehung der Werte.* Frankfurt am Main: Suhrkamp.

Jonas, H. (1984). *The Imperative of Responsibility – In Search of an Ethics for the Technological Age.* Chicago: University of Chicago Press.

Josefson, I. (1987). The Nurse as an Engineer – the Theory of Knowledge in Research in the Care Sector. In B. Göranzon & I. Josefson (eds.), *Knowledge, Skill and Artificial Intelligence.* New York: Springer Verlag.

Judt, T. (1997). The Social Question Redivivus. *Foreign Affairs,* 75(September/October), 95–117.

Jung, C. G. (1953–78a). *Psychology and Alchemy, Collected Works 12.* Princeton, NJ: Princeton University Press.

Jung, C. G. (1953–78b). *The Structure and Dynamics of the Psyche, Collected Works 8.* Princeton, NJ: Princeton University Press.

Juran, J. M. (1951). *Quality Control Handbook.* New York: McGraw-Hill.

Jørgensen, K., Kristensen, F. S., Lund, R. et al. (1998). *Organisatorisk Fornyelse – Erfaringer fra 24 Danske Virksomheder.* København: DISKO projektet, Erhvervsfremmestyrelsen.

Kandel, E. & Lazear, E. P. (1992). Peer Pressure and Partnerships. *Journal of Political Economy,* 100(4), 801–817.

Kant, I. (1781). *Critique of Pure Reason* (1971 ed.). London: Macmillan.

Kant, I. (1785). *Grundlegung zur Metaphysik der Sitten* (1962 ed.). Hamburg: Verlag von Felix Meiner.

Kay, I. T. (1997). *Ceo Pay and Shareholder Value: Helping the U.S. Win the Global Economic War.* St. Lucie Press.

Kay, J. (1997). The Stakeholder Corporation. In G. Kelly, D. Kelly & A. Gamble (eds.), *Stakeholder Capitalism.* London: Macmillan.

Kelly, G., Kelly, D. & Gamble, A. (1997). *Stakeholder Capitalism.* London: Macmillan.

Kerr, N. L. & Kaufman-Gilliland, C. M. (1997). "... and besides, I probably couldn't have made a difference anyway": Justification of Social Dilemma Defection via Perceived Self-Inefficacy. *Journal of Experimental Social Psychology,* 33(3 May), 211–230.

Kierkegaard, S. (1843). *Fear and Trembling* (1983 ed.). Princeton, NJ: Princeton University Press.

Kleist, H. v. (1808). *Michael Kohlhaas – Aus einer alten Chronik* (1976 ed.). Weimar: Greifenverlag zu Rudolstadt.

Knight, J. A. (1997). *Value Based Management: Developing a systematic approach to creating shareholder value.* New York: McGraw-Hill.

Knouse, S. B. (1995). *The Reward and Recognition Process in Total Quality Management.* Milwaukee, Wisconsin: ASQC Quality Press.

KPMG (1998). *Sociale Regnskaber – et Værktøj til Virksomhedens Udvikling.* København: KPMG.

Krogsgaard, O. T. (1992). *Ledelse og vildledelse – Virksomhedsledelsens brug og Misbrug i Teori og Praksis.* København: Børsen Bøger.

Kuhn, T. S. (1996). *The Structure of Scientific Revolutions.* Chicago: University of Chicago Press.

Kvale, S. (1993). En Pædagogisk Rehabilitering af Mesterlæren? *Dansk Pædagogisk Tidsskrift,* 1, 9–18.

Kvalitetsprisen for den offentlige sektor – vejledning (no year). Den Danske Kvalitetspris, European Foundation for Quality Management, Centralorganisationernes Fællesudvalg, Forbundet af Offentligt Ansatte, Kvalitetsinstituttet for Servicesektoren.

Kylling, A.-B. (1994). *Virksomhedernes Sociale Engagement.* FormidlingsCenter Aarhus.

Lakatos, I. & Musgrave, A. (1975). *Criticism and the Growth of Knowledge.* Cambridge: Cambridge University Press.

Langlois, R. N. & Everett, M. J. (1992). Complexity, Genuine Uncertainty, and the Economics of Organization. *Human Systems Management,* 11, 67–75.

Latané, B. & Darley, J. M. (1968). Group Inhibition of Bystander Intervention in Emergencies. *Journal of Personality and Social Psychology,* 10(3), 215–221.

Latané, B. & Darley, J. M. (1970). *The Unresponsive Bystander: Why doesn't he help?* New York: Appleton-Century-Crofts.

Lave, J. & Wenger, E. (1991). *Situated Learning – Legitimate Peripheral Participation* (1996 ed.). Cambridge: Cambridge University Press.

Lehmann, H. & Roth, G. (1993). *Weber's Protestant Ethic – Origins, Evidence, Contexts.* Cambridge: Cambridge University Press.

Lepper, M. & Green, D. (1978). *The Hidden Costs of Reward: New perspectives on the psychology of human motivation.* Hillsdale, NJ: Laurence Erlbaum.

Lerner, M. (1997). *The Politics of Meaning – Restoring Hope in an Age of Cynicism.* Reading, MA: Addison-Wesley.

Locke, J. (1690). *The Second Treatise of Government – An Essay Concerning the True Original, Extent and End of Civil Government* (1976 ed.). Oxford: Blackwell.

Luhmann, N. (1985). *Soziale Systeme: Grundriss einer allgemeinen Theorie.* Frankfurt am Main: Suhrkamp.

Lukes, S. (1974). *Power – A Radical View.* London: Macmillan.

Lunati, T. M. (1997). *Ethical Issues in Economics: From altruism to cooperation to equality.* London: Macmillan.

Machiavelli, N. (1513). *The Prince* (1929 ed.). London: Alexander Moring.

Machiavelli, N. (1513). The Prince. In J. Plamenatz (1975) Machiavelli – *The Prince, Selections from The Discourses and other Writings.* London: Fontana/Collins.

MacKinnon (1993) The Longevity of the Thesis: A critique of the critics. In H. Lehmann & G. Roth (eds.), *Weber's Protestant Ethic: Origins, evidence, contexts.* Cambridge: Cambridge University Press.

Magee, J. F. & Boodman, D. M. (1967). *Production Planning and Inventory Control.* New York: McGraw-Hill.

Magretta, J. (1999). *Managing in the New Economy.* Cambridge, MA: Harvard Business School Press.

Malik, F. (1984). Evolutionary Management. In H. Ulrich & G. J. B. Probst (eds.), *Self-organization and Management of Social Systems – Insight. Promises, Doubts, and Questions.* Berlin: Springer-Verlag.

Mandeville, B. (1924). *The Fable of the Bees – or Private Vices, Publick Benefits* (1988 ed.). Indianapolis: Liberty Press/Liberty Classic.

Manganelli, R. L. & Klein, M. M. (1996). *The Reengineering Handbook: A step by step guide to business transformation.* New York: Amacom.

Mannheim, K. (1940). *Man and Society in an Age of Reconstruction* (1950 ed.). London: Routledge & Kegan.

Maslow, A. (1996). A Theory of Human Motivation. In J. S. Ott (ed.), *Classic Readings in Organisational Behaviour.* Belmont: Wadsworth.

Maturana, H. R. & Varela, F. J. (1980). *Autopoiesis and Cognition: The realization of the living*. Dordrecht: Reidel.

Mayo, E. (1933). *Human Problems of Industrial Civilization*. New York: Macmillan.

McCormick, J. (1997). Mapping the Stakeholder Society. In G. Kelly, D. Kelly & A. Gamble (eds.), *Stakeholder Capitalism*. London: Macmillan.

McCrone, J. (1998). Gut Reaction. *New Scientist* (20 June), 42–45.

McGregor, D. M. (1957). The Human Side of Enterprise. *Management Review* (November), 22–28, 88–92.

McIntyre, A. C. (1981). *After Virtue: A study in moral theory*. Notre Dame, IN: University of Notre Dame Press.

McKergow, M. (1996). Complexity Science and Management: What's in it for business. *Long Range Planning*, 29(5), 721–727.

McKinnon, A. (1993). Kierkegaard and "The Leap of Faith". *Kierkegaardiana*, 16, 107–125.

McTaggart, J. M. & Kontes, P. W. (1994). *The Value Imperative: Managing for superior shareholder returns*. New York: The Free Press.

Meyer, T. & Arentz, T. (1997). *DIALOGOS – Den Etiske Læreproces. In V. C. Petersen & M. S. Lassen (eds.), Værdibaseret Ledelse – Et alternativ til styring, regulering og kontrol?* København: Dansk Industri.

Milgram, S. (1974). *Obedience to Authority: An experimental view*. London: Tavistock Publications.

Mill, J. S. (1863). *Utilitarianism, On Liberty, and Considerations on Representative Government* (1977 ed.). London: J. M. Dent & Sons.

Miller, A. (1994). *An Enemy of the People adapted from Henrik Ibsen, En Folkefiende*. London: Longman.

Miller, N. E. & Dollard, J. (1969). Imitationslernen: Versuche mit Kindern. In M. Irle (ed.), *Texte aus der experimentallen Sozialpsychologie*. Neuwied: Luchterhand.

Mingers, J. (1995). *Self-producing Systems: Implications and applications of autopoiesis*. New York: Plenum Press.

Minsky, M. (1986). *The Society of the Mind*. New York: Simon and Schuster.

Modig, M. (1989). *Den Livsvigtige Ulydighed* (1989 ed.). København: Fremad.

Moon, D. J. (1994). *Constructing Community – Moral Pluralism and Tragic Conflicts*. Princeton, NJ: Princeton University Press.

Morscher, E. (1981). Inwiefern ist die Sprache ein Soziales Phänomen? In R. Haller (ed.), *Sprache und Erkenntnis als Soziale Tatscahe*. Wien: Hölder-Pichler-Tempsky.

Moser, P. K. & Nat, A. v. (1987). *Human Knowledge: Classical and contemporary approaches*. New York: Oxford University Press.

Néda, Z., Ravasz, E., Brechet, Y. (2000). The Sound of Many Hands Clapping. *Nature* (February), 849–850.

Newborn, M. (1997). *Kasparov versus Deep Blue: Computer Chess Comes of Age.* New York: Springer Verlag.

Nielsen, A. (1999). *Værdibaseret Ledelse i Min Bank: Casestudier i Jyske bank om Etisk Adfærd, Styring og Ledelse: Fra regler hen imod værdier.* Silkeborg: Jyske Bank.

Nietzsche, F. (1886a). *Jenseits von Gut und Böse* (1968 ed.). Berlin: Der Goldmann Verlag.

Nietzsche, F. (1886b). *Således talte Zarathustra* (1983 ed.). København: Jespersen og Pio.

Nietzsche, F. (1887). *Zur Genealogie der Moral: Eine Streitschrift, Werke* (1969 ed.) München: DTV.

Nonaka, I. (1991). The Knowledge-creating Company. *Harvard Business Review,* 69(6 November–December), 96–104.

Nonaka, I. (1994). A Dynamic Theory of Organizational Knowledge Creation. *Organization Science,* 5(1 February), 14–37.

Nonaka, I. & Takeuchi, H. (1995). *The Knowledge-creating Company: How Japanese companies create the dynamics of innovation.* New York: Oxford University Press.

OECD Principles of Corporate Governance (1998). Paris: OECD.

Ogburn, W. F. (1964). *On Culture and Social Change.* Chicago: University of Chicago Press.

Olson, M. (1973). *The Logic of Collective Action.* Cambridge, MA: Harvard University Press.

Omachonu, V. K. & Ross, J. E. (1994). *Principles of Total Quality.* London: Kogan Page.

O'Neill, O. (1996). *Towards Justice and Virtue – A Constructive Account of Practical Reasoning.* Cambridge: Cambridge University Press.

Orwell, G. (1945). *Animal Farm – A Fairy Story* (1995 ed.). London: Secker and Warburg.

Pædagogiske principper for forsvaret (1984). København: Forsvarskommandoen.

Paine, L. S. (1996). *Cases in Leadership, Ethics, and Organizational Integrity: A strategic perspective.* Richard D. Irwin.

Parsons, T. (1951). *The Social System.* Glencoe: The Free Press.

Parsons, T. (1960). *Structure and Process in Modern Societies.* Glencoe: The Free Press.

Patching, K. (1999). *Management and Organisation Development – beyond Arrows, Boxes and Circles.* London: Macmillan.

Paton, H. J. (1986). *The Moral Law – Kant's Groundwork of the Metaphysic of Morals.* London: Hutchinson.

Paul, E. F., Miller, F. D. & Paul, J. (1993). *Liberalism and Economic Order.* Cambridge: Cambridge University Press.

Paul, E. F., Paul, J. & Miller, F. D. (1985). *Ethics and Economics.* Oxford: Basil Blackwell.

Penrose, R. (1989). *The Emperor's New Mind – Concerning Computers, Minds, and the Laws of Physics* (1990 ed.). London: Vintage.

Perrow, C. (1984). *Normal Accidents: Living with high-risk technologies.* New York: Basic Books.

Petersen, V. C. (1975). *Ikke-metrisk Multidimensional Scaling.* Århus: Aarhus Universitet.

Petersen, V. C. (1985). *Planlægning og Samfundsudvikling – fra 30'erne til idag, 3 vols.* Stockholm: Nordplan, Nordiska Institutet för Samhällsplanering.

Petersen, V. C. (1994). Upholding or Breaking Ethical Rules? – Responses to Ethical Problems. In H. D. Geer (ed.), *Business Ethics in Progress?* Berlin: Springer-Verlag.

Petersen, V. C. (1995). Når Løsningen Bliver Problemet – om Etik og Personligt Ansvar. *Kritik,* 28(115), 10–19.

Petersen, V. C. (1996). Resultatløn og Snavsede Kaffekopper. *Berlingske Tidende* (9 November 1996).

Petersen, V. C. (1997). *Mere Katolsk end Paven? – Ledelse, Holdninger og Værdier i en Storbank.* Århus: CREDO/The Aarhus School of Business.

Petersen, V. C. (1998). *Tacit Ethics – Creation and Change.* Aarhus: Working Paper, Department of Organization and Management, The Aarhus School of Business.

Petersen, V. C. & Jensen, F. D. (1996). Balls! *Ledelse i Dag,* 6(22), 16–18.

Petersen, V. C. & Lassen, M. S. (1997). *Værdibaseret Ledelse – et Alternativ til Styring, Regulering og Kontrol?* København: Dansk Industri.

Piaget, J. (1952). *The Origins of Intelligence in Children.* New York: International Universities Press.

Piaget, J. (1965). *The Moral Judgment of the Child.* New York: The Free Press.

Pirsig, R. M. (1974). *Zen and the Art of Motorcycle Maintenance: An inquiry into values.* London: Bodley Head.

Platts, M. (1991). *Moral Realities – An Essay in Philosophical Psychology.* London: Routledge.

Polanyi, M. (1958). *Personal Knowledge – Towards a Post-critical Philosophy* (1962 ed.). London: The University of Chicago Press.

Polanyi, M. (1962). The Republic of Science: Its political and economic theory. *Minerva,* I(1), 54–73.

Polanyi, M. (1967). *The Tacit Dimension.* London: Routledge and Kegan.

Pratt, J. W. & Zeckhauser, R. (1985). *Principals and Agents: The structure of business.* Boston, MA: Harvard Business School Press.

Probst, G. & Büchel, B. (1997). *Organizational Learning – The Competitive Advantage of the Future.* Hemel Hempstead: Prentice Hall.

Prusak, L. (1997). *Knowledge in Organizations.* Oxford: Butterworth-Heinemann.

Purser, R. E. & Cabana, S. (1998). *The Self Managing Organization: How leading companies are transforming the work of teams for real impact.* New York: The Free Press.

Quattrone, G. & Tversky, A. (1986). Self-deception and the Voter's Illusion. In J. Elster (ed.), *The Multiple Self.* Cambridge: Cambridge University Press.

Quinn, J. B., Anderson, P. & Finkelstein, S. (1998). Managing Professional Intellect. In *Harvard Business Review on Knowledge Management.* Boston: Harvard Business School.

Rapoport, A. (1970). *Two Person Game Theory – The Essential Ideas.* Ann Arbor: The University of Michigan.

Rappaport, A. (1997). *Creating Shareholder Value: A guide for managers and investors.* New York: The Free Press.

Rawls, J. (1971). *A Theory of Justice.* Cambridge, MA: Belknap.

Rawls, J. (1985). Justice as Fairness – Political Not Metaphysical. *Philosophy and Public Affairs,* 14(3), 223–251.

Rawls, J. (1988). The Priority of Right and the Ideas of the Good. *Philosophy and Public Affairs,* 17, 251–276.

Rawls, J. (1993). *Political Liberalism.* New York: Columbia University Press.

Reber, A. S. (1989). Implicit Learning and Tacit Knowledge. *Journal of Experimental Psychology: General,* 118, 242–244.

Reber, A. S. (1993). *Implicit Learning and Tacit Knowledge: An Essay on the Cognitive Unconscious.* New York: Oxford University Press.

Reder, A. (1995). *In Pursuit of Principle and Profit: Business success through social responsibility.* New York: G. P. Putnam's Sons.

Retningslinier om etik i pengeinstitutternes rådgivning (1994) København: Finansrådet.

Retningslinier om etik i realkreditinstitutioner (6 September 1995). København: Forbrugerstyrelsen

Richardson, H. S. (1994). *Practical Reasoning about Final Ends.* Cambridge: Cambridge University Press.

Ridley, M. (1996). *The Origins of Virtue.* London: Viking.

Ring, P. S. & Ven, A. H. v. d. (1989). Formal and informal dimensions of transactions. In A. H. v. d. Ven, H. L. Angle & M. S. Poole (eds.), *Research on the Management of Innovation.* New York: Ballinger.

Roethlisberger, F. J. (1941). *Management and Morale.* Cambridge, MA: Harvard University Press.

Roos, J. (1996). What You Can Measure You Can Manage. *IMD Perspectives for Managers,* 26(10 November), 10.

Roos, J. (1998). Exploring the Concept of Intellectual Capital. *Long Range Planning,* 31(February),

Ross, W. D. (1930). *The Right and The Good* (1950 ed.). Oxford: Oxford University Press.

Rousseau, J.-J. (1755–58). Discourse on Political Economy, The Social Contract (1994 ed.). Oxford: Oxford University Press.

Runciman, W. G. (1966). *Relative Deprivation and Social Justice.* Berkeley: University of California Press.

Runciman, W. G. (1998). *The Social Animal.* London: HarperCollins.

Russell, B. (1912). Appearance, Reality, and Knowledge by Acquaintance. In P. K. Moser & A. v. Nat (eds.) (1987), *Human Knowledge: Classical and contemporary approaches.* New York: Oxford University Press.

Russell, J. A. & Fernández-Dols, J.-M. (1997a). What Does a Facial Expression Mean? In J. A. Russell & J.-M. Fernández-Dols (eds.), *The Psychology of Facial Expressions.* Cambridge: Cambridge University Press.

Russell, J. A. & Fernández-Dols, J.-M. (1997b). *The Psychology of Facial Expressions.* Cambridge: Cambridge University Press.

Ryle, G. (1949). *The Concept of Mind* (1950 ed.). London: Hutchinson.

Saavedra, M. d. C. (1998). *Don Quixote.* Oxford: Oxford University Press.

Salamon, L. (1994). The Rise of the Non-profit Sector: A global associational revolution. *Foreign Affairs,* 73(July/August 1994).

SAP SEM – Enabling Value Based Management (1999). White Paper. Walldorf: SAP AG.

Sarma, K. M. (1998). Protection of the Ozone layer – A success story of UNEP. *Linkages/Journal,* 3(3, 28 July),

Sartre, J.-P. (1943) *Being and Nothingness: A phenomenological essay on ontology* (1993 ed.). New York: Washington Square Press.

Sartre, J.-P. (1992). *Notebooks for an Ethics.* Chicago: Chicago University Press.

Sashkin, M. & Kiser, K. J. (1991). *Total Quality Management.* Seabrook, MD: Ducochon Press.

Schelling, T. C. (1980). *The Strategy of Conflict.* Cambridge, MA: Harvard University Press.

Schelling, T. C. (1984). Self-command in practice, in Policy, and in a Theory of Rational Choice. American *Economic Review,* 74(2), 1–11.

Schildknecht, R. (1992). *Total Quality Management: Konzeption und State of the Art.* Frankfurt am Main: Campus.

Schmidt, H. (1998). *Auf der Suche nach einer öffentlichen Moral. Deutschland vor dem neuen Jahrhundert.* Stuttgart: Deutsche Verlags Anstalt.

Schmidt, J. (1993). *Die sanfte Organisations – Revolution. Von der Hierarchie zu selbststeuernden Systemen.* Frankfurt am Main: Campus.

Schön, D. A. (1983). *The Reflective Practitioner: How professionals think in action.* New York: Basic Books.

Sculley, J. (1987). *Odyssey – Pepsi to Apple. A Journey of Adventure, Ideas, and the Future.* New York: Harper & Row.

Searle, J. (1980). Minds, Brains and Programs. In D. Hofstadter (ed.), *The Mind's I.* Harmondsworth: Penguin.

Selbach, S. J. (1996). Dansk Legetøj er ikke Lavet af Børn. *Ledelse i Dag* (23), 44–46.

Seligman, A. R. (1998). *The Problem of Trust.* Princeton, NJ: Princeton Universty Press.

Sellitz, C. (1969). *Methods in Social Relations.* London: Methuen.

Sen, A. (1985). The Moral Standing of the Market. In E. F. Paul, J. Paul & F. D. Miller (ed.), *Ethics and Economics.* Oxford: Blackwell.

Sen, A. (1987). *On Ethics and Economics.* Oxford: Basil Blackwell.

Shand, A. H. (1990). *Free Market Morality – The Political Economy of the Austrian School.* London: Routledge.

Sidgwick, H. (1907). *The Methods of Ethics* (1962 ed.). London: Methuen.

Simon, H. A. (1945). *Administrative Behavior – A Study of Decision-making Processes in an Administrative Organisation* (1957 ed.). New York: The Free Press.

Simon, H. A. (1956). *Models of Man – Mathematical Essays on Rational Human Behaviour in a Social Setting.* New York: Wiley.

Simon, H. A. & Newell, A. (1958). Heuristic Problem Solving: The next advance in Operations Research. *Operations Research,* 6, 1–10.

Skinner, B. F. (1953). *Science and Human Behavior* (1965 ed.). New York: The Free Press.

Skocpol, T. (1979). *States and Social Revolutions: A comparative analysis of France, Russia, and China.* Cambridge: Cambridge University Press.

Smart, J. C. C. (1990). Distributive Justice and Utilitarianism. In M. W. Hoffman & J. M. Moore (eds.), *Business Ethics: Readings and cases in corporate morality.* New York: McGraw-Hill.

Smith, A. (1776). *The Wealth of Nations* (1974 ed.). Harmondsworth: Penguin.

Snow, D. A., Rochford, E. B., Worden, S. K. et al. (1986). Frame Alignment Processes, Micromobilization, and Movement Participation. *American Sociological Review,* 51(August), 464–481.

Sommers, A. T. (1978). A Collision of Ethics and Economics. *Across the Board,* 1(5), 14–19.

Soros, G. (1998). *The Crisis of Global Capitalism – Open Society Endangered.* London: Little, Brown and Company.

Spender, J. C. (no year). *The Individual and Collective Dimensions, and Dynamics, of Organizational Knowledge.* Newark, NJ: Preliminary version of paper, Rutgers University.

Stacey, R. & Parker, D. (1994). *Chaos, Management and Economics: The implications of non-linear thinking.* London: IEA (Institute for Economic Affairs) Hobart Paper.

Sternberg, R. J. & Wagner, R. K. (1992). Tacit Knowledge: An unspoken key to managerial success. *Creativity and Knowledge Management*, 1(1 March) 5–13.

Stewart, T. A. (1991). Brainpower: How intellectual capital is becoming America's most valuable asset. *Fortune* (2 June), 44–60.

Stewart, T. A. (1994). Your Company's Most Valuable Asset: Intellectual capital. *Fortune* (3 October), 68–74.

Stewart, T. A. (1997). *Intellectual Capital: The new wealth of organisations.* London: Nicholas Brealey Publishing.

Stone, C. (1988). *Earth and other Ethics: The case for moral pluralism.* New York: Harper & Row.

Storey, J. (1996). *Blackwell Cases in Human Resource and Change Management.* Oxford: Blackwell.

Sufrin, S. C. (1989). *Ethics, Markets and Policy – The Structure of Market Ethics.* Lund: Studentlitteratur.

Sugden, R. (1986). *The Economics of Rights, Co-operation and Welfare.* Oxford: Blackwell.

Sveiby, K. E. (1994). *Towards a Knowledge Perspective on Organisation.* Edsbruk: Akademitryck.

Sveiby, K. E. (1997). *The New Organizational Wealth.* San Francisco: Berrett-Koehler.

Swift, J. (1726). *Gulliver's Travels* (1992 ed.). London: Wordsworth.

Taylor, F. W. (1911). *The Principles of Scientific Management.* New York: Harper & Row.

Tennyson, A. L. (1854). *Poems* (1908 ed.). London: Macmillan.

Thierauf, R. (1999). *Knowledge Management Systems for Business.* Westport, CT: Quorum.

Thomas, W. I. (1966). *On Social Organization and Social Personality.* Chicago: University of Chicago Press.

Thoreau, H. D. (1849/1866). Resistance to Civil Government, or Civil Disobedience. Found at http://www.vcu.edu/engweb/transweb/civil/civildisobedience.htm.

Tilly, C. (1978). *From Mobilization to Revolution.* Reading, MA: Addison-Wesley.

Tingsten, H. (1966). *Från Ideer til Idyll – Den lyckliga Demokratin.* Stockholm: Norstedt.

Tissen, R., Andriessen, D. & Deprez, F. L. (1998). *Value-based Knowledge Management.* Amsterdam: Longman.

Tjosvold, D. (1984). Cooperation Theory and Organizations. *Human Relations,* 37(9), 743–767.

Townsend, P. L. & Gephardt, J. E. (1992). *Quality in Action: 93 lessons in leadership, participation, and measurement.* New York: Wiley.

Tsoukalis, L. (1997). *The New European Economy – The Politics and Economics of Integration.* Oxford: Oxford University Press.

Turner, V. W. (1969/1982). *The Ritual Process – structure and anti-structure.* New York: Aldine.

Ulrich, H. (1984). Management – A Misunderstood Societal Function. In H. Ulrich & G. J. B. Probst (eds.), *Self-organization and Management of Social Systems – Insight, Promises, Doubts, and Questions*. Berlin: Springer-Verlag.

Ulrich, H. & Probst, G. J. B. (1984). *Self-organization and Management of Social Systems – Insight. Promises, Doubts, and Questions*. Berlin: Springer-Verlag.

Varela, F. J. (no year). *Autopoiesis and a Biology of Intentionality*. Paris: CREA, Ecole Polytechnique.

Varela, F. J., Thompson, E. & Rosch, E. (1991). *Embodied Mind: Cognitive science and human experience*. Cambridge, MA: MIT Press.

Vogel, S. K. (1998). *Freer Markets, More Rules – Regulatory Reform in Advanced Industrial Countries*. Ithaca, NY: Cornell University Press.

Vroom, V. H. (1996). Work and Motivation. In J. S. Ott (ed.), *Classic Readings in Organizational Behavior*. Orlando: Harcourt Brace.

Vygotsky, L. S. (1978). *Mind in Society*. Cambridge, MA: Harvard University Press.

Waal, F. de (1996). *Good Natured – The Origins of Right and Wrong in Humans and other Animals*. Cambridge MA.: Harvard University Press.

Waddington, C. (1957). *The Strategy of the Genes*. London: Allen and Unwin.

Waddock, S. & Graves, S. (1997). *Finding the Link Between Stakeholder Relations and Quality of Management*. Social Investment Forum, Winning Paper, Moskowitz Prize 1997.

Waxman, C. I. (1969). *The End of Ideology Debate*. New York: Simon & Schuster.

Weber, M. (1905). *Die Protestantische Ethik* (1969–72 ed.). München: Siebenstern Verlag.

Weber, M. (1920). *Gesammelte Aufsätze zur Religionssoziologie, 3. Bde*. Tübingen: J. C. B. Mohr.

Weber, M. (1930). *The Protestant Ethic and the Spirit of Capitalism* (1989 ed.) London: Unwin Hyman.

Weber, M. (1956). *Wirtschaft und Gesellschaft* (1956 ed.). Tübingen: Mohr.

Webster's Encyclopedic Unabridged Dictionary of the English Language (1989). New York: Portland House.

Weick, K. E. (1995). *Sensemaking in Organizations*. Thousand Oaks, CA: Sage.

Werhane, P. & Freeman, E. R. (1998). *Blackwell Encyclopedic Dictionary of Business Ethics*. Oxford: Blackwell.

Willetts, D. (1997). The Poverty of Stakeholding. In G. Kelly, D. Kelly & A. Gamble (eds.), *Stakeholder Capitalism*. London: Macmillan.

Williamson, O. (1981). The Economics of Organization: The transaction cost approach. *American Journal of Sociology*, 87(3), 548–577.

Williamson, O. E. (1975). *Markets and Hierarchies: Analysis and antitrust implications – A study in the economics of internal organisation*. New York: The Free Press.

Williamson, O. E. (1995). *Transaction Cost Economics, 2 vols.* Aldershot: Edward Elgar.

Wilson, E. O. (1978). *On Human Nature.* Cambridge, MA: Harvard University Press.

Wilson, E. O. (1998). *Consilience: The unity of knowledge.* New York: Knopf.

Wittgenstein, L. (1953). *Philosophische Untersuchungen.* Oxford: Blackwell.

Wittgenstein, L. (1958). P*hilosophical Investigations* (1971 ed.). Oxford: Blackwell.

Wittgenstein, L. (1969). *On Certainty/Über Gewissheit.* New York: Harper.

Wittgenstein, L. (1970). *Schriften 5: Das blaue Buch, Eine philosophische Betrachtung, Zettel.* Frankfurt am Main: Suhrkamp.

Wittgenstein, L. (1976). Cause and Effect: Intuitive awareness. In P. K. Moser & A. v. Nat (eds.), *Human Knowledge: Classical and contemporary approaches.* New York: Oxford University Press.

Wittgenstein, L. (1980). *Bemerkungen über die Philosophie der Psychologie, Band I und II.* Oxford: Blackwell.

Wolgast, E. (1992). *Ethics of an Artificial Person: Lost responsibility in professions and organizations.* Stanford: Stanford University Press.

Woodham-Smith, C. (1953). *The Reason Why* (1998 ed.). New York: Barnes & Noble.

Yergin, D. & Stanislaw, J. A. (1999). *Staat oder Markt.* Frankfurt am Main: Campus Verlag.

Young, J. S. (1988). *Steve Jobs: The journey is the reward.* London: Scott, Foresman and Co.

Zinck, K. J. (1995). Total Quality Management: Begriffe und Aufgaben – Ein Überblick. In D. B. Preßmar (ed.), *Total Quality Management II.* Wiesbaden: Gabler.

Index